PARTS PER MILLION

ALSO BY JOY HOROWITZ

Tessie and Pearlie: A Granddaughter's Story

PARTS PER MILLION

THE POISONING OF BEVERLY HILLS HIGH SCHOOL

Joy Horowitz

VIKING

VIKING
Published by the Penguin Group
Penguin Group (USA) Inc., 375 Hudson Street, New York, New York 10014, U.S.A. ▪ Penguin
Group (Canada), 90 Eglinton Avenue East, Suite 700, Toronto, Ontario, Canada M4P 2Y3
(a division of Pearson Penguin Canada Inc.) ▪ Penguin Books Ltd, 80 Strand, London WC2R
0RL, England ▪ Penguin Ireland, 25 St. Stephen's Green, Dublin 2, Ireland (a division of
Penguin Books Ltd) ▪ Penguin Books Australia Ltd, 250 Camberwell Road, Camberwell,
Victoria 3124, Australia (a division of Pearson Australia Group Pty Ltd) ▪ Penguin Books
India Pvt Ltd, 11 Community Centre, Panchsheel Park, New Delhi – 110017, India ▪ Penguin
Group (NZ), 67 Apollo Drive, Rosedale, North Shore 0745, Auckland, New Zealand (a division
of Pearson New Zealand Ltd.) ▪ Penguin Books (South Africa) (Pty) Ltd, 24 Sturdee Avenue,
Rosebank, Johannesburg 2196, South Africa

Penguin Books Ltd, Registered Offices:
80 Strand, London WC2R 0RL, England

First published in 2007 by Viking Penguin,
a member of Penguin Group (USA) Inc.

1   3   5   7   9   10   8   6   4   2

Excerpt from "Ballad of Jed Clampett" written by Paul Henning. © 1962 (renewed)
Carolintone Music Company, Inc. All rights reserved.

LIBRARY OF CONGRESS CATALOGING IN PUBLICATION DATA
Horowitz, Joy.
Parts per million : the poisoning of Beverly Hills High School / by Joy Horowitz.
p.   cm.
Includes bibliographical references and index.
ISBN 978-0-670-03798-8
1. Class actions, (Civil procedure)—California. 2. Liability for hazardous substances
pollution damages—California. 3. Toxic torts—California. 4. Beverly Hills High School—
Trials, litigation, etc. I. Title.
KFC1017.H67 2007
346.79403'8—dc22   2006034357

Printed in the United States of America
Set in Celeste with Avenir
Designed by Daniel Lagin

For Shirley and Mike Horowitz, my parents,
who taught us not to be afraid of the truth.

CONTENTS

Everything that we see is a shadow cast by that which we do not see.

—Martin Luther King Jr.

From my parents' balcony—looking west from South Camden Drive, circa 1928.
(Courtesy of Joy Horowitz.)

I fell in love with an old photograph that now sits propped up on a bookshelf over my desk. The quality is lousy and the surface hopelessly scratched, but I adore it anyway. My sister, Shari, discovered the picture bundled inside a thick sheaf of tattered real estate papers from the house where we grew up on South Camden Drive in Beverly Hills. When I began working on this book, she gave it to me as a keepsake, a sepia-toned image full of hints about an unrecoverable past.

The picture is a still life of snowfall in Los Angeles from the 1920s, taken from the vantage point of our parents' upstairs balcony—looking west toward the Pacific. There is a dreamy cast to the snapshot, the Spanish-tiled rooftops dusted in freshly fallen snow which, of course, is a rarity in southern California. The sky is ominous, heavy with gray clouds, but if you look closely you can spot two starlings perched on the telephone wires overhead. The landscape doesn't yet include the 20th Century Fox studios or Century City development, once lima bean fields.

But in the distance, on the horizon, there are seven giant oil derricks, rising from hilly terrain. They stand as lumbering reminders of the oil boom that helped spawn a mad dash for money by wildcatters and outlaws here at the turn of the last century. And just behind a rooftop is Beverly Hills High School, built in 1927 by local tycoons so their children wouldn't have to travel all the way to Hollywood.

It's impossible for me to look at this picture and not think of that moment from *The Wizard of Oz* right before the tornado smacks Dorothy in the head, signaling the advent of Technicolor somewhere over the rainbow. Only here, there will be no munchkins or wizards or witches, only oil barons and movie stars and real estate developers, settling a town that the rest of the world would come to see as a sort of glittering Emerald City, a symbol of the American dream.

Beverly Hills, in other words, is nothing if not a place of illusion, of sleight of image. Just like my old photograph, it bespeaks possibility at the same moment that we see beneath its facade, unearthing oil and money and the unexpected.

Certainly, nothing was more unexpected—or unwelcome—in February 2003 than the arrival of the environmental champion Erin Brockovich, the subject of the 2000 Hollywood blockbuster that depicted her transformation from white-trash paralegal to fetching demagogue in a tank top. Armani, no less. Now she was at it again, claiming there was a connection between the cancers of a group of young Beverly Hills High School graduates and the oil fields that lay beneath the campus.

It was greed, and greed only, she believed, that had caused these students—as well as faculty and nearby residents—to grow sick with a variety of illnesses: with a 5 percent overriding royalty from the operations that offered a promised $50 million over forty years for the city, its residents, and school district, dangers to schoolchildren went ignored for decades.

Brockovich's claim was, of course, deeply unsettling. For the society-minded denizens of Beverly Hills, it struck directly at the self-image of their community—an enclave of wealth and privilege, to be sure, but one that was also devoted to its public schools: people moved to Beverly Hills for its schools, just as my family had from the Midwest back in the mid-1960s when the schools were considered top-notch, among the best in the nation.

The high school, in particular, enjoyed a reputation as a sort of public private school. There was the Swim Gym, featured in the dance scene from the classic *It's a Wonderful Life,* the phenomenal faculty, the plethora of over-achieving students, whose parents might be industry scions or Holocaust survivors or chauffeurs at the Beverly Hills Hotel. It didn't matter where you came from, really. What mattered, more than anything, was that you had arrived.

There were snobs, of course, and the social misfits you'd find in any small town. But at school, class struggle was more about curriculum than money consciousness. We took so much for granted then—the perks of living in Beverly Hills, which included the oil that flowed miles beneath the paved streets and cement sidewalks and classrooms, too.

Oil production at the high school was supposed to be a win-win proposition—good for the school district, which owned the land, good for the city coffers, and good for the residents who reaped royalty payments from mineral rights. Not to mention how it lessened everyone's dependence on foreign oil.

It wasn't supposed to make young mothers die from stage IV Hodgkin's disease. Or cause young men to become sterile. What Brockovich had managed to expose was a hidden anxiety within Beverly Hills itself and the rest of America, for that matter: parents' horror at the possibility that they had been slowly poisoning their children for decades.

It is this anxiety that still haunts us, even now, looking back.

From earthquakes to tar pits to smog, the story of Los Angeles—a desert that sits atop a giant basin of hydrocarbons—is really a story about oil. And nowhere has that tale taken a more frightening turn than in Beverly Hills, a place that despite its mythology is really just another American town, albeit one with a giant oil derrick decorated with brightly painted flowers on the high school football field.

Growing up there in the sixties and seventies, no one thought twice about the wells behind the football bleachers at the high school; the bobbing heads of pump jacks, like praying mantises, were simply part of the landscape. One caught fire in the early sixties from an electric transformer. Sometimes they'd cast a fine spray of petroleum on the football players at practice. My brother, Steve, was one of them. In keeping with the ethos of the time, my mother complained that she could never clean Steve's football jersey because it was stained with droplets of oil. That's what the oil wells meant to us: the need for better detergent.

Clearly, we didn't think of them as any kind of hazard. Nobody did. Indeed, we felt a sort of smug pride in the knowledge that they provided an added source of income for the school district. The bobbing wells would morph years later into a sprawling derrick with eighteen wellheads beneath it, an offshore platform under the school's athletic field.

Now, it seemed, Beverly Hills could be paying a steep price for its apparent shortsightedness: might the very thing that had made our community so rich also cause so much illness and heartache years later?

It occurred to me that the story here might be a microcosm of the hidden dangers of petroleum, in general, beyond the realm of global warming. After a century of producing and reaping the benefits of this abundant natural resource, it appeared that now we could be facing a grim reminder of its true cost—the legacy of our Faustian bargain.

I'm not what you'd call a Beverly Hills High School junkie, but I do have fond recollections of the place. It offered ample opportunity for a classic overachiever, such as myself, to excel: I ran track, played violin in the orchestra, sang in the Madrigals, organized the school's first Earth Day celebration, and wore a cute, short pleated skirt every Friday night with a big B on my chest as a cheerleader for Beverly.

But mostly, the place was about the people. My best friend Amy Spies, who walked to school with me most mornings from sixth grade on, lived across the street on South Camden Drive. It was not unusual for us to bump into the likes of John Provost, the child actor on *Lassie,* on his skateboard, or Walt Disney on the bowling green at Roxbury Park, or Groucho Marx at the pharmacy where we bought *Betty and Veronica* comic books, or the actress who played Ellie May on *The Beverly Hillbillies,* because she was dating our friend's father. When it came time for college, Amy and I would be roommates at Harvard. Later, she was the maid of honor at my wedding. My children can't quite believe how my life remains entwined with my old pals from high school, like Amy, who would go on to become a television writer for *Beverly Hills, 90210.* But we forged a bond as south-of-the-track toughies and then, when our children were born, shared the juggling nightmare of motherhood and writing careers. Those are lifelong connections, the most precious commodity.

It was Amy with whom I first spoke in early 2003 about the problem at Beverly. The evening news had run an alarming piece about the possibility that Beverly could be a "toxic" school, suggesting a link between cancers among recent graduates and leaks from the oil wells. The local CBS station broke the story during "sweeps" week, a key time period when ratings are determined for news outlets. Soon after, the *Los Angeles Times* followed suit: CANCER CLUSTER IN BEVERLY HILLS ALLEGED. Amy, whose two sisters had been stricken with breast and ovarian cancer and whose mom died of lung cancer, urged me to check it out.

I was, of course, deeply skeptical. For starters, I was troubled by the Hollywood angle, namely Erin Brockovich—the va-va-voom paralegal who was making the charges and seemed to be looking for more than her fifteen minutes of fame. Not only had she become the star of her own cable TV series, *Final Justice,* but she and her boss, the bombastic lawyer Edward L. Masry, had told *Daily Variety* columnist Army Archerd that "the film rights are up for grabs." Was this Beverly Hills story simply a phony celebrity-launched cause that was just another money grab?

Besides, making the connection between cancer and environmental exposures to toxins is almost impossible. There are too many confounders—genetics, lifestyle, age, diet. The fact is that one in every three women and one in every two men will get cancer. And even if there were an excess of cancers in Beverly Hills, that didn't mean they could be linked to the oil wells, which are ubiquitous in Los Angeles. As a local oil attorney once quipped: "They ruined a perfectly good oil field by building a city on top of it." Indeed, the history of the town is predicated on petroleum production, from Edward Doheny to Armand Hammer, the Medicis of Lotus Land.

But the Beverly story wouldn't go away for me. Having attended my thirtieth high school reunion the previous summer, I occasionally logged on to an Internet chat group of my classmates. And it was in reading those missives that I began to wonder if maybe there really was something going on. One person after another wrote about thyroid problems or lymphomas. There were naughty recollections, too, of passionate kissing by the oil wells and of white gym shorts stained with black tar. But mostly, the e-mails were like this one:

> Date: Tu, 18 Feb 2003
> 09:54:37—0800
> From: Madeline Fries
> mfries@winnr.com
> Subject: BHHS thyroid/cancer problems
>
> Hi Everyone:
> Last weekend I had dinner with Debi Genson Fries. Some of you may remember her. She went to Beverly for a couple of years. Anyway, I mentioned last week in these Emails that she has Graves Disease (thyroid problem), and her sister, Betsy, also a Beverly student, had a thyroid condition.

Debi pointed out to me that her husband, Tom, another '71 grad, had Hodgkins Disease in his mid-twenties, which led eventually to his untimely death at the age of 47.

I don't know the status of the investigation into the Bev High oil fields, but I thought I'd put this out there.

Madeline Cantillon Fries

Not everyone who was sick, though, had graduated from the school. Worried that the city might be closing ranks, a psychologist named Lee Bova wrote a letter that was published in the *Los Angeles Times*:

I have lived one block downwind of the oil pump since 1991, and I was diagnosed with non-Hodgkin's lymphoma a year ago. My kids, grads in '90 and '91, are OK so far. Anybody ask around the neighborhood for cancer incidences? I hope the good city fathers (and mothers) put property-value considerations aside and explore this diligently and with integrity. It would be sad to see a modern version of Henrik Ibsen's "An Enemy of the People" in Beverly Hills.

Now, my journalist's skepticism gave way to worry as I set out to unravel the facts. It turns out that writing a book about toxins in the environment is really an exercise in confronting a series of obstacles, especially when a lawsuit is part of the equation. When I tried to gain access to public records from the city of Beverly Hills, I was told that key documents about the oil wells would be off-limits because they had been deemed "privileged." The city attorney would neither tell me what records were being withheld nor offer a privilege log, a list of what public records were exempt from disclosure because of attorney-client confidentiality.

I hit another stumbling block with the air pollution agency, the Air Quality Management District. I figured if I could gain access to internal government documents detailing pollution emissions, a piece of the puzzle might be revealed. Months after requesting public records through California's Freedom of Information Act, I was denied access to certain documents: a lawyer at the agency claimed that "trade secrets" protected the oil and gas companies from having to release what they considered proprietary information. Other reports were missing from files or redacted with a Sharpie.

Even more troubling was my attempt to secure public records from California's Department of Health Services. Since the cancer registry in Los Angeles had reported a threefold excess of thyroid cancer rates among young men in Beverly Hills, I wondered if documentation about the use of radioactive iodine-131—a substance which is injected into oil wells to check for flow rates and leaks in casings but is also known to "nuke" people's thyroid glands—might offer clues. The only known cause of thyroid cancer is radiation exposure.

Again, my public-records request was denied. But this time, the reason offered seemed truly far-fetched: I was told by a bureaucrat that releasing the information "might jeopardize the public health and safety in light of 9/11." In other words, the government's concern about terrorists getting their hands on the stuff would preclude any reasonable discussion about who was potentially being exposed—namely, schoolkids. Or could this be a case of the government protecting the interests of the oil and gas industry?

The story, it seemed, was as much about the suppression of public information as anything I had ever encountered in my thirty years as a journalist.

I had to find out.

You would have to call me an unlikely chronicler of Beverly Hills High School's environmental problems. Certainly, many of the town's leaders have thought of me that way. My first book was a family history, a memoir of my two ninety-something grandmothers. It was a true labor of love. This book is more of a love-hate affair: I care deeply about the place but hate how difficult it is to get at the truth. Just asking questions made a lot of people angry. Not surprisingly, this was not a quest that appealed to civic boosters. Many of them wouldn't return my phone calls. Frankly, for a while I was relieved not to have to talk to them.

So I started researching and found myself, in the course of exploring the science of cancer causation, talking to dozens of public health researchers, cancer specialists, geologists, toxicologists, epidemiologists. I also interviewed teachers, classmates, and high school administrators I hadn't seen for more than thirty years. That led me to the next place: the human heart. Reflecting on children and the parents who love them—and the wishful thinking that we all embrace just to get through the day—really brought me back to this look at my old town. It wasn't denial I was seeing, I thought, so much as shame.

Until now, I did not realize how much writing a book about the environment is an open invitation to fear. For more than four years, the story about the possible connection between the industrial sites at the high school and elevated cancer rates has inhabited my life. It's been a very uncomfortable time for me, like taking the gauze from my eyes and seeing the truth for the first time: we pay lip service to our children's safety but get so wrapped up in our daily lives that we refuse to pay close attention. We allow industry and schools to exist side by side—and we look the other way.

As one high school parent told me: "For too long, we never really paid attention to what effect this might be having on our children. Then, we finally woke up."

And that's what this book is about: waking up. It's partly an environmental primer about a place that has the flash and allure of wealth and glamour but, in reality, is not so different from any other American town. Perhaps because it is a story at the nexus of celebrity, law, science, and politics, it tells us more about the way our world works than we may want to know: if it could happen here, in one of the world's wealthiest communities, it could happen anywhere.

Early on, the plaintiffs' lawyers were caricatured as either fear-mongering extortionists or humanitarian do-gooders. Unfortunately, as often happens in high-profile cases, much of the initial information about them was either factually wrong or irrelevant and misconstrued. While there might be elements of both of these extremes in these particular people, they are largely neither of these things. The intent of this book is to try to better understand the real story behind their pursuit of justice, nuanced and complicated though it may be.

This is not a book about certainty. It is, instead, intended to pose a range of questions. At its heart lies a fundamental one: is it possible that a community could care more about money than about the health of its children? Having grown up in Beverly Hills, it seemed impossible. The town was filled with too many good people, too many savvy and loving families, too many well-educated professionals who would never tolerate their kids being placed in harm's way.

No matter what its stereotype, Beverly Hills remains a cozy enclave of Little League games and farmers' markets on Sundays and sunbathing *bubbes* in the park, gathering at the senior center for drama classes. Many residents are renters who live in modest apartments, and most of them do so to send their children to the public schools. As a school board member told me: "We're really Mayberry RFD with a little Botox and lip gloss." The paradox of the place is that it's also inhabited by developers with get-rich schemes and deep pockets.

Of course, people want to know what I really think: is there solid proof of a connection between environmental exposures and illness at Beverly Hills High School? The question could take decades to answer with any degree of certainty. Even then, there may be no clear-cut resolution; science takes years to catch up with common sense. In the well-known case of Woburn, Massachusetts, depicted in the book and film *A Civil Action,* scientists looking for a causal link between trichloroethylene-laced water wells and childhood leukemia came up empty-handed until, twenty years later, a peer-reviewed journal published a correlation between prenatal exposures—what the mothers drank while pregnant in Woburn—rather than childhood exposures. Initially, the wrong question was being asked about the wrong population.

Still, there is much that we *do* know.

We are at a crossroads, environmentally speaking, in drawing more precise connections between illness and hazardous substances. If we live in a toxic soup of goop, we also increasingly understand how to tease apart fact from fiction, how environmental factors are not going away in cancer statistics. And, how children are affected may be the most striking product of all.

Despite rosy pronouncements from the Centers for Disease Control and Prevention, cancer rates are on the rise—and we now know that most cancers are caused by environmental factors, not genetic ones. In the word "environmental," though, scientists lump together everything that isn't genetic, meaning exposures to toxins and diet and "lifestyle" choices. But even those distinctions have become meaningless, because it turns out that every cancer is both environmental and genetic, a delicate interplay of many causes.

We don't hear more about environmental contributions to disease—herbicides and non-Hodgkin's lymphoma, cadmium and prostate cancer, polycyclic hydrocarbons and breast cancer—because our methods of quantifying causality are still in their infancy. It wasn't until the last few years, for example, that the federal government formally acknowledged that children are more vulnerable to the effects of carcinogens than adults. The extent to which this is true, however, remains unknown. As with so much else in science, the best answer is: "We just don't know."

As science plays catch-up, the judicial system offers relief. I know too well about the difficulties of proving causation. My father was the first American to successfully sue a cigarette company in a court of law. He died of mesothelioma, a cancer of the lining of the lung caused only by exposure to asbestos. His exposure came from smoking Kents, which were promoted by the Lorillard Tobacco Company as the "health" brand in the 1950s because of their Micronite filters. In fact, the filters were made of asbestos. The United States Supreme Court upheld his verdict in 2000 after his death. I had been opposed to the lawsuit when he was so ill, but he and my mom insisted it was the right thing to do. Making the connection between cancer and environmental factors, they taught us, is not only possible—it's imperative.

PART 1

The meek shall inherit the Earth, but not its mineral rights.

—J. Paul Getty

Come and listen to a story about a man named Jed
A poor mountaineer, barely kept his family fed,
Then one day he was shootin' at some food,
And up through the ground came a bubblin' crude.

Oil that is, black gold, Texas tea.

Well the first thing you know ol' Jed's a millionaire,
Kinfolk said Jed move away from there
Said Californy is the place you ought to be
So they loaded up the truck and moved to Beverly.

Hills, that is.
Swimmin' pools, movie stars.

The Beverly Hillbillies!

—Paul Henning, "Ballad of Jed Clampett,"
from *The Beverly Hillbillies* TV show (CBS, 1962–71)

CHAPTER ONE

FROM CEDARS-SINAI TO THE BEVERLY HILLS HOTEL

I the summer of 1996, they met in the doctor's office. It seemed an unremarkable moment, one that only reveals itself as something of profound consequence looking back.

Not until seven years later—lucky seven—would they embark on a quest together, their search for truth stamped with a case number, BC297083, and reduced to a state court file name: *Lori Lynn Moss et al. v. Venoco, Inc. et al.*

But when they first were introduced to each other in the oncologist's office that day, Lori Moss and Dana Goodman kept to themselves. What else could they do but wait? They didn't yet understand, of course, how their separate paths would intertwine, destined for a moment of justice. Or at least a rough approximation of it.

Upstairs on the sixth floor of the Cedars-Sinai Medical Towers, an imposing black-glass-and-granite structure a few blocks from Beverly Hills, the Tower Hematology Oncology Medical Group was usually crowded on Friday mornings, a zone of anxious efficiency. You checked in at the glass-block receptionist's desk and tried not to think about too much, maybe leafed through a periodical called *Lymphoma Today* or stared at one of Lance Armstrong's inspirational brochures: cancer research is worth the ride!

Just about every patient here appeared to be in his or her sixties or seventies, the age when most cancer diagnoses are made. Many dressed with style—Prada bags, cashmere coats, Hermes scarves—but the gestures at sartorial elegance did little to mask the sallow faces, wigs, and oxygen tanks.

Lori Moss was twenty-one and quite beautiful, a student at California State University, Northridge; Dana Goodman, a schoolteacher, was twenty-seven. Both were being treated for Hodgkin's disease, a rare form of cancer that attacks the lymph nodes and organs that are part of the body's immune system. Some doctors theorized that the cancer might be caused by exposure to a virus, like mononucleosis or Epstein-Barr, but no one knew for certain. In the United States, Hodgkin's disease is diagnosed in three of every one hundred thousand people, or fewer than ten thousand cases a year. Its occurrence is on the rise nationally among young adults and among people older than fifty-five, but it is unclear why.

Given how young Lori and Dana were compared to the other patients, it was impossible for the two not to notice each other. Still, just dealing with the task at hand—waiting and getting through the next treatment—was more than enough for anyone. Step by step.

The waiting, of course, was the hardest part—just like that old Tom Petty and the Heartbreakers song. It was a sort of purgatory: waiting for test results, especially over a long weekend. Waiting for blood to be drawn. Waiting for the poisons in plastic bags to be dripped into your veins, a circus of cisplatin and all the other chemo drugs with alphabetized nicknames. Adriamycin, bleomycin, vinblastin, decadron. ABVD.

Not that the people in this office weren't great. They were. The nurses called you "honey," the linen guy made sure your blanket was warm. Even the pastel tones and floral upholstery felt homey. And wasn't that the point? Anyone who'd been treated for cancer would tell you how the smallest gesture—the simplest act of kindness—meant everything, like a prayer.

But it was, finally, a lonely endeavor, agonizingly so. You stared at the carpet, the color of grass and red wine. There was a coffeemaker and that burned-coffee smell, magazines so worked over that their paper had become as limp as silk. On the wall, there were prints of flowers and a large digital clock near a bubbling fish tank, welcome signs of life and the forward movement of time.

The waiting could make you play mind games, though, like in the middle of the night when you'd launch into a round of hide-and-seek with your cancer cells, the seeds of death. You made bargains and promises, even ridiculous ones, to get through.

Lori Moss knew, for example, how strange it might seem that at a time like this her main concern was her hair. She understood that vanity and chemotherapy were an absurd combination, but she didn't care. When she first learned she had cancer, the only thing that went through her mind was that she'd rather jump off a building than lose all her beautiful, long hair. If people thought she was shallow, let them, she thought.

After her doctor told her to expect to lose all her hair, she did some research and discovered that chemotherapy patients had once been offered helmets with ice in them to prevent hair loss. The ice packs, though, were banned when doctors realized that they diminished the prognosis for patients with brain cancer. But since she had a form of lymphoma, her doctor gave her the go-ahead to freeze her scalp.

So, every other Friday for six months, she taped twelve-pound ice bags to her skull before each chemo session. She slept with a mirror in her bed to check her progress. She considered it a triumph that she lost only 40 percent of her hair. No doubt, it was thinner and curly now. But she beat the odds. She could handle this.

Lori squeezed her mother's hand. She felt so lucky to have her mom's support. Judy Herman worked at a domestic agency on Beverly Drive, the commercial thoroughfare in downtown Beverly Hills. She took off work—she'd do anything, of course—to be here with her daughter. Like so many mothers and daughters, they were as different as could be. Take shopping for clothing, for instance: Lori loved it; Judy hated it. That hardly mattered, though. They thought of each other as best friends. Lori's cancer diagnosis and treatment only strengthened that bond.

The ordeal started on a February morning in 1996, when Lori stepped out of the shower. As she was toweling herself off, she felt a lump under her right arm. At the time, she was living at home with her mother and brother in an apartment on South Rexford Drive. The lump didn't worry her at first. Her doctor thought she had a swollen gland, and she had no family history of cancer. But after a round of antibiotics, the lump grew larger. When she couldn't turn the steering wheel or grab her car keys because of pain, she had a needle biopsy. It was benign. Still, she didn't feel right. She went in for surgery to biopsy her lymph node, and the surgeon knew right away it was malignant. When the lymph nodes were removed, she had a mass the size of a baseball under her arm. It was stage III Hodgkin's disease.

In the hallway, between the waiting room and the examining rooms, Lori and Dana were introduced by their oncologist, a beautiful young cancer specialist with long brown hair. She mentioned that they had a lot in common. Not just Hodgkin's disease, but also Beverly.

"Beverly" was Beverly Hills High School, long considered one of the premier public schools in the nation. In recent years, though, the school had lost some of its academic bona fides when the locals began to eschew it in favor of private schools, like Harvard-Westlake or Crossroads. Still, the mythology of the place endured, thanks largely to its illustrious roster of graduates, including Hollywood celebrities like actors Angelina Jolie, David Schwimmer, and Carrie Fisher. And of course Beverly High was best known as the setting for TV shows and movies, such as *Beverly Hills, 90210* and *Clueless.* Never mind that everyone in town knew that the high school wasn't in the 90210 zip code, nor was the show or movie filmed there.

Lori had never been a particularly great student at Beverly, nor had she distinguished herself much there. She'd tell you that she was more socialite than academic, preferring time at the beach with her girlfriends or going to Friday football games to hitting the books.

Mostly, she remembered returning home from Beverly every day with crushing headaches, needing to nap.

"The big joke from my parents was that I had a brain tumor," she later recalled. Some joke.

The waiting.

Dana Goodman wanted to put it all behind her. The sooner the better. "I lost all my hair, lost a lot of weight," she later told a TV news reporter. "I was yellow." She joined a support group for young adults with cancer the following year. Like others, she discovered that just when you're lucky enough to be "cured," and everyone expects you to feel grateful, you can cross over to the dark side of what it means to be "cancer free." Decreased fertility. Early menopause. Thanks to life-saving treatments, young survivors of Hodgkin's lymphoma and other cancers are likely to suffer later in life from second cancers, cardiovascular disease, hearing loss, and even blindness.

When Dana's hair started growing back, she bleached it platinum blond. It was her way of moving on beyond the ranks of the survivors.

Seven years would elapse before the South Coast Air Quality Management District (AQMD) launched one of its most high-profile inspections in the organization's fifty-six-year history. It was a cool February afternoon in 2003. As the sun shone on a small patch of land in southern California—in a town known primarily for its wealth and privilege—a half dozen air quality engineers and inspectors drove west from the agency's headquarters in Diamond Bar along the 10 Freeway and headed to the southwestern edge of Beverly Hills. Armed with globe-shaped stainless-steel canisters and "organic vapor analyzers" that resembled golf clubs attached to briefcases, the inspectors arrived at an industrial compound where a towering oil derrick, brightly painted with flowered designs, was located less than one hundred meters from the track and football field at Beverly Hills High School. A gate opened, and as school district officials barred a TV camera crew from tagging along, the inspectors set to work.

After placing some of their air-sampling gear on the football bleachers, the inspectors reached their final destination: an oil-and-gas operation on less than an acre of land, including eighteen oil wells that pumped night and day with slant-drilled pipes extending a mile east beneath the residential neighborhood streets to exclusive Rodeo Drive, the world-famous shopping district. On the other side of a service road, they could see a hospital and a steam-generating power plant for the giant skyscrapers of Century City, the commercial neighborhood of office buildings, hotels, condominiums and shopping malls. The area had previously been part of the back lot of the 20th Century Fox Film Studios until the studio had to sell its land to developers in 1961 after the budget for *Cleopatra,* its epic film starring Elizabeth Taylor and Richard Burton, spun out of control.

The inspectors could hear students exercising on the track and playing fields nearby. They worked quickly. While some gathered one-minute "grab" samples of ambient air for the lab to analyze for hydrocarbons (reactive gases that mix with combustion gases and sunlight to make ozone, the main ingredient in smog) and toxic chemicals, an inspector named Katsumi Keeler snapped photographs to document their work.

Keeler wasn't scheduled to work that day, but he'd agreed to fill in for an inspector who had called in sick. Thanks to cars, diesel exhaust, and oil refineries, the Los Angeles Basin (along with Houston and the San Joaquin Valley) has the worst air pollution in the United States: one thousand four hundred people out of one million will contract cancer from exposure to hazardous chemicals in the air emitted mostly by petroleum combustion— emissions of about four hundred times federal limits, according to AQMD data. That means that as many as fourteen thousand people living in Los Angeles can expect to get cancer simply by breathing. Children bear the brunt of it; a recent study sponsored by the nonprofit National Environmental Trust found that a two-week-old baby in Los Angeles has already been exposed to more air toxins than the federal government deems acceptable over a lifetime.

California has long been at the forefront of regulating air pollution, setting higher emission standards than the federal government. It is up to Keeler and other air-quality "cops" to enforce the arcane provisions of both federal law and state mandates to protect the public health from industrial polluters. They have their work cut out for them; the AQMD has about a hundred inspectors to regulate more than thirty thousand businesses in an area of about eleven thousand square miles.

The fact that much of what is now the congested Los Angeles area sits atop huge oil fields has long been a source of concern for residents. Crude oil and pressurized gases often seep into the basements of homes. In 1985, methane escaping from underground deposits in the city's Fairfax district sparked a fire that burned for several days and caused an explosion inside the Ross Dress for Less store. Twenty years earlier, the Baldwin Hills dam collapsed as a result of subsidence from high-pressure water being injected into an oil production site. In 1999, plans to revamp the Belmont Learning Center, a downtown high school built over an old oil field, were scrapped when geologists realized that an earthquake fault lay beneath the property, which had explosive pockets of methane gas. Environmental hazards associated with oil wells, in other words, are ever present, if ignored. Like earthquakes or fires, these hazards are just risk factors in a desert town where oil and gas experts say there is more petroleum per acre of land than anywhere in the world, including Saudi Arabia.

Before long, Keeler grew worried. While checking out the equipment near the high school for leaks—the on-site structures included a tank farm with approximately four one-thousand-barrel tanks; two three-phase separators; a "water knockout" unit that separated oil, gas, and water; a pump house; a twenty-by-twenty-five-foot compressor house; an office building; and a six-foot-high brick wall separating six parking spaces—he and his colleagues discovered that the facility had been illegally "venting" 230,000 cubic feet of well gas into the air over the playing fields that day. Normally, Venoco, Inc., the Santa Barbara–based company operating the oil wells, sold its natural gas to the gas company through a pipeline for use in its service area. How long Venoco had been venting waste gas was unclear.

Later that evening, the Venoco company foreman, who had gone home for the day, was contacted by the inspectors. He agreed to return to the site to shut down the wells until further air tests could be conducted and a laboratory could analyze air samples for chemical components. Having won awards from oil industry regulators, Venoco prided itself on its operations in "sensitive" areas, such as Beverly Hills. In addition to owning several offshore oil platforms in Santa Barbara, the company, which had been financed by the Enron Corporation prior to that company's notorious bankruptcy, also worked an oil field in the Hagerman National Wildlife Refuge in Texas.

Upset by what he had seen, Katsumi Keeler shot off a note to his boss when he returned to the office. He rarely communicated with his chief executive officer, Barry Wallerstein, but he sent him an e-mail anyway, attaching a photograph:

> Barry, no matter how the sample analyses turn out, this photo shows my greatest concern: the small figures on the left-hand side are kids on the athletic field. I think that any parent would be concerned about their kids in this kind of environment.

Keeler ended his e-mail with a hope—that the test results would come back showing no problem.

> Even negative results are important, if only for peace of mind.

Peace of mind, though, would prove to be in short supply for Barry Wallerstein. What Keeler didn't yet know was that his boss was already intimately familiar with the site.

A 1971 graduate of Beverly Hills High School, Wallerstein had worked out on the track by the oil wells, which bobbed up and down like giant birds, back when he ran cross-country there. He had grown up in Beverly Hills on Ambassador Drive, up north in the swank section of town, and he gave credit to Mr. Porter, his teacher at Hawthorne Elementary School, for his lifelong interest in science. After receiving a doctorate in environmental science and engineering from UCLA, he worked for industry before taking a job in 1984 with the AQMD, a public agency that some environmentalists have ranked in American mythology right alongside the Tennessee Valley Authority for its broad powers and commitment to the area's economic development.

As home to the nation's first air pollution control program, the South Coast air district boasts a reputation for innovative and stringent air pollution policies; the agency is credited with greatly cleaning L.A.'s air during the past three decades. But critics charge that since the mid-1990s, the behemoth bureaucracy has fallen under heavy pressure from politicians and business leaders, who fear that the smog policies are harming California's economy. In a stinging rebuke of the AQMD's newly lenient air-pollution policies, the agency's esteemed scientific advisers resigned en masse in August 1996. The following year, Wallerstein took over his post.

Though he favored crisply tailored suits and sported a diamond pinkie ring, Wallerstein, at fifty, still looked much like the eighteen-year-old pictured in *Watchtower,* his high school yearbook. He had a wide face, wire-rimmed glasses, and a longish mop of straight brown hair punctuated on top by a bald spot.

Days before Keeler's e-mail, Wallerstein had received a phone call from Drew Griffin, an investigative reporter at KCBS, the local CBS television affiliate in Los Angeles. Griffin asked Wallerstein to go on camera to discuss the disturbing results of some air tests run on samples Griffin had obtained from an unspecified location in Beverly Hills.

When Wallerstein asked to see the data to prepare for the interview, he was puzzled by what Griffin showed him. Though the data had been analyzed by a reputable local lab, it was not what Wallerstein normally found in ambient air in southern California. Instead, the sample contained high levels of benzene, a known carcinogen, which is a widespread contaminant in the air and groundwater and comes from gasoline, car exhaust, industrial sources, and cigarette smoke. Where in Beverly Hills could this sample have come from? Based on the presence of certain pollutants—n-hexane, a powerful neurotoxin, and methane gas, which is not toxic but potentially explosive— he figured the source might be an auto body shop. Or maybe they had put a sampler curbside on Santa Monica Boulevard next to an idling car.

After some negotiations, the KCBS team disclosed to Wallerstein that the air samples had been taken on the field at Beverly Hills High School, right next to the oil wells. Wallerstein, in turn, agreed to let the TV crew film his inspectors arriving at the site to take air samples and then to share their results after the lab analyzed the samples, using complex instruments such as a gas chromatograph and mass spectrometer for toxic chemical detection. The chromatograph breaks up chemicals into their components, and the spectrometer identifies them by comparing them to libraries of known substances. With readings from both, scientists can usually identify a chemical.

"Okay," Wallerstein would later remember telling Griffin. "We want to make sure we have the right science. We'll go sample. I haven't offered this to anyone before. But this is obviously a serious allegation."

At that point, Wallerstein called the superintendent of schools in Beverly Hills to tell her that he intended to come to the school and pull some air samples. School officials, in turn, informed Wallerstein that the story was the subject of pending litigation by a personal-injury law firm from Westlake Village called Masry & Vititoe—the same firm that employed the celebrity-cum-environmental-activist Erin Brockovich.

"That frankly doesn't change what we do, right?" Wallerstein asked rhetorically. He was sitting at a long conference table in his office, nervously shaking his leg. "My obligation to the kids and the parents, the employees of the school district, and the people that live and work around the school site and the oil well is to make an independent, scientific determination as to whether or not there are elevated levels of air pollutants at the site. Plain and simple.

"Admittedly," he added, "because of the involvement of the Masry firm, it's generated a lot of publicity. Unfortunately, what that has also done is heighten the anxiety rate among the students and the parents at the school."

Still, it was Wallerstein who agreed to have his inspectors on camera, arriving at the school. And it was Wallerstein who would invest in new monitoring equipment after the lawyer Ed Masry accused his agency of not following the testing protocol of the U.S. Environmental Protection Agency.

Five days later, it was rainy and dark when Katsumi Keeler returned to inspect the Venoco site at Beverly Hills High School. The metal gratings were slippery. The lights kept flickering and going out, so he used a flashlight to see.

Even though the oil wells had been shut down, the hydrocarbon emissions from the oil-water separator unit in background readings were so high that Keeler feared for his own safety and chose to abort his inspection early. He had intended to check for hydrocarbon leaks from one thousand component parts but settled on four hundred instead, because of concerns about explosive levels of gas. Most toxic air pollution is not from refinery smokestacks but from leaks in equipment, such as valves, flanges, and hatches, known as "fugitive emissions."

He noted in his report that his gas probe, or organic vapor analyzer, kept "flaming out," meaning that concentrations of volatile organic compounds were so high that they could not be read by his instruments. The probe "flames out" above one hundred thousand parts per million, which is the explosive limit for methane gas. Keeler observed gas bubbling out from hatches.

In an e-mail to his boss on the morning of February 12, 2003, he wrote:

> I can't stress enough that this is becoming an immediate health and
> safety issue, not because of chronic effects, but due to the possibility
> of explosion.

Keeler recommended contacting the Beverly Hills Fire Department, and
added:

> We should note that these emissions existed when the ambient
> temperature was low. At higher temperatures, and in a confined space,
> hydrocarbon emissions are probably much worse. . . . Note also that the
> integrity of the facility's electrical system is suspect. . . . And, of course,
> there is no vapor recovery to speak of. Therefore, I think we should act
> with an abundance of caution here.

Wallerstein, however, seemed more concerned about alleviating "the
anxiety rate" in Beverly Hills than in publicly airing his inspector's safety
concerns. Public reassurances about the school's safety were key. Wallerstein
appeared on the *Today* show in May 2003 to announce that there were "no
abnormal" levels of toxins in the air at the school. He failed to mention that
the oil wells had been shut down when some of those tests were conducted.
And, he told *People* magazine, he'd send his own children to Beverly.

Everything, in other words, was safe.

A consummate bureaucrat, Wallerstein hedged his bets about safety by
pledging further air testing—a flagrant cop-out to many, who charged that
political expediency was taking precedence over science. Three weeks later,
the oil wells were up and running again.

Not every scientist agreed with Wallerstein's rosy assessment. In San
Francisco, I spoke with Jack Broadbent, director of the U.S. Environmental
Protection Agency's air division for California and a former AQMD staffer. I
was meeting Broadbent at a delicate time. Frustrated by the Bush administration's pro-industry environmental policies, he had just announced his resignation from his EPA post to head up the air district in the San Francisco
Bay area, which might account for his candor with me.

I told him that Venoco had temporarily been shut down for air violations, and I showed him the AQMD's data; one air sample taken from a leaking tank on February 11, 2003, for example, showed thirty-six parts per

billion of benzene, nearly double the California reference exposure level. But the agency said it was not representative of air at the school, since the sample was taken one inch from the leak.

"I wouldn't want a facility like that adjacent to my kids' school," Broadbent said bluntly. "And I wouldn't want my kids to go there."

When I reminded him that Wallerstein said he'd send his own children to Beverly High, he laughed derisively. "That's because he went to school there," he said.

The day after her last treatment in 1996—six months of chemotherapy and daily doses of radiation for a month—Lori Moss didn't feel much like celebrating. Her cousin dragged her out of the house to get some lunch on Beverly Drive, and that's when she met Randy Moss, a handsome marketing executive.

"I told Randy in our first conversation, 'I have cancer,' and it didn't scare him off," Lori recalled. They were married just two years later, looking forward to starting a family. Those plans were upended in October 2001, when Lori felt another lump in her neck. She thought she was overreacting, so she asked Randy to feel it too.

Another biopsy followed and then the call from her oncologist.

"Is somebody there with you?" she asked Lori on the phone. "You're not alone, are you?"

This time, it was thyroid cancer. Two cancers by the time she was twenty-seven. "The first one was horrific," Lori recalled. "But the second time it was: holy shit."

It's possible that the second cancer had been caused by radiation treatments for the first one, but it's unclear precisely why or how it evolved. The only known cause of thyroid cancer is radiation exposure.

Lori found herself back at Cedars for more radioactive treatments, but this time the ordeal was even more surreal. The hospital room's floors were covered in paper. Everything else was layered in plastic—the toilet seat, the arms of the bed, the phone, the light switch.

"They asked Randy to leave the room. They took out this pill and they had to witness that I swallowed my pill. They checked inside my mouth and under my tongue to make sure I didn't have it, and they left the room and said: 'We'll see you in three days.'

"I wake up in a room by myself with some foreign object in my body, and I'm looking out my window at Jerry's Deli across the street, and I can't eat anything. I couldn't be within six feet of my husband. I couldn't sleep in the same bed for a week. I couldn't be around pregnant women for a month.

"I basically was exuding radiation out of my body."

In the weeks that followed, Lori Moss fell into a funk. She had no energy. Her thyroid felt like it had gone haywire: she had no desire to do anything. Randy convinced her that she should get out of the house.

Lori had heard that the environmental activist Erin Brockovich was doing a book signing at the Beverly Hills Public Library for her new self-help book, *Take It from Me: Life's a Struggle but You Can Win.*

"You have to go," Randy said. "*We* have to go."

"I didn't want to go," Lori recalled, "but we went."

Lori and Randy stood in line for three hours so she could talk to the woman whom she admired, thanks to Julia Roberts's portrayal in the Academy Award–winning film *Erin Brockovich.* The movie, of course, tells the story of how Brockovich and Masry spearheaded a major lawsuit against the Pacific Gas and Electric Company, when she discovered that the highly toxic rust inhibitor hexavalent chromium had leaked into the groundwater of the desert town of Hinkley, California; the giant utility ultimately paid $333 million in damages to more than six hundred Hinkley residents—the largest toxic tort settlement in U.S. history at the time. The real-life story was slightly less black-and-white than the film version, however: despite the chemical contamination of groundwater, a state cancer study never found an excess of cancers in the area's residents.

At forty-two, Erin Brockovich seemed larger than life to Lori for reasons beyond her newfound celebrity status. Her physical stature—she's five foot nine and big boned—lends her an Amazonian presence, like a female warrior. And her trademark cleavage, a result of the almost comical breast implants that gave her the desired Barbie-esque proportions, imparts a sort of self-mocking air, like the bombshell from *The Producers:* if you've got it, flaunt it.

Indeed, much of how Brockovich was portrayed on screen is apparent in person: She makes unexpected movements and gestures. There is a languor about her that shifts without warning to passion, matched by sudden rises in the volume of her voice. She gnashes gum like this could be her last piece, favors designer heels, and sports skirts that add a sort of floozy appeal. Her hair color can change without warning. She always seems to be trying to tweak convention. A registered Republican, she regularly votes Democratic.

She generally abhors lawyers but works for one. She is endearing and appalling all in the same moment. On the board of the nonprofit advocacy organization Children's Health Environmental Coalition, she believes her most important job is to protect children's health.

At the front of the line, Lori Moss couldn't see anything about Erin Brockovich except her heart. She thought it was big and open.

"I'm a cancer survivor," she told Brockovich.

"Oh, my God," Brockovich said. "I'm really sorry."

"I just got back from getting more scans in the hospital," she said.

"You've been standing in line a very long time," Brockovich said, checking her watch. "As a matter of fact, it's been three hours."

"Well," Lori said, "I just really wanted to see you."

She told Brockovich about the Hodgkin's disease and thyroid cancer. Lori noticed that Brockovich's strong, self-assured voice had the flat ring of Kansas, where she was born, the youngest of four children. There was something remarkably rock-solid and poised about her.

"Look, I'm not a doctor," Brockovich said, "but, wow—two cancers. That's a bummer, to say the least."

Lori said she had grown up in Beverly Hills and attended the high school there. She said: "I don't know why I have cancer. Nobody in my family has it."

Brockovich asked her if there was anything unusual about Beverly High, any industrial, chemical, or environmental concerns.

"There's an oil derrick there," Lori said.

An oil derrick at a school? Brockovich thought that sounded odd. "I don't know anything about the school," she said. A resident of Thousand Oaks in the San Fernando Valley, Brockovich rarely "went down" to Beverly Hills except to shop. She suggested that Lori find out if any other people from Beverly High were sick. That might yield some clues.

Lori noticed that Brockovich had tears in her eyes as they said good-bye. She hugged Lori. "I'll call you if I find out anything," she said, handing Lori a business card. On it, she goes by Erin Brockovich-Ellis, a name change since her 1999 marriage to Eric Ellis, an actor she met in an airport.

Months passed, and Lori didn't hear anything. She tried calling Brockovich, but her call was never returned.

Nonetheless, Lori was determined to answer the question Brockovich had asked: what about other Beverly graduates? With a furious intensity, she set out to find them.

She began to keep a journal. Using her 1992 *Watchtower* yearbook, she started researching other young graduates who had fallen ill, writing down the information she gleaned beneath various headings. Name. Graduation date. Disease.

She tracked down Dana Goodman, of course, the woman she had seen six years earlier in the oncologist's waiting room. Through the friend of a friend, she heard of another young woman from Beverly Hills, Stephanie Meyers, a thirty-two-year-old social worker now living in San Francisco who had been in Dana's support group at the Wellness Community, a cancer support center in nearby Santa Monica. Stephanie's younger brother had been in Lori Moss's class at Beverly.

Stephanie's family lived on South Roxbury Drive, just a few blocks from the high school. She didn't attend Beverly—her parents sent her to Westlake, a private girls' school—but her family did receive royalty checks from the oil company for the oil that flowed beneath their home. "A couple hundred bucks a month—it was really cool, getting that check every month or so," she later recalled. "It was like free money."

Stephanie Meyers was working as a special-education teacher in Culver City when she began to develop sharp stomach pains in the fall of 1996. At times, the pain was so excruciating that she couldn't stand up. She pleaded with her students, a classroom of young boys with attention deficit hyperactivity disorder (ADHD), not to be rambunctious. But the stomach pains didn't go away.

On March 26, 1997, she was diagnosed with non-Hodgkin's lymphoma (stage II), a blood-borne cancer that has been linked to benzene exposure among petroleum industry workers.

A 1997 National Cancer Institute study of workers in Shanghai, China, where benzene exposure is far higher than in the United States, concluded that workers with ten or more years of benzene exposure had a risk of developing non-Hodgkin's lymphoma more than four times that of the general population. A more recent NCI benzene study published in the journal *Science* in December 2004 concluded that benzene causes diseases of the blood, even at levels below those considered safe by the U.S. government, "particularly among susceptible subpopulations." In response, the American Petroleum Institute, an industry trade group, challenged the U.S. government study by financing a $27 million study of its own, paid for by BP, Chevron-Texaco, ConocoPhillips, ExxonMobil, and Shell Chemical; the petrochemical giants have final approval over their data.

What constitutes a "safe" level of benzene exposure has been debated since the late 1940s, but for almost twenty years, one part of benzene per million parts of air has been considered the maximum acceptable exposure for workers in an eight-hour workday. Barry Wallerstein's air samples from the rig's vent pipe at Beverly High contained benzene at four times that level, but that didn't reflect what students were breathing on the athletic fields.

"It's unsettling," Stephanie Meyers later said, "to think my cancer could have been prevented."

Just as Lori Moss was struggling with her second cancer at Cedars-Sinai, three thousand miles away in New York City, another Beverly Hills High School graduate, Carrie Powers, was facing a health crisis of her own.

Accustomed to the fast-paced, high-stress work of convertible bond trading on Wall Street, Carrie suddenly became plagued by terrible headaches. "I'd start a sentence, and halfway through, I couldn't remember what I was saying," she later recalled. "On a trading desk, that just can't happen. People kept saying, 'What is wrong with this woman?'"

Her internist told her that she was too stressed from both work and an impending divorce, and recommended antidepressants. "I said, 'I'm not depressed. I'm in pain.'"

She had long been anemic, so she figured that her exhaustion was due to her blood counts being off since the birth of her daughter in 1993. An MRI at New York-Presbyterian Hospital proved otherwise: Carrie Powers was diagnosed with a brain tumor, a meningioma, pressing on her cortex. She underwent surgery immediately to have it removed.

But several months later, Carrie, who used to hold the banner for the marching band on the football field at Beverly, still wasn't feeling right. She consulted a hematologist, who did a bone marrow biopsy. She was diagnosed with MGUS—monoclonal gammopathy undetermined significance. She learned that about one fourth of the people with MGUS, which is a protein deficiency, develop a form of bone marrow cancer, called multiple myeloma—and she was one of them. Multiple myeloma is a cancer in which the average age at diagnosis is seventy. Carrie was forty-five.

While it is generally accepted that, at certain levels, benzene exposures can cause leukemia, scientists argue about the level of risk posed by exposures to lower levels, and about whether benzene may also cause other blood-related diseases. When Carrie Powers consulted Dr. Brian Durrie, a multiple myeloma expert at Cedars-Sinai Medical Center, one of the first questions he asked her was: "Have you ever had petrochemical exposure?"

Lori Moss was beginning to see a connection. She tracked down another Beverly graduate with Hodgkin's disease, Carl Wilson, who worked both as a chef at a Venice café and a drummer in a rock band. The son of the famed Beach Boys drummer Dennis Wilson, Carl had graduated from Beverly two years before Lori. He and his brother were raised by their mother, Barbara, in a modest triplex near La Cienega Park at the edge of town, a section she called "Barely Hills." A single parent and psychotherapist, Barbara Wilson had moved to Beverly Hills to send her sons to a "safe" school.

In his early teens, Carl loafed through school, spending lots of time skateboarding down the ramps of nearby parking garages on Wilshire Boulevard and surfing as much as possible. "We were little surf rats," he later recalled.

At Beverly, the first thing he did every morning was run around the track in PE. "At eight o'clock in the morning for four years I'm going out onto this field," he recalled with some anger. "It's the first thing I do every day, you know? And you know, my mom won't let me have chocolate cereal in the morning 'cause it's bad for me, but she'll let me go run in the benzene? It's not like we knew anything about it."

In the summer of 1998, he was diagnosed with shingles. His dermatologist told him that it was unusual for a twenty-five-year-old to get shingles but didn't think much of it. Not long after, he was walking on the beach and wearing a backpack, his hand resting on the strap, when he noticed a lump on the side of his neck. He tried to ignore it but couldn't.

"It was like the size of a walnut, but it wasn't round. It felt like it had a weird shape and it even seemed to almost have a horn coming out of it. It wasn't symmetrical. It was hard, you know, and it felt like I could grab it: I could almost get behind it and grab it.

"And I remember being scared, like I had gotten this feeling over me like, this doesn't feel right. By the time the doctor saw me, he pointed out that there were four other smaller pea-sized lumps that were running up the side of my neck." A biopsy followed.

His cell phone rang while he was driving with his mom down Crescent Heights Drive to a coffee shop, and his doctor delivered the bad news: it was Hodgkin's disease, stage IV. When he saw his oncologist, Dr. Peter Boesberg, he was reassured that Hodgkin's disease is highly curable. Still, not all of Boesberg's patients with Hodgkin's disease had happy outcomes. The doctor felt a deep attachment to one in particular, who, like Carl Wilson, had been diagnosed as a twenty-five-year-old. Tom Fries, a sound editor with a young family, died at age forty-seven from complications arising from his treatment. He also was a graduate of Beverly Hills High School. In fact, he graduated in the same class as Barry Wallerstein, the AQMD chief. The same year I did.

Lori Moss hadn't yet heard about Tom Fries. But her list was growing, and almost everyone on it seemed to have either Hodgkin's disease, non-Hodgkin's lymphoma, or thyroid cancer.

With a renewed sense of urgency, she called and left another message for Erin Brockovich, who had begun doing some sleuthing of her own.

The Los Angeles personal-injury law firm of Masry & Vititoe, where Erin Brockovich works as director of research, sits atop a green hillside on the western edge of the San Fernando Valley in Westlake Village. Located in the cul-de-sac of a commercial park lined with flowering plum trees, the law offices are housed inside a two-story cream-colored stucco building with darkened windows. The front entrance, framed by a fountain and an iron banister, has a faux Italianate feel.

Upstairs, the lobby is decorated with burnished woods, nautical paintings, and gold-gilded furniture: it looks like a set designer's idea of what a law firm should look like, but not the schlocky one depicted on film. The walls are lined with framed magazine articles comparing their real and movie selves. Certainly, their real-life operation is predicated on a simple routine: Brockovich, using her celebrity status, acts as a veritable media magnet, and Masry plays the grandstanding lug, sometimes abrasive and insulting, but a brilliant tactician nonetheless.

"We're road warriors, like Click and Clack," Brockovich said of their partnership, referring to the hosts of *Car Talk,* the National Public Radio program devoted to car issues, because she and her boss drive up and down the state together in pursuit of new cases. After Masry gave her a $2.5 million bonus on the Hinkley case, she bought a silver BMW. She traded that car in for a black Hummer, not exactly standard issue for someone with environmental leanings, and then moved on to a Toyota Prius.

When Brockovich first told Masry about meeting Lori Moss in Beverly Hills, he was distinctly unimpressed. She knew it would be hard to get him to agree to take the case. So she dug in.

She conducted a public-records search of the city of Beverly Hills, of the oil and gas industry, of internal government documents from the AQMD.

Though her allure may be about breast size, her genius resides in her organizational mania—gathering, filing, underlining, and memorizing boxloads of information, perhaps to compensate for her dyslexia.

What she found was a big-time oil operation. Pumping 740 barrels of oil and 330,000 cubic feet of natural gas a day, Venoco's eighteen active wells next to Beverly High now brought the school system and the city a combined $700,000 a year in royalties. But before the field was worked over, it had been far more lucrative: in 1973, public records showed, the city, schools, and residents stood to make more than $25 million in royalties; other documents suggested that royalties could be twice that amount. It was, Brockovich now believed, a cash cow that no one wanted to lose—regardless of the danger.

In fact, while production increased at the site during the 1980s, public records showed that repeated complaints and warnings about bad odors and noise from nearby residents were ignored by the Beverly Hills City Council. In April 1985, for instance, dozens of residents of the Century Park East condominiums, located directly across the street from the high school on Olympic Boulevard in Los Angeles, communicated with city officials, to no avail.

"It's common knowledge," wrote one, "that twelve hundred Beverly Hills families divide $75,000 per month from the operation. I have been told that because of this we haven't got a chance to reverse your rulings, which changed an area that was residential to an ugly industrial area. Money shouldn't be everything; human values, no?"

Another resident, Ruth Goldstein, complained: "The wind brings in the oil odor which is sickening." A resident named Elizabeth Biegler said: "We have called Beverly Hills police at night. They stopped until police went and then started again. It deposits oily dirt on my window sills. Why were we not asked to vote on this project before it was started?"

Abraham Gottfried said: "Four hundred eight residences (the number of condominiums at Century Park East) if located in the Beverly Hills flats (south of Wilshire) would take up 15 square blocks. If this many residences were negatively impacted in Beverly Hills, surely you would sit up and take notice. For 24 hours a day, 7 days a week, the rumbling of the machinery and the operation of the oil tanker trucks, make it impossible for us to open a window in our apartment, located as we are on the East side of the building. Even with all the windows closed the noise permeates our apartment. When the actual drilling or the change of the oil pipes is taking place, the noise is deafening."

Brockovich began wading through a 1978 Environmental Impact Report prepared by the Beverly Hills Oil Company for the city of Beverly Hills. On page 158, she found a passage that read: "Air quality monitoring data cannot indicate the air quality at the site since local emissions are substantially dispersed within a few thousand feet."

She stuck a Post-it on the page with the notation, "BULLSHIT!"

Then, as a reminder, she attached another note: "Never, ever did any air monitoring or health risk assessment."

But Brockovich could go only so far with public-record searches. What she really needed was air, soil, and water samples to secure evidence of contamination. She'd take them herself, since she had been certified by California's Occupational Safety and Health Administration to do so. But she was allergic to sulfur and carried an epinephrine "pen," an autoinjector of epinephrine, for emergencies. Her brother, Tommy, died of anaphylactic shock in 1992. She didn't know how much hydrogen sulfide might be in the natural gas at Beverly High, so she'd need to get Jim Drury, the firm's "environmental specialist," to take samples.

Drury had already tried to pull some air samples at Beverly, but he had been kicked off the campus. Now he'd have to sneak on the field in the dark of night. And the lab testing was going to cost at least $50,000.

Brockovich steeled herself. She walked into Masry's office and told him what she needed, hoping for his approval.

"This is goddamn Beverly Hills!" he screamed at her. "Forget it."

Brockovich, of course, was accustomed to such dismissals. Having worked for Masry for ten years, she had a sign taped up behind her desk that read: "Obstacles are what you see when you take your eyes off the goal."

"Edward," she persisted, "what do you want me to do with this information?"

No one understood the difficulties of securing "exposure" information better than Masry, who practically revolutionized the way community groups try to keep regulators and industrial polluters honest. In June 1994, he and Brockovich represented residents of the northern California town of Crockett, near the Unocal refinery, after a chemical release there coated the neighborhood with sticky goo. For years, hundreds of people thought their respiratory ailments and illnesses were related to odd smells around Unocal, but there was no way to monitor what was coming out of the refinery.

While Masry and Brockovich were working in Crockett one day, the plant sprang a sulfur leak and made them both sick. Masry called the local air control district and asked what substance had escaped so he could tell their doctors. But he was told that company air monitors showed there was no problem. Indignant, he decided to equip his clients with air-sampling equipment and surround the plant with air monitors so they could gather their own data on what the plant was releasing. But the airtight, stainless-steel containers, known as Summa canisters, were, at $1,000 each, too expensive. Masry asked an environmental engineer to come up with a cheaper model, and they devised an air-sampling bucket that cost $300 to produce.

"That was just really exciting when that happened," recalled Denny Larson, who now directs the Refinery Reform Campaign in Richmond, California. "When they unveiled those things at that first meeting out there—oh my God, the people in the community just went nuts, you know, because they'd always wanted something like that.

"They knew that if somebody would just test the air when these guys were blowing this stuff out at you, they would find that it was full of toxic chemicals and harmful. But nobody, of course, would ever do that. The inspector would show up an hour late. Or he wouldn't have his canister with him. Or the monitoring station would always get put two miles away from the fence line, when everyone wanted to put it at the fence line." The cheaper buckets, according to data later compiled by the EPA, produced results comparable to the pricey Summa canisters.

With the data they gathered, Masry and Brockovich won their cases against Unocal in 1997, collecting $80 million for six thousand residents. Data supplied by polluters, who often calibrated monitoring equipment so chemicals could be detected only at very high levels, was unreliable; Larson viewed the cheaper buckets as a "missing link." Masry then donated thirty of the air-sampling buckets to a local environmental justice group, Communities for a Better Environment. And Larson set up "bucket brigades" in dozens of so-called fence-line communities across the country—from industrial hot spots in northern California to towns in "Cancer Alley," a hundred-mile stretch along the Mississippi River between Baton Rouge and New Orleans where more than one hundred petrochemical plants are located. Beverly Hills, though, was another story.

Back at her office desk, Brockovich picked up the phone to call Lori Moss. Excited, Lori shared her own findings about the other young Beverly graduates—more than twenty now—with different forms of lymphoma and thyroid cancer, and desperate to know why.

With a larger client base, Brockovich knew that Masry would start to get interested too. He sued anybody when he thought he could rationally expect a settlement that exceeded the cost of litigation. To prevail at trial, the burden of proof in a personal-injury case is the preponderance of the evidence, as opposed to a scientific certainty.

The risks inherent in toxic tort cases, though, are sizable: not only is proving causation an almost impossible task, given the number of "confounders" that can turn a seemingly airtight case into a murky one, but the financial burdens can be steep. On average, it costs at least half a million dollars to mount a case, usually more, on a contingency basis. And going up against a platoon of corporate lawyers has its own set of headaches, including an avalanche of legal delays and costly court appearances. According to one insider, the Beverly Hills case could prove to be "the Mount Everest of toxic torts."

Masry hadn't been inside a courtroom in more than a decade. One of his strengths resided in knowing how to partner on a big case. In the Hinkley litigation, he relied on the well-respected Los Angeles trial lawyers Thomas Gerardi and Walter Lack for support. In the Beverly Hills case, he would team up with a forty-year-old Southern Baptist from Texas by the name of Allen M. Stewart. The baby-faced lawyer was a partner at Baron & Budd, a Dallas-based law firm that is one of the largest plaintiffs' firms in the nation, specializing in asbestos cases. Stewart's partner, Frederick M. Baron, had been president of the Association of Trial Lawyers of America and an early supporter of John Edwards's 2004 presidential bid.

Exactly what the public gains from Masry's work is unclear. He's a poor substitute for EPA lawyers who are charged with protecting environmental laws. But he and Brockovich have thrived, at least in part because enforcement and regulation of the federal Clean Air Act by the EPA has grown weaker in recent years.

Not only did the Bush administration cut the agency's enforcement staff by 270 positions, it also allowed industry to pay less to pollute. In 2002, the number of penalties recovered from polluters in civil cases settled in federal court declined by half compared to the previous three years. At the same time, the EPA admitted that toxic releases had increased by 5 percent. A 2004 review of toxic air emissions by the nonprofit Environmental Integrity Project found that the EPA routinely underreports the amount of refinery and chemical-plant carcinogens to the public, particularly when plant "upsets" or disruptions in normal operations occur that require refinery operators to dispose of gas through flares or vents.

In 2005, a scathing report by the Government Accountability Office, the investigative arm of Congress, criticized the EPA's ability to ensure that tens of thousands of chemicals in commercial use did not pose a health risk, especially to children. Unlike pharmaceutical and pesticide producers, the manufacturers of most chemical substances are not legally required to supply human toxicity information before selling their products to the public. The burden, in other words, remains on the public to show harm—usually after the fact.

"When Erin first told me about Beverly Hills," Masry later recalled, sitting in his corner office overlooking the mountains, "we didn't know what the hell was going on. All we knew at that time was there seemed to be an abnormal amount of certain types of cancer coming from graduates at the school. We didn't know if it was the population as a whole. We had no idea what we were going to find."

This time, he gave Brockovich the go-ahead. But there was a caveat. Masry insisted that the air sampling be documented by a news outlet. Publicity, he figured, would help to attract more clients. As mayor of the bedroom community of Thousand Oaks, Masry sat on the city council with a KCBS-TV producer, Claudia Bill–de la Peña. He called her and asked if Drew Griffin, an investigative reporter who also lived in Thousand Oaks, might be interested in a big story.

The law firm's air sampling would find high levels of the carcinogen benzene, the neurotoxin n-hexane, and methane, a substance in natural gas, at the high school bleachers. Benzene in one air sample was measured at eighteen parts per billion—twenty-eight times higher than the average concentration found in ambient air in L.A.

By the time the TV station aired its story, "Toxic School?" during sweeps week, Beverly Hills was facing a public relations meltdown.

The fallout was swift.

The day after the story aired in February 2003, school district officials met with Masry, who had invited Dr. Gwen Gross, the superintendent of schools, to discuss the results of his law firm's air sampling. The meeting, though, was a disaster.

Gross never showed. Instead, she sent David Orbach, the school district's attorney, and an environmental consultant named Mark Katchen, who last conducted air tests for the school district back in 1999, when parents were worried about toxins inside portable bungalows after their children at

Beverly Vista Elementary School grew ill. Those air tests revealed extremely high levels of benzene and formaldehyde inside classrooms, according to Katchen's secret "draft" report, which was never released publicly.

Katchen arrived at Masry's office in Thousand Oaks with Venoco's attorney, Gisele Goetz, who had not been invited, as well as the company's haz-mat supervisor, who demanded the raw data from the law firm's air sampling.

Orbach, the school district's attorney, accused Masry of putting Beverly High in the untenable position of possibly going bankrupt if he pursued such a frivolous lawsuit. If Masry and Brockovich cared so much about the students at the high school, why had they waited for months to share their information?

Brockovich shot back that money concerns were tacky.

"I was worried about people with cancer, not bankruptcy," she later said. "At the time, we had just begun our investigation. They weren't willing to discuss our findings and how this was potentially exposing the students and faculty."

"The superintendent stood us up and sent her henchmen over," Jim Drury, the Masry & Vititoe environmental specialist, added. "Then they put me on the spot and gave me the third degree. At the time, we said, 'Hey, enough is enough. See you boys later,' because they're trying to impeach the fact that I walked onto that property, placed a Summa canister with a flow controller, and sampled for eight hours, which anybody could do."

The meeting ended abruptly. It seemed a harbinger of the bare-knuckle legal fight that would ensue.

On a sunny Thursday afternoon in early March 2003, the phones were ringing off the hook inside the offices of Masry & Vititoe. Since the KCBS report, hundreds of Beverly graduates with cancer had called, and hundreds more were interested in the law firm's evidence.

Wearing high-heeled boots, low-waist blue jeans, and a cream-colored hippie shirt with turquoise beading, Brockovich was conferring with a Malibu filmmaker about how best to sell their case to a sophisticated audience at an upcoming "community" meeting in Beverly Hills: how to convince potential plaintiffs that the oil operation on the school campus caused their cancers and that the city, the school, and the oil companies, including Venoco, were to blame. The day before, a crew from the *Today* show had interviewed them for a feature piece.

Brockovich spoke in clipped cadences, like an old-fashioned cop from an episode of *Dragnet*. Dates were rarely uttered with the name of the month, for example, but rather with numbers, as in "two-oh-six-oh-three." There was something distinctly noirish about her, save for her flair for fashion.

When Masry padded into her office, he kissed her on top of the head. She smooched the air in return.

"Hi, babe," he said to her, having just returned from a morning of dialysis, which he underwent three times a week.

She polished off a leftover slice of pizza from the office kitchen and then topped it off with an orange jelly candy from Costco.

"You okay?" she asked him as he slumped into the chair in front of her desk. She called him "Edward"; he called her "kid." He wore black drawstring pants and a loose-fitting silk shirt.

At seventy, Masry looked pale and fleshy and appeared quite frail, despite his combative reputation. His hands trembled, and his mind could wander.

"I always tell him he's a roach," she said, joking about his multiple health issues, including five-way heart bypass surgery and chronic leukemia, to which he had yet to succumb—much to the dismay of his naysayers, who viewed him as little better than a skilled extortionist. "Fearmonger," "ambulance chaser," "slimeball," were some of the kinder names he was called.

Yet Masry also had a distinctly avuncular bearing. His boutique firm was clearly a family affair: His ex-wife, Jackie, worked in the accounting department. His daughter Louanna Masry-Weeks, a lawyer, worked there, as did his son, Louis Masry. So did his wife Joey's sons, Chris and Tim, who tended to the computer department downstairs. "This is kind of a family deal," Masry said.

Even so, troubles had surfaced. In May 2000 a paralegal named Kissandra Cohen, described by the *Los Angeles Times* as both a child prodigy and "coltish," sued Masry for wrongful termination, sexual harassment, and slander. She claimed a lawyer in the firm gave her a lollipop shaped like a penis, rubbed her thigh, caressed her neck, and marked up a copy of the *Jewish Journal,* which had profiled her, with the words, "Cool and kosher!! No pork on these gams!" In response, Masry insisted he fired her for poor work performance and, during a TV interview, referred to her as one of many "people coming out of the woodwork," in hopes of profiting from him after the release of the film *Erin Brockovich*. He also said Cohen had joined in the office teasing, as when she gave Masry a G-string at a party. While Cohen lost on her claims for sex harassment and wrongful termination, she proved that

Masry had slandered her—and was awarded $120,000 by the jury. Masry, ever the fighter, said the money was "worth it."

Born in Paterson, New Jersey, Masry grew up poor. He was the son of immigrant parents from Syria and France who started a silk apparel business that failed. When his family headed to California, they bought a tiny bungalow in the San Fernando Valley. For three years, he and his brother had to sleep in a tent outside. One of his happiest memories was the day his father bought him a bed. The experience drew him both to representing underdogs and to wanting to make large sums of money like lawyers in movies. He attended Valley Junior College and later earned a law degree from Loyola University in Los Angeles, having done well on a placement exam but never graduating from college. "I was always a party freak," he once explained.

Over the years, Masry represented politicians, judges, prostitutes and pimps, a stripper named Lucky Wynn, a religious cult, former *Baywatch* star Pamela Lee Anderson, and, at one time, more than half of the Los Angeles Rams football team. Other clients included the rock band Steppenwolf of "Born to Be Wild" fame and a televangelist for whom Masry burned a court order on television. Accused by the state attorney general's office of bribing a lieutenant governor and of theft of funds, he was jailed five times, but the comedian Danny Thomas once bailed him out from serving sixty days.

In 1991, while defending a $1.5 billion money-laundering case, he suffered a heart attack in court. After a two-week recess the trial resumed, but when it was over he promised his wife he'd never go back to the courtroom.

A lover of Las Vegas, Masry mostly trafficked in the lucrative, high-stakes poker game called environmental tort cases, having originally represented defendants accused of polluting Lake Arrowhead's marina. Since the original PG&E case, he and Brockovich had shadowed a procession of deep-pocketed energy and oil companies. In the late 1990s, for instance, Masry won property damage settlements from Unocal Corporation for sixty residents in Avila Beach, a coastal town north of Santa Barbara, where the oil company was forced to clean up a 400,000-gallon oil spill by digging up the entire town and removing tons of contaminated soil.

To be sure, Masry also lost a few of his environmental cases, most notably one against the defense contractor Rocketdyne in 1997, but even some of his defeats make him look farsighted. Most recently, his firm has represented the environmental group Communities for a Better Environment in a suit against a raft of oil companies for contaminating groundwater with benzene and MTBE from leaking underground storage tanks throughout California. MTBE, a fuel additive that the EPA upgraded from being a "probable" to a "likely" carcinogen in 2005 after California banned it, has contaminated the water supplies of communities in more than thirty-six states.

"We filed that on behalf of the citizens of California," he said. "We've become a private attorney general, which is good because we went to the attorneys general. We had meetings with them. No question they would have taken this case except they didn't have the resources."

Clearly, Masry's goal is less about muckraking and more about the money to be made in his line of work. Even his planned public meeting at the Beverly Hills Hotel would ultimately reveal his multiple agendas: he wanted to inform the public about a possible danger in the community, but he also needed more claimants than he already had attracted to his Web site for the case, in order to earn millions more in legal fees.

Jim Drury, a large, burly man wearing a Yankees baseball cap, poked his head in the door to Brockovich's office. He waved a sheaf of papers at Brockovich, having just received more lab results on the Beverly Hills case.

"Oil leak slop pit," he said. "Tics off the charts. Weird stuff in there."

"Slop pit?" I asked. "Tics?"

Tics, she translated, stood for "tentatively identified compounds"—a term used by the laboratory before final results of the chemical analysis could be determined.

"Yeah," she said, "and there's some scary shit in it: 740 parts per billion (ppb) of acetone. Two hundred ninety ppb of benzene. So benzene keeps cropping up. We've got 300 ppb for toluene. Ethyl benzene 59 ppb. N-butyl benzene. Naphthalene. So there's some crap in that slop pit.

"It's helpful to understand that this is obviously a big process," she added of the oil production at Beverly High. "It generates hazardous waste. What do you do with the waste? You're at a high school. So they're injecting a lot of the brine water and waste back down in the wells. On the other side of that wall where the derrick is and the football field, there's this big huge slop pit where they're dumping this stuff. And this is what we're starting to see from it."

Ed Masry could barely contain his excitement.

By 7:15 p.m. on Wednesday, March 12, 2003, the Crystal Ballroom at the Beverly Hills Hotel was packed, and people were still pouring in—down the green-carpeted stairway, under the art nouveau ceilings and giant crystal

chandeliers. The valet parking attendants in their pink oxford shirts had already begun to move cars to neighboring side streets because the parking
garage was full.

The impish lawyer with silvery hair and spectator glasses had called
community meetings before. But nothing like this—an overflow crowd of
more than six hundred people in one of America's grandest banquet rooms.

It seemed fitting to hold the meeting here. For one thing, the opulent
setting suggested that Masry's personal-injury law firm would spare no expense. The truth, however, was that it cost only $500 for the room on a week-
night, a bargain. But there was also the historic value. Constructed in 1912,
the elegant pink hotel once served as the center of community life: it was a
theater, a meeting place, a church. Now, the community was gathering here
once again, riven though it was by discord over the oil wells.

More people kept streaming in—from Hawaii, from northern California, from the San Fernando Valley. And they had one thing in common: Beverly Hills High School. Hundreds of alumni, students, parents, teachers, and
neighbors had cancer, or knew graduates who did, and they wanted to hear
Masry's evidence. Others were just plain curious: would Brockovich be anything like the cinematic folk hero created by the director Steven Soderbergh?
Still others, worried about their children at the high school, expressed outrage that the public school system might go bankrupt because of Masry's
shameless money grab.

Since the original news report just a month earlier, rumors were rampant. Was it true that a mother of a student at Beverly High had offered to sit
atop the oil rig in protest, like the guy who refused to climb down from an
old oak tree? Did Masry refuse to share his data with district officials? Was
the school district really being run by its lawyers now?

Out in the lobby, amid alums with name tags, it was easy to spot Brockovich. All you had to do was look for the lights and cameras, and she'd be the
one with the microphone thrust in front of her face. She could work it, pleading their case to the reporters on hand, and offering concise, provocative
sound bites to the TV cameras she'd invited. MSNBC. CBS. CNN. PBS.

As the guests filtered in, some seeing each other for the first time in
years, Brockovich and a small platoon of lawyers worked the room, handing
out business cards and making small talk. Brockovich swooped into conversations, comforting victims. The Erin-and-Ed show was in full swing, and
they seemed to be taking Beverly Hills by storm. You couldn't script it any
better than this.

Masry instructed a handler to announce that they'd begin in another five minutes to accommodate the late arrivals. Let them wait, he thought. It'll build the anticipation.

But Brockovich knew she had to be on her best behavior tonight. No righteous rants, like her recent testimony before a state senate hearing about a key scientific study rejecting claims that hexavalent chromium released into the groundwater at some Pacific Gas and Electric facilities could poison nearby residents. Brockovich charged that the report was "corrupt, skewed and biased" because two members of the blue-ribbon panel that contributed to it were paid consultants of the giant utility.

She had been working on transforming her trailer-trash image anyway. Her New Year's resolution had been to clean up her "potty mouth." She knew how to stick to a narrative that would sell and didn't have to worry about straining credulity so long as she stayed on topic: too many people in Beverly Hills were sick, and they deserved to know why.

Of course, she made sure to dress the part, too—black Armani suit, four-inch stilettos that had her towering over Masry. Together, they looked slightly cartoonish, a little like Boris and Natasha without the trench coats. If Masry, dressed in a tweed sport jacket, came off as "a little teddy bear," as one of his clients said, then Brockovich was the vixen who kept him in line. Nothing pleased her more than being called "Ralph Nader with cleavage," a tag line she relished.

When she glided onto the dais, after Masry playfully introduced her as "the girl who gets my coffee," she quipped: "He's quite confused about who's the boss and who's not." The audience roared its approval. Given the reception, it seemed a truism that no one had gotten a better deal from Hollywood than Erin Brockovich.

A cellular phone played "Hava Nagila" and someone in the audience wondered aloud if she could order room service. But the humor couldn't mask the tension in the room. The fact that the meeting was held in the days just prior to the American invasion of Iraq, when the price of oil was still $30 a barrel, only seemed to help the plaintiffs' attorneys' quest to demonize the oil companies, especially Venoco.

"This is not a publicity stunt," Brockovich began, immediately warding off criticism. Weeks before, she had told Army Archerd, the *Daily Variety* columnist, that the film rights for the Beverly Hills case were "up for grabs." But she later said the comment had been made in jest, and now onstage as the lights were dimmed and a gigantic image of the flower-painted derrick—the Tower of Hope—was projected onto a screen, she added: "There is no movie being sold here."

A hush descended on the room. She told the story of how the case came to her, at a book signing, when she was approached by Lori Moss. After doing some preliminary research online, Brockovich discovered an EPA document about oil spills that concerned her.

"'In Los Angeles, the oil industry has developed creative facades to mask oil operations occurring amid the glamour of Beverly Hills,'" she read from the document.

She said she didn't like that word "mask."

She continued reading: "'In Southern California, where over 9 million residents live on the third largest oil field in the country, the oil industry has been forced to adopt several strategies seeking to minimize the impacts of their operations on other land uses.

"'Seeking to improve the appearance of oil wells and minimize pump noise, the oil industry has responded in a variety of ways. For example, on Olympic Boulevard in Beverly Hills, the Venoco oil company has built a 16-story tower covered with vinyl material painted in a floral design to hide a well. The so called "Tower of Hope" rises above the Beverly Hills High School football field, and was painted by terminally ill children.'"

The crowd groaned with disgust.

She continued to read from the government report. "'One of the wells extends a mile and a half under a tony shopping district along Rodeo Drive. "They don't even realize that there is an oil field here," said Bill Giardino, production foreman of Venoco's Olympic Boulevard facility.'"

Brockovich said her firm took air samples, and she was "stunned" by how high the levels of benzene, a known carcinogen, were at Beverly Hills High School. She then took a comparison air sample at the 405 Freeway and Santa Monica Boulevard. "The benzene levels at Beverly Hills High School were five times higher than at the 405 and Santa Monica Boulevard," she said.

After receiving the Environmental Impact Report from the city of Beverly Hills, she looked for details about possible environmental hazards at Beverly High.

She found none.

In fact, the school had never been tested for health effects by any government agency. An Environmental Impact Report from the 1980s when the rig was restarted addressed only noise-abatement and aesthetic issues. Yet the same EIR contained several "MAYBE" responses from the oil company to questions as to whether there might be negative health effects.

"Will the proposed drill site result in health hazards or unnecessary exposures to people?

"Their response," she said, showing the audience a huge blown-up copy of the environmental report, "was 'MAYBE.'

"Nobody," Brockovich added, "has addressed the health effects. We don't know whether there is or isn't too much cancer at this school. Nobody knows a thing."

Additionally, she said, the girls' softball field was built over four abandoned wells with no safeguards. There was a collective gasp from the audience at some rather shocking photographs of the site as it was before the fields were built: a huge industrial rectangle behind the bleachers. The facility under the rig, she charged, was not well maintained in comparison to normal safeguards used at a refinery.

In the past month, she said, her law firm had received 550 inquiries, including from 170 people who said they'd been treated for cancer—147 of them Beverly Hills High School alums, ten teachers, and thirteen residents. About one-third of those cancers were lymphomas.

"Our intention is absolutely not to create a public scare," she said. "We're trying to put the information out there. We want to be sure the children are safe."

The law firm's expert, a medical doctor and toxicologist named Dr. James Dahlgren, who is on the adjunct clinical faculty at UCLA Medical School, presented the preliminary data he'd received on Beverly alumni graduating between 1975 and 1997: an epidemic of illnesses compared to national cancer rates for lymphomas; leukemia; multiple myeloma; and thyroid, breast, testicular, and other tumor sites. Hodgkin's disease was occurring at sixteen times normal levels, thyroid cancer at fourteen times normal levels. "These all could be an aberration," he said, "but you have a whole cluster of rare and unusual cancers. That's why it's probably more than a statistical blip."

Dahlgren, who received $400 an hour from Masry, said the average age at diagnosis was thirty-three. But he didn't mention whether that average age reflected a self-selected group of cancer victims who were Internet savvy. Nor did he discuss whether the rate of oil production at the high school correlated to the rate of illness.

All these cancers, he believed, could be related to emissions from the rig. Testing carried out by using EPA-approved methods revealed very high amounts of benzene, toluene, n-hexane, and methyl ethyl ketone on the athletic fields. For example, benzene was found at eighteen parts per billion (ppb), whereas a government agency had found that only 4 ppb will cause chronic neurological effects.

"We're looking," he said, "at a unique experiment."

Young cancer victims sobbed. Parents in the audience were irate. One, in particular, was fuming. A short, articulate redheaded woman named Jody Kleinman refused to be ignored. She frantically waved her hand so Masry would call on her when he fielded questions. She stood up so he could see her in the throng. Her sixteen-year-old daughter Marisa—the youngest of three daughters and a sophomore at Beverly High—sat beside her, looking embarrassed that her mom was at it again.

As far as Kleinman was concerned, Brockovich and Masry couldn't care less about Marisa's health; otherwise, why weren't they filing an injunction to shut the wells down? For the past month, Kleinman had barely slept, given her worry about the oil wells. She was the first parent to speak before the school board, requesting that the wells be shut down. Or, at a minimum, she wanted the athletic fields closed so students wouldn't be playing sports so close to the rig. She had begged her daughter to lead a revolt during PE, but all Marisa wanted to do was put a paper bag over her mother's head. Teenage kids are funny, Kleinman thought. They think they're invincible.

A former Berkeley activist, Kleinman was a full-time mom who led nature hikes up in Franklin Canyon. Her optometrist husband, Jeff, had attended Beverly High and graduated in 1969, the same year she graduated from "Uni," University High School, in West Los Angeles. Kleinman believed in the scientific method, but she had also lived through the ordeal of her best friend's daughter having been diagnosed with thyroid cancer at age nineteen. With neither solid proof of a cancer "cluster" nor convincing evidence of the oil well's safety, she wanted one thing: accurate information. It was hard to come by.

Now she was convinced that the truth would be clouded by legal posturing and personal agendas. As a mother, she wanted to protect her children to "a neurotic level." She'd do whatever it took to minimize their risks, and she had nothing to gain but their well-being.

She wanted to know why Masry's air samplings of benzene and methane differed so markedly from samplings by the AQMD, which found the air quality at the high school to be no different from that of ambient air in the rest of L.A.

Finally, he nodded at her. She told him that she applauded his efforts here, but she also wanted to know if he'd be willing to do side-by-side testing—or split-sampling—with the AQMD.

Masry said he had tried to do so, but that the AQMD had double-crossed Brockovich, promising to show up on one day but taking samples on another. "They never went out and tested before we got there," he reminded the group.

My God, Jody Kleinman thought. It's like we've all been asleep, but now we're awake.

The remarkable scene at the hotel ballroom melded all of Erin Brockovich's many worlds: the groups of sick people; the TV cameras and clutches of reporters who questioned her motives; the smooth contingent of lawyers signing up clients at the back of the room; and her new career as a motivational speaker facing the same need to win over a restless audience with a familiar story to tell—a story about greed at the expense of public health.

Not everyone would buy it, though. Storming out into the foyer, a chubby woman with ample cleavage named Norma Zager was shaking her head. "They're a bunch of slime," she said to no one in particular.

A former stand-up comic, Zager was the editor of the local newsweekly, the *Beverly Hills Courier,* "the best-read newspaper in Beverly Hills." She approached a graduate with cancer for a quote.

"Could you spell your name for me, honey?" she asked sweetly, then tapped his answer into her laptop while leaning on one of her Jimmy Choo mules.

I asked her what she thought of the meeting. "They're a bunch of liars," she said of Masry and Brockovich. "You think the people in this town don't love their children? They're Jews. They'd die for their children before they'd let anything happen to them."

Zager viewed herself as "the mama of the community," a protector of the chamber of commerce. Born in Detroit, she was determined to present a cheery picture of Beverly Hills, much as she had always written up stories about homes in the area inhabited by famous people. "The bottom line is everything is okay," Zager said. "When it's time to panic, we'll panic."

What shocked Barbara Wilson, who attended the meeting with her son Carl, was not the sadness of those who were ill but the anger of those who were not. Denial, she thought, must be a defining part of the human condition.

"You try to protect your kids from everything. But the bottom line is something slips under the radar, and you really start facing the uncertainty that exists. That's what people don't want to live with, the uncertainty.

"It's too threatening. So they'll see Ed Masry or the alleged victims as being troublemakers, because it disrupts their lives, too."

Another mother there that night was an African American social worker named Geneva Day. It was her birthday, her first one since the death of her daughter, Janet. Geneva Day did not live in Beverly Hills, but she had sent four of her children to school there. Janet, a star basketball player and 1984 graduate, had been in remission from Hodgkin's lymphoma but had died suddenly just three months earlier, over Thanksgiving weekend.

Geneva Day later recalled driving back home to South Central L.A., after the community meeting, with her daughter Janine, Janet's twin sister: "We talked about what a tragedy it was to send the child to one of the best schools in the city—in the nation, I think—and then she had to come into this type of situation where she contracted cancer from the drilling of oil under the school."

CHAPTER TWO

THE TOWER OF HOPE:
A MITZVAH MAKEOVER

Tower of Hope (courtesy of Patricia Williams).

Beverly Hills oil field, circa 1910 (courtesy of Library of Congress).

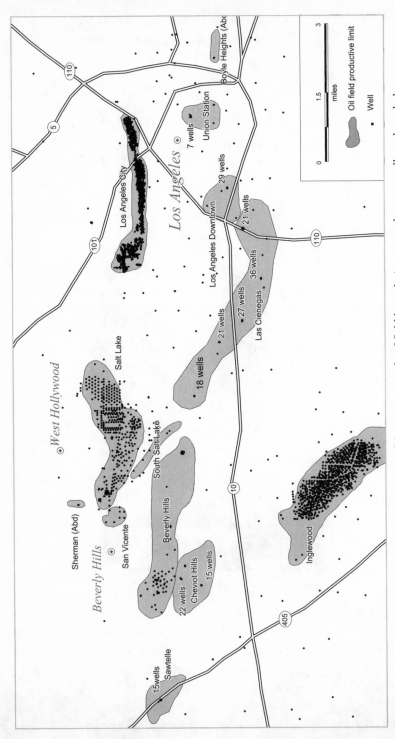

Location map of the oil fields of central Los Angeles. Well locations outside of field boundaries are exploratory wells and coreholes. (Map by Jim Spriggs, California Department of Conservation, Division of Oil, Gas and Geothermal Resources.)

D oheny Drive slices through Beverly Hills along its eastern edge. Lined by thick magnolias in the modest residential neighborhood of "the flats," where even the shabbiest houses sell for millions of dollars, the road gives way to gated estates on the crest of a hill atop Sunset Boulevard. Driving along Doheny, it's easy to see how black gold has defined the town's identity, if not its soul. Named for the so-called Emperor of Oil, Edward L. Doheny—the scrappy gold miner from Wisconsin who first discovered petroleum in Los Angeles in 1892 and created one of the world's colossal fortunes—the avenue, from end to end, is marked by oil.

At Doheny's southern tip, just past the city limits in a commercial district known for its kosher restaurants on Pico Boulevard, a giant chimney towers over the neighborhood. It belongs to BreitBurn Energy, an oil-and-gas production facility formerly owned by Occidental Petroleum. The oil operation, which resembles a flagstone-faced mausoleum from the street, is open twenty-four hours a day and takes up two city blocks, near apartment houses, a Jewish preschool, and the Beverlywood Bakery across the street. Thanks to a vast network of crisscrossing underground pipes originating at BreitBurn, local residents have received royalty checks since the mid-1960s for oil that is slant-drilled beneath their homes along the eastern Beverly Hills oil field. In recent years, a band of local residents led by rabbis and doctors who were concerned about health effects from hydrocarbon emissions unsuccessfully protested the facility's expansion.

At Doheny's northern end, there is a city park called Greystone, which used to be the private residence of the oil tycoon's son, Ned. Arguably the most opulent estate in Beverly Hills, the gated compound once stretched over four hundred acres, with towering trees, a lake, a waterfall, a fire station, riding stables, horse trails, a swimming pool, tennis and badminton courts, a bowling alley, and a greenhouse. Built of limestone and slate, the 46,054-square-foot castle stands as a grim reminder that fortune has a dark hidden side, as the English Tudor–styled mansion has come to be called the Palace of Grief.

Just five months after moving into his hilltop home with his wife and five children, Ned Doheny was mysteriously murdered on February 16, 1929, with his secretary. It was the first murder in the new city of Beverly Hills, providing a sort of cautionary tale about how oil money was tied to both scandal and tragedy: if Doheny was a Midas, his golden touch led to his only son's death. The oil baron was accused of bribing the U.S. secretary of the interior in the infamous Teapot Dome oil-lease scandals that shattered the presidency of Warren D. Harding, and of employing his son to deliver the bribe money. Though Doheny was eventually acquitted, it was presumed that his egotism and hubris had killed his heir.

Now, Greystone has the feel of a haunted house, albeit a well-landscaped one with a sloping lawn and terraced gardens. From 1969 to 1981 the mansion housed the American Film Institute, and it was subsequently used as a site for location shoots; Steve Martin and Lily Tomlin danced together in the great hall, and the Green Goblin plotted against archnemesis Spider-Man on the marbled landing. Visitors, however, are no longer allowed inside, save for occasional chamber music concerts.

Instead, city bureaucrats have turned the site into a "passive" park. No picnics. No dogs. No throwing balls. No loud noise. No picture taking. Weddings, however, are permitted. The actor Kirk Douglas and his wife, Anne, recently renewed their vows on the manicured grounds.

But when I visited Greystone early on a weekday morning in the spring of 2004, no one was around. A solitary park ranger patrolled in his pickup. It was remarkably quiet. Squirrels skittered in the bushes. A lone coyote howled. "It's kinda a hidden secret here," the ranger told me, smiling.

Hidden assets have always been a mainstay of Beverly Hills, especially as they relate to its favorite thing—real estate, both what is on the land and what lies beneath it. Even before millionaires and industrialists like Doheny, Firestone, and Hearst swept into town, movie stars created showplace homes in the foothills west of Hollywood. In 1919, Douglas Fairbanks Sr. suggested erecting a wall around the six-square-mile city to keep it exclusive. The wall never materialized, but an invisible economic wall would set Beverly Hills apart for the likes of Mary Pickford, Gloria Swanson, Charlie Chaplin, Marion Davies, and Will Rogers, the wisecracking humorist who, as the town's first "honorary" mayor, waged a fierce battle to prevent Beverly Hills from being annexed by Los Angeles.

That isolationist mentality explains in part how the city of thirty-four thousand has emerged as its own little island, smack-dab in the middle of Los Angeles—halfway between downtown, where wildcatters first struck it rich, and the beach. Real estate developers from the 1930s initially lured prospective buyers to the area in precisely the same manner, by pitching it in promotional brochures as the "center of the next million."

Over the years, though, the heady mix of money and celebrity made for something of a superiority complex among its denizens, who were rightly proud of their first-class library, public schools, and police and fire departments. But they also seemed to have fallen dangerously in love with the town's own Hollywood-encrusted mythology. They would boast it was the sister city of Cannes. They would construct diagonal crosswalks at intersections and enlist the gardeners from Disneyland to landscape their public parks, as tour buses loaded with gawking tourists veered past movie-star homes, and local sidewalk vendors on Sunset Boulevard kept selling guide maps to their gated enclaves.

Beverly Hills still loves its image of exclusivity. At night, the local cops don't hesitate to question you for walking down the street or to knock on your door for making too much noise past ten o'clock. If the police used to tap on the windshields of teenagers for making out in parked cars in the 1960s, by the 1980s they would develop a reputation for stopping African Americans, including the president of the local bar association, just for driving through, a dubious infraction some called DWB, or "driving while black." The practice led to racial-profiling lawsuits and eventual settlements by the city. To many, this seemed an obvious outgrowth of a place where local home owners' associations in the 1920s had restrictive covenants prohibiting the sale of homes to blacks. Jewish residents flocked to the area because covenants in nearby Hancock Park refused them. Current demographics reflect past practices; the city, which has thriving Jewish and Iranian communities, is 85 percent white, 7 percent Asian American, 4 percent Hispanic, and less than 2 percent black.

The town also became famous for the creation of a phenomenon in real estate known as "the teardown," in which big old houses were demolished in favor of even bigger ones because land was at such a premium. One of the first teardowns reportedly occurred on North Roxbury Drive, where the actor Jimmy Stewart doubled the size of his property by buying the house next door and demolishing it for his beloved garden. To get more bang for their buck, realtors would even label parcels of property that bordered the city limits as Beverly Hills "adjacent" and Beverly Hills "post office." Protecting residuals and the real estate value of that land, inch by inch, was big business. It always had been—ever since an oil boom led prospectors there to strike it rich.

Beverly Hills' first commercial enterprise was a lima bean farm, built by the hotel owners Charles Denker and Henry Hammel in the 1880s. Back then, the land was densely wooded, with streams cascading down hills in the north and gathering near the southern boundary, where a *ciénaga,* or swamp, formed in the rainy season. Originally, the land had been deeded for a cattle ranch by the Mexican governor of California.

At the turn of the century, a down-on-his-luck miner named Edward Doheny discovered oil with a shovel and a pick in Los Angeles, and soon he became the richest man in America. His partner, Burton Green, bought a rancho about five miles west for $670,000 in 1905 to extract oil for the Amalgamated Oil Company. But when Green twice failed to find oil on the land, the Rodeo Land and Water Company was formed as a subdivision. A city was planned with wide streets with palm, acacia, eucalyptus, and pepper trees. It was named Beverly Hills, after Beverly Farms, Massachusetts, because Green thought the name sounded pretty. Planned as an estate community, with lovely homes, large estates, and seven miles of bridle paths, the city was incorporated in 1914—and promptly banned oil drilling within its borders. By 1930, horses were also prohibited to make way for cars.

Before there was a movie industry, before there was an aircraft industry, Los Angeles had oil. About 23 million years ago, under the heat and pressure of a continental collision, large masses of rocks in southern California began to bend. When they broke—in a series of long, jagged parallel lines—oil and gas migrated from deep in the earth into cracks and folds in the rocks. By geological standards, California oil is considered young. It is also heavy and thick, and often contains a lot of nitrogen, metals, and sulfur, which makes it harder to take from the ground and harder to turn into gasoline and other products. A typical oil or gas reservoir in California is found in porous grains of sandstone.

Over time, oil profoundly affected what Los Angeles would become. In the past century, more than 8 billion barrels of oil have been produced in a county of 10 million residents. Nowhere else in the world has that much petroleum—beneath so many people.

Once Doheny peered into the La Brea tar pits and saw a fortune after punching a hole in the dirt, he understood that steamships and locomotives would no longer be powered by coal but by petroleum. As the boom hit at the turn of the century, the town's first oil was produced on a strip between Elysian Park and Vermont Avenue. More oil was struck to the east and to the west, and in 1904 the new Salt Lake Field came in at what is now the Farmers' Market neighborhood in the Fairfax district. All this drilling was on front lawns and in backyards, cheerfully put up with by homeowners because the royalties compensated for the foul odors and spattering.

In the industrial exuberance of the 1920s, black gold spouted in far greater volume at Montebello, Huntington Beach, Santa Fe Springs, Baldwin Hills, Venice, and Wilmington. Signal Hill was so covered with derricks that it was nicknamed "Porcupine Hill." Los Angeles had an oil surfeit comparable to that of one of the Arab states today and was ranked the fifth-largest oil producer in the world. Standard Oil, a prime employer and property owner, virtually ruled the coastal towns of southern California: the city of El Segundo, for instance, which means "the second" in Spanish, was given its name because it was the site of Standard Oil's second oil refinery.

Low oil prices were key to California's—and America's—efforts to survive the Great Depression and emerge as the world's leading industrial and military power. After World War II, when the American economy relied on increased energy consumption, oil production peaked as the car culture, freeways, smog, and sprawling suburbs became a way of life. Los Angeles was considered the most productive industrialized region in the country because its sixty vast oil fields provided a cheap source of fuel. Even the official government seal of the county of Los Angeles featured a drawing of three oil derricks.

Currently, California is the fourth-largest oil-producing state, after Alaska, Texas, and Louisiana. Oil company executives like to say that there is more oil per acre in Los Angeles than in Saudi Arabia, and geologists estimate that there are about fifteen to twenty years' worth of economically viable oil reserves still in the ground. But as land values have increased, urban development of declining oil-producing sites has become popular, because some of the most scenic ocean views come from these properties.

Since 1900, thirty thousand wells have been drilled in the L.A. Basin, and most of them remain idle or are "orphans," meaning they've been abandoned. Some experts suggest that at least 10 percent of them were never abandoned with proper environmental safeguards, which since 1976 have required complicated procedures involving dynamite, methane barriers, and cement plugs. As a result, when many abandoned wells are tested they are found to be leaking gas from the pressure of shallow sands.

What's left is about five thousand oil wells operating along freeways, in public parks, and nestled between apartment buildings. From fifteen wells at the exclusive Hillcrest Country Club to twenty-two wells at the municipally owned Rancho Park golf course to forty wells operating next to Cedars-Sinai Medical Center in West Los Angeles, oil production is ubiquitous—if hidden, as required by law. The practice of disguising oil operations dates back to the 1950s, when the city of Los Angeles first permitted oil development in residential and business districts with the proviso that drill sites be masked or enclosed.

Thus, by sinking drill bits with permits in neighboring areas of Los Angeles, the "majors," such as Standard Oil and Occidental, could suck up black gold beneath the flats of Beverly Hills. First, the oil beneath the public lands of Roxbury Park and La Cienega Park was tapped by the Standard Oil Company, later Chevron. To the west, in what would become Century City, Gulf Oil would develop twenty-five oil wells right next to the high school. To the south, the drilling and pipelines from the Hillcrest Country Club and Rancho Park, both technically in Los Angeles, would feed into the valuable property of Beverly Hills.

On the grounds of what is now Beverly High, amid signs proclaiming "Dig We Must," the first wells were drilled in 1906—predating the school by twenty years. The wells on the site operated on and off for years. Some, including those under what is now the school's football field, were abandoned and capped, but their precise locations are in doubt. In the 1950s, two pump jacks became operational on school property next to the girls' athletic field across from the 20th Century Fox back lot, the site of twenty-five oil wells (abandoned by Chevron in the early 1990s for real estate development). The ground beneath the Science Building was previously used as a sump for oil wastes.

By the 1970s, when petroleum prices skyrocketed and new technologies allowed for drilling at deeper sands, the school district's annual earnings from the wells exceeded $1.5 million, helping Beverly High to pay its highly regarded faculty some of the most handsome teacher salaries in the country. At the same time, other California schools faced draconian cutbacks in state funding due to Proposition 13, the property tax initiative that permanently slashed public school revenues.

"If we had all the money in the world and didn't need an oil field on campus maybe we'd say we don't want it," Beverly Hills assistant superintendent Reuben Cordova told the Associated Press in 1978. "But this is the real world and we're very pleased that whoever created this land a couple of million years ago put oil there."

In the early 1980s, with production declining and the oil market slumping, the owners drilled seventeen new wells, which continue to pump today. To accommodate oil development and fill its coffers, the city council had amended its municipal code in 1979 so that oil drilling would be prohibited everywhere in town *except* at the high school. The city and schools both stood to make 5 percent of the royalties. A handful of residents, most of them across the street in the city of Los Angeles, objected. But hundreds of Beverly Hills residents didn't mind. They liked their royalty checks, which helped to offset property taxes. Even when new state environmental regulations took hold in 1987 and Chevron issued letters to thousands of residents, advising them of the use of hazardous chemicals "located on or beneath your property" to keep the well operating and make the oil flow more easily, no one in Beverly Hills expressed concern.

Over the years, though, the rig has had its share of unpublicized "upsets." In 1989, for example, the Houston-based Wainoco Oil Company paid a $500 fine for violating air pollution rules when volatile gases escaped from a five-hundred-barrel crude oil tank. A notice of violation was also issued against Wainoco on October 17, 1994, by the Los Angeles County Health Hazardous Materials Division when corrosion of a portion of the six-inch oil pipeline caused oil to seep into three underground vaults at the nearby PacBell plant in Century City. Nevertheless, the Beverly Hills fire marshal stated that the facility had excellent compliance records. And the city manager believed that the drill site was "by far the cleanest and best maintained" urban oil well in Los Angeles.

Since 1995, the oil rig—which operates much like an offshore oil platform with eighteen wellheads—has been operated by Venoco, Inc., the company that found its niche by running producing properties in "very sensitive" areas: from offshore California in the Santa Barbara Channel, to the campus of Beverly High.

Begun in 1992, Venoco was one of the new wave of independent oil companies in California, squeezing oil out of places the so-called Seven Sisters, such as Exxon or Chevron, no longer believed made economic sense. Venoco's two partners, Timothy Marquez and Rod Eson, were modern-day wildcatters; Eson was a mechanical engineer, and Marquez a former Unocal roustabout.

Oil wells don't normally run dry. Not completely. Most of the big players drain about 40 percent of a field and then leave the rest. Pulling out the remaining oil doesn't make economic sense for big companies with large overheads, since the process requires more cash per barrel. With a decline in real prices for oil, which began with a crash in 1986, the majors fled to concentrate their efforts overseas. By the early 1990s, domestic oil fields were relatively cheap and more independents snapped them up— especially in the decidedly anti-oil environment of California. It was, after all, the massive 1969 offshore oil spill in Santa Barbara that had led to the creation of the EPA.

But Marquez and Eson liked to think of Venoco as "a new kind of oil company." Just as British Petroleum would morph into BP—Beyond Petroleum—and promote itself as a "green" company, Venoco would display a Toyota Prius hybrid-electric sedan bearing the company motto, "Energy, Safety, Community." Not only did the company hand out thousands of desk calendars showing local wildlife coexisting with energy facilities, but its PR spokesman guided tourists on boat tours of offshore platforms, pointing out the dolphins, fish, and sea lions while emphasizing the company's belief that natural oil seeps surpassed man-made ones. Venoco made sure to donate to art museums, to create a baseball field, to offer scholarships. The company gave generously—as much as $800,000 one year—to the Boys and Girls Club, schools, the Avocado Festival, and the chamber of commerce. By 2000, it was honored as the business of the year by three local organizations in Santa Barbara.

Its beginnings were humble enough. On April Fools' Day, 1994, after drawing on their credit cards and families to raise $110,000, Eson and Marquez bought their first oil patch in a residential neighborhood of Whittier, California. Exactly one year later they purchased the Beverly Hills field, and they would soon install new pumps and dig two new wells to increase the lifespan of the reservoir by about ten years. Not long after, the company was ranked one of the fastest-growing private oil companies in America. Revenue soared from nearly $6 million in 1996 to $94 million in

2000. Bill Richardson, the former energy secretary turned governor of New Mexico, was among its board members.

To its credit, Venoco received a sizeable equity infusion from another company that was successfully rethinking the energy business, the Enron Corporation. In 1998, Venoco sold six thousand preferred shares, about 30 percent of the company, to Enron for $60 million—all in anticipation of the company's going public.

It looked like the guys at Venoco could do no wrong. In Beverly Hills, just as they were primed to expand drilling operations, their public relations juggernaut rolled into city hall: they'd turn the beautification of their rig into an act of charity, or a mitzvah, with a code name—Project 9865. It was, by all accounts, a stroke of marketing genius.

The redbrick wall outside the oil derrick on the south side of Beverly High is enshrined with photographs, now faded, of terminally ill children. The memorial tells the heartrending story of how sick children, who could not use their hands, were given special shoes attached with paintbrushes to decorate the vinyl soundproofing panels that cover the derrick. Others, who could not leave their hospital beds, had sections brought directly to them. Kids in wheelchairs used "telescope" brushes. Those who couldn't use their arms or feet employed a fruit-flavored mouth paintbrush.

The commemorative plaques explain how the community, including hospitals throughout California and local corporate heavy hitters, came to view the beautification of the rig as an act of philanthropy. It was, they proclaimed, the Tower of Hope—an irony not lost on those who would come to believe that poisons from the rig would cause a generation of students to grow ill.

The inscriptions exhaust hyperbole, including one that suggests that the 165-foot tower is taller than the Statue of Liberty. "The children painted a surface area nearly three times the size of the Sistine Chapel ceiling— creating the largest monument in the western United States." Less prominent at the front gate is the posted warning, required by state law, about toxic chemicals there that could cause cancer or birth defects.

After Erin Brockovich descended on Beverly Hills, a cartoon in the student newspaper, *Highlights,* would call it "The Tower of Hope You Don't Get Cancer." But Project 9865 had nothing to do with alarmist ideas about toxic exposures. It was all about aesthetics and good works.

On Sunday afternoon, June 11, 2000, the commemoration ceremonies for the unveiling of the sixteen-story Tower of Hope took place on Nickoll

Field, the football field at Beverly High where President Ronald Reagan used to touch down in his helicopter. School board president Barry Brucker, a 1977 graduate of the high school who bore a slight resemblance to the beefy actor John Goodman, called it "an artistic masterpiece."

"This Tower symbolizes the work of children afflicted with illness and those that are healthy coming together in the spirit of hope, love, and peace," he said. Posters that were distributed bore a logo: "Helping children experience happiness while coping with illness."

The mood was jubilant. There were balloons, a marching band, sandwiches from Subway, popcorn, ice cream, and cotton candy. Hundreds of high school students gathered alongside busloads of sick children from hospitals throughout the state. And there were local dignitaries too, including the mayor and city council members, who spoke of the transformation of an oil rig—the drab gray exterior panels surrounding the drilling rig were brightly repainted with a floral motif by every schoolkid in Beverly Hills—into a public artwork.

The governor even proclaimed the date Tower of Hope Day. Donors of $150 could receive watches or rings with the same floral motif as the tower. Financial backers included civic-minded corporate sponsors, from ABC Television and Universal Studios to the Bank of America. Of course, Venoco had also sponsored the endeavor. Even ardent environmentalists, like U.S. senator Barbara Boxer and state senator Tom Hayden, endorsed the art project as a worthy cause.

And there were the Beverly High students and participants from neighboring private schools who felt pride because it gave them an opportunity to do "community service." In the weeks after publishing stories such as "Teens Get Thrill Shoplifting" and "More Teens Consider Plastic Surgery," *Highlights* featured a story about the oil well's redo, using the vernacular of the community's cosmetic-surgery obsession: DERRICK GETS A MAKEOVER.

Every student in the school district had been enlisted to help. As an elementary-school teacher, whose students stenciled flowers onto the panels later told me: "In retrospect, all we were doing was hiding these wells. But who knew? We all just thought how wonderful we were getting this revenue. Little did we think it might be killing us."

There was, however, one skeptic on the field that day, and his name was Willie Guo. An honors student at Beverly who would go on to attend the University of Pennsylvania, Guo asked the hard questions that everyone else was too polite to raise: was it possible that the oil wells could be endangering the health of students at the school?

"The response we got," he later recalled, "was, 'This is the tallest freestanding monument west of the Mississippi. These kids are deceased. This is their last contribution on Earth. It would be sacrilegious to tear it down now.'"

Within months of its unveiling, the beautification project had worked its magic. The state Department of Conservation's Division of Oil, Gas and Geothermal Resources, which regulates oil wells in California, conferred one of its most prestigious awards—a Lease Maintenance Award—on Venoco for going "the extra mile to be good neighbors." In July 2000, Venoco was also honored by the U.S. Department of Energy for its "contribution to nearly four thousand seriously ill children as well as its environmentally responsible energy operations in an urban setting."

It was, for Marquez and Eson, a dream come true. Even so, it was a dream that couldn't last, especially since no one was talking about the non-permitted pollution scrubber hidden *inside* the Tower of Hope.

If the denizens of Beverly Hills were unfazed by decorating their derrick, they had history and Hollywood on their side. After all, the art of camouflaging oil drill sites dated back to the 1950s, when companies worked to "harmonize" industrial equipment with existing structures. Oil well sites were disguised to look like everything from high-rise office buildings to a lighthouse. In Long Beach, offshore rigs would even be designed to look like condominiums with fake palm trees.

At the 20th Century Fox studio lot, which was located on the Beverly Hills oil field, Universal Consolidated Oil Company excavated two "islands"; after drilling fifty-two wells, the company removed the derricks and screened the islands with plants and shrubbery, leaving no visible evidence of the production operation from nearby properties. From Beverly Hills, the search spread to nearby Cheviot Hills, where Signal Oil & Gas Company's geologists identified a potential oil field in a neighborhood that boasted some of the area's most expensive homes, including those owned by John Wayne, Fred MacMurray, Nelson Eddy, and Jeanette MacDonald.

The company's exploration chief settled on a brushy ravine inside the Hillcrest Country Club's golf course as the ideal drill site. The exclusive country club was the province of an affluent membership drawn from the worlds of finance and show business. Comedian Jack Benny, one of the club's members, quipped, "Perhaps if we sign up with Signal, we will be as rich as Bob Hope or Bing Crosby someday." Signal also secured a lease on the nearby municipal golf course, Rancho Park.

Signal's acoustical engineers enlisted the help of Hollywood's sound-stage experts to soundproof the drilling derricks on the two golf courses. To conceal the derricks from golfers, Signal planted sixty-foot-tall palms and Canary Island pines. The company enhanced the camouflage by painting the jackets grass green at ground level, grading to sky blue at the top.

By the time the Los Angeles Open was convened at Rancho Park in 1958, there was no noise, odor, or vibration from the nine-thousand-foot well—proof, to many, that if golf pros could play critical shots in the shadow of a drilling rig without being bothered by it, urban oil wells would pose no problem anywhere else. Signal Oil went on to drill fifteen wells from its Rancho Park site and thirty-three from Hillcrest Country Club, the social enclave for those in Beverly Hills who were unwelcome at the nearby Los Angeles Country Club, which excluded Jewish members.

Of course, turning a dilapidated oil derrick into a work of art took considerable skill and assets, especially in a town like Beverly Hills, where public art ranged from the sublime to the pretentious. In the grand rotunda of City Hall, for instance, a classic bronze torso by Auguste Rodin is permanently exhibited; blocks away, on the median at Burton Way, there are what appear to be smashed pieces of metal, painted reddish orange, that some residents liken to a bloody car wreck; the city paid half a million dollars for the Alexander Lieberman sculpture, known as *Sisyphus*. Equally controversial on Rodeo Drive's Walk of Fame is Robert Graham's shiny *Torso*, a blindingly erotic aluminum sculpture that appears to satirize the local shopping mavens—giant ass, erect nipples, and no head.

But two brothers, Eddie and Bernie Massey, had impressive marketing credentials. Eddie was the charismatic artist who loved to provoke debate; Bernie was the promotional maven who understood his audience. A former staffer with the Anti-Defamation League, Bernie lobbied the Jewish community in California to lead the way in making contributions to the $1.5 million tower project to cover costs for everything from paint to the special vinyl soundproofing; he told the *Jewish Journal* that painting the tower offered an opportunity for *tikkun olam*, a way of repairing the world.

By cleverly focusing on the value of art therapy and avoiding references to oil production or the derrick, the Masseys, who had both attended Beverly High, were able to negotiate an impressive array of bipartisan support for the landmark's redo.

Over time, the fact that the project had anything to do with an oil derrick would be downplayed in promotional materials. A press release from the City of Hope, a major cancer care center, for instance, curiously omitted any reference to the derrick: "CITY OF HOPE PEDIATRIC CANCER PATIENTS TO HELP CREATE THE LARGEST ART MONUMENT IN THE WESTERN UNITED STATES."

"Ultimately," the announcement read, "the designs will cover a 165-foot tall tower in Beverly Hills—13 feet taller than the Statue of Liberty! The completed tower will be situated at the gateway to Century City and Beverly Hills."

For Hathaway Dinwiddie, the construction company that built the massive Getty art museum and helped to construct the panels on the Tower of Hope, promotional materials focused on the tower's visibility and potential audience: "Because of its prominent location on the Beverly Hills/Century City border, the completed project will be viewed by millions of people annually."

Originally, Eddie Massey conceived the idea for the tower while he was running around the track after work one day. He thought the gray soundproof paneling on the derrick, which had been installed in 1981 by the Beverly Hills Oil Company, looked tattered.

Though the lease agreement stipulated that the rig be removed three years after drilling began in the early 1980s—an agreement that was flagrantly ignored over the years—the Masseys later insisted that the tower become a permanent part of the landscape. "Kids would ask how long it would last," Eddie later recalled, "and we'd say, 'It has the life of a flower.'"

The Masseys were no strangers to controversy. Prior to the oil rig project, they had caused a stir with their campaign against sexual assault, a sculpture of a crumpled-up rape victim writhing on the floor that was prominently displayed in a storefront window not far from a middle school in Santa Monica. In New York City, they had encountered opposition to their campaign to have sick children paint taxicabs. But their flower-powered crusade took off at Kitty Hawk, North Carolina, where they enlisted children with cancer to paint a plane with their signature flower motif. Even a blimp, underwritten by a mortgage company in need of PR help, was launched through their "Portraits of Hope" program, dedicated to "improving the human condition."

To convince the Beverly Hills City Council that the tower would be beautiful, the Masseys agreed to tone down their psychedelic color scheme, a prerequisite of the city's art commission. "Even for the children who don't survive," Ed Massey reminded the city council, "their parents can drive by and see something their son or daughter left behind."

After viewing an emotional appeal on videotape, the Beverly Hills City Council was moved to tears when it approved the project. "I have sat up here for close to nine years and there are only a few moments when I have felt like things were happening that were extraordinarily special, and that's the way I feel tonight," said city councilman Allen Alexander. "This is a brilliant, brilliant idea." Others suggested that the Tower of Hope would be to Beverly Hills what the Eiffel Tower was to Paris.

Not everyone adored the aesthetic, though. Many of the locals were furious about the giant psychedelic daisies that resembled something out of the 1970s flower-power period—somewhere between the sets from *Laugh-In* and *The Brady Bunch*—with its mix of muted gray, bright green, and teal flowers. "They're selling this by saying it's being done by handicapped children," a local gallery owner sniffed. "This is just bad art."

Others felt pressured to keep quiet. "You don't dare say anything, because they made such a cause out of it, taking it to children with cancer," said Peggy Kaus, a longtime resident whose husband, Otto, was a California Supreme Court justice and whose son, Mickey, is a well-known journalist and Internet blogger. "I particularly disliked the painting, which is really awful," she added. "It used to just blend in with the sky. Frankly, I'd rather not be aware of the oil wells."

It was never an easy sell, of course. But the Masseys prevailed.

"No one thought we could do it," Bernie later recalled.

"Yeah," Eddie added, "everybody kept saying, 'No way!'"

The Masseys had another important asset—Eddie's wife, Dawn Harris, a Julia Roberts look-alike who worked as a dental hygienist in Beverly Hills. One of her patients was a veteran Beverly Hills High School teacher named Leonard Stern. While having his teeth cleaned one day, the history teacher listened with rapt attention as the beautiful technician described the art project. Stern, a budding artist himself, was instantly smitten. He was convinced that Massey's social-action art was "awesome."

"He was out there," Stern recalled with admiration. Having taught both English and history for thirty-seven years at Beverly High, Stern plunged into Project 9865. For three years he became the project's school liaison and official photographer. It was easy, since his portable classroom was located just a few feet from the derrick. And with the support of a school board member, he coordinated efforts to provide community-service "credit" to students for their participation in decorating the derrick.

"It was a wonderful art project," he said. "We believed in it with all our hearts. I wanted to go to the hospitals and tell the kids, 'When you get well, you'll drive to Beverly Hills and you'll be a star.' That's enormous motivation to a kid in Merced with leukemia.

"My whole life," he added, "was Project 9865. It gave a lot of meaning to me. If I had the guts, I would have quit my job at Beverly and just worked on the project. I was too afraid to change my life, too afraid to leave Beverly." On weekends, he visited the Project 9865 headquarters at the Westside Pavilion, an indoor mall a few miles west of Beverly Hills, where shoppers made donations by purchasing wooden miniatures of the tower. Stern also enlisted his students to bring canvases to the girls' gym, roll up their sleeves, and paint.

"Why decorate an oil well?" I asked him.

"Why not decorate everything with art?" he replied. "That's what an artist does—challenge convention. Why live with garbage if we can beautify something?"

But the first rumblings of trouble began even in the months preceding the tower's dedication. After attending a conference on air pollution in Los Angeles put on by the local chapter of the Sierra Club, the student activist Willie Guo wanted to open up public discussion about the oil derrick's safety.

He had learned that despite inroads to clean up the air in southern California, public health problems from air pollution seemed to be growing worse. Guo was shown mounting scientific evidence that air pollution has chronic adverse effects on pulmonary development in children, leading to a permanently reduced ability to breathe. Microscopic particles from soot and diesel fuel can cause a variety of health problems, including aggravated asthma, decreased lung function, chronic bronchitis, and premature death, particularly in sensitive populations such as children and the elderly.

More than a dozen studies linked particulate matter to premature birth and infant deaths. At the Harvard School of Public Health, researchers concluded that as many as 11 percent of infant deaths in the United States—about three thousand per year—may be due to microscopic particles in the air.

At the conference, Guo was shown a map of "toxic hot spots," most of which were in neighborhoods in southeast Los Angeles, where industrial facilities tend to be located in low-income neighborhoods. The green dots on the map, "People of Color and Toxic Release Facilities in Los Angeles County," represented facilities listed on the U.S. Environmental Protection Agency's "toxic release inventory," a public database of annually reported toxic chemical releases from certain manufacturing or processing facilities. The inventory was established in response to the Bhopal disaster of 1984, when sixteen thousand people were killed by lethal gases from Union Carbide's plant, and it provides the public with information about toxic releases in their communities.

Guo studied the map. Blacks and Hispanics in Los Angeles, as elsewhere, were disproportionately impacted. But Guo was surprised to find a "toxic release facility" right in his neighborhood in Beverly Hills, next to his high school.

Worried, he shot off e-mails to everyone he could think of, including the Beverly Hills City Council and the school board. It hardly seemed to matter, though, that Guo played football and poker with the mayor's son. No one from city hall responded. At school, an administrator called him out of class one day and insisted that the derrick had been there a long time and posed no health hazards. "I basically got yelled at for meddling in affairs that didn't concern me," Guo recalled.

Undaunted, he sent a series of e-mails to some local environmental groups, including one to the head of the Coalition for Clean Air, a nonprofit advocacy group based in West Los Angeles.

> Sent: Wednesday, March 08, 2000 8:29 PM
> Subject: Beverly Hills High School
>
> Dear Mr. Carmichael,
> My name is Willie Guo, and I'm a junior at Beverly Hills High School.
>
> I am extremely concerned about the environment, so I joined the Sierra Club Student Coalition and became the Regional Coordinator for California. I was wondering if you need the assistance of any high school or college level students in your program, as I have many people willing to work for a better environment.
>
> I also have a personal concern: there is an oil derrick right next to our high school. They release some sort of black smog and terrible odor. They must be violating some sort of law, right? Who should I contact to report such an offense? Thank you.
> Willie Guo

Guo's e-mail was forwarded by the environmentalists to public officials in the city of West Hollywood, which is located due east of Beverly Hills.

"I thought it was cute, at first," West Hollywood mayor Jeffrey Prang said of Guo's e-mail. But then Prang discovered that Venoco and the school district had agreed to a cogeneration plan in which extra gas from the oil wells would be diverted for heating and air conditioning at the high school. Soon, Prang would come to believe that Willie Guo's fears were justified.

The problem, as he saw it, was that Venoco intended to use an inferior pollution-control system for its gas turbine that could create ammonia "slip"—hazardous particulate matter that prevailing winds could carry three miles northeast into West Hollywood. Ammonia is listed as an "extremely hazardous substance" by the EPA's Superfund, the federal program that locates the most contaminated waste sites in the United States. Prang said: "I thought they were cutting costs at the expense of the potential health of kids."

After making a round of phone calls, Prang learned that the school district had never received appropriate permits from the city of Beverly Hills to develop the cogeneration project. He dispatched a letter to the Beverly Hills mayor. "I am not convinced that the environmental concerns with this project have been adequately addressed or that the city of Beverly Hills has been adequately informed," he wrote.

In the meantime, on March 30, 2000, an inspector with the Beverly Hills Building and Safety Department issued a "stop work" order against Venoco for violating the municipal code: the company had installed underground gas pipes without bothering to secure permits. According to a negligence and breach-of-contract lawsuit filed against Venoco by school officials on May 2, 2001, high-pressure gas lines had been "installed in wrong locations," without inspection, and without meeting "minimum standards." The minimum allowed for piping is two feet belowground. Venoco's contractor installed pipes just two *inches* below the service road between the oil wells and the Sempra power plant behind the high school.

When Eson, the oil company's president, threatened to countersue the school district for $1.6 million, claiming that his company had "at all times been in compliance with applicable codes and regulations," the lawsuit was quietly dropped.

Litigation, though, had become a way of life at Venoco. Just a year after its glorious Tower of Hope dedication, Venoco's fall from grace came hard and fast.

One evening in August 2001, Marquez and his CFO sat down to dinner in Santa Barbara with two Enron officials who oversaw the company's investment, Jesse E. "Jempy" Neyman and Richard Lydecker. Venoco didn't know at the time that Enron desperately needed cash to cover up its mounting losses. Just three months later, the company would file the largest bankruptcy in United States history.

At the dinner, Neyman and Lydecker offered Enron's shares back to Venoco for $65 million, which would be financed through the issuance of high-risk corporate bonds, or "junk bonds." The deal included a $10 million payout to Venoco's principals.

Over drinks at the Four Seasons Biltmore, Marquez read over the Enron proposal. He was worried that the deal would saddle Venoco with interest payments it couldn't afford. "This is a nonstarter," he told them.

According to court records, the Enron executives were furious. "If Venoco wants to fuck with Enron," one of the Enron officials shouted, "Enron will fuck Venoco." The dinner ended just short of a brawl.

In the months that followed, a bitter power struggle erupted within the company. While he was still CEO, Marquez fired his old partner Eson and his CFO and filed suit against them, claiming that company e-mails proved they had conspired with Enron officials to dump him from the company as an act of revenge. In fact, that is precisely what happened.

On June 30, 2002, the board of directors, which included the Enron officials and Eson's wife, voted to terminate Marquez. He filed a second lawsuit, this time a $10 million breach-of-contract suit against Venoco and its major shareholders. Meanwhile, a Delaware judge declared that Eson had breached his duties to the company, but the firm should not have fired him. He returned to his job. "I used to think life was like an engineering equation," Eson told a reporter. "You plug in the right variables and the right answer comes out.

"And that's just not the way it is."

By the time Erin Brockovich descended on Beverly Hills, fingering Venoco as the culprit of so much cancer in Beverly Hills, the company had already imploded. Marquez had moved to Denver to set up his own company, and Eson would rely on one man, Mike Edwards, to act as the public face of Venoco in Beverly Hills.

When I first met Mike Edwards for a tour of Venoco on the morning of April 22, 2003, he diligently handed me a hard hat and goggles to wear as we entered the facility at the alley that borders the high school, just east of the Century City Medical Building by Olympic Boulevard. The thing that is both marvelous and ridiculous about visiting oil wells is you're given something to cover your head and protect your eyes, but what you really want is a gas mask to cover your nose.

The air was heavy with petroleum fumes. When I asked Edwards to identify the odor, he dodged my question.

"What does it smell like to you?" he asked. "That's the question. This is a closed-loop system, so we're not impacting air quality."

I felt as if I had now officially entered the Theater of the Absurd: here's a business that reports emissions of more than 14 tons a year of hydrocarbons and gases to government regulators, but it's magically "not impacting air quality"? Even more astonishing, though, was the proximity of these industrial operations to the track and the softball field, just a few feet away.

Edwards, a warm and friendly man, has the square jaw and good looks of a television anchorman. When I first arrived, he showed off his son's photograph that hangs on the brick wall outside the facility, along with those of the other kids who helped to paint the big flowers on the vinyl panel of the Tower of Hope. Edwards lives in Santa Barbara with his wife and two children and has worked for the company since 1994. He got his start doing land work, traveling to courthouses and researching titles for surface and subsurface ownership rights.

Here, he explained, the school district owns the surface and mineral rights, which end on Spalding Drive. East of there, eight hundred residents share in royalty payments.

Edwards said that oil is brought to the surface from eight thousand feet below the ground under four thousand pounds per square inch of water pressure. The facility has nineteen wells—fifteen producing ones, three waste-injection wells where waste water is pumped back underground, and one idle. All the equipment operates off a hydraulic pump, located thirty feet below the surface. Once it gets to the surface, he said, gas is released "kind of like a soda pop can."

I asked what chemicals were stored in a giant plastic tank next to the Tower of Hope. The tank, which was labeled "Techni-HIB603," had an advisory that read, "Caution, may cause irritation. May be harmful."

"I don't know," Edwards said, "but the main thing would be corrosion inhibitors." Additives such as corrosion inhibitors are mixed with acids to prevent acid attack on tubing and casing and to prevent formation of in-soluble sludge. Venoco also uses refrigeration and compression to remove liquids and gases.

When crude oil is brought to the surface, the final production step is to reduce it to the form in which it will be sent to the refinery for processing. Contaminants such as sediment and water are removed, and volatile compo-nents are separated and treated by the use of separators. Natural gases must be treated to remove water vapor and acid gases, such as carbon dioxide and hydrogen sulfide. Water vapor may be removed by bubbling the gas through a solid or liquid desiccant; the acid gases may also be removed from a natu-ral gas stream by adsorption or absorption with a liquid or solid desiccant. This process of removing acid gases from a natural gas stream is commonly referred to as "sweetening."

Edwards pointed to an array of pipes: green pipes were for "vapor recov-ery"; red pipes were for a fire-suppression system; brown pipes contained gas to be sold to the Southern California Gas Company. These were near a massive gas storage tank and the company's recently installed gas chromatograph.

"For all those tanks we maintain a vapor recovery system," he said. "If there are vapors on the tank, they don't go to the atmosphere. They're all contained in the vapor recovery system, which goes back and pulls the va-pors back in the gas pump."

I asked if I could see the wellheads, located just a few feet from the soft-ball field's third-base dugout. A 2002 report by California's EPA found that samples of "oily sludge" extracted from these wells exceeded threshold limits for lead, one of the most toxic substances for children because it can accumu-late in their bones. "No," Edwards told me. "For safety reasons, we're not going down there."

He told me that my Radio Shack tape recorder might pose a danger be-cause its batteries could be a "sparking source" at the site. I offered to leave it in the office, a trailer decorated with an Ansel Adams photograph of Yosemite. He still said no.

Then I pointed out that not far from the compressor "house," a couple of employees were taking a smoking break just a few feet from the high school track. "That's a designated smoking area," Edwards said.

Not long after my visit to the Venoco site, I noticed that *Explorer,* the magazine of the American Association of Petroleum Geologists, published a laudatory story about the company. It was called "Winning Minds by

Winning Hearts." "In addition to official commendations for its clean operations, the company recently won kudos for supporting a project to decorate its 165-foot working derrick with artwork from terminally ill children," the article noted. "Called the Tower of Hope, it provides a colorful counterpoint to the negative Brockovich publicity."

Los Angeles oil fields, circa 1890 (courtesy of the California History Room, California State Library, Sacramento, California).

CHAPTER THREE

BLAME IT ON JULIA ROBERTS

Sunset Boulevard, circa 1911 (courtesy of the Seaver Center for Western History
Research, Los Angeles County Museum of Natural History).

W hen people in Beverly Hills spoke about what they called "the oil wells" or "the incident at the high school," some meant the series of allegations that had led to the June 9, 2003, filing of a lawsuit, with subsequent complaints filed in Los Angeles Superior Court, on behalf of more than one thousand former students, faculty members, and residents who believed that their cancers, immune diseases, skin rashes, or fear of contracting cancer in the future (which the California Supreme Court had said was a legitimate claim) resulted from toxic chemical exposures at Beverly Hills High School. Others meant not the allegations, which they saw as either outright inventions or representations of facts open to interpretation (the phrase "good science" got heavy usage), but rather the national attention that followed those allegations, the invasion of Beverly Hills by what its residents called "you people" or "the media," and the appearances by Erin Brockovich on the *Today* show, *Good Morning America,* and even *Real Sports with Bryant Gumbel,* since so many cancer victims were athletes who worked out by the oil derrick.

Beverly Hills High School, of course, was accustomed to frenzies of unwelcome press scrutiny. The homicidal Menendez brothers and infamous White House intern Monica Lewinsky, who had all attended the school, took care of that when they were creating headlines. Still, no one had ever suggested the school might be contaminated. It didn't help matters that media outlets from London to Tokyo pounced on the story. The *Today* show lead-in announced: "Erin Brockovich goes Hollywood again." And CNN's Aaron Brown intoned that this was a tale that "not even the writers of *Beverly Hills, 90210* would dream up."

Even for those critics who questioned why the press wasn't investigating schools in low-income neighborhoods that were *really* getting clobbered by industrial pollution, the symbolism of Beverly Hills could hardly be ignored: if it could happen here, it could happen anywhere.

The fallout was immediate. City and school district officials quickly launched a preemptive strategy of damage control. It began with posting an environmental "fact sheet" on the school district's Web site, which included reassuring dispatches from the chamber of commerce's preferred hometown paper, the *Beverly Hills Courier,* written by editor Norma Zager.

The environmental fact sheet did not mention a petition signed by eight English teachers at the school, asking for indoor air sampling in the old Business Education Building not far from the oil wells and right next to the Sempra power plant. Nor did it refer to the editorial entitled "This School Stinks," published months earlier in the school newspaper *Highlights,* complaining about gaseous odors and petrochemical smells on campus that repeatedly went ignored by the administration.

But image is everything in Beverly Hills. And the stakes were potentially enormous. The city council, unhappy with the publicity the city was receiving, was even less happy with parents who were making noise about moving or pulling their children from the high school. They thought it irresponsible for people to give the impression that there might be a major health crisis without factual evidence to back up their claims. This, after all, was Beverly Hills—the tourist mecca that spent millions each year to promote itself in glossy travel magazines as "the province of Beverly Hills." How could the legendary town that boasts of a two-minute response time from the fire and police departments, that enriches its schools by $6.6 million every year, handle the "panic" and "hysteria" created by cockamamie reports of high cancer rates? Members of the chamber of commerce warned privately about declining property values. Might there be an "exodus of business"? The city would have to make this go away.

It was, as one longtime resident wryly explained, time to adopt the Beverly Hills Motto: "No problem. No problem." To many, living in Beverly Hills represented the fulfillment of the all-American dream—the zip code, the ogling tourists, the fine homes with swimming pools and tennis courts. The denizens' sense of bounty was hard-won; in their world of entitlement and excellence, there could be no pollution: there was simply no room for it, no room for the inconvenience. There was no problem from environmental toxins, they believed, because they did not see it—nor would they really look.

Beverly Hills mayor MeraLee Goldman, who was leaving office, insisted that public safety was key. "It's a question of doing what is right—namely, getting the perfect experts," she said at the time.

"Have you read John Grisham's *King of Torts*?" she continued. "It's a blueprint for this kind of lawsuit. It's not a great novel, but it's fascinating reading and extremely instructive."

How employing more hired guns would protect the safety of students and faculty at Beverly Hills High School was unclear. But it would undoubtedly protect the city's economic interests, which were substantial. The town boasted an annual budget of $258 million, the largest treasury of any small town in America.

At his installation at city hall, the newly elected mayor, Thomas Levyn, promised transparency. The white-haired fifty-four-year-old real estate attorney, who had a daughter at the high school and was married to a former school board member, vowed to meet regularly with school officials. As promised, every Tuesday morning at 7:30 the brainstorming occurred—behind closed doors.

"I feel it's absolutely safe to put my daughter there," he said of Beverly High. Publicly, the school board president made similar pronouncements of safety; privately, he accused the plaintiffs in the lawsuit of being "litigation sluts."

The lack of information only served to fan the flames of alarmism and gossip.

Some parents fled. The film director Amy Heckerling didn't want to take any chances with her daughter, Olive,* and pulled her out of school soon after a hematologist detected trace amounts of benzene in Olive's blood. "I hate to be Chicken Little here," said the director of *Fast Times at Ridgemont High* and *Clueless*, "but my kid's got pulmonary problems."

Heckerling had some reason for her paranoia. After her divorce two years earlier, she had moved back to New York with Olive "to make a new life." Olive's first day of high school was September 11, 2001; that night, she had difficulty breathing. In the days that followed, New Yorkers were told that keeping wet towels under cracks in doorways would keep out pollutants. Meanwhile, residents of lower Manhattan observed workers in hazmat suits coming and going from EPA offices. "It made me wonder about the so-called watchdogs," Heckerling said.

---

*Name changed upon request.

As it happened, Heckerling's skepticism was later justified by an internal government investigation which revealed that the White House purposely directed the EPA to give New Yorkers misleading assurances that there was no health risk from the debris-laden air after the World Trade Center collapse. With Olive coughing all the time, her mother decided they'd move back to L.A.—only to confront allegations of a contaminated school at Beverly High.

"I didn't like what I was hearing from the school," Heckerling recalled. She met with Ben Bushman, the football coach turned principal. "'We're handling it' is what I heard. He said, 'We have our own people coming and taking tests, and we'll have the results soon.' I'm like, 'don't you keep the kids home until you hear the results are good?' Some parents suspected administrators wanted to keep students in school before environmental testing results were available because they didn't want to lose money: in California, school districts receive funding based on student attendance.

"They were telling me it's perfectly healthy. I said, 'I don't think it's perfectly healthy to have my child running around on a toxic field. I'm a mother, and I have some rights about my child's health.' Bushman said, 'Okay, she won't have to take PE.'"

Olive finished her senior year by taking GED exams at home and spending lots of time at Starbucks. She also analyzed episodes of *The Simpsons* for her mother, including one called "Who Shot Mr. Burns?" about slant-drilling for oil beneath the fictional Springfield Elementary School that would make the school flush with petrodollars and usher in "an era of unbridled spending."

None of which was funny to Joel Pressman. The outspoken choral music teacher, who had reigned as impresario of the high school's fabled Vocal Music Department for nearly three decades, viewed Olive's departure as a sure sign of the media madness that had saturated the culture.

"I just hate to see this kind of public hysteria," he later said. "This is about what happens when people don't know the truth and assume the worst. It's a study in social panic and media hype. So we're going to spend a huge amount of money to show it's nothing. Why do these people have any credibility at all? It's an ugly case of manipulation of the media.

"I think we're all fighting the fact that everyone loves Julia Roberts," he added. "Whenever she was on screen [in *Erin Brockovich*], violins played inspiring music and she fought for the little guy."

Pressman had a point, of course. Without the imprimatur of the Oscars and Julia Roberts's Academy Award–winning performance, Erin Brockovich's credibility might be at issue. It was not. At a moment in California history when Arnold Schwarzenegger, the action star and former body builder, could orchestrate a recall election and become governor of the state, the populace was clearly hungry for heroes, especially celluloid ones. Celebrity meant everything. Erin Brockovich-cum-Julia Roberts, it seemed, was untouchable.

Beverly Hills would need to change all that.

In the court of public opinion, defendants in lawsuits are usually guilty until proven innocent. No one took this maxim more to heart than the five-member Beverly Hills City Council, three of whose members were, like Mayor Thomas Levyn, attorneys. To shift public perception would require significant work and considerable resources. The town's officials were ready to dole out both, since they were convinced that they were not being sued for anything they had done but rather for what they represented—a deep-pocketed community with extravagant tastes and money to burn. To them, the allegations were pure hokum perpetrated by a couple of skilled extortionists mau-mauing the community.

In the weeks following the temporary closure of the oil wells on February 6, 2003, city and school officials closed ranks. Parents, desperate for information, were told nothing by the school board except that air sampling showed that the air was "not abnormal," according to the AQMD, and that environmental testing would soon be carried out by a nationally recognized engineering firm, Camp Dresser & McKee (CDM).

What was not discussed publicly, however, was the fact that CDM had been hired by the city's defense law firm, Lewis Brisbois Bisgaard & Smith; that way, any evidence from CDM that might be helpful to Masry's case, as well as to Brockovich and the one thousand plaintiffs and other potential claimants, would be protected by the attorney-client privilege and thus exempt from public disclosure.

Some residents were already demanding that the city shut down Venoco's operations for good. To appease them, the mayor conducted small "focus groups" at city hall, ostensibly to permit community members to vent their concerns. Ironically, however, the meetings, which one parent characterized as "divide and conquer," were not open to the public; they were by invitation only.

There would be no town hall meetings, no public debate, no righteous rants. Mayor Levyn, a short man with blue eyes behind wire-rimmed glasses, was famous for presiding over city council meetings with the forced gaiety of a talk show host, striding down the aisles in city hall chambers and mugging for ceremonial photo ops. But now he insisted that small private meetings enabled people to speak more candidly.

It was, in other words, time to batten down the hatches. But that's not exactly how the game plan to manipulate public opinion was presented. "Our quest," the mayor said, "is to find out what the truth is and report back as quickly as possible."

In fact, the quest was geared toward thwarting liability claims, limiting exposure to further lawsuits, and developing a strong public relations front. As defendants in a lawsuit, the school district and city faced the possibility of being held liable for millions of dollars in damages. Needing to protect taxpayers from that type of liability, the city leaders were obviously reluctant to make admissions—publicly or privately—that might sway a jury later on. One unfortunate possible consequence of being held liable was that the school district could, in fact, face bankruptcy. Though Masry had initially invited school officials to join him in the suit, he wasn't worried when they rejected his offer. He was certain the schools' lawyers would simply cross-complain against certain defendants when they had to.

Even so, the city and school district had a signed lease agreement with Venoco until 2016 and worried that they might be held in breach of contract if they insisted on stopping operations. It was not as easy as simply shutting the oil wells down. Theoretically, no one wanted Venoco to continue its operations at the high school. But in reality, the potential for damages didn't just consist of what the school district and city made in royalties, namely about $1 million a year. The potential loss of the oil company's revenues needed to be considered. And with the price of a barrel of oil rising daily, now that the war in Iraq was in full swing, revenues kept climbing. It created a conflict that was irreconcilable as far as fact-finding was concerned.

The greater imperative, of course, was public safety, when measured against potential legal liability. The assumption by outsiders was that if you were concerned, you would take your child out of the school. But there was only one high school in Beverly Hills. If you sent your child to a private school instead, you could expect to pay $25,000 a year. Sixty percent of residents in Beverly Hills were apartment renters. No matter what the rest of the world thought about their community, many parents simply didn't have that kind of money.

Despite its cosmopolitan allure, Beverly Hills operates like a small town. From the soccer fields and Little League diamonds to the produce aisle at the

Whole Foods Market, word spreads fast. No doubt, the town is a quirky mix of Persian émigrés and plastic-surgery freaks who tend to avoid voting booths and civic boosterism. Though the town is primarily made up of liberal Democrats, few of them bother to vote in local elections. Still, the suburban enclave of high hedges and mansions is an off-kilter clash of the bucolic and cosmopolitan, a hotbed of gossip à la *Peyton Place.*

Chatter buzzed on the Internet grapevine. E-mails were flying among the PTA intelligentsia. "The school board, superintendent, and the city council have our best interests at heart," wrote one PTA mom. That line of reasoning, embraced by the majority, left little room for skepticism.

So when Beverly parent Jody Kleinman first contacted the school's PTA president and threatened to climb atop the oil derrick if answers weren't forthcoming about its safety, small-town politics prevailed—the PTA president contacted the school principal, who in turn quickly e-mailed the police chief: who is Jody Kleinman and what do you know about her?

Kleinman, her husband, Jeff, and their three daughters lived "north of the tracks," just down the street from mogul David Geffen's lavish estate in the hills. Despite its name, most people in Beverly Hills live in the flats, once divided by train tracks that ran along Santa Monica Boulevard and split the town in two. North of Sunset Boulevard, where the most expensive homes are located, is the swank part where Jody Kleinman lived. As a student at UC Berkeley in the sixties, she marched at People's Park; as PTA president of the middle school at Stephen S. Weiss Temple, she led an investigation into methane gas leaks that swore her off of PTA involvement forever. Now, she drove a hybrid car and ate organic vegetables.

With neither solid proof of a cancer cluster nor convincing evidence of the oil well's safety, she asked: "Does it make sense to have an oil well operating on a high school campus?" Was it possible, she wanted to know, that Beverly Hills and its school district had ignored health risks to its students for the sake of money, as Masry alleged? What is a school's obligation to minimize toxic exposures, especially for children whose immune systems are not fully mature?

Kleinman wanted to rattle some cages—at city hall, at school board meetings, wherever she could. "They're worried about their lawsuit," she insisted. "They're not worried about our kids."

Frustrated, in early April 2003 she drove downtown to the Los Angeles cancer registry, based at USC's Keck School of Medicine, to formally request an epidemiological study of Beverly Hills alumni: was the cancer incidence among graduates higher than the norm? She wanted facts, not hype.

But Dr. Thomas Mack, one of the few epidemiologists in town with access to the confidential records of cancer patients dating back to 1972, was hardly eager to oblige. As a director of the Los Angeles County Cancer Surveillance Program, he was skeptical about environmental links to cancer clusters.

Like many others in his field, he subscribed to a twenty-five-year-old study by the researchers Doll and Peto that found only 2 percent of cancer deaths were from pollution and 4 percent were due to occupation, whereas tobacco accounted for 30 percent and diet 35 percent. Over the years, that study had been cited in more than four hundred scientific articles and used by many to suggest that "cleaning up the environment" wouldn't make much difference in cancer statistics. Mack was also the author of a forthcoming cancer-mapping book of Los Angeles. Though his statistical analysis found geographic clusters for at least six forms of cancer, including for non-Hodgkin's lymphoma and thyroid cancer, he believed "no evidence of a malignancy caused by a strictly environmental carcinogen has yet been confirmed."

What Kleinman didn't yet know was that Mack, a respected cancer researcher who was a member of California's Carcinogenic Identification Committee, had already provided an affidavit for a defense law firm representing an oil company with operations at Beverly High.

"How credible is the suggestion in the first place if I tell the National Cancer Institute that Julia Roberts was the one who suggested the study?" the cancer researcher asked me, his voice coated in sarcasm.

After signing a joint-defense agreement, in which members of the school board and city council agreed not to discuss the case publicly and to share confidentiality among their lawyers, a carefully orchestrated campaign was waged to counter Brockovich's allegations and besmirch her integrity: public relations experts, a Web site devoted to promoting the defense's side of the story, and the hiring of two prominent defense teams—one well known for its "win at any cost" tactics—were crucial.

By the end of March 2003, the city had hired the Sugerman Communications Group, a Los Angeles public relations company accustomed to handling crises for corporate clients. Steve Sugerman, who served as deputy mayor to former Los Angeles mayor Richard Riordan, also counted the Playa Vista Development Corporation as a client. Environmentalists had vehemently objected to the development of Playa Vista, because of potentially explosive methane gas seeping up from old oil and gas wells there; Sugerman, though, worked successfully with CDM scientists to have the project green-lit. He believed "it is the words we urge our clients not to say that end up making the difference."

To oversee the legal team, Beverly Hills relied on its goateed city attorney, Laurence S. Wiener, a 1979 Beverly High graduate who resembled the filmmaker George Lucas and whom Norma Zager likened in print to Moses. Zager was captivated by Wiener's "puppy dog eyes," "boyish innocence," and "sweet smile," seeing "goodness written all over his face."

A senior partner in the well-respected downtown law firm Richards Watson Gershon, Wiener (pronounced Wee-ner) hired tough-as-nails environmental defense specialist Christopher P. Bisgaard of the downtown firm Lewis Brisbois Bisgaard & Smith. Tall and portly, Bisgaard had successfully commandeered taxpayer money to finance the cleanup of the Stringfellow Acid Pits in Riverside, one of the first sites in the United States designated by Superfund, the federal program begun in 1980 to clean up abandoned hazardous waste sites. His client, the owner of the toxic dump site, avoided liability.

But if Bisgaard was well regarded for his gentlemanly approach to mounting a legal defense for corporate clients, the city also counted on the mayor's good friend Louis "Skip" Miller of the Century City law firm Christensen, Miller, Fink, Jacobs, Glaser, Weil & Shapiro for a sustained attack. If this was war, attack dogs would be necessary, and Miller was known among his peers as a lawyer who would stop at nothing to represent his clients. They called him the Prince of Darkness.

In the 1990s, for instance, Miller had defended the city of Beverly Hills in a racial-profiling lawsuit that accused the local police department of discriminating against young black men for "DWB," or driving while black. The suit dragged on for years, resulting in an undisclosed settlement, though critics suggested it could have been settled much earlier had it not been for Miller's scorched-earth tactics. In May 2000, Miller was disciplined by the California bar for professional "misconduct" and publicly reproved for improper contact with a former juror during a trial. When he was first retained by the city in the oil wells case, the Beverly Hills Weekly in an editorial labeled him "the wrong lawyer at the wrong time."

In any case, the high-priced advisers would cost taxpayers at least $300,000 per month—about the cost of a good epidemiological study.

Together, they embarked on a stealth campaign of spin and evasion, enlisting friendly journalists, like town yenta Zager, to impeach Brockovich's credibility in print. Zager, the ultimate Beverly Hills loyalist, was only too happy to comply.

"That bitch is going down," she said of Brockovich. "I'm a thorn in her side and I'm proud of it. I've cost her a lot of money.

"She chose the wrong town to pick on. I'm the head boob in Beverly Hills—and mine are real."

Since the city was under attack, it effectively ignored the pleas of a handful of parents in search of objective information and, perhaps most important, denied the existence of inconvenient facts: not only had Venoco persistently violated air pollution rules and admitted to venting its gas for longer than anyone cared to mention—for at least twenty days, by the AQMD's calculations, maybe longer—but the Sempra power plant in Century City adjacent to the high school was considered a "major source" of toxic air pollution by the U.S. Environmental Protection Agency. Venoco too had been identified by the AQMD in 2002 as a "major source," meaning it was one of the top three hundred polluters in Los Angeles since it emitted at least twenty-five tons a year of hazardous air pollutants. But the AQMD exempted the company from reporting requirements after Venoco, taking advantage of a regulatory loophole that discounts "fugitive" leaks from valves and tanks, submitted its own emissions estimates that showed it released less than half of what AQMD said.

The city's savvy legal strategy also required that the voices of school board members, most with children in the school, be silenced. Only Superintendent Gwen Gross, a Geraldine Ferraro look-alike from Wisconsin, had authority to speak.

Her proclamations about the school's safety, vetted by lawyers, also suggested that Masry was a schlockmeister because he wouldn't share his "data" with the school district. Masry disputed this, saying he turned over everything he had. But he also seemed to relish taking potshots at the superintendent, calling her "that Gross woman" in public meetings.

After months of repeated requests and dodged phone calls, I was finally granted an interview with Gwen Gross just after graduation ceremonies in late June 2003.

I asked her why the California Department of Toxic Substances Control (DTSC), which oversees the cleanup of hazardous materials on school sites, had been prohibited from conducting an environmental assessment at Beverly High.

"I'm not going to make a statement on behalf of the district that hasn't been fully planned and discussed," she told me, sitting beside the PR flak, Sugerman. "We are in a lawsuit mode. The strategy has been—strategy's not really the right word—our efforts have been focused on getting information."

Wearing pearls and ballet slippers, she folded a leg under her thigh and pulled her skirt down to her knee. She looked miserable. I felt sorry for her.

Why would a school with an oil well and power plant next door not conduct air monitoring over the years?

"I can't answer that question," she said.

"Does Venoco notify the school district when it's using radioactive materials at the site?" I asked.

She shook her head no.

The following month, with another year left on her contract, she submitted a letter of resignation to the school board.

No one was more of a team player than principal Ben Bushman, the former football coach who had worked his way up the ranks of the administration at Beverly since 1965. Tall and athletic with piercing blue eyes, he ran a tight ship. Known for his willingness to roll up his sleeves when times were tough, he'd personally serve up doughnuts at school events or fix a stopped-up toilet, if necessary.

Bushman was a big believer in promoting good news about Beverly, not negativity. He was especially proud that the school had been honored as a "New American High School," one of ten in the country given that recognition by the federal government in 2000. Other accolades followed: Beverly was a national "Blue Ribbon" school and one of a handful of "distinguished" schools in California.

When the oil well story broke, he dutifully declined reporters' requests for interviews, with one exception: *In Style* magazine wanted to talk to him about Beverly High being a "cool school" because of its illustrious roster of Hollywood alumni.

Putting out fires, though, was part of his job. When Venoco was shut down, he made sure to have a chat with Floyd Leeson, an operations engineer with the state Division of Oil, Gas and Geothermal Resources (DOGGR) whose job it was to oversee Venoco's operations. The agency's employees, like Leeson, called themselves "doggers."

As Bushman walked out on the football field with Leeson, the engineer assured the principal that if the company was venting gas, then the air pollution agency must have given Venoco permission to do so. Leeson told Bushman that the real worry with an oil well was not cancer, but fire and explosions.

Leeson was intimately familiar with the site: his first job in 1980 out of the USC graduate school of engineering was as a mud engineer at the Beverly High oil wells. In 1985, when the price of oil had dropped precipitately, he left for state regulatory work. "I was a mud man," he liked to quip, "and now I'm a dog man."

Dressed in blue jeans and a green zippered jacket, the mustachioed Leeson wore a baseball cap and clip-on sunglasses. "This site has been operating safely for twenty-five years," he reassured Bushman. "This whole thing is all media-driven craziness."

The catch-22 for the company, he believed, was that oil wells don't like to be shut down. They sometimes don't come back. Sand and sediment can flow with the oil, and sand will fall back down and plug up the bottom of the well. Then you get a "burp" of carbon dioxide, a real nightmare for the operator.

For Leeson, any worries about explosive levels of methane gas at the football field were misplaced.

"I didn't see pyres aflame," he said with some sarcasm.

Ben Bushman stormed into room 253, the journalism classroom run by a young teacher named Jennifer Moulton, a tall and attractive former reporter. It was the middle of March 2003.

Bushman was livid. He had just hung up the phone with the superintendent. One of Moulton's students, Parinaz Farzinfarid, had left a message requesting that Gwen Gross debate Ed Masry for the Norman News Service, the broadcast journalism program at Beverly that conducted press conferences to bring opposing viewpoints together.

"You can't let the kids do this," Bushman warned Moulton. He refused to allow the television studio to be used for such purposes.

Moulton said she didn't think that Bushman could legally restrict the use of school equipment, paid for by taxpayers. Since there was nothing obscene about such a debate, nor would it be a breach of school district or state rules, she saw the prohibition as a violation of her students' First Amendment rights.

"Bushman assumed Parinaz was on Masry's side," Moulton later said. "But she honestly was trying to find out if she and her friends were in danger. She was asking the questions out of concern and a position of neutrality."

Bushman fumed: "You've gotta keep a tighter rein on these kids."

Moulton rolled her eyes at the memory. "Gosh, what do they think will happen?" she asked. "They get very uptight."

Every two weeks, Bushman returned to Moulton's office, complaining bitterly that she wasn't controlling her kids. An editorial published in *Highlights* opined: "[T]he wall of secrecy that seems to go up whenever the news media, especially Beverly student journalists, ask questions and attempt to report the news thoroughly only makes the possibility of lawsuits and carcinogens more threatening."

The following school year, despite nothing but positive evaluations, Jennifer Moulton's contract was not renewed.

Besieged by worried parents, Bushman did the best he could to answer questions about the high school's safety; the regulatory agencies said there wasn't a problem, and he believed them.

Still, many found it hard to get straight answers about the air quality at the high school. One such parent was a university professor who had attended Ed Masry's community meeting at the Beverly Hills Hotel and thought the presentation was more show than substance.

"I'm neither an environmental activist nor a Greenpeace member," said Menashi Cohen, a professor of engineering at Purdue who was spending the year as a visiting professor in the Department of Civil and Environmental Engineering at UCLA. "If anything, I'm a Republican, probusiness guy."

Cohen was quick to point out that he was not an expert in air pollution science. But he did have twenty-five years of experience in developing scientific experimental research programs and had served on numerous national review panels for the National Science Foundation.

The principal agreed to send him the AQMD report from Barry Wallerstein, including his raw data, which had not been made public. Cohen, in turn, promised that his interpretation of the data would be "exploratory." He didn't want to alarm anyone.

But when he reviewed the AQMD memorandum, Cohen was convinced that Wallerstein had presented "a clear misinterpretation of the data." Even a cursory look, he thought, would not support Wallerstein's conclusions that air quality at Beverly Hills High School was safe, or that the levels of pollutants were "NOT abnormal." Rather, Cohen wrote in a memo, "there is clear indication that the AQMD readings suggest that levels of air pollutants in the vicinity of the Venoco vent (this includes the football and track fields, bleachers, etc.) is markedly higher than levels in areas further away."

For example, he saw that levels of the neurotoxin n-hexane at Beverly High were 400 percent higher than levels measured at City of Commerce, an industrial city used by Wallerstein as a comparison. He also questioned why there was no measurement of wind direction, time of day, or temperature, which would impact ambient air measurements.

Cohen sent his memo to school officials who forwarded it to the AQMD. "It is only prudent that immediate steps be taken by appropriate government officials and private citizens to shut down the Venoco production," Cohen wrote.

In a March 4, 2003, e-mail, flagged as "high importance," AQMD engineer Mohsen Nazemi told Wallerstein:

> Barry, I suggest that a response to Dr. Cohen's memo be included in your next memo.

But Wallerstein chose to ignore the advice.

"I thought I'd get a respectful response," Cohen later said. "I wish they would have responded officially. Nothing." Cohen's son left Beverly High for Harvard-Westlake that year.

"Whenever there is a gap in knowledge," he said, "you should err on the side of caution, especially when children are involved."

Parents and teachers who questioned officials were quickly labeled "troublemakers." Many were ridiculed and ostracized, especially those of Iranian descent. One of them was a real estate developer named Abraham Assil.

Knowing that the school district was facing more budget cutbacks from the state, Assil, a fifty-three-year-old father of four, offered to donate $30,000 for independent environmental tests. The school district said no. "We, as parents, really don't know whom to trust," he told the school board one evening in March 2003.

Weeks later, he would return to present a petition signed by four hundred parents, the Parents Association for Safe Schools, demanding that the wells be shut down until it could be proven that they did not pose a risk to students and staff. One couple, who had gathered many of those signatures at the baseball diamond at nearby Roxbury Park, yanked their son from the baseball team in protest. High school administrators responded by assigning him to a dance class. "He's an athlete," his mother, a defense lawyer, said. "He can't spend four years in a tutu."

How many more of our children, Assil wanted to know, must get sick before something is done? During the first week after the story about the oil wells broke, he didn't sleep. "Everybody was terrified," he said. "I was terrified. My wife was scared. My children were pretty paranoid."

Assil spent an hour and a half talking to Bushman in his office one day. "He was insulting me because I was questioning him," Assil later said. "Although I'm not American-born, I am a citizen now and have been for fifteen years. And I know enough about this country, of course, to know that I have the right to ask my government, or any government, what they can do. Checks and balances.

"Ben Bushman questioned my loyalty, or my patriotism, to this country. He said that in this country, we believe in our government. I told him that it would be a misplaced thing for him to be a principal in this school and teach our children the values of democracy and make a statement as out of place as this. And I told him he should go and check the Constitution of the United States. Read the First Amendment.

"This has nothing to do with where I come from," Assil added. "It has to do with the children."

Even more than the personal attacks, Assil was offended by what his children had been asked to do. "The thing that truly bothers me is they have that chimney, that exhaust chimney, on the school site. And they had the kids—our kids—paint those daisies. It's just like the Germans who would have hired all these concentration camp people to be, you know, the ones who redefine the area of the death camps. That is how insulting it is to me."

While parents asked the school district to support an epidemiological study, other residents requested a citizens' oversight committee. Neither was forthcoming, though the school district did hire its own toxic tort lawyer who, in turn, retained the school district's environmental consultant.

Frustration also arose when parents contacted the state Department of Toxic Substances Control for help. Surely, if state law prohibited cigarette smoking twenty-five feet from a school campus, an oil rig and power plant must be restricted too, they reasoned. Not necessarily. The state agency would need a signed contract with the school district to get involved.

When DTSC division chief Hamid Saebfar, who had worked to clean up the Love Canal for the federal EPA back in the 1980s, contacted school district officials, he was rebuffed twice—first by the school's in-house counsel and then by the city's lawyer, Christopher Bisgaard: don't call us, they told Saebfar, we'll call you.

Within weeks, Ben Bushman was announcing his retirement after thirty-eight years. He had had enough.

"It's just so sad," he later said.

It was just before 7 p.m. on Tuesday, April 29, 2003, when Jody Kleinman took out a chit to speak before the school board inside the Salter Family Theater at Beverly High.

Her knees were shaking. She hated public speaking. But in the days prior to the meeting, when her husband was out of town on a golf trip, she found herself snooping around the empty lot next to Century City Hospital and Medical Center, a former oil-drilling site with twenty-five wells abandoned and buried beneath it by Chevron. She was stunned to learn that the local fire department considered the land "contaminated." She also found several discarded fifty-five-gallon drums for waste disposal sitting on the gravel fill.

At five feet two, Jody Kleinman was a small but forceful presence, her big green eyes going wide, and her curly red hair blow-dried for the occasion. On this night, she wore her regular uniform—sneakers, blue jeans, and a lavender T-shirt.

Kleinman's activism came unbidden. Like everyone else, she understood how easy it was to be relegated to wacko status in Beverly Hills and ostracized for speaking out. Several parents who four years earlier had insisted on environmental monitoring of portable classrooms had pulled their kids from the schools for precisely that reason. There was also the legendary case of the PTA president who was so adamant in her opposition to auctioning off wine at a school fund-raiser, going so far as to call the police department as the sale was taking place, that she was expelled from office.

Kleinman wasn't interested in joining the ranks of the local crackpots. She spoke a little too loudly and had an annoying habit of interrupting, but she was not some sort of environmental kook.

Neither hip nor glamorous, she considered herself obsessive-compulsive, especially when it came to protecting her children.

Just the weekend before, one of her daughter's best friends, a ponytailed honors student and softball player named Brittany Darwell, had told her about playing a doubleheader on the softball field right next to the Tower of Hope after the oil wells had been reactivated.

"In the second game, it started to smell really bad," Brittany said. "It was so bad your eyes were burning and your nose was burning. My little sister had to sit in the car for the second game because of the fumes. Even the umpire said he'd never experienced anything like it. I went to softball practice the next day, and you could tell the wells were running again because of the smell—a sort of chemical celery smell."

It was hard to get relief from the fumes. "Nobody likes to use the water fountain there," she added. "People say it tastes like cancer. So now, no one drinks from it anymore." Kleinman convinced Brittany to report what she had encountered to the AQMD, hoping the agency might investigate her complaint.

Standing at the podium, her voice faltering, Kleinman reminded the school board members that they had more than a legal duty—they had an ethical one, too. She understood that the school district and city didn't want to "put out food for the ants" by admitting liability if they could avoid it, but she also couldn't sit idly by and not speak out. She would keep nudging everyone into doing the right thing, even if it meant they'd think of her as some lunatic.

She injected words like "standard of care" and spoke of the need for a "robust" investigation: get it out in the open and deal with it, she advised. It wasn't just a matter of defending against a possibly scurrilous lawsuit. It was a matter of doing right by the kids. If tort law was based on a reasonable-man standard, then Kleinman, who had no interest in any litigation, wanted to hold Beverly High to an even steeper one: the Jewish mother standard. They had a golden opportunity; why not just do the right thing?

Don't just test the air and the soil at the school for toxic exposures from the oil wells, she pleaded. A serious investigation should also look at Sempra Energy's steam-generating power plant adjacent to the school, which provided heating and cooling to Century City.

Through her research online, Kleinman discovered that the energy plant reported emitting more than 10 tons of toxic organic gases, nearly 2 tons of reactive organic gases, 16 tons of carbon monoxide, 10 tons of nitrogen oxides and more than 1 ton of particulate matter in 2002; Venoco reported emissions that year of 9.2 tons of toxic organic gases and 5.1 tons of reactive gases. What about the cumulative effect of both facilities?

In response to her plea, the school board members said nothing. She understood that what was legally appropriate might have nothing to do with moral imperatives.

But she was feeling hopeful. She thought she was starting to get to them. "They were *plotzing*," she would later recall.

Anna Harari was wearing her favorite red T-shirt, the one with the message "You Say Tomato, I Say Fuck You." With her chestnut-colored hair tied back in a scrunchie, the seventeen-year-old junior considered herself typical of "the average kid at Beverly who doesn't really care what's going on."

In fact, she did care, or why operate the sound system for the student-run TV station, KBEV, to broadcast local school board meetings? From her spot at "master control," Anna was a study in surliness, the perfect adolescent blend of eye-rolling and intelligence.

At 7 p.m. on Tuesdays, she cued the music that signaled the start of another school board meeting. It was a weird sci-fi techno blend of synthesized wa-wa pedal and thumping drum machine; afterward, the Pledge of Allegiance was recited in a small theater draped in royal blue velvet curtains.

Despite all the recent publicity about cancer at her school, the news vans parked on the street in front of Beverly's rolling front lawn, the seemingly endless lineup of worried parents asking the school board for answers, Anna could not understand what the big deal was. "I was in my own world, obsessed with my social life," she would later explain. "I didn't run track, so I didn't think anything was going to happen to me."

Besides, all Anna really wanted was to get her satirical soap opera, *A Student Body,* on the air at KBEV. It was the story of a naive freshman girl and a "hottie" senior whose make-out session in the boys' locker room is suddenly interrupted by a locker that pops open, revealing a corpse. Initially, suicide is suspected, since the dead student had bipolar tendencies.

In high school, Anna believed, everyone is capable of murder. She especially wanted to make fun of failed screenwriters turned teachers, of which she had had two at Beverly. Plus, she loved her last line of dialogue, "So teachers really are evil!"

No doubt, Anna Harari had filmmaking in her blood. Her mother is the novelist Amy Ephron of the Hollywood writing dynasty that includes her aunts Nora and Delia, both of whom have their photographs hung in the main hallway of the high school's Alumni Wall of Fame.

Still, Anna believed that Beverly was mostly "excellent at encouraging conformity and followers." If there was a moment of serious conformity at Beverly, Anna thought it had to do with the oil well controversy, which had led to a siegelike us-versus-them mentality.

"All the stuff we heard was kinda like antimedia," she said. "Like all the news crews coming down to Beverly were all against us." Anna was convinced that the whole thing was a publicity stunt perpetrated by Erin Brockovich, looking to bolster her TV career.

"The only thing I thought was weird was they never talked about it at school, you know? They really tried to quiet it down as much as possible, and nobody else really seemed to notice.

"Then to come home and have my mom, like, flipping out, you know? And she was giving me all these facts about the oil pipes that ran under our house on Camden and all the people in our neighborhood with cancer. But then, when I was at school, these facts didn't exist.

"It was a fake contract, like: go to school and never mention it. And if it was brought up, it was like, 'Oh, no. It's fine. It's all BS.' Like, whatever. It didn't feel real. It was the oil well, then Erin Brockovich, or Julia Roberts, so it can't be real.

"Because of the celebrity factor, it became like a dream."

Barry Wallerstein was not happy. On Wednesday morning, April 30, 2003, one of his top chemical engineers, Pang Mueller, discovered more problems at Venoco: excessive amounts of the carcinogen benzene were leaking from the Tower of Hope.

Mueller, a forty-seven-year-old mother of two daughters, had conducted a series of "source tests" on a piece of equipment, an amine unit, used to remove carbon dioxide gas from the produced gas stream prior to its being sent through pipelines to the Southern California Gas Company.

But the giant carbon filters which are supposed to absorb hydrocarbon gases on the amine unit kept malfunctioning. They failed to trap benzene, for example. One test showed 213 parts per million of benzene; another was as high as 915 parts per million, an amount that exceeded emissions even for some giant coal-burning factories. Cancer risk is assessed in terms of exposure over a lifetime. Normally, the "gold standard" of risk is set at one in a million, meaning that it is permissible for one person in a million to get cancer from exposures to a particular substance. The AQMD has set its "significance threshold" for cancer risk from air toxics at ten in a million. But Pang Mueller's source testing determined the cancer risk from benzene ranged from thirty to eighty in a million. Venoco's equipment, in other words, was creating a cancer risk that was at least three times higher than what was permissible.

"The problem is you can put carbon in there," Mueller said of the amine unit, "but you keep having toxic contamination way too quickly." For Mueller, this simply meant that Venoco's pollution control system needed to be better designed and upgraded. She believed the engineering problem didn't necessarily indicate high levels of public exposure to benzene. Since the benzene content of undiluted well gas had originally been measured as less than .01 percent, she wasn't too worried, especially since vapor leaks become diluted quickly in the atmosphere. As for high cancer risks, the modeling results from the faulty amine unit were based on a twenty-four-hour-per-day, 365-day-per-year and seventy-year lifetime exposure—far more than any student would ever receive.

As the head of a regulatory agency, Wallerstein believed he had to apply rules in an equitable manner for the twenty-eight thousand facilities on his watch. In his view, he had some discretion but very little. He had already allocated resources and manpower to conduct air samples on six different occasions in Beverly Hills. Each time, he had determined that the ambient air at the high school was "not abnormal," though on most of those days the oil wells had been either shut down or had not been operating at full capacity.

What Wallerstein did not disclose until months later, however, was the fact that on four separate occasions, his inspectors had returned and discovered more leaking equipment at the Venoco site. They had quietly issued "notices of violation" against the company for faulty equipment and leaking tanks with rusted components. One was found to be leaking 500,000 parts per million of volatile organic compounds—1,000 times the permissible level.

Historically, according to internal AQMD reports, the oil-and-gas production site had flagrantly ignored air pollution laws. Back in 1981, for example, an AQMD engineering memorandum noted: "Facility has been partially built . . . did not know we required permits."

As a precautionary measure, Wallerstein decided to revoke the facility's permit for its amine unit inside the Tower of Hope. The permit, which no one had bothered to review until Erin Brockovich started making noise, had been languishing in the AQMD's files for three years—yet another embarrassment for Wallerstein.

"I don't want to have to go out there and babysit them all the time," he grumbled.

Even so, the current air tests wouldn't tell the story of what had happened fifteen years earlier, when Lori Moss was a student, returning home from high school every day with crushing headaches.

"There's so many of us who are sick," she said, "and the numbers keep growing. It seems like the parents in Beverly Hills are in la-la land. When you're told everything's okay, you want to believe it.

"Denial is the way it goes."

CHAPTER FOUR

THE CURSE OF THE
ENGLISH DEPARTMENT

At the top of a sloping green lawn, Beverly Hills High School is a stately looking building of pink brick, with a watchtower, a red-tiled roof, and a gymnasium that opens onto a swimming pool. The sprawling campus, bird-of-paradise landscaping, and Norman-style architecture suggest a fine hotel more than a high school. Even the producing oil wells at the football field have long given Beverly the enviable sense of prosperity and privilege.

Over the years, surprisingly little has changed on the twenty-six-acre campus. The so-called new building—a three-story addition with underground parking, a TV station, and a planetarium—opened the year of the devastating 1971 Sylmar earthquake, which cracked its foundation. The most striking shift in the school's appearance is its backdrop: the looming skyscrapers of Century City, developed as "the ultimate industrial city" after it was the back lot of the 20th Century Fox movie studio, where cowboys were filmed loping off into the sunset, multiplied. The first high-rise office buildings were the forty-four-story "twin towers," designed by the architect Minoru Yamasaki, who also created New York's ill-fated World Trade Center. The Century City towers were finished with anodized silver to reflect the sun's rays.

Like most public schools across America, Beverly has had to fight against more than urban growth. Encroaching budget cuts, particularly due to Proposition 13 in 1978, created a grim reminder that the school was losing its luster as test scores declined and demographics shifted; 51 percent of students now have a first language other than English, and 35 percent are foreign born, most of them from Iran, Russia, Israel, and Korea. Locals began drifting away in favor of private schools, such as the tony Harvard-Westlake and Buckley schools, located over the hill in the San Fernando Valley.

Earnings from the school's oil wells supplemented dwindling revenues. But when the price of oil plummeted in the mid-1980s, the school district looked for new income streams, including the licensing of a Beverly Hills High School logo to clothing manufacturers. A loyal cadre of fund-raisers helped to make up for lost revenues through an education foundation. But it was the city council that came to the rescue in the 1990s. With property values pegged to the school's stellar reputation, the city committed $6.6 million annually to its schools, especially the crown jewel, Beverly High.

All of which meant a Cadillac educational system for Beverly Hills students—and their teachers. While the annual per capita expenditure for American pupils was $3,449 nationally (Los Angeles could afford but a paltry $2,554), Beverly Hills spent a whopping $8,488 per student. That commitment, of course, meant better conditions and higher salaries for teachers, many of whom spent entire careers at Beverly.

But by the spring of 2003, as the oil-well story was gaining traction in the media, one aspect of the controversy that was utterly ignored by the press was the one that fascinated me most: if industrial emissions were, indeed, causing young graduates to grow ill, what about the faculty, whose exposures were potentially the greatest? Certainly, the duration of their exposure—decades, in some cases—and proximity couldn't be ignored.

With a couple of exceptions, I had not seen any of my teachers for thirty years. When I contacted them, they couldn't have been more gracious with their time or their memories. Those teachers and administrators whom I met for the first time were equally generous.

What they revealed to me—about repeated complaints that went unheeded, anecdotal accounts of "too much" cancer among faculty and staff, ambivalence about the lawsuit due to lack of information—suggested a struggle for the soul of a place. And shame.

Here are their voices:

Lou "Mr. V" Versace (English teacher, 1966–86): I came to Beverly when I was twenty-six years old, fresh out of college. I got a B.A. from Princeton, a master's in teaching from Harvard, and an M.A. in English from Berkeley. I did twenty years of hard time at Beverly before I got out.

Coach Gerald "Carp" Carpenter (history teacher and football and golf coach, 1964–88): I grew up in Newton, Iowa, home of Maytag. I was working at a brand-new high school in the suburbs of Chicago, called Lake Park High School. And I had been on a Fulbright program to India.

When I finally arrived at Beverly, we had this U-Haul and three little kids. We literally could not find the school. It took us most of that day to figure out that little alley that goes up by the oil wells is not Beverly Hills. There's no sign there or anything. It was 1964, no Century City.

Marilyn "Mickey" Freedman (English and history teacher, 1967–2001): I was thirty-seven when I started at Beverly, and the school was almost totally white and Jewish. I was hired as an English teacher. I came midyear. They neglected to tell me that the woman I replaced was shot by her estranged husband during the holidays. The kids told me.

I loved the kids, which is why I stayed so long. I had one English class that first semester that had five of the top kids in the class. They all went to Stanford and Harvard, Yale and Princeton. It wasn't an honors class. It was regular English.

For the most part, the administration never bothered anybody. We had a series of goofy superintendents. One of them slept through every meeting and sent out hysterical missives to staff with a purple mountain on it. That was the butt of a lot of jokes. Then we had a guy who was very elegant looking and drove a Jag. Then when the teachers' strike came, they canned him.

Lou Versace: I had a class once, one of my more memorable classes, loaded with Motown. I had Berry Gordy's kid, Marvin Gaye's kid, and Smoky Robinson's kid all in the same room, and I had to teach them to write. My students used to say, "Mr. V, when are you going to get a real job?" and I'd say, "When I'm tired of this."

Herbert Dodge (history teacher from 1962 to 1988 and chair of the Social Studies Department for six years; started the AP history program at Beverly High): My first teaching job was in Grosse Point, Michigan. They were on the cutting edge of education there. They had an AP program started by a professor of history at Williams College. I wanted to go to the best school system in California. Beverly Hills High was considered that at the time.

When I wanted to start an AP history program at Beverly, I received nothing but encouragement. We had the leading AP program west of the Mississippi. I wrote to *Time* magazine. I said, "Why don't you run an article on public schools?" In the summer of '63, they sent a reporter to Beverly and published a story, "As Private As Public Can Be." I can't say enough about the quality of the kids. The students were just superb.

Lou Versace: It's gotta be one of the strangest places I've ever spent some time in, Beverly Hills High School. The first year I came, 1966, they still had a lot of money. They were pretty fashionable and high flying. They had an opening breakfast for the faculty at the Beverly Hilton. This was a posh affair. I was an impressed, neophyte little teacher. Everyone's making speeches about how great the school is and how fortunate we are to work there. This one woman with a very thick German accent says, "You may haf hert that Beverly Hills High School is the best. Vell, vee are." I knew at that point I was in trouble.

I mean, I've never been at a place that takes itself so seriously. Yeah, it's a good school. But there are lots of good schools. But everybody thought they were the be-all and end-all.

THE CURSE

Mickey Freedman: I did feel that something was wrong on the third floor. We lost I don't know how many English teachers from that third floor. I kept wondering, How come we had so many cancers when there were so few people?

Lou Versace: We used to call it the Curse of the English Department. It was incredible. There was like a death a year, starting with Barbara Schenkel. She had breast cancer. I remember going to her funeral.

Mickey Freedman: Barbara O'Brian had breast cancer. Barbara Schenkel, breast cancer. Barbara Sussman, also breast cancer. The three Barbaras— they all worked up on the third floor. Also Marilyn Willinger, who died of cancer, was on the third floor. Ilene Collins, who worked in the school treasurer's office in the student store. Also on the third floor. Breast cancer, but she survived. Gail Shafran, who had lung cancer, worked on the third floor. She chaired the English Department. Lou Versace worked on the third floor, and he's got prostate cancer.

It's just a lot of coincidence, maybe. But odd. You can see why some people would speculate. Who the hell knows?

Jane Wortman (math teacher, 1977 to present; chair of the Math Department; 1971 graduate): It was spooky—the fact that people who taught in those classrooms up on the third-floor patio kept getting cancer. It was weird, like, what's going on?

Leonard Stern (English and history teacher, 1966–2001): I started there when I was twenty-three and left when I was sixty-one, so really my whole life. There's an enormous amount of illness among faculty. I'm getting tired of funerals, frankly.

THE WARNINGS

Coach Dick Schreiber (football and swimming coach, 1959–97): I do remember one day at football practice, the oil well exploded. We had dignitaries visiting from Japan. It spouted oil across the football field and all the way across the street onto the apartment buildings. Our practice gear had oil stains on it a couple of years until it wore out. The district had to pay for new suits for the Japanese visitors and to repaint the apartment buildings across the street where the oil was sprayed. I was coaching football, the sophomore and freshman teams. We wore our practice pants for a week and turned them in to get a clean pair, then we wore the clean ones to the game. As the season went on, you'd get more mixed and matched. All the practice jerseys kept the oil on them.

F. Willard "Robbie" Robinson (principal, 1959–75): The oil wells were never that important. They enabled us to pay the salaries of three teachers. For all the headaches, it probably wasn't worth it. We only had one problem: it blew out one time and blew oil spots on cars. The district paid to fix them up. It blew some kind of gas; there were flakes of oil within the gas.

There was a fire one time. I remember that too. There were about five wells there, and they'd move the derrick to service the hole.

Ken Peters (principal and superintendent of schools, 1950–80, in a letter to Clifford Enger, Beverly Hills Oil Company, October 31, 1963): I wish to report that we have not at any time found a pumper or employee of the Beverly Hills Oil Co. on the site. Further, the emergency sign posted at the entrance to the site lists the number OL. 46852 for emergency calls. I find it can hardly serve this purpose because dialing several times to this date results in no answer.

An additional provision in the April 4, 1961, Consent and Agreement, requires that the site be kept in a clean, orderly, safe, attractive condition. It does not qualify on any of these points. Your lack of attention to these matters creates a significant public relations problem and a vital pupil welfare concern.

Joyce Banzhaf (health education teacher, 1973–2001): I was a runner. I'd work out on the track every morning and you'd smell the fumes. So, I called the AQMD. They'd say, "Methane vented doesn't smell."

Every time I phoned about venting from the oil well, it would stop for a few days. This would go on for years. You wouldn't smell the gas for a few days and then they'd start again. It was so reliable. I sent a letter to the physical education teachers and superintendent and assistant superintendent. They could be calling. If we all called, they could fix it.

The only thing that happened was the superintendent told me to butt out.

"Coach" Chuck Kloes (history teacher and track and football coach, 1965–2000; currently assistant football coach): I arrived in 1965. I've been out on that track longer than anybody. When you're out there on the field, particularly during track season, you can smell the fumes. Sometimes, they're more noxious than others. When you work out at the track, you can't help but get a whiff of the oil wells. It used to smell kinda sweet, like celery. If the wind was blowing, it wasn't noticeable.

On the so-called upper field, you've got kids playing there all the time—soccer, freshman football, summer football. My son, who coached and taught softball, said there were always days he could smell it up there. But no one complained about it causing any adverse health effects.

Initially, they didn't vent it well in the eighties. There were days, depending on the prevailing wind, you could really smell it. Three or four summers I was teaching, it got pretty bad. Joyce Banzhaf, the health education teacher, called about it. The oil company vented it more efficiently, maybe by the early nineties.

Mari-Ann Strandwall (track and tennis coach, 1967–92, quoted in *Highlights,* **April 13, 1973, "The Oil Well Is Not Well; Causes Problems in PE" by Michael Ross and Sue Frankel):** It's disgusting; [the oil wells] stink to the point where you can't breathe anymore.

"Coach" Jason Newman (golf and basketball coach, 1982 to present; 1969 graduate): Over the years, there have been sporadic bad smells. I don't know what they did [to fix it]. We just didn't think about it. We took it for granted. It could be a costly mistake in ways more important than money.

Linda Tromblestein* (Beverly Hills Unified School District teacher 1970s to present): I was in room 504; that's where the student activity center used to be in the Business Education building, where they had the Pigskin Prom and taught shorthand and typing. It was divided into three classrooms. Room 504 has a fireplace and a kitchen. It's all brick and glass. I was right on that alley by Century City.

There was black stuff coming out of the vents in the ceiling. It's like coal, black.

THE POWER PLANT

Lou Versace: There was a big generator with smokestacks that was more noticeable than the oil wells. I always used to look up at those when I parked in the Business Education lot, and I'd think: what the hell is that? When the new building came, I moved to the third floor.

Joyce Banzhaf: I think it's just astonishing they built a power plant between a hospital and a school.

Jane Wortman: People in the BE Building were complaining the vibrations were driving them crazy from the power plant.

---

* Name changed upon request.

Joyce Banzhaf: I was teaching in the southernmost building, the BE Building. The windows face the power plant.

My kids' desks rattled. There was this constant rumbling sound. My kids would ask me, "Ms. Banzhaf, why is my desk rattling?"

I finally had it checked out. People from the L.A. County Health Department came and tested and said, "This is illegal for schools." They measured it at ninety decibels. So the guy from the health department said to me, "We'll help you fight it." The principal at the time wasn't willing to fight it; it's the Century City power plant, and that's kinda scary. They'd need to build a very thick wall. Nobody was willing to take this power plant company or Century City to court.

Jane Gifford (substitute teacher, 1971–83, and special education teacher, 1984–96): I was in room 103 in the old building across from Business Education. I was right above the warehouse—above the Swim Gym. Every afternoon, there would be this electricy, acidy, burning smell. Really pungent. I called the AQMD maybe five times. The last time I called, they never contacted me. I called them from January to June 1996.

The AQMD told me "it'll take us an hour to get out there." I said, "If it takes you an hour to get here, the odors don't last that long." I thought it was at the hospital, behind the building. They said, "There's an oil well there."

You just get to a point where you say to yourself, "I'm outta here." You get worn down.

Herbert Dodge: There was all that steam—a cloud of it—coming off that plant. I'd drive up that back entrance and see all that steam and wonder if it had negative effects. I remember driving through the steam one day and going to the teachers' lounge. I told one of my colleagues, "I just passed through that cloud again."

Jane Gifford: The AQMD said to me, "Is it toxic or just noxious?" I said, "It's a horrible smell." I know people in the Business Education Building were complaining about the horrible smell too. Something was going on there. But people gripe all the time. If it doesn't affect you, you slough it off. I think the AQMD sloughed it off too.

Nobody did anything. That's the bottom line. People complained, but no one did a thing.

MORE CANCER

Mickey Freedman: Mari-Ann Strandwall, the track and tennis coach, had a double mastectomy and died of cancer.

Leonard Stern: Chuck Reilly, who was a basketball coach, had a massive tumor on the side of his head. It was an egg on the side of his face. It killed him. He was thirty-seven years old.

We were all so naive. Nobody thought it might be environmentally caused. Everyone just thought, "I'm glad it's not me" and went on their merry way.

Jason Newman: I lost my kidney and half a colon. I was fifty. When I got a colonoscopy, they found a tumor in my colon. The surgeon said it was a surprise, because I had had no symptoms. Then they did a scan on my kidney and lower abdomen and found a tumor on my kidney too. The doctors were struggling to figure out why.

I went to see a holistic doctor, who told me my immune system was compromised. My killer cells were almost nil, which means I didn't have cells to kill off the bad ones.

Susan Messenger (AP Spanish teacher, 1977 to present): I taught in a classroom where it seemed like an inordinate number of teachers with health problems had also taught. It was room 228, the choir room. I've had three diagnoses of breast cancer myself. When I was seven months pregnant with my third son, they induced his birth and then I started chemo and radiation ten days after he was born. Three years later, I had a lumpectomy and all my nodes removed. I had chemo all year.

After my third diagnosis, I had a full mastectomy. I was a lovely bald bride. I spent my honeymoon at the City of Hope—very romantic. So, you could say I have definite health issues.

Lou Versace: I was diagnosed with prostate cancer on New Year's Day, 2003. I had a transurethral resectioning of the prostate, a medieval term for Roto-Rooter.

Then I had the radiation treatments because I couldn't have surgery. So, I had radiation—a giant machine that just rotates around you and zaps you with invisible rays. It's real Star Wars stuff; you can't see anything, you can't feel anything. You just hear some buzzing. They zapped me on four little black dots they tattooed on me for thirteen seconds each. They basically fry the prostate. They make it toast.

They can't narrow it to just the prostate. They'll fry a little of your bladder and a little of your rectum. So there are some side effects, which I'm going through now.

What's Erin Brockovich like? Nothing like Julia Roberts? Or are there similarities? If I were not in the throes of ongoing hormone therapy, I'd ask about how her boobs compare to Julia's, but at this point, I'm just not interested (and I used to be).

Joel Goodman: (history teacher, 1967–70; 1962 graduate): After being diagnosed with prostate cancer at the age of fifty-two in December 1996, I subsequently underwent radical prostatectomy surgery, intensity-modulated radiation therapy, two rounds of hormone ablation therapy and thalidomide therapy. At the moment, I'm on an off-cycle from the hormone ablation therapy, but expect to begin my third cycle with chemotherapy within a few months.

The first year I was there, I taught in the BE Building. That's nearer to where the fumes are; the girls' athletic field was next to it. I taught all my classes my second year in the BE Building, where the student lounge was converted to a classroom. I taught "Problems of Democracy" there.

THE LAWSUIT

Gerald Carpenter: Not once in those twenty-four years did we ever have any kind of discussion of potential harm of those oil wells. Not once.

It's kinda like the cigarette thing. Everyone knew cigarettes weren't good for you, but even when they put it on the package people weren't sure. But it's not something we ever thought about. And it was never mentioned. We knew it was really important to the finances of the district, but other than that we didn't pay any attention to it.

Jane Wortman: It seems like every time we turn around, someone else on the faculty is being diagnosed with cancer. But schoolteachers in California also have a higher incidence of breast cancer, so what are we to make of that?

I honestly don't see a connection to the oil wells. It just seems like a big publicity thing to me. Personally, I'd be more worried about fumes from cars on Olympic Boulevard.

Jason Newman: Initially, I was scared when I heard about this, like everyone else. Then I started thinking, why is the one oil well in Beverly Hills the magic one? There are oil wells everywhere in L.A. If this had some type of relationship to developing cancer, you'd think people working around it would have the greatest incidence of cancer.

I'm going to wait for the scientific data to come out. You'd think in the public interest, if Masry and Brockovich found something bad they'd present their information to be part of the solution. But they're hiding it.

I really don't want to think it was responsible for my situation or that we're exposing our kids to it. To me, it makes no more sense for me to be working near an oil well than living in Los Angeles. I remember when we could see smog. Now, it seems not so bad as it used to be. We're all doing our kids a disservice, living in L.A. How many of us are willing to move out of state?

In a way, [having an oil-and-gas production facility on campus] probably doesn't make sense. Why introduce something additional that potentially isn't good for kids to be around? In a perfect world, no one would build an oil well there. My parents got $30 a month from the oil under their house.

Mickey Freedman: Until all of this was well publicized, I didn't know that many of the people I worked with had cancer. They never mentioned it. There are also many teachers who have cancer who are not filing suit. I can't imagine anybody being that fucking loyal. That's just plain stupid.

Jason Newman: Maybe I don't believe it because I don't want to believe it. If somebody did know about the dangers or should have known or buried information, I'd join the lawsuit. But they don't have a causal link.

I trust the school board. I trust their integrity. Hopefully, they're doing what's in the best interests of the kids. It does make sense to do an epidemiological study. Who would fund it, I don't know. If they do a study, someone will be responsible if there's a problem.

Susan Messenger: I don't want to come off litigious or like I'm on a bandwagon. I went to a couple of informational meetings at lunch here. There's too much that's not known still. Nobody has convinced me that I shouldn't come here to teach.

Mickey Freedman: Some of these people [in the lawsuit] want money. Not that I don't want money. But I decided to join the suit because we have to force them to find out what's really going on. There's no sense exposing more kids to this crap if we don't have to. Maybe it will force these people to do something. At least find out. It's absurd to not find out if this is causing all these illnesses and deaths.

Susan Messenger: I got a big packet [from the law firm] in my mailbox. I don't know who put it there. When I signed the papers to join the lawsuit, I felt such anxiety about it.

Herbert Dodge: To be honest, when I first heard the news reports about the lawsuit, I thought there might be something to it because of the Belmont School downtown. [A high school discovered in 1999 to be contaminated with hazardous gas from old oil wells that lay beneath it; parts of the school had to be demolished and rebuilt.] Then you think about the first Gulf War and the burning oil wells and being in close proximity to oil wells. My daughter is a lawyer. Her first reaction was it would be very, very difficult to prove.

Mary Ann Baum (AP English teacher, 1977 to present): This whole lawsuit is ridiculous. Things happen. People die of cancer. A lot of healthy people have been teaching here a long time. You might as well worry about breathing car fumes. There are all sorts of things people can get sick from. It's laughable, to tell you the truth. Beverly Hills is as far removed from reality as it can be. People in Beverly Hills need something to stimulate their boring lives, so they develop these panicky attitudes. I teach, so I don't get involved with all this nonsense.

Lou Versace: I heard about the lawsuit from one of my colleagues, Mary Ann Baum. She saw the story on TV and sent me a printout over the Internet. She sent me an e-mail saying, "How does this one grab you?"

Mary Ann Baum: Some of my students were pulled from school. People are acting like this is an Ebola epidemic and people are dropping like flies. There are more people that are healthy than not. You need to do a comparative look at schools with oil wells. I'm more interested in my salary and getting air-conditioning here. People are just being neurotic about things they can afford to be.

Lou Versace: I just cannot understand the apathy and downright hostility of a majority of teachers at Beverly Hills High School against their own. I don't know anyone who has died because of the oil wells, but if I did, I would be out for blood. This is not just a lark for me. I want very much to see the bastards—oil conglomerates and the greedy bureaucrats of Beverly Hills—to go down, hard.

The Norman motto is "Today well lived." Dylan Thomas says you "rage, rage against the dying of the light." I try to live every day I can, being an old Norman, having as much intensity as I can. That's what this lawsuit means, in some ways, doesn't it?

Mary Ann Baum: The [oil well] has been there for fifty years, and all of a sudden it's a problem? To me, it seems amusing. There's been little factual information released that would cause me to worry. That could change, but for right now I focus on teaching.

Lou Versace: I'm not terminal. I don't have lymphoma or leukemia, like some of these poor bastard kids did. If I did, I'd be enraged. Not if I were them, but if I were their parents. I mean, how irresponsible can you get in the name of money? My God, you drill for oil on a high school campus and you kill the students while you're doing it? What about having terminally ill children decorating their own tomb? At the ceremony, bowing down to the god of hope while they're ingesting the fumes and killing themselves? It's just too bizarre. Too bizarre. The fact they're denying it up and down shows something: they won't face reality or the truth.

Gary Thorpe (AP chemistry and biology teacher, 1967 to present; academic decathalon coach): I volunteered to be on the superintendent's environmental committee. I was turned down. I said, "Excuse me, I wrote a book about it. My kids go to school here." If there is contamination, there is something called remediation. There are ways of dealing with it.

But problems don't exist in Beverly Hills. It would affect too many people and businesses. Your image would be destroyed. This is Oz. It's like the emperor has no clothes.

Gerald Carpenter: I really feel terrible for those people who got sick. If they can prove that the oil thing caused their illness I have no qualms that they deserve whatever support they can get out of it. But I'm just praying that it doesn't hurt that district.

There are other oil wells, and I never heard anything about those being a problem. In fact, we had oil rights from one of our houses. We had our little duplex on Corning, and they were slant-drilling. We lived only a few blocks from the wells on Pico.

Mickey Freedman: We've got a lot of staff who were so proadministration that if Howdy Doody were running the place, they would have thought he was a genius. But people kept dying off, and nobody paid much attention—until now. Did you know the staff kept lists of the dead and dying?

Chuck Kloes: This oil well was looked at as a boon because of the money it brought in. Now, it's a bane because it's viewed as a cause of illness. To hold the school district responsible for something they didn't have any idea about—well, a lot of people don't want to get called into court to testify one way or another.

On a philosophical level, you think about education and the purpose of Beverly Hills High School: you have all these kids getting a good education and you have the people who taught there. It's not easy to get a job there. The lawsuit has the potential to bring the whole thing down. If I were ill, I'd have a whole different take on it.

Jane Gifford: Our daughter, Jane, teaches in Beverly Hills. She said the district explained that this was all trumped up and pooh-poohed the idea. She came home saying, it's really nothing.

It's a matter of whose propaganda you listen to.

As far as I'm concerned, there's just too much cancer there.

MONEY AND LOVE

Ken Peters: When I arrived, the school district got no money from the oil well. It was old and antiquated. I wanted to shut the darn thing down because the girls always wanted more room for their physical activity up there. We used to call it the "girls' field."

Then a number of years later, an oil engineer came in and, in effect, said, "You guys are crazy. Century City is drilling like mad, right up against your boundary. You have to realize oil goes where the drilling is, and they're getting all of your oil." So that resulted in sessions with Century City. They hired an expert in oil. I forget the title. And they began exploring. Along the way, they put out bids to contract for drilling.

There were continued discussions and concern we all had about safety. But it had no relation to the toxic deal and so forth. We never heard about that until recent years. The concern was: you're going to have an oil deal here and oil trucks; that sounds dangerous.

Arthur Malin (school board member, 1969–77): We never thought about the health part of it, I can tell you that. We only thought about the money: we've got an oil well—what, it makes $2,000 a year? What the hell is that?

Bernie Grenell (school board member, 1976–80): It's the only site in Beverly Hills where you could put an oil well. You can't put one in the city. I was involved in asking for a greater royalty for the school district. The city put in their order for royalty payments. I don't think it was high on our agenda. I think the city was pushing for it.

Ken Peters: With our oil attorney and oil engineers, it was figured out where it would be located and with direct access from Olympic it would really take less of the girls' field than the old thing that had been there for years. That was when there was the assurance they'd put up this rather attractive brick wall. There would be no trucks on campus, other than from the Olympic entrance there.

But before they had a drop of oil, I retired. I retired in '81. So, as I tell people, I was very unhappy because I didn't get an oil change for my car after all this money floating around.

Initially, the city said they wanted no part of it. And they didn't want the school district to get involved either. But the school district, through county counsel, reminded the city that the school district was an entity of the state, and if the district really wanted to go ahead they could go ahead. After the city got more into it, they realized it could be rewarding financially. The city's main concern was noise. We didn't understand toxicity then.

Gerald Carpenter: I know we were pretty excited when they developed Century City. It was a fantastic thing for the district, for the school. We always had the image of being an ultraspecial place. Then, to back up right against Century City, it was more of a university feeling. I used to go over there and walk during my lunch hour. It was a great feel for a little country kid. That's the end of the boundary line. Beverly Hills ends right there, right by the school. So they didn't have any control over it, other than putting their two cents in if something was going to be developed and they didn't like it.

Lou Versace: In 1972, I got a note in my typewriter from a teacher who had just come to the high school. She wrote, "I am your new office mate, and you have to clean up this place." By October, we were having a mad affair. In February, my wife found out about it. I decided to leave my wife and kids for this woman. We lived at the beach together. I divorced my wife.

Her name was Charlie Atol, and she was the love of my life. We lived together for four years, and it was the happiest four years of my life. Her dad was a pit boss in Vegas. It was her thing to entertain people. She loved it. She made a movie for the fun of it. One night, we gave a great Fourth of July party. We were driving to Westwood and got into an accident on Bundy and National. The car was broadsided and rolled over. She went through the sunroof and died instantly. I walked out without a scratch. I went back to Beverly for summer school.

If I had not taught at Beverly, I would not have met Charlie Atol. She was thirty-three when she died; I was thirty-six. I had asked her to marry me three times. She said no each time. There was an unwritten law you couldn't teach at the same school and be married. She loved teaching at Beverly Hills High. Her strong point was comedy.

My work saved me, and the students saved me. It was either that or blowing your brains out, and I thought about that too. So, there's a special place in my heart for Beverly Hills High School.

CHAPTER FIVE

THE "STEAM" NEXT DOOR

W hen Zack Anderson asked his friends in the math patio during lunch to help him start an underground newspaper at Beverly Hills High School, the long-haired brainiac had yet to discover four discarded computer monitors in the alley behind the apartment he shared with his mother, a psychotherapist, on South Roxbury Drive. Nor had the seventeen-year-old techie with a fondness for Starbucks Mocha Frappuccinos and the sound track to *Pulp Fiction* set out to investigate what the "steam" from the power plant adjacent to the high school might be spewing onto his campus. Neither had Anderson, winner of the 2002 Los Angeles County science fair for his computerized robot that detects obstacles via sonar and zips by them, been admitted early to MIT nor invited to testify at a California Senate investigation into possible contamination of his high school—the first public forum to address the issue.

Anderson, a tall and lanky tennis player, hadn't done any of this when he was sitting in his honors English class in the spring of 2003 and, during a not-too-lively discussion of British literature, a friend randomly complained that major chunks of what she had written for the student paper *Highlights* had been edited out. "Jokingly, I said, 'We should start an underground newspaper and print the entire thing,'" he later recalled.

But what started as a lark took a decidedly different turn when the science geek discovered that his English teacher, the chair of the department, was going on medical leave to be treated for lung cancer. And no one at school was talking about the oil wells anymore. That's when he hauled the computers from the trash bins to his bedroom and, in an effort to promote stories the administration wanted suppressed, cobbled together a new Web site, www.beverlyunderground.com.

"The school is kind of going along with the city, and trying to cover it up—keeping it a hushed subject," he said, sitting in one of his favorite haunts, the Starbucks on the corner of Santa Monica Boulevard and Lasky Drive, across the street from the swank Peninsula Hotel. "It's like propaganda: everything's healthy and safe. Don't panic. There's nothing to worry about."

On his Web site, Anderson began asking the tough questions—albeit, in the edgy parlance of adolescence—that the grown-ups in town seemed to want to ignore: "With the oil well, why can't they just take that shit down?" one of his contributors asked in an editorial.

"No amount of money is worth having a safety risk for students. Last year in PE, it smelled like shit on a lot of days.

"I mean if they don't care about students getting diseases and cancer, why not put a nuclear reactor or maybe a toxic waste dump there? Hell, how about a prison? They would get a lot more money with that. Take it down!"

Beneath a photograph of the Tower of Hope was the heading "Why?" And the answer: "We thought we should spare the BS, and once and for all, enlighten the public as to the motive—$50 million." Another editorial suggested that the school motto be switched from "Today well lived" to "Tomorrow not lived."

Hate mail began pouring in.

"Get a Fucking Life Loser," wrote steeltoe@yahoo.com. "Jesus Christ, you people are the biggest fucking pussys [sic] in the world. 'Oh, I'm scared I might have cancer, help shut down the school immediately.'

"Only in fucking Beverly Hills can kids sit around on their parents' computer and complain about a fucking oil well."

The son of a school board member accused Anderson of being a liar. "You think my mother would want me to go to that school and keep the oil well running if it were dangerous?" he asked in an e-mail.

From "identity concealed," there was this: "All of you are probably social outcasts that sit home on the weekends writing these horribly-written stories for your loser website that gets almost no visits."

Over time, the site attracted more than eighty-seven thousand visitors and 2.5 million hits. But not before Anderson, whose favorite fashion statement was a leather belt etched with an image of Che Guevara, would be threatened with suspension by high school administrators for a prank involving photographs of pole dancers at open house.

About twenty miles northeast of Beverly Hills, in a bright corner office of a concrete-and-glass government building near the railroad tracks at the foot-hills of Glendale, Hamid Saebfar's phone was ringing off the hook.

It was late one afternoon in April 2003, inside a branch of California's Environmental Protection Agency. Parents from Beverly Hills High, who had no interest in suing anyone, were calling. They wanted any shred of informa-tion they could get to determine if their kids were safe: what would he do if he was in their position?

Saebfar, a handsome and friendly man and the father of three children, is the chief of the division in California's Environmental Protection Agency that evaluates and cleans up hazardous substances on school properties in Los Angeles. His agency, the Department of Toxic Substances Control (DTSC), could offer objective information unrelated to litigation issues. First, though, he'd need a signed contract with the school district to get involved.

Saebfar was a veteran of hazardous-site cleanups. Having worked for the EPA in Washington, D.C., in the 1980s, when he was assigned the cleanup of Love Canal, he was well acquainted with the thicket of environmental laws protecting public health. He also knew the laws' shortfalls. When Congress enacted the Superfund legislation in 1980, for example, one hazardous sub-stance was exempted from regulation: petroleum.

In California, state law granted broader authority for cleaning up petroleum wastes, at least in theory, since petroleum and its by-products—organic compounds, heavy metals, and solvents—were defined as hazardous "materials." In practice, though, the distinction proved laughable for regulators like Saebfar, as evidenced by a little-noticed but highly charged DTSC report, "Oil Exploration and Production Wastes Initiative." The 2002 study found high levels of lead contamination, for example, in samples of oily sludge from the Venoco site at Beverly High. But "economic concerns" and political pressure from the governor's office prevented the agency from doing anything about it.

Saebfar wasn't optimistic about helping the parents who begged him to provide an independent investigation in Beverly Hills. "The biggest problem is when you've got a school district that knows they've got a problem but don't want to address it," he would explain.

That, unfortunately, is precisely what would happen in Beverly Hills. The DTSC, the one state agency equipped to handle the contamination of schools, would not be allowed in. And there was nothing Saebfar could do about it.

Mandated to carry out federal environmental laws in California, the DTSC was created by the state legislature in 2000 to assess school sites, but was funded to monitor only *new* schools; existing schools must pay for environmental reviews. Thus, the glaring catch-22: without proof of an "imminent" hazard, the law stipulates, school districts aren't required to do a thing.

If budget-conscious districts, including Beverly Hills, aren't interested in engaging the services of bureaucrats like Saebfar, nothing can force them to do so—not even the judgment of toxicologists and other DTSC experts that children could be at risk. Since Beverly Hills viewed soil and air sampling as possibly handing evidence to Brockovich and Masry, its officials would stubbornly refuse to sign a contract with Saebfar.

DTSC scientist Jennifer Jones, a tall and lithe Ph.D. candidate in environmental science at UCLA, was assigned to manage the Beverly High evaluation.

"At first," she later said, "we thought, this is a powerful community with a lot of money. Other communities with no money are able to lobby to get us in. So why doesn't Beverly Hills?

"The thing is, they have better lawyers. They know they don't have to."

By the time Saebfar arrived for a preliminary meeting at Beverly High on a Friday morning in early May 2003, he knew that politics would prevail over science. Touring the high school campus and adjacent sites with a geologist and petroleum engineer, Saebfar and Jones believed that an investigation was warranted. They worried about potential impacts from historical oil production—abandoned oil wells, an underground storage tank—and from Venoco's and Sempra's current production operations.

After touring Venoco's site, they walked around the corner from the hospital in Century City and visited Sempra's plant. They were surprised to see that it was located so close to the school campus; you could actually throw a ball from the outdoor basketball courts to the cooling towers next door.

Saebfar wasn't sure which toxic air contaminant was more poisonous, the trace amounts of benzene coming from the oil wells or the hexavalent chromium, a known lung carcinogen, once used in the cooling towers at Sempra. But he had toxicologists on staff who could help him assess what chemicals might have the greatest effect on children's developing bodies. In some cases, the chemicals of most concern might not necessarily cause cancer.

Public records from the AQMD's files show that one of the chemicals for which Sempra quietly paid annual "emissions fees" to the local air pollution agency was acrolein, a toxin that the state's Office of Environmental Health Hazards Assessment lists as being especially dangerous for children because it is thought to exacerbate asthma. Even so, state and federal regulators hadn't gotten around to monitoring it yet. According to the federal Centers for Disease Control's Agency for Toxic Substances and Disease Registry (ATSDR), acrolein is produced by oxidation of propylene and is mostly used as a biocide to control algae, fungi, rodents, and microorganisms. Acrolein, which the EPA lists as a "possible" human carcinogen, has also been used as a warning agent in gases, as a test gas for gas masks, in military poison gases, and in the manufacture of colloidal metals.

Even at low concentrations, the ATSDR's Web site states, acrolein "is severely irritating to skin, eyes, and mucous membranes. Inhalation of acrolein may result in respiratory distress and delayed pulmonary edema. The mechanism by which acrolein produces toxic symptoms is not known, but the compound is highly reactive. Exposure to acrolein produces severe respiratory problems and individuals with pre-existing breathing difficulties or skin disease may be more susceptible to its effects."

The day before they toured the campus, Saebfar and Jones met at city hall with school and city officials and their attorneys to discuss the scope of a DTSC investigation. Not only would they need soil and soil-gas tests, they explained; they would also want to assess the AQMD's air-testing data for quality-control purposes and to review the work of Camp Dresser & McKee, the company hired by the city's defense law firm.

"That's when the project died," Saebfar recalled, adding that AQMD chief Barry Wallerstein refused during a telephone conference call in that meeting to share his agency's data as a courtesy. "We didn't get any of it."

Wallerstein was convinced that neither Venoco nor Sempra was a major toxic emitting source: the "fugitive" emissions at ground level from storage tanks and leaky equipment from Venoco were inconsequential. He also believed that the total mass of emissions from Sempra might shoot out of stacks at higher temperatures and with greater velocity, but by the time they were dispersed at such high elevations, their concentrations were much lower. The risk, he believed, wasn't significant.

But it wasn't just internecine battles that waylaid the DTSC chief. A crucial part of his process also required setting up a community meeting to inform the public about his findings. Saebfar was convinced, however, that the defense lawyers were purposely avoiding public input. His repeated telephone calls and letters to school district administrators, city officials, and their attorneys went unreturned.

As a courtesy, he sent out another letter in early June, reminding school and city officials that time was of the essence if they hoped to realize their goal of finding answers about the school's safety for the upcoming school year. Unless the contract "is signed promptly," he wrote, "the investigation may not be completed prior to the next school year." Saebfar also asked the mayor to sign the agreement and requested that CDM's work plan be submitted for his review. But the mayor never signed the agreement, nor would CDM submit its work plan.

The problem with the CDM analysis, Saebfar believed, was that it was limited to one area of the campus by the oil wells. Saebfar wanted to look at the entire campus, inside and out, reasoning that the oil field beneath it was not shallow and could be leaking methane gas or toxic chemicals from old, abandoned wells. Since the area had once been inhabited by wildcat operations, Saebfar thought it important to look for evidence of oil sumps on campus too.

According to schools superintendent Gwen Gross, such a study was deemed "too comprehensive."

As the weeks passed, Saebfar's hopes of providing objective information to the parents who had contacted him dimmed, especially when he learned from his boss in Sacramento that a Beverly Hills High School parent named John Millan had accused him of "lobbying" for the job. It was a sentiment shared by many others in town. As it happened, John Millan would be elected to the school board that fall.

"I wanted to deal with the science and the facts," Saebfar later said, "and they wouldn't let me do my job."

Hamid Saebfar shook his head.

Sitting in his office six months later, he sounded exasperated as he recalled the events in Beverly Hills. "When there's money involved," he said, "people don't care who they hurt."

He continued, "I finally got a call that they were willing to sign a contract, but only if we did a limited investigation that they wanted to do: in other words, we couldn't ask for more data. I said, 'That's not acceptable.'"

Larry Wiener, the Beverly Hills city attorney who graduated from Princeton and UCLA Law School, where he had edited the *Journal of*

Environmental Law and Policy, claimed that the city decided not to work with the DTSC because "it would take too long."

"That's a lie," Saebfar countered. "That I dispute. They never submitted a work plan to us—period.

"They defend a lawsuit rather than address the entire situation. I don't blame 'em, because they've got so much money riding on this thing."

Even more infuriating to Saebfar, though, was the soil and soil-gas analysis by CDM. Not only did CDM's report conclude that "no basis exists for believing that students or staff would show any adverse health effects from exposure to chemicals in soil or soil gas," but it added that in terms of cancer risk, "the State of California would not require any type of cleanup or action at the high school."

The CDM report stated that it was "conducted in accordance with Cal-EPA DTSC guidance."

I asked Saebar if his agency had, indeed, offered guidance to CDM in its data collection.

"Absolutely not," he replied. "It would be like consulting with an architect to build a house and then not use his plans. We talked about drafting a plan; it ended there. They have zero approval from us. Big zip."

In the third issue of his underground newspaper, Zack Anderson published his first investigative piece, "'Steam' from Century City Building Isn't Just Water Vapor." In it, he cast a spotlight on the power plant—owned by Sempra Energy, the Fortune 500 energy giant, with revenues of $9.4 billion, and the parent company of the Southern California Gas Company—located between the school's southwest parking lot and Century City Medical Plaza.

"It is important to know," Anderson wrote, "that the Oil Well is not necessarily the only possible source of carcinogens: the seemingly harmless cloud of 'steam,' in reality, contains much more than just water vapor—it contains harmful toxins and massive amounts of pollution.

"What people don't know," he added, is that "the owners of the complex have been cited on various occasions for releasing illegal and harmful amounts of chemicals into the air."

Until now, no one had bothered to mention the toxic emissions from the steam next door, other than Jody Kleinman during her evening forays before the school board.

No one had to.

Sempra, in compliance with state law, had taken out a tiny ad earlier that year on page 2 of the *Beverly Hills Courier,* warning the community of chemical releases from its plant. It read: "Sempra Energy Solutions wants you to know that detectable amounts of some of these substances (chemicals considered by the state to cause cancer, birth defects, other reproductive harm) may be found in and around its facility located at 2052 Century Park East, L.A., CA. Potential sources of these substances can include common products such as gasoline, oil, natural gas, paint, welding rods and cleaning solvents."

But it was such an innocuous warning, like the ones posted at California gas stations, that few people paid attention. The only other public discussion of Sempra's Central Plant in Century City had to be dug out of court filings in the *Moss v. Venoco* litigation, in which Sempra would be named as a defendant.

Despite demurrers filed by company lawyers, denying that the energy giant had anything to do with cancer cases in Beverly Hills, a court order would require the owners of the power plant to turn over internal documents that might offer clues about the health impacts of toxic exposures there. In the meantime, Zack Anderson used the Internet to do some sleuthing of his own.

Opened in 1965, Sempra Energy's Central Plant is one of the largest commercial heating and air-conditioning systems in the world. The plant provides chilled-water and hot-water energy services twenty-four hours a day, seven days a week, for 11 million square feet of residential and commercial buildings in Century City, including the hospital, the Century Towers, and the Century Plaza Hotel.

In essence, the giant boilers heat water by burning natural gas. The complex houses four gas-fired boilers, three steam-driven centrifugal chillers totaling 16,000 tons, three electric-driven centrifugal chillers totaling 7,500 tons, and four steam-powered absorption chillers totaling 3,500 tons. The boilers produce high-temperature water for heating and steam for running turbines to produce cooling. The heated steam and the burned natural gas are then released into the atmosphere next to Beverly High.

According to the U.S. EPA, Sempra's Century City facility is considered a "major source" of air pollution, one of about three hundred facilities in Los Angeles that release twenty-five tons or more of pollutants every year. In 2000, Sempra released more than two hundred tons of nitrogen oxides, sulfur dioxide, carbon monoxide, organic gases, and particulate matter. AQMD documents also reveal that Sempra pays "emission fees" for its re-lease of hazardous air pollutants, including formaldehyde, a known lung carcinogen; acetaldehyde, a carcinogen that is ranked as one of the most hazardous compounds to ecosystems and human health; and benzene.

The amount of pollution released into the air by the complex is so vast that the AQMD has fined Sempra on many occasions. In 1996, for example, the facility paid more than $13,000 for emitting nearly two tons of nitrogen oxides beyond what was permitted. The company also received "notices of violation" for disconnecting its emissions-monitoring system, for not prop-erly reporting emissions data, and for exceeding its permitted allocations of nitrogen oxides.

That same year, when the plant suffered "a catastrophic failure," or natu-ral gas explosion, government records indicate that the AQMD cared more about Sempra's bottom line than about public health. Despite complaints from faculty and neighbors about "pungent" and "burning" odors, the AQMD hearing board granted Sempra a variance from complying with air pollution rules to avoid "economic harm."

Sempra is part of the AQMD's "cap and trade" program, called Reclaim, which permits companies to trade in pollution "credits." Basically, the pro-gram allows polluters to buy credits from nearby facilities that are not using up their allotment, resulting in concentrated pollution sources—or "hot spots"—in particular areas.

"The problem with the Sempra facility," Zack Anderson wrote, "is that they often buy these credits so that they can legally emit far more pollutants than their own permit allows."

Until 1990, when the federal government banned the use of hexavalent chromium in water-treatment chemicals for open water-circulating systems, the Sempra plant used hexavalent chromium in its cooling towers to protect equipment and piping from corrosion and to control algae growth. During the cooling process, chromium emissions were released into the atmosphere in the form of water droplets.

How much was released over time is unclear.

While "chromium 6" compounds are among the most efficient and cheapest corrosion inhibitors, they are also highly toxic; one study estimated that chrome emissions from cooling towers in the South Coast Air Quality Management District alone may have caused as many as seven hundred additional cancers over a seventy-year exposure period. In 1990, they were banned by the state of California for that use.

Hexavalent chromium, of course, is the same poison that made Erin Brockovich famous. Of the two hundred chemicals reviewed by a scientific advisory panel for the state of California, chromium 6 is one of the most potent carcinogens—second only to dioxin. It is more potent than arsenic, butadiene, diesel exhaust, formaldehyde, trichloroethylene, and methylene chloride.

When, in the fall of 2004, AQMD officials tried to determine how much hexavalent chromium had been used at Sempra in the past, the plant operators refused to provide that information to the government agency. Nor did the law require them to do so. So long as Sempra considered that information proprietary, meaning its release could give other companies a competitive edge, it would remain secret.

"Whether the toxins released by the complex are harming the students and faculty or not," Zack Anderson wrote on his Web site that fall, "it is evident that the cooling plant poses a palpable risk to the students and staff of Beverly Hills High School."

In the weeks that followed, one person who clicked onto the Beverlyunder ground.com Web site was a soft-spoken man named Roger Dunstan, who was a consultant for the Health and Human Services Committee of the California Senate in Sacramento. Already, Dunstan had spoken with Erin Brockovich and Ed Masry about Beverly High: they had been lobbying State Senator Deborah Ortiz, the chair of the committee, to hold a public hearing.

Ortiz, a Democrat from Sacramento, had unsuccessfully introduced a bill three times in the state legislature to promote the practice of biomonitoring—collecting blood samples to pinpoint chemical components and thereby help researchers better understand environmental exposures. The politician, whose mother had survived thyroid cancer but died of ovarian cancer, was also deeply committed to revamping laws to better protect children at schools and to enforce criminal sanctions against corporate polluters.

When she agreed to convene a hearing with the Senate Environmental Quality Committee in the coming months, she asked Dunstan to put together a roster of key witnesses, including Erin Brockovich and Jody Kleinman, and the heads of regulatory agencies.

For a student perspective, Dunstan e-mailed Zack Anderson, asking him if he might be willing to testify. The idea, he explained, was to help the legislature better prevent health risks in California schools; it was not to be a forum about the pending litigation.

Zack Anderson was flattered by the invitation. He quickly accepted. A high school junior who was taking four advanced placement classes at once, he was happy for the diversion. He knew a lot could happen between now and the hearing.

CHAPTER SIX

PR WARS

On a bright Saturday morning in May 2003, just as the jacaranda trees were bursting with purple blossoms, a white van pulled up to the curb on Moreno Drive and parked across the street from Beverly Hills High School. Slung over one side of the van was a large banner: BEVERLY HILLS HIGH SCHOOL CANCER STUDY; ROBERT LIFSON, MD, CLASS OF 1971.

Standing beside the van was a short, friendly man with a trim beard and sunglasses, a cell phone clipped to the waist of his khaki pants and a clipboard in his hand. His name was Bob Lifson, and he was an emergency-room physician who had worked for several years in the California prison system.

Lifson, a 1971 Beverly High graduate, was looking for clues as to why so many of his classmates had been stricken with a variety of medical maladies and had died young. He wanted to find out if there was, in fact, a significant health risk associated with attending Beverly High.

"Nobody's looked," he said. "Nobody's really studied it."

He walked to the back of his van and pulled out a questionnaire. Smiling, he handed it to a pedestrian, a Beverly alumnus who eagerly began to fill out the form.

"If we don't start to look at something, we won't have any answers," Lifson said. "I went to Beverly. I live in Beverly Hills. I want to know what the hell is going on."

He began to jot down information.

I asked him if he was filling out a medical form on himself.

"You bet, baby," he said.

———

Lifson's timing couldn't have been worse. At least that was the perspective of many of the hundreds of alumni who had flocked to the front lawn that day for the high school's seventy-fifth-birthday bash beneath a giant arch of floating orange and white balloons. They believed it was in poor taste to remind people about such matters at a celebration.

By the flagpole, the elite high school choral group, the Madrigals, broke into song. Wearing a tuxedo, the group's conductor, Joel Pressman, kept time with a baton as he eyed the van across the street with undisguised contempt. He had heard of ambulance chasers, but now it appeared that this guy Lifson was actually driving the van.

Lifson, though, remained unfazed by the criticism. He said he'd go to his "higher power" when people attacked him. Nor did he want to antagonize anyone, especially the Madrigal singers, since he had once been part of that ensemble. He was, in fact, my singing partner when we'd don scarves and knitted caps to sing Christmas carols, most of us Jewish kids happy to comply with the demands of holiday performances.

In the weeks prior to Beverly's birthday celebration, Lifson had asked permission to set up a booth on campus to distribute medical information. But the alumni association, which had organized the event, forbade it. Its officers viewed his presence that day as part of a public relations ploy by personal-injury lawyers to drum up more business and remind the community that this messy business about elevated cancer rates in Beverly Hills wasn't going away—despite recent evidence suggesting that allegations of a cancer epidemic in Beverly Hills were unfounded.

Ten days earlier the Los Angeles Times had reported that a statistical review by the local cancer registry, entitled "Community Cancer Assessment Regarding Beverly Hills, California," had concluded that there was no cancer cluster in Beverly Hills. The story was headlined: CANCER STUDY FINDS NO ELEVATED RISK IN BEVERLY HILLS.

The report, which was conducted in response to a request from Jody Kleinman, was authored by Dr. Wendy Cozen, an epidemiologist at the University of Southern California Cancer Surveillance Program, where she maintained the cancer registry for the county of Los Angeles through funding from the state of California, the U.S. Centers for Disease Control and Prevention, and the National Cancer Institute (NCI).

Studying cancer registry data through 1999, Cozen concluded that Beverly Hills residents between the ages of fifteen and forty-four were "at the upper limits of normal" for developing Hodgkin's disease and non-Hodgkin's lymphoma. Despite Jody Kleinman's original request, Cozen failed to take into account high school graduates who had moved away. But her report did quote from a 1996 medical textbook, *Cancer Epidemiology and Prevention,* to support her view that a higher rate of Hodgkin's disease among young adults in Beverly Hills would be expected due to socioeconomic factors, not chemical exposures. "There is evidence that risk of Hodgkin's lymphoma in young adults is associated with higher education, higher social class, fewer siblings, less crowded housing, early birth position. All of those factors foster susceptibility to late infections with the common childhood infections."

Cozen also found that young men in Beverly Hills had a threefold excess chance of developing papillary thyroid cancer, but she dismissed those results, saying the numbers were too small to be statistically significant and that thyroid cancer was on the rise in other parts of West Los Angeles too. Part of the increase could be explained by better diagnosis of smaller lesions, she noted, adding that thyroid cancer was also linked to higher socioeconomic status.

"The main risk factor for this type of thyroid cancer," the report stated, "is radiation, either ionizing (as in X-rays) or atomic (as in radioactive material). Again, there is no evidence linking petroleum or petroleum products to an increased risk of this cancer."

Whatever its true merits or failings, the USC study created an immediate public sensation. The findings would be interpreted by the school district and city officials as proof that no harm existed, despite the fact that Cozen herself cautioned that her analysis was only a cursory review of census tract data of Beverly Hills residents, not alumni or faculty of the high school.

Cozen's negative findings would also be cited by the director of toxic epidemiology for the Los Angeles County Health Department to reassure parents that they "should not feel any trepidation" about sending their children to Beverly Hills High School.

In turn, county health officials assured state investigators that a risk assessment in Beverly Hills wouldn't be necessary. That, of course, was a relief for an underfunded and overworked bureaucracy in northern California.

Ultimately, Cozen's report appeared to be a textbook case of what happens when government agencies agree to conduct cluster investigations in response to citizen inquiries: it is more often done to make a problem go away rather than to confirm the existence of a hazard.

In a seminal study, "Truth and Consequences: Health Agency Responses to Environmental Health Problems," Dr. David Ozonoff of the Boston University School of Public Health revealed how it is easier for public officials to banish uncomfortable results instead of erring on the side of caution: they invoke a lack of statistical significance rather than public health significance.

"Departments of public health have become departments of public reassurance," Ozonoff wrote in 1987. "A public health catastrophe is a health effect so powerful that even an epidemiological study can detect it."

Dr. Marilyn Underwood, a toxicologist at the California Department of Health Services' Environmental Health Investigation Branch in Oakland, believed that "the essential bugaboo" with environmental health investigations, like Cozen's, was that they relied on epidemiological evidence, not information about toxic exposures that could provide useful data about internal dose, internal effects, and biological markers.

Moreover, Underwood said, Cozen's report was inherently flawed, since it failed to look beyond epidemiology, or the statistical study of disease in large populations. "It's like trying to use binoculars to see something microscopic," she said. "The information doesn't prove anything.

"It just shows you how imprecise these reviews really are. We're using tools not designed to tease apart information in any useful way."

Underwood added: "Wendy and [her husband] Tom [Mack] have a very strong bias toward not believing a lot of environmental effects. I see this in doctors, too. They think diet and smoking are a big deal. But individuals next to an industrial site have additional risk.

"Many people just don't see it. That's why [it's] called the cancer registry—not the environmental cancer registry."

For Lifson, Cozen's report provided little meaningful information, since it didn't compare the cancer cases to a healthy cohort. He thought that government officials had acted precipitately in using the report to declare a "clean bill of health" at the school.

A graduate of the Tulane Medical School, Lifson was an idealist. He was an adherent to the philosophy of a kundalini yoga teacher, Guru Singh, and signed e-mails with the salutation "Have a grateful day." He also subscribed to conspiratorial theories about corporate malfeasance and Big Oil. He thought that Venoco, for instance, was really Chevron, because Venoco pipelines, he said, offloaded to Chevron ships.

Lifson had developed a Web site with James Dahlgren, the toxicologist originally hired by Edward Masry. On it, they had compiled an extensive list of research studies taken from the occupational literature, showing a correlation between exposure to chemicals in the petroleum industry and a variety of illnesses, including bladder cancer, brain cancer, and leukemia.

The two doctors had worked together on other litigation involving toxic exposures. They had performed medical exams in Columbus, Mississippi, for example, where exposures to creosote in canals near the Kerr-McKee plant, they believed, had caused hundreds of children to grow ill. They believed that the medical community was far too slow in recognizing the perils of environmental toxins.

Lifson had a theory about the Beverly Hills case. He believed that constant low-level exposure to benzene and other carcinogens had damaged the immune systems of graduates and faculty and residents in the area. He suspected, but couldn't prove, that benzene and other chemicals alter DNA function. Usually, he said, a healthy, vigilant immune system will attack and kill aberrant cells. But if the immune system has been damaged, as Lifson speculated, a malignant cell stands a far greater chance of surviving and proliferating. He thought that so many cases of thyroid disorder and autoimmune disease were a sure sign of that.

But now, Lifson—in high school he was Bobby, but preferred as an adult to be called Bob or Robert—was trying to contact as many Beverly graduates as possible. He and Dahlgren had been hired by Hunter Lundy, a toxic tort lawyer from Lake Charles, Louisiana, and the author of a nonfiction book about Jimmy Swaggart called *Let Us Prey,* to conduct an epidemiological study.

They said they were conducting a medical study of alumni to determine if there was an increase in immune dysfunction disorders compared to a control group, though no such study was ever published. In previous weeks they had presented medical information at meetings a few blocks away, inside a ballroom of the Beverly Hilton Hotel on Merv Griffin Way. Conveniently, a paralegal for the Lundy law firm was passing out forms at the back of the room to solicit more clients at those meetings.

Lifson said he was not working for Masry on this case; he didn't trust him. As if there weren't enough conflicts already, jealousy and competition between and among the plaintiffs' law firms were mounting. The lawyers and their experts traded accusations about misconduct that poisoned the atmosphere.

Whatever the internal conflicts, though, the law firms would ultimately need to work together as a team, with Baron & Budd as top dog.

As Lifson approached passersby to fill out medical questionnaires, he didn't tell them that he was working on behalf of the plaintiffs' expert, just that he wanted medical information in order to conduct an epidemiological study. He had also tried to sign up his classmates over the Internet through a Classmates. com site and a Yahoo! site started by members of the class of 1971.

Not everyone, of course, was cheered by his e-mails, as evidenced by this posting on the Web site:

> From:☺ "Phillip Berman" <pb@d . . . >
> Subject: Lifson's solicitation for Erin Brockovich
>
> As a member of the class of 1971, a cancer survivor (embryonal cell testicular cancer in 1985) and a physician, I think this whole ad hoc and unscientific solicitation of random epidemiological experience through a Yahoo! group is absolutely bullshit. It should be buried as a ridiculous attempt to manufacture money for lawyers and bankrupt a school district.

Less than a year after firing off that e-mail, though, Phil Berman tapped out another e-mail from his BlackBerry.

> From: Phillip Berman MD
> To: Joy Horowitz
> Subject: Hey, round 2
>
> Joy,
> Thought I'd drop you a note. Haven't seen anything in the press vis-a-vis the oil well stuff lately. But I've now joined the cancer club a second time. This time its metastatic lung cancer (no, I never smoked). Pretty rotten stuff as you probably remember from your Dad. But I'm doing pretty well so far.
>
> Anyways, I still don't feel like signing up for the plaintiff's squad, but thought I'd try & get an update from someone trying to play it down the middle.
>
> Hope things are healthy & happy for you.
>
> All the best,
>
> Phillip Berman MD/ Blame the typos on my handheld.

Up on the fourth floor of the Norris Cancer Research Center at USC, not far from downtown Los Angeles, the signs on Wendy Cozen's door read "Keep your laws off my body" and "Kick 'em Out! Vote Democratic." Wearing a diamond pendant necklace, silk blouse, and black trousers, she has long, curly black hair and a mellifluous voice.

Cozen works in a small office next door to her husband and mentor, Dr. Thomas Mack, a jolly-looking man with an ample belly, gray beard, and mop of black hair. Married for a year, the academics are collaborators and colleagues. Since 1972, Mack, a professor of preventive medicine and author of a book of cancer maps in L.A., *Cancers in the Urban Environment: Residential Patterns in Los Angeles County,* had been at the helm of the population-based cancer registry. If anyone has access to cancer data, it is Mack and Cozen, an osteopathic doctor with a degree from LaVerne University.

With the exception of cancers caused by atomic radiation, asbestos, and arsenic—the three A's, they call them—Mack and Cozen don't believe in the existence of environmentally caused clusters. All other geographical clusters, they believe, are either largely speculative or not statistically significant. Chance plays too big a role.

Most cancers, they say, have less to do with where you live than with who you are: influences such as race, ethnicity, smoking, diet, and other genetic and lifestyle factors. The fact is that one out of every three women and one out of every two men will get cancer in their lifetime, even in Beverly Hills.

To do a serious analysis of high school graduates would require a cohort sample of healthy graduates from a similarly affluent neighborhood. Such a study would need to focus on a single type of cancer, not a bunch of them, with a big enough sample size. To do it right would take years and require interviews with tens of thousands of people, asking questions about diet, gathering medical histories, getting DNA samples.

The most reliable health data is derived from house-to-house interviews because "shoe leather epidemiology" will always be more thorough than fixed databases, but that method is expensive and time-consuming. Neither Cozen nor Mack was inclined to commit resources to such an exhaustive study. Indeed, both Cozen and Mack were well known in public health circles for their deeply skeptical views about environmental links to cancer. One colleague affectionately referred to them as "pigheaded" on the subject.

Only a handful of cluster investigations have ever uncovered a preventable cause. One of the first medical reports of a cancer cluster involved young boys with scrotal cancer who worked as chimney sweeps in London in the eighteenth century; by crawling though narrow chimneys, they were exposed to soot from coal. In the 1970s a rare vaginal cancer most common among older women began showing up in young women; scientists tracked the cause to the drug DES, which the girls' mothers had taken during pregnancy to prevent miscarriage. In the 1980s, a cluster of Kaposi's sarcoma and pneumonia in healthy gay men led to the discovery of AIDS and the virus known as HIV. In occupational medicine, physicians have long known about the link between mesothelioma and asbestos or between angiosarcoma of the liver and vinyl chloride, but these were cases where the exposures for workers were high and prolonged.

Still, these medical discoveries were primarily due to motivated researchers and physicians who found an excess of very rare cancers among their patients.

Mack thought Masry's numbers were highly dubious anyway. If cigarette smoking increases the risk of lung cancer ten times, how could an oil well cause a twenty-fold increase? He didn't think it made sense. There was also the denominator question. Though it's not uncommon for people to draw a ring around a certain area and presume the number of cancers is abnormal (called the "Texas sharpshooter fallacy" in epidemiology), defining a population is critical. Did the cancer cases include alums who had moved away? Residents who didn't attend the school? Faculty who lived elsewhere?

Besides, what would be the biological cause of the cancers? Exposure to airborne benzene? Radiation? As far as Cozen and Mack were concerned, there wasn't one. No doubt, some research supported the connection between benzene exposure and non-Hodgkin's lymphoma and some forms of leukemia. There was also a Danish study connecting Hodgkin's disease and benzene exposure from urban traffic patterns. Cozen preferred to think about the relationship between viruses, like HIV, and non-Hodgkin's disease. She subscribed to the theory that Hodgkin's disease, which is more common among people of higher social classes, is the result of delayed infection with a common childhood virus like Epstein-Barr—a theory predicted on the "hygiene hypothesis": lack of early childhood exposure to infectious agents increases susceptibility to autoimmune diseases later in life. According to one recent study, children who attend day care or nursery school for at least one year before going to kindergarten are about 36 percent less likely than those not in preschool to develop Hodgkin's lymphoma as young adults. Hepatitis C, she thought, could be a strong risk factor too. But oil wells?

"I'm not saying it's totally implausible," she said, "but there are oil wells all over L.A."

Still, Mack allowed some room to wonder about the reported ages of the litigants. The average age at diagnosis was twenty-eight. Hodgkin's disease and thyroid cancers are diseases of young people, but he wasn't sure they were usually that young.

In any case, Wendy Cozen had no interest in pursuing a serious study of Beverly Hills. "Cancer clusters are just a big mess," she said. "The CDC agreed to stop investigating them, because they're a total waste of taxpayers' money. Most health departments around the country won't do them anymore." A CDC spokeswoman flatly denied any such policy existed, but Cozen's blanket condemnation reflected a deeper frustration among scientists and shed light on the political realities of why cancer research fails to track environmental pollutants.

Unlike infectious diseases, chronic diseases are not monitored in the United States. Among the diseases and disorders not counted and tracked are asthmas, birth defects, autism, and many forms of cancer—especially childhood cancers. And though the U.S. Environmental Protection Agency sets limits on how much toxic agents can be put in the environment, it does not track these agents to discover if they are linked with human disease.

In September 2000, the Pew Environmental Health Commission at the Johns Hopkins School of Public Health issued a startling report, stating that the nation's public health system was "woefully inadequate" in understanding, identifying, and preventing illnesses that may be linked to toxic chemicals and other environmental contaminants. Citing an epidemic in Libby, Montana, of diseases associated with asbestos exposure from mining, that had gone undetected for two decades, the panel urged the U.S. Centers for Disease Control and Prevention to establish a nationwide tracking center to investigate cancer clusters.

Currently, no such center exists. In 1996 a survey by a national group of epidemiologists found that forty-one health departments reported 1,900 inquiries, most resulting in a finding of no increased cancer incidence. Without a tracking system to identify suspected or confirmed clusters, though, no one knows precisely how many reported clusters there are.

Instead, cluster investigations are carried out as statistical reviews by epidemiologists who are loath to conduct them, because isolating an environmental link to cancer is almost never achieved. In all of medical history, there has never been a successful neighborhood-cluster investigation. Even though the public might suspect a pattern of illness in a particular neighborhood, scientists usually can't confirm any such thing. For instance, after an eighteen-month investigation in Fallon, Nevada, the Centers for Disease Control and Prevention concluded in 2003 that the presence of a cluster of children with leukemia could not be linked to an environmental cause, though government scientists detected high levels of tungsten and arsenic in the urine of residents near a naval air station there.

Since scientific methods for showing or proving causality are crude and inadequate, the public remains largely in the dark about environmental contributions to cancer—much to the dismay of women in Marin County, California, who have the highest rate of breast cancer in the world; the only risk factor that researchers have been able to tease out of scientific data thus far in Marin is the influence of drinking two glasses of wine a day. On the other hand, after ten years of study, researchers with the Long Island Breast Cancer Study found that exposure to polycyclic aromatic hydrocarbons (PAHs), like benzene, might be associated with a slight increase in breast cancer risk, but they recommended further study.

Frustrated by years of unsuccessful cluster investigations, researchers in California have just begun to analyze the state's cancer registry to better understand links between childhood cancer and hazardous air pollutants, for instance. Epidemiologists from the state Department of Health Services reported in 2003 that lower ambient air quality appears to raise the likelihood of developing certain childhood cancers, particularly leukemia.

New studies also offer clues to tracing how the deadliest air pollutants cause chronic disease. At UCLA, in one of five particle-pollution research centers in the United States, a team of researchers has shown how the tiniest air pollutants—ultrafine particles—penetrate deep inside a cell and damage its mitochondria, causing cells to die off and reduce overall lung function. The particles, which contain toxic metals and hydrocarbons, are carried by the bloodstream from lung tissue to the brain. The result in laboratory animals is inflammation of the brain as well as heart disease and strokes.

Still, Cozen was reluctant to get involved in the Beverly Hills case. Never mind that her ex-husband graduated from Beverly High in 1972. Contacted by the city of Beverly Hills to be an expert witness in the litigation, she declined because she thought it was important to stay "neutral," given her role with the cancer registry.

Yet, there was one crucial finding that she had downplayed in her report on Beverly Hills: young male residents in four contiguous census tracts, including one adjacent to Beverly Hills High School, are at high risk for developing papillary thyroid cancer—a finding that was almost certainly not due to chance alone.

In other words, Erin Brockovich might unwittingly have stumbled upon a very real point of medical inquiry. "This increase," Mack said, "is a real source of scientific concern, as opposed to the oil well, and additional studies to understand the reason should get priority. Unfortunately, when people are obsessed with litigation, they are reluctant to participate in necessary studies, and when they do, they downplay responses to anything other than the source of current concern."

Mack added that he and Cozen had applied for a federal grant to pursue their hypothesis about elevated rates of thyroid cancer in the area, but he declined to say what his hypothesis might be so as not to influence responses by potential study subjects.

"Isn't that a bugger?" he asked.

Jody Kleinman was growing infuriated. When she first contacted Cozen, asking for an investigation to see if Beverly High alumni have cancer rates above the norm, the soccer mom thought she was doing the right thing. After all, no one from the city or school district was rushing to find out.

To the contrary, in their zeal to discredit Erin Brockovich, the city's lawyers devised a clever strategy to subpoena her evidence of toxic exposures at the high school in a public relations effort to prove that her case was based on "junk science"—a common tactic embraced by corporate defendants, including the tobacco industry, who attack junk science while simultaneously creating and relying on it.

Kleinman wanted objective data, not information from a hired gun. She had no idea that she was walking into a minefield—what she would later come to see as both corruption of the scientific process and the politics of cancer research. Kleinman felt "like a pawn," used by the city of Beverly Hills for political purposes and by the researchers for their career advancement.

But worse, she believed, was the hypocrisy of Cozen and Mack. While Cozen professed "neutrality," her husband had quietly been retained as a consultant for Irell and Manella, a law firm representing Wainoco Oil, one of the oil companies in the litigation.

After the *Los Angeles Times* published an account of the arrangement by the reporter Martha Groves, Mack declined payment to avoid the appearance of a conflict of interest. Still, the intention of his work—thwarting liability claims and developing a strong public relations front—was being achieved.

Mack was an effective spokesman. He had already signed an affidavit stating that the oil wells were not a cause for concern. And he'd repeat that opinion to reporter Eric Umansky of the *New Republic.* In an article entitled "Erin Brockovich's Weird Science," Umansky quoted Mack as saying "You're just as likely to get cancer from your car stereo." Umansky used that same quote in a piece for the *Columbia Journalism Review,* never bothering to mention Mack's role on behalf of the defense counsel.

"Oh, God, I'm embarrassed about this," Mack later said of his work for the oil company in the case. "It was stupid and thoughtless. It was the first and last time I'd do such a thing—I assure you."

Despite his contrition, critics questioned whether his consulting work and his wife's industry-friendly report might have been influenced by a $5 million gift to USC from ChevronTexaco, another defendant in the Beverly Hills case. Others asserted that was nonsense: it was no different from Stanford University's $225 million Global Climate and Energy Project being financed by ExxonMobil.

For Jody Kleinman, though, the damage had been done. The question of whether a cancer cluster existed among high school graduates would remain as elusive as ever. She was now convinced that the process of conducting an objective inquiry had been corrupted by the researchers themselves. Cozen's report, she had come to believe, was little more than "a joke."

On the east side of Crescent Drive, between Santa Monica and Little Santa Monica boulevards, Beverly Hills City Hall stands as a palace of splendor. It was built in 1932, when the rest of the country was impacted by the Great Depression; its gold-topped tower is offset by a low classical base of Spanish Renaissance design—a magnificent symbol of both the town's charm and its excess, just a block from Jimmy Choo's.

In a conference room on the second floor of the city attorney's office, Laurence S. Wiener and the public relations maven Steve Sugerman hastily convened a press conference on Monday afternoon, May 5, 2003, to announce the results of ambient air testing at the high school by Camp Dresser

& McKee, the environmental-engineering firm hired by the city's defense law firm.

Clearly, the city needed as much good press as it could get. Just a week before the press conference, as the oil wells were shut down again by the AQMD, Ed Masry and Erin Brockovich had drawn more headlines by filing hundreds of administrative claims against the city and schools, a precursor to filing a lawsuit. Each round of publicity, of course, could mean more clients—and more legal headaches for Beverly Hills.

Earlier that morning, the CDM engineers had met with a handpicked group of parents and announced that their ambient air tests showed that there was no difference between the air at Beverly High and the rest of Los Angeles. "There is no basis for believing that the ambient air on the campus is adversely impacted by oil well operations," they noted in their report. Many, of course, were gratified by the good news.

Others remained skeptical. Dean Vlahos, a forensic architect whose son was a freshman at the high school, thought the city was showing its due diligence by testing, but he was also convinced that it was simply part of a PR campaign to collect just enough test data to say there was no problem. Despite the mayor's promise that all "raw data" would be made available, Vlahos pointed out that the test results were, in fact, attorney work product.

"Let's not kid each other," he said. "You don't ask the question unless you know the answers beforehand.

"They're trying to give the impression they're being responsible, but it's clear they're more worried that the lawsuit will put the district and city in financial chaos."

When the CDM scientists repeated their findings to the press—that based upon four days of air testing over spring break, there was no reason to believe that a problem existed at the high school from oil well operations—they were confronted by a host of questions they simply could not answer.

Did the samples reflect the plume? (Don't know.) Did the samples take into account the fact that it had rained the day before? And what about installation of a new fertilizer system on the playing fields? (Don't know.)

A reporter asked what the rationale was for gathering ambient air samples rather than classroom air samples. Mark Katchen, the industrial hygienist who had been hired as the school district's environmental consultant, was sitting beside the city's PR flak at the conference table that day, his hair gelled back and his celadon green suit jacket neatly pressed. "Those data should be available sometime next week," Katchen said of his classroom air tests. Months later, when Jody Kleinman begged for Katchen's data, he told her, "The lawyers have it."

In addition to conducting air sampling inside classrooms, Katchen had also been meeting with teachers to discuss their concerns. He had last taken air samples in 1999, when parents were worried about toxic chemicals inside portable classrooms, and he had detected surprisingly high levels of airborne benzene and formaldehyde—results that were never widely disseminated. When parents asked for copies of his report, they were told they'd be required to bring their own copying machine to school district headquarters.

Now, four years later, when reporting to the public about current test results, Katchen did not also reveal he was an expert for the defendants in the case.

According to documents obtained through the California Public Records Act, Katchen's "dual" role prohibited him from publicly revealing "unfavorable results."

In a letter to an insurance company executive, school district attorney William E. Ireland of Haight Brown & Bonesteel described the "unavoidable overlap" between Katchen's work as being both "litigation oriented" and intended to fulfill the school district's responsibility of ensuring a safe environment.

"As defense counsel," Ireland wrote,

> I need to be involved in ensuring that there are no reports being generated by consultants who are experts on behalf of the School District, which can or will be evidence in support of the plaintiff's contentions that dangerous conditions existed at the school. There is no information currently available regarding conditions at the school during the times when many if not all the plaintiffs attended the school. While the plaintiffs will not necessar[ily] agree that evidence of the lack of current exposure proves no past significant exposure, if the new reports are inartfully phrased or have unfavorable results, the plaintiffs will seek to capitalize upon those.

One has to wonder if Ireland's strategy in defending the lawsuit inevitably blocked disclosure of information about the current state of the air at the high school.

On a cold and rainy evening in April, Erin Brockovich and Ed Masry conducted a second informational meeting in a Beverly Hills Hotel ballroom. It was just a few nights before Passover, the same week that CDM had begun collecting air-sampling data.

The turnout was meager, with fewer than one hundred people present. Masry, wearing an oversized sweater, blamed it on the weather: no one goes out in L.A. when it rains, he said.

In attendance that evening was a twenty-two-year-old realtor with a brain tumor. Justin Greenberg had graduated from Beverly in 1998. In some ways, he considered himself lucky; he had pituitary adenoma, a benign cancer that two thousand Americans are diagnosed with every year. Greenberg thought it odd, given how rare the illness is, that his brother's friend, who had also graduated from Beverly, had the same tumor.

"Me, I'm nothing compared to what some of these people have," he said, dismissing his fears about the surgery he'd undergo in the coming weeks to have his brain tumor removed.

Another young Beverly graduate tapped him on the shoulder. "Greeny?"

Greenberg turned around to find his old friend Carl Wilson standing before him. They greeted each other with high-fives and a big bear hug. Wilson, a drummer in a rock band and chef at a restaurant near the beach in Venice, explained that he was being treated for Hodgkin's lymphoma.

Like so many others who were sick, Greenberg had spent a great deal of time on the athletic fields at Beverly, where he had volunteered as a soccer coach. Recent studies published in the *Lancet* and the *New England Journal of Medicine* had concluded that athletes are especially vulnerable to air pollutants, since their exposure is magnified; when you're exercising, you're breathing in up to thirty times as much air as when you're sitting still.

Another athlete who came to that night's meeting was Ralph Punaro, a standout in baseball, basketball, and football at Beverly in the 1960s. When Punaro was diagnosed with non-Hodgkin's lymphoma about twenty-five years after he graduated, his doctor asked him if he had been exposed to benzene. Like so many others, Punaro didn't make the oil well connection at the time.

Punaro, a physical education teacher at South Pasadena High, later developed leukemia from radiation treatments. The development of secondary cancers from radiation treatments is not uncommon. Sound editor Tom Fries, a shaggy-haired baseball player who graduated from the high school in 1971, was diagnosed at twenty-five with Hodgkin's disease, for which he received a "sandwich" treatment of chemotherapy and radiation.

The radiation burned his lungs and weakened his heart. After several heart surgeries and the removal of his sternum, he died at forty-seven.

His widow, Debi Genson-Fries, said: "Tommy was very young and very sick, and this lawsuit isn't going to bring him back to me or to our three daughters. I realize that. But if there's some way that we could have finality on it, or evidence that pointed to the possibility that this did have something to do with the illness he suffered for so long, it'll be worth it. That needs to be known for other kids.

"Did he have some sort of weakness in his system that made him more susceptible to it? Who knows? But if that is indeed the case, then he's the last person that should have been on that campus."

Questions like these were circulating in the audience when Erin Brockovich took the stage. She was wearing a poncho and blue jeans, a funky getup that belied the seriousness of her message: the number of cases of cancer "are staggering—and they continue to grow," she said; they were now approaching three hundred.

"I'm going to share with you just for a few minutes nothing about the law and nothing about the science. I'm going to share with you some information that I know personally.

"I'm going to take you back in time twelve years to when Ed Masry and I started the Hinkley litigation. If you think for one minute while we were doing that case we ever stopped and thought, 'Hmm, it's going to settle for $333 million, somebody's going to come along and make a movie about it, and oh yeah, Julia Roberts is going to play moi—'"

The audience roared with laughter.

"—and they'll name the movie after you and then you get a big bonus to boot. We absolutely never stopped at any moment to wonder what the outcome was going to be. But we did know one thing, and it's the exact same thing that we know on this case: something went wrong and people are sick."

Now, she added, "People have lost their lives. Human health has been destroyed. And we're going to have to stand strong—and we're going to have to stand together to see an outcome."

Justice, she said, requires perseverance. "You're going to hear rumors. You're going to read rumors. You're going to get different stories from the AQMD. You're going to get different stories from Beverly High. You're going to hear different things from us.

"But we're not in this for the fun of it. There is a problem. We believe in this case. We are going to move forward. There are too many children with cancer. It's not normal. I believe in the tests we have taken. I believe in the doctors that we have. And I don't believe it's normal to have this many cancers from one isolated place."

Nothing, she said, was more important than human health and life. "It's the greatest gift we have. Three hundred people have had that gift taken away. They need some justice. Money isn't going to give that to them or to you," she said. "But coming together as a group, and standing up for what you believe in, and preserving and protecting the dignity of those who have been harmed, and making certain that this doesn't happen to another is a fight worth fighting."

The intention of the lawsuit, she said, was to get some answers about why so many young people had cancer.

With that, she turned over the dais to Al Stewart, who was now the lead attorney on the case.

Stewart had a mop of brown hair and the honey-soaked voice of a southern gentleman. A senior partner at Baron & Budd, the largest law firm in the United States that deals exclusively with toxic tort cases, he was an exacting trial lawyer, one who was used to winning. *American Lawyer* magazine had named him one of its top "40 under 40" because of his succession of victories in the courtroom.

Before he agreed to take the case, Stewart made a point of walking around the perimeter of Beverly Hills High School. He had the righteous streak of a preacher when he spoke. "I'm just a farm boy from the South," he later said, "but as soon as I saw that school, I knew instantly that I'd never send my children there.

"When I was standing out on the sidewalk I was looking at the derrick thing there, and I was also looking over at Sempra. And I watched a dozen high schoolers during PE run right by there—like it was nothing."

The legal team, he told his audience, was continuing to gather documents and information. Until a lawsuit was filed, though, it would be very difficult to obtain documents from the defendants.

"The bulk of the documents we will get in this case," he said, "we will get because a court of law forces the opposition, after lots of haggling and motions and re-motions and threats, to cough up the documents. After they cough up the documents, there will then be motions and re-motions and hearings for them to cough up the real documents. They don't give up the real documents the first time.

"After they cough up the second round of documents, there will be motions and hearings and arguments to cough up the real documents."

He smiled. "At the beginning of the case, they say the case has no merit. At the middle of the case, they say the case has no merit. When you're talking to a jury, they say it has no merit. They're never going to say it has merit; it's not coming."

He spoke of the need for medical record reviews, "exposure profiles," causation experts, and historical exposure modeling. Already, one of his experts had crunched the numbers and found an excess of Hodgkin's disease in addition to a disproportionate number of thyroid cancers among graduates of the high school.

The process, he added, would require one other thing: "You have got to spill your guts to us," he said, "And I mean that. You've got to give us the information. Information is power."

He added: "It's a long, laborious process. It's a lot of fighting. Here's the good news: I like to fight. I mean that sincerely. I tell my wife all the time, I come home and she says we don't need that here. It's pleasurable to me. Good lawyers like a good fight.

"This," he said, grinning, "is going to be a good fight."

The first time opposing counsel confronted each other was not in court. It was during a televised debate on the CNN program *NewsNight with Aaron Brown,* when Erin Brockovich and Beverly Hills mayor Tom Levyn were interviewed, seated in separate studios beside their lawyers, Al Stewart and Skip Miller.

"Let's go to the mayor," Brown said after a commercial break.

The camera switched to Tom Levyn as he absently looked around the studio, unaware he was on the air. Levyn fumbled with his earpiece. Without a studio monitor, he appeared uncomfortable and shifty-eyed.

Brown asked: "Mayor, has there been ongoing monitoring of the air around the wells in the high school and the adjacent areas leading up to the filing of these claims?"

Levyn changed the subject. "Aaron, thank you for inviting us here this evening," he replied.

He continued. "You started off by saying that you had both sides. We're really on the same side. And let me tell you what that means to me. It doesn't mean lawsuits and lawyers."

It seemed an odd thing to say, given that he was sitting beside his lawyer, Skip Miller. "What it means to me is my daughter, who's an eleventh-grade student at the high school, my son, who's recently graduated; all of us on the city council and the school board have children at the high school.

"And we say categorically today that Beverly Hills High School is safe."

Levyn then shifted into attack mode, accusing Brockovich of scaring the community and refusing to share her data with city officials.

He challenged her to turn over her evidence.

"Have you turned over all of the relevant data so they have a chance to look at it?" Brown asked Stewart. "Because, you know, maybe they got a problem they don't know they have a problem, they'd like to solve it, you know?"

Stewart replied, "Simply, the answer is yes. That data has been turned over."

"Okay," Brown said.

Miller invoked his experts, whose tests showed no unsafe chemical exposures, and the Cozen report. He denied that the city had ever received Brockovich's data.

Levyn said: "I will be at Mr. Masry's office at ten o'clock on Tuesday, May 13, to collect the information, the raw data from their test, how they did their testing, who did it, when they did it, and what equipment they used."

But Levyn never showed. After he sent Masry a hand-delivered letter, he received a fax in return, calling his bluff. Masry told him he could pick up everything he asked for under one simple condition: turn over all the air monitoring of the campus since 1975.

Of course, there had been none.

Nonetheless, Brockovich was good to her word. The information the mayor asked for was forwarded to the offices of the Beverly Hills City Council, the Beverly Hills Unified School District, and the mayor. It was information they had already received.

Watching himself on TiVo later, Levyn told his wife, "We're not going to win a PR battle with Erin Brockovich."

They'd need to try to beat her in court instead. Miller would need to invent another way of discrediting her evidence.

The grandstanding by lawyers on television that May was a sharp contrast to the private pain being endured by Lori Urov in a New York hospital. At thirty-six, the mother of four-year-old twins had been diagnosed with Hodgkin's disease, stage IV, and her lungs were coated with tumors. She was bleeding everywhere from scratching, a symptom of the disease. She was due to undergo a final desperate stem cell transplant, but pneumonia had set in.

In her final months, she had learned about Lori Moss and joined the lawsuit to help others discover whether there was, indeed, a problem in Beverly Hills. Despite her weakened state, she had become a "Glamour girl"—posing bald for an article in *Glamour* magazine and a story for ABC's *Good Morning America.* "I just felt like someone had opened my mouth and poured Hodgkin's disease down my throat," she said at the time. "And here I am with probably less than a year to live and two kids to raise. I felt literally poisoned."

At Beverly High, Lori Urov ran track before graduating in 1984. She had been a member of the school's backpacking club and climbed Mount Whitney. In the summers, she had worked with children for the city's parks and recreation program at the Greystone mansion. The youngest of four children, she lived on South Camden Drive—the same street where I lived. Her father died of melanoma; her mother was a breast cancer survivor.

When the two Loris conferred about the impending lawsuit by phone, their conversation was brief. They wanted to make sure it never happened to anyone again and vowed to find out what caused so many people from Beverly to grow ill. "She was coughing a lot," Moss later recalled. A few days later, Lori Urov was dead.

At 10:30 a.m. on Monday, June 9, 2003, Al Stewart stood before a bank of microphones and cameras at the head of a conference table inside the Masry & Vititoe offices in Westlake Village. Beside him stood Erin Brockovich, Ed Masry, and Lori Moss.

Two months had passed since their last hotel meeting, and they were now announcing the filing of their lawsuit against the city of Beverly Hills, its school district, and a raft of energy company defendants, including Chevron, Venoco, and Sempra Energy, the power plant owner. It would subsequently be known in court as *Lori Lynn Moss et al. v. Venoco, Inc. et al.,* case number BC297083.

"This case," the complaint began, "is about the inexcusable and knowing failure of the oil and gas industry and municipal and administrative bodies to protect school children, the most vulnerable members in society, at the places that should be the safest—schools.

"Instead, these same companies and governmental bodies opted to place royalties and profits before the health of a generation of school children, slowly poisoning them while continually denying that there was any cause for concern."

The complaint was filed on behalf of twenty-one Beverly Hills High School graduates, who had contracted Hodgkin's disease and had attended the school between 1977 and 1996. Some had died. The plaintiffs did not fit any stereotypes of Beverly Hills; they were rich and poor. The lawsuit was the first one to be filed; more would follow that would include other cancers.

The defendants, Stewart said, "emit toxic chemicals on a daily basis and have been doing so for decades." The lawsuit, he said, was intended to point out that residents in Beverly Hills and students at Beverly Hills High School were at increased risk of getting cancer.

A reporter asked Stewart how he could prove that Hodgkin's disease was a direct result of whatever it was these plants emitted. Stewart admitted that there would be disagreement in the case about what caused Hodgkin's lymphoma, and "that's what makes it ripe for a lawsuit."

What about the local cancer registry report, which found that there was no elevated incidence of cancer in Beverly Hills?

The report, Stewart said, was "clever but misleading." It stated that the cancer registry tracked cancer from 1972 to the present, even though doctors weren't required to report cancers until 1988, leaving a sixteen-year gap of complete information.

"I think this complaint demonstrates pretty effectively that we could find the numbers that that cancer registry couldn't," Stewart added.

Another reporter asked Lori Moss if she was certain that the oil wells had caused her Hodgkin's disease.

"Yes," she said, without hesitation. "Where else did it come from except inhaling the fumes as your body is developing and maturing?"

"And that's what your doctor told you when you were diagnosed?"

"No," she said. "It was never discussed when I was diagnosed."

There was one thing Lori Moss didn't talk about that morning, a part of her life that didn't quite mesh with her narrative of illness. It was, she believed, nothing short of a miracle: she was pregnant, and for the first time in a very long time, she was looking forward to her future.

P A R T   2

The tragedy of benzene is that it has taken so long for science to be translated into protective action. Many thousands of workers and other persons in nations around the world have suffered unnecessarily and died prematurely while regulatory agencies, industry and the courts debated the carcinogenicity of benzene and argued about the need for protective regulation. In the current era of global proliferation of toxic chemicals and hazardous technologies, all who are involved in the production and use of benzene have a heavy responsibility and a duty to protect their workers and the general public against this highly toxic and carcinogenic compound. The debate over whether benzene is carcinogenic has long since ended, and controversy about the need to protect humans against benzene must not continues.

—Dr. Philip Landrigan, MD, MSc, DIH, FAAP, professor and chairman, Department of Community and Preventive Medicine, professor of pediatrics, Mount Sinai School of Medicine, New York; editor-in-chief, *American Journal of Industrial Medicine.*

I am fascinated with the oil industry. All my friends have in one way or the other been involved in the oil industry.

—George W. Bush, *A Charge to Keep*

CHAPTER SEVEN

RAZZLE-DAZZLE

M arch 25, 2004. I'm sitting in the conference room of Haight Brown & Bonesteel, the law firm representing the Beverly Hills Unified School District. Before me are six huge cardboard boxes containing thousands of pages of documents—the response to a public-records request I had filed months earlier. Not everything I asked for is here, of course, thanks to the pending litigation, which provides a convenient excuse for keeping secret that which is public, including e-mails from administrators concerning the oil wells on campus.

My head is throbbing as I pore over old board of education minutes, letters, agendas, newspaper clippings, and notebooks filled with insurance company information that I'm hoping will shed light on a key question: what did school officials know and when did they know it?

A handsome young associate from the firm is sitting beside me. Apparently, he has been assigned to babysit me and make sure I don't steal anything. He leafs through old issues of *Highlights,* the high school newspaper, and smiles at me. Whether these documents will reveal anything, I have no idea. But I know I have to keep looking.

I find school board minutes from November 14, 1978, which indicate that "upon [the assistant superintendent's] advice that the City Council has approved and adopted the documents, which have been signed by Mr. Enger of the Beverly Hills Oil Company, a motion was made, seconded and passed unanimously, accepting the agreement and Amendment to the Oil and Gas Lease dated October 30, 1978." This is a reference to the municipal code that would be rewritten to allow for oil drilling in Beverly Hills—but only at the high school. School officials agreed to the lease because they were promised more space for athletic fields—and oil royalties. Initially, the promise by Chevron was for $25.7 million: $8 million for the city, $15 million for residents, and $2.7 million for the school district. Then the company revised its calculations and promised $50 million.

Twenty-five years later, there would be another reference to the lease. In a June 20, 2003, letter to the general counsel of Venoco, Inc., Peter Rosen, a lawyer at Mayer Brown Rowe & Maw hired by the city of Beverly Hills, demanded that the oil company defend and indemnify the city against claims for all costs and attorney's fees, in accordance with its "indemnity agreement" in the 1978 lease.

In other words, Rosen expected Venoco to pay the bills for Christopher Bisgaard of Lewis Brisbois Bisgaard & Smith, for Skip Miller of Christensen, Miller, Fink, Jacobs, Glaser, Weil & Shapiro, and for Camp Dresser McKee, the environmental-testing firm that conducted ambient air sampling and soil testing at the high school in the spring of 2003.

It is hush money, I think.

If the city of Beverly Hills is demanding payment from the operator of the oil wells for legal costs, how can anyone rationally expect the city or schools to conduct an objective health investigation? It is, of course, an impossibility. A sham, really. Or maybe this is simply the cost of doing business.

In the file, I rifle through a series of desperate letters from David Orbach, the school district's legal counsel, to a number of insurance carriers. One is dated July 22, 2003, and is addressed to Natalie McMeans at the Highlands Insurance Group, the insurance carrier for Wainoco Oil from 1985 to 1986. Orbach explains in his letter that in addition to the first twenty-five claimants, who say they are suffering from Hodgkin's lymphoma, non-Hodgkin's lymphoma, or thyroid cancer as a result of their exposure to toxic chemicals, the damages claimed for the 213 existing claimants are as follows:

1 *adenoid cystic carcinoma*
1 *Bell's palsy*
1 *bladder cancer*
7 *bone cancer*
23 *breast cancer or tumor*
26 *cancer of the reproductive organs*
1 *ganglion cysts*

17 *gastro-intestinal problems*
1   *Graves disease*
28 *Hodgkin's lymphoma*
2   *immune disorders*
3   *leukemia*
2   *lung cancer*
3   *lupus*
28 *neurological problems*
15 *Non-Hodgkin's lymphoma*
2   *organ problems*
6   *prostate cancer*
21 *respiratory problems*
1   *Sjogren's syndrome*
26 *skin cancer and or tumors*
53 *thyroid cancer or disorder*
1   *Waldenstrom's lymphoma*

On August 7, 2003, Natalie McMeans replied: "I have reviewed the Wain-oco Oil & Gas Co. policies and regret to inform you that BHUSD is not listed as an additional insured under the policies issued to Wainoco." Other insurance carriers responded that a "pollution exclusion" precluded coverage, including for a custodian employed at Beverly High who now had chronic myelogenous leukemia.

I'm bleary-eyed.

I look out the window and take in the view of the San Diego Freeway and a green hillside cemetery across the way. In fact, it is called Hillside. Al Jolson is buried in the mausoleum there. On the east side of the property, my parents are buried beneath a melaleuca tree.

I decide to visit them.

It is warm and sunny, a Thursday afternoon, when I drive up to the Mount of Olives section, park my car, and walk to my parents' graves. I sit on a bench, marked "Horowitz."

To my surprise, I begin to sob—big, fat, belly sobs. Eight years have passed since my dad died. Just a week after we buried him, my mother learned she had a recurrence of her breast cancer. She died the following year. My grief for both of them isn't as sharp as it once was. Still, it comes in waves, and on this day I realize I wish I could call my mom, just to chat. One in seven women in the United States will get breast cancer, and more than forty thousand of them die each year from it. The cancer researcher Irving Selikoff once said statistics are people with the tears wiped off. My mother is now a statistic, but I'm still crying for her. I watch my tears fall on her grave.

With no history of breast cancer in our family, we wondered how she got it. Was it the fifteen years of hormone replacement therapy, which is known to increase your chances of breast cancer by 25 percent? Was it the fact that she's from an upper socioeconomic bracket? Was it a particular genetic-environmental reaction—hydrocarbons from the oil pumping at Roxbury Park, where she loved to jog? Or from the high school bleachers, where she watched my brother's football games and my track meets? Or from an exposure as a child? Or just rotten luck? We'll never know, of course.

I'm also crying for all the other sick people from Beverly Hills. All the pain and sorrow they've endured, the lives cut short. The frustration I feel for not knowing, for sure, who's accountable—if anyone.

Here is what I want to tell my mother and my father:

Thank you.

Thank you for fighting.

Thank you for teaching me to keep fighting, because the will to fight is the answer to those smiling faces, now gone, looking back at me from the *Watchtower* yearbooks. They remind me how lucky I am to keep questioning.

I dry my tears. For a moment, anyway, I feel hopeful. It occurs to me that if I hold on to my patience, a clearer picture might emerge of the real story in Beverly Hills. Looking for answers, I'm bound to hit any number of dead ends. That I come to realize this in a cemetery—a dead end, get it?—is an irony I'd rather not contemplate right now.

On a bright, breezy Tuesday in May 2003, I tagged along as a group of about fifty geologists and petroleum engineers stepped off an air-conditioned tour bus and gathered in front of a multimillion-dollar home on Broad Street in Newport Beach, the beachside town where the popular TV show *The OC* is filmed. There, on the first stop of their bus tour of the Los Angeles oil fields, the scientists, who were casually dressed in khakis, Hawaiian shirts, and sneakers, studied a ten-foot pole topped by a tiki torch—a noxious gas vent—embedded in the front lawn by an olive tree. The rotten-egg smell of hydrogen sulfide, a remnant of an old oil field that once operated in this residential neighborhood, hung in the air.

"This particular vent has burned for thirty-two years," explained one of the group's leaders, John Jepson, an engineer with the California Division of

Oil, Gas and Geothermal Resources, otherwise known in the industry as DOGGR, which is the state agency that oversees the subsurface operations of oil and gas producers. Created in 1915, it was the state's first agency to regulate wildcatting operations during the oil boom, and it has enjoyed a cozy relationship with the industry ever since.

Part of a combined conference of the American Association of Petroleum Geologists and the western region of the Society of Petroleum Engineers, the field trip promised scientists the chance to study the petroleum legacy of Los Angeles. I was interested in understanding their attitudes. Technically, the tour was called "Rigs to Roofs, Pumps to Parks: The Oilfields of the Newport Inglewood Fault," but I felt as if I had crashed a secret club when I asked about possible health consequences of these old, leaking oil fields.

"One article in the newspaper and property value goes plummeting," a group leader warned me as I took notes.

"Yeah, they'd have a field day with this," said another.

"The mommies, especially, get hysterical," said a third. "A lot of this can be controlled very easily. If you burn methane and hydrogen sulfide together, it doesn't smell so bad."

Methane gas sensors and alarms are commonplace in Los Angeles, thanks to real estate development atop old oil and gas fields. From the underground parking garages of the vast Playa Vista housing development, built over old oil and gas fields, to the dressing rooms of Abercrombie & Fitch at the Grove shopping mall, which sits atop the old Salt Lake field in the Fairfax district, warnings abound. "Methane Gas Alarm," reads the Abercrombie sign. "Evacuate building and call 911." Dangerous methane seeps from old oil fields have been cited as the reason for federal prohibitions against building an underground subway on the west side of Los Angeles for the past twenty-five years.

Mostly, though, these geologists viewed the tiki torch and subsequent stop at a hospital, which harnessed leaking underground gases to provide for the facility's energy needs, as creative solutions—nothing short of engineering marvels.

What the petroleum engineers were less keen to discuss was the health costs associated with oil production. In 2002, the Harvard Medical School's Center for Health and the Global Environment issued a report detailing the threats posed by the extraction, transportation, refining, and combustion of oil. It was the first such health study not financed by oil companies. Among its findings: occupationally related fatalities among workers in the oil and gas extraction processes are higher than deaths for all other U.S. industries combined. Oil workers risk injury and chronic disease from exposures to chemicals, including cadmium, arsenic, lead, and polycyclic aromatic hydrocarbons. Petroleum by-products, such as benzene, threaten workers' health from cancer, especially leukemia. Chemical and particulate air pollution are related to heart and lung disease, including asthma, and to premature death.

As a group, the American Association of Petroleum Geologists tended to be ideologically connected to its product. In 2006, for example, it would vote to confer its annual journalism award to science fiction writer Michael Crichton for his 2004 novel, *State of Fear,* which dismisses global warming as a scientific hoax. Never mind that researchers with the National Academy of Sciences had found in 2003 that the impact of greenhouse gases—particularly methane from oil and gas production in the southwestern United States—had been vastly underestimated, or that most mainstream scientists had come to believe that the burning of fossil fuels was changing the atmosphere's chemistry in potentially catastrophic ways. Petroleum production and consumption were vital to the country's national security, a view promoted by President Bush.

At the same time, the oil industry had important connections inside the Bush administration to cast doubt on the link between greenhouse gases and rising temperatures. Philip A. Cooney, a lawyer for the American Petroleum Institute—the industry's key lobbying group—became chief of staff to the White House Council on Environmental Quality. Two days after the *New York Times* revealed that he was altering White House documents to downplay the impact of climate change, Cooney resigned and took a job at Exxon-Mobil—the company that, according to one investigation, spent at least $8 million to fund a network of groups challenging the existence of global warming.

So when I posed questions about toxic air emissions to these petroleum engineers, it wasn't surprising that they tossed them off as inconsequential. The general consensus on this tour was that environmental concerns, particularly air-quality regulations, had driven a stake into the heart of a business that has allowed this country to become the richest one in the world.

I asked, for example, about hydrogen sulfide, which is toxic and can cause brain damage in high enough doses. At Beverly High, government records showed, the "venting"—or release into the air—of waste gases occurred when the Southern California Gas Company refused to accept Venoco's natural gas because sulfur compounds in it exceeded four parts per million. According to studies conducted at the University of Southern California, central nervous system damage can occur even at levels as low as one part per million, a level that is much lower than workplace standards allow.

Were the gas leaks we saw in Orange County the result of wells that were never properly "abandoned"—plugged up with cement and dynamited—by the oil companies that once worked here? Natural gas and hydrogen sulfide are often coproduced with oil. While natural gas is marketed as a separate product, hydrogen sulfide gas constitutes a waste and is flared or injected into disposal wells alongside other waste fluids.

"Nobody knows the answer," a retired geologist named Mel Wright said with a wink, making accountability by oil producers an elusive proposition. At Beverly Hills High School, air quality inspectors from the AQMD discovered in February 2003 that gas was being illegally vented through the top of the Tower of Hope. By April, their testing found that a pollution-control scrubber was adsorbing hydrogen sulfide—but not the so-called BTEX chemicals

Salt Lake field at Fairfax Avenue, site of the Grove (courtesy of Seaver Center for Western History Research, Los Angeles County Museum of Natural History).

(benzene, toluene, ethyl benzene, and xylene) defined as "hazardous air pollutants" by the federal government in 1998.

The highest allowable airborne exposure for benzene for a short time is five parts per million, and the level at which officials become concerned (the official "action level") is 0.5 ppm. The amount of benzene emitted from the oil derrick at Beverly Hills High School in April 2003, causing it to be to be shut down a *second* time, was 915 ppm—nearly 1,900 times the action level. But that standard is for workers, not students, over an eight-hour workday. What was the actual exposure to the kids?

That point was not lost on an environmental advocate named Bernard Endres, who was viewed as a renegade among this group of engineers. Endres presented a paper the following day at the geologists' conference, entitled "Environmental Hazards Posed by the Los Angeles Basin Urban Oilfields: An Historical Perspective of Lessons Learned." A geologist and lawyer, he had worked as a consultant for the Masry & Vititoe law firm to help conduct air and water sampling at Beverly Hills High School before the lawsuit was filed. His tests would provide evidence about toxic exposures there.

As the tour bus slowly cruised through residential neighborhoods, there were pumping wells that pecked at the earth like huge prehistoric insects. One was next to a Taco Bell, another next to a cemetery. Several were in backyards near a middle school, whose teams were nicknamed the Oilers. The mix of land use was breathtaking—hundreds of new homes, wetlands, commercial real estate development, and parklands where oil fields had been sucked dry or were just starting to operate again after forty-five years. It was, finally, a matter of simple economics: over time, the ocean location had grown more valuable than the mineral wealth beneath the sandy soil, and the major oil producers unloaded their real estate, sometimes without taking the requisite environmental precautions to properly shut down wells. In Huntington Beach, where three drills lurk in the parking lot at city hall, a group of parents had just begun to link their children's rare form of brain cancer with oil production there—a connection disputed by the local health department.

Driving from Long Beach to Inglewood to Beverly Hills, the bus tour finally stopped at BreitBurn Energy on Pico Boulevard. The project manager, an affable man named Steve Lyles, distributed hard hats and goggles to us as we walked inside.

Camouflaged by a stone wall, the facility spans two city blocks and is located across the street from an assortment of kosher delis. Currently, twenty-five wells are operating there, but since its walls were raised and the diesel rig was converted to an electric one, the city of Los Angeles permitted it for forty more wells, including one to be horizontally drilled all the way to Rodeo Drive and Olympic Boulevard in Beverly Hills.

"I just tell people this rig is 90210," Lyles quipped, drawing a big laugh.

Weeks earlier, the local air agency had cited BreitBurn for air emissions violations; while maintenance work was being performed on a sump pump, oil and sludge backed up into a drainage trench. I asked Lyles about the infraction.

"They're here all the time now with everything going on at Beverly Hills High School," he said, batting away my concern.

"What happened?" I asked again.

"Only good," he replied, angered by the line of questioning.

Six months later, Lyles would lose his job for failing to repair a leaking wellhead "in a timely manner."

The conferees snapped photographs of each other as they took turns manning the rig, looking like little boys playing Nintendo. Only here, they were running a massive rack-and-pinion drilling rig with an eight-thousand-foot drill pipe, the same kind used to drill utility lines under fjords in Norway.

"For engineers," one of them said, pulling a lever and tapping another button at the control panel as we watched the gargantuan rig overhead, "this is better than having an orgasm."

Night after night, when she couldn't sleep, Jody Kleinman surfed the Internet to discover everything she could about the toxic chemicals in question: benzene, a known carcinogen; methane gas, which has the potential for explosions; and the neurotoxin n-hexane, among others. "There has to be an accounting," she said at the time.

What she learned was deeply disturbing: chronic diseases among children are increasing every year, and the suspected culprit is toxic chemicals in the environment. Exposures to lead, mercury, and polychlorinated biphenyls (PCB's) are key. Cancer, after injuries, is the leading killer of American children. In California, long considered a pioneer in air-pollution research, studies suggest links between toxic air contaminants and low-birth-weight babies, childhood leukemia, and even brain cancer.

But a huge gap exists between research findings and regulatory action. The federal government considers chemicals safe unless proven harmful: we use first, ask later. Of three thousand high-use chemicals in industry, only 43 percent have been minimally tested. Of those, only 10 percent have been tested to examine their effects on children.

One of the few known human carcinogens that has been tested repeatedly is benzene, but government standards for what is considered a "safe" exposure are the subject of heated debate. Questions about chronic low-dose exposures remain, especially in light of a landmark 2004 National Institutes of Health study of Chinese factory workers, showing that such exposures—even at levels below the current legal exposure limit of one part per million—destroy several types of blood cells. Short-term exposure to benzene can cause temporary nervous system disorders, immune system depression, and anemia, while long-term exposure can cause chromosome aberrations and cancer.

But what did that mean, exactly, for the kids running around Beverly High's track and athletic fields? No one could say with clarity if benzene was the real culprit. What about the emissions of "steam" from Sempra's power plant next door to the high school? Or were the actual toxic exposures from these sources so tiny as to be inconsequential?

When she called the plant safety manager one day, Jody Kleinman was told that the steam from the plant was no different from water vapor from a tea kettle—though government records showed that the company had reported releases of tons of particulate matter and other pollutants from the plant every year.

The differences in the biology of children are critical for assessing risk but remain poorly understood. Children are very different from adults because pound for pound, they're more heavily exposed. Two critical points for determining exposure are weight and duration, but the effect of certain neurotoxins on a child's brain development may have more to do with *timing* of exposure than amount. Even growing teenagers, who can weigh as much as adults, tend to metabolize toxic chemicals more quickly, since organs that break down drugs, such as the liver, or excrete chemicals, such as the kidneys, take years to mature. The rate of blood flow to the skin and lungs is also higher in children, so topical or inhaled agents may be more rapidly absorbed.

At Clark University in Boston, Massachusetts, EPA researcher Dale Hattis recently recommended that the federal government's "safe" levels of chemical exposure be reevaluated because of age-related differences in cancer susceptibility. Hattis's research, which combines biological and statistical analyses, has shown how toxic exposure in early life is more important to overall cancer risks than exposures during adulthood. The most sensitive periods for children, he found, are from birth to weaning and from ages three to fifteen.

Hattis has found that the liver does a lot of work in making toxins more soluble so they can be excreted, and that process has a side effect. Vinyl chloride, for example, is harmless by itself. But as it's metabolized to a DNA-reactive compound in the liver, that compound will be harmful. Benzene also requires metabolic activation. "There's a period in adolescence," Hattis told me during an interview, "where those chemicals would create more risk per unit of dose than exposures later on." The risk for teenagers is at least three times that of adults, but current regulatory schemes have yet to incorporate that finding.

Like Hattis, scientists at Columbia University's Center for Children's Environmental Health have also shown that there can be critical "windows of exposure" during a child's development, even before birth. In one study, more than five hundred pregnant women in New York City pulled on backpacks with devices that trapped the chemicals they breathed. By "fingerprinting" chemicals in umbilical cord blood, the scientists could actually trace how airborne toxins—the polycyclic aromatic hydrocarbons found in cigarette smoke, power-plant emissions, car exhaust, and other combustion sources—breathed in by the mothers during pregnancy caused DNA damage in their newborns.

Now, Jody Kleinman was beginning to understand that long before the science comes in, the harm has been done. Risk analysis is based on mathematical calculations about the likelihood of causing harm. Uncertainty is a key component. The precautionary principle, on the other hand, recognizes the limits of science—and the fact that scientific uncertainty is an unavoidable breach into which ordinary citizens sometimes must step. Jody Kleinman was about to do just that.

Still, she believed in the truth of science. In the absence of direct data, you get interpretation. She needed someone to help her interpret the government's assurances that all was safe.

Sitting at her computer in the family room, next to an old-fashioned Coke machine and with a view of the pool out back, Kleinman began to Google air-monitoring experts. In 2000, air pollution researchers in Los Angeles produced the landmark Multiple Air Toxics Exposure Study, which quantified for the first time the relationship between toxic air contaminants and cancer: breathing the air in L.A. results in fourteen thousand extra cancers every year.

One of the technical advisers on that panel was an air-modeling expert named Bill Piazza. He had done consulting work for Communities for a Better Environment, the environmental justice advocacy group in East Los Angeles. Piazza had also coauthored research on kids and pollution from roadways. As it turned out, he was one of the few air-risk assessors in southern California. When Kleinman discovered that he had also been conducting health risk assessments for the Los Angeles Unified School District for more than two decades, she thought she had hit pay dirt.

She picked up the phone to call him. Excited, she left a voice message.

In 1977, a year before the city of Beverly Hills changed its municipal code to accommodate oil drilling at its high school, researchers with the environmental epidemiology branch at the National Cancer Institute in Bethesda, Maryland, began sounding the alarm "to clarify the risk of cancer among various groups of petroleum workers and to evaluate the possible effects of petrochemical emissions released into neighboring communities."

At the time, the cancer researchers were concerned about two studies that suggested "indirect evidence of a hazard": a national survey showed that lung cancer deaths were higher among men in counties with petroleum manufacturing, and a Los Angeles study found higher lung cancer rates in neighborhoods where airborne levels of hydrocarbons were emitted, in part, from refineries. "White male residents of the petroleum industry counties had significantly higher average age-adjusted mortality rates for cancer of the lung, nasal cavity and sinuses, stomach, rectum, testes and skin than those of control counties with similar demographic characteristics," reported the International Agency for Research on Cancer, an arm of the World Health Organization.

But it wasn't just men who were at issue. Studies from Russia at the time also showed that a high proportion of women working in petroleum-processing plants were sterile, and the rate of spontaneous abortion was also high. Moreover, U.S. government scientists reported in the journal *Science* that high rates of lung cancer among female residents in the petroleum-industry counties "raise the possibility of a pollution hazard spreading beyond the workplace."

Thirty years later, Jody Kleinman would wonder if a "pollution hazard" was spreading from the oil wells to Beverly Hills High.

Answers were hard to come by, though, given a long-standing pattern of delay and denial by the petroleum industry, which had been the beneficiary of special exemptions from environmental oversight for decades. In 1980, for instance, under intense lobbying by the industry, Congress temporarily exempted from EPA regulation the numerous carcinogens and neurotoxins that contaminate the drilling muds, brine, and fluids associated with gas and oil production. Seven years later, federal regulations overseeing toxic waste from oil and gas operations were again deemed unnecessary—even though the EPA recognized that the industry generated more than 12 billion barrels of liquids and mud containing hazardous substances, including benzene, lead, arsenic, and barium. At the time, the EPA's decision was based on the "financial burden" of regulation for the oil industry, which threatened to reduce domestic production and pass on as much as $4.5 billion in costs to consumers.

In 1991, the National Academy of Sciences acknowledged the dilemma with regard to environmental exposures and public health. A distinguished panel of scientists found that "insufficient data [were] available for evaluating the impact on public health of exposure to [toxic] substances." Calling for action, the scientists recommended that "a margin of safety be provided regarding potential health risks."

Instead, more delays followed. The EPA's Science Advisory Board warned in 1998 that the current regulatory system relying upon Toxic Release Inventory (TRI) data—self-reporting by companies—was deeply flawed. Exposure data was incomplete, the report concluded, because it was based on estimates, not on actual emissions that were carefully monitored. Not all facilities were required to report TRI data to the government, nor were all chemicals emitted from a facility required to be reported. Even so, by 1998 the EPA had labeled hundreds of them "extremely hazardous air pollutants."

In a 1999 congressional investigation, "Oil Refineries Fail to Report Millions of Pounds of Harmful Emissions," the House Committee on Government Reform found that oil and gas facilities vastly underreported leaks from valves and hinges, releasing more than 15 million pounds of toxic pollutants. In 2001, the General Accounting Office called on the EPA to improve its oversight of emissions reporting. But the agency responded by weakening monitoring rules; now, monitoring would be required only once every five years. Not surprisingly, the EPA admitted its biggest one-year increase of toxic emissions ever in 2003, including an additional 15 million pounds of benzene—ranked by the federal government as one of two chemicals posing the greatest national cancer risk.

The fact that Venoco had slipped under the radar of reporting benzene emissions pointed to yet another loophole. The National Emissions Standards for Hazardous Air Pollutants for oil and gas sites only apply to "major" sources of pollution, meaning a mere 330 of 250,000 facilities nationwide. The oil and gas production site at Beverly High was not one of them.

Nor did regulators have the authority to assess the "cumulative impact" of both Sempra and Venoco. "That's a hole we need to fill in our regulatory scheme," John Brock at the EPA's Air Toxics Enforcement Division in San Francisco told me in an interview. "There's a real difficulty in quantifying cumulative risk. If you've got the same contaminants, it's easier to add risks. But with multiple contaminants, you've got some risks that could have a synergistic effect. It makes it even worse.

"We haven't figured out how cumulative risks can be applied, so we don't have rules yet," he added.

One evening after his weekly softball game, Bill Piazza returned Jody Kleinman's phone call. At forty-four, he was a wiry man with dark eyes and a mustache, a mulletlike hairdo from the 1980s, and a wardrobe to match— blue jeans, pointed boots, and a pressed shirt and vest. In his off hours, he was a ballroom-dancing devotee and an antique-car buff with a special love for his 1929 Model A four-door sedan. As director of health and safety for L.A. schools, he believed part of his job was to goad the system by keeping bureaucrats honest about technical matters.

Kleinman told him she needed help demystifying the scientific jargon. Was her daughter safe at the school? Were assurances that there was no evidence of adverse effects from the oil well operation based on the best available science, or on politics?

Piazza told Kleinman that he was skeptical of Brockovich's claims of a cancer cluster. But he also had had many years of experience working with the AQMD, and he was convinced that the agency, headquartered in a gleaming edifice he called "the house that smog built," purposely looked the other way when it came to protecting kids at schools from toxic exposures. As for Camp Dresser & McKee, the engineering firm hired by the city's defense lawyers, some of those guys worked down the hall from him at school headquarters; he respected them, but he also knew on which side their bread was buttered.

The quantification of health risks from exposure to hazardous air toxics is an imprecise science. Of 188 air pollutants deemed "hazardous" by the

EPA, only a handful have information on human health effects, derived mostly from animal and occupational studies. Still, Piazza thought this Beverly Hills assessment was "a no-brainer."

In his opinion, the school district needed to conduct a "cumulative" risk assessment by analyzing emissions from all sources in the area—including the oil wells, the power plant, the hospital, the roadway. He had conducted about three hundred risk assessments over the years, including one for a school built on an oil well property in Brea-Olinda, where he found no significant risks for students.

Piazza was less worried about toxic chemical emissions than about methane gas from the old oil field beneath the school. "There's explosion potential," he told Kleinman. His concern was that methane could build up from beneath buildings, seep out of cracks, and blow up a classroom. That was the real issue, he believed—subsurface gas migration. He'd seen it at other schools: a teacher turned on a light switch—and boom.

"I think people are being taken for a ride," he added. "There's money being wasted on attorneys. They could have had the damned thing done by now." In Piazza's experience, the oldest trick in the book was to grab an air sample and then say no problem existed, because 99 percent of the time, chemical analyses will come back as a "nondetect," meaning below measurable levels.

"They go out and look like they're doing something, so it's okay on a political level," he later said. "You want to be careful of guys who stick an eight-hour Summa canister outside, willy nilly. It's a dog and pony show. It doesn't tell you where benzene is coming from. You have no idea if it's from the road or an area source."

Piazza said he needed to review the data. Risk assessment has two main components: how a chemical hurts the body and the probability of coming into contact with it. To assess all exposures, he'd need to review empirical data, site data, engineering data. He recommended that Kleinman obtain emissions reports submitted to government regulators by Venoco and Sempra. The reports were annual and reflected estimates, not actual monitoring data, and they wouldn't include the "burps" or "upsets" or numerous "venting" episodes; but they would help to piece together a picture, uncertain though it might be.

The focus should be the safety of the children, he said.

It had been months since Jody Kleinman first asked the school board for a health risk assessment, and no one had taken her seriously until now. "I couldn't stop crying," she later said of her relief from that phone call with Piazza. "I felt so grateful he was willing to help. I offered, but he wouldn't take any money. It was the first night I slept in weeks."

Even so, Piazza cautioned that there would be caveats. Current assessments wouldn't reflect historical exposures, from when her husband and two older daughters had been at the school. And ambient air measurements would give only a snapshot in time; wind speed, temperature, and humidity could all impact testing results. The appropriate method of analysis would require a mathematical model of air dispersion.

Traditionally, exposure assessments have relied on external or ambient exposure monitoring of airborne toxins. The process involves measuring a chemical either by area sampling with a monitor in a fixed location, or by personal monitoring in which small air pumps are worn. But that method often underestimates total exposures because it measures only one "pathway of exposure," namely what is breathed in, and fails to include chemicals absorbed through the skin or ingested through tainted water or food.

At Beverly High, students ate lunch outside on the front lawn or in the outdoor patio by the cafeteria, so they were constantly bombarded with airborne particles. Differences in absorption at similar exposure levels may occur in children because of their increased respiratory rate and because their surface-to-volume ratio is larger than adults'.

Kleinman agreed to provide Piazza with the data she had gathered so far. She told him she had gotten hold of leak reports, describing Venoco's leak rate. All oil wells and refineries leak, he said. They'd need to see if it was leaking more than it should.

The key question, Piazza believed, was: Are children being exposed to chemicals that are potentially causing risk?

"I can't wait to get my hands on the data," he told her.

The first published medical reports linking benzene exposure to destruction of human bone marrow date back to 1897, when cases of aplastic anemia were documented in Sweden among young women working in bicycle tire factories. In humans, and in all laboratory animals tested, benzene produces destruction of bone marrow precursor cells that are responsible for mature red blood cells, platelets, and white blood cells. This is accompanied by chromosomal damage. The expansion of industrial uses of benzene would be accompanied by a vast increase in the number of reported cases of aplastic anemia.

In 1922, Dr. Alice Hamilton, the first female professor at Harvard Medical School, published an article in the *Journal of the American Medical Association* entitled "The Growing Menace of Benzene Poisoning in American Industry." Hamilton pointed out that the outbreak of war had created a demand for benzene and toluene for the manufacture of explosives, and of aniline for the manufacture of dyes and rubber. An over-supply of coal-tar distillates created markets for benzene, especially for tires, footwear, and hose; in sealing mixtures for tin cans; for cement; in certain processes in the making of straw hats; and as a substitute for gasoline in automobile fuel.

"If a man is susceptible to benzene it takes only a small quantity to poison or even to kill him," Hamilton noted. "[I]n acute benzene poisoning the blood in the heart and vessels is fluid, in the veins of the abdomen, engorged. There are hemorrhages into the gastric mucosa, bloody foam in the air passages, no benzene odor, and no benzene demonstrable chemically." Hamilton recounted medical episodes of factory workers who experienced "profound blood destruction." In one case, a worker had "bleeding from the nose and mouth, black and blue spots over the body, secondary anemia, and breathlessness"; a fifty-seven-year-old woman employed in the same factory "died in the hospital after hemorrhages from the intestine, kidneys, and nose, and into the skin."

Today, benzene—a component of crude oil—is one of the most widely used chemicals in the United States, with total usage about 11 billion gallons per year. An estimated 238,000 people are occupationally exposed to it in petrochemical plants, petroleum refineries, and other operations. It is impossible to avoid low-level environmental exposures: it enters the air through vehicle emissions. It can seep into a house from an attached garage when benzene in gasoline evaporates from the car's engine or tank. It is also one of the many hazardous constituents of cigarette smoke.

After the introduction of benzene into gasoline, its carcinogenic effects on many organ systems in animals and humans became known. Based on studies showing that exposure to high levels causes leukemia in workers, researchers have noted that benzene can damage genetic material in cells. The damage is cumulative and irreversible, and evidence of it can take decades to emerge as cancer—of the lung, prostate, skin, brain, and breast, among other organs.

In 1948, the American Petroleum Institute issued a toxicological review of benzene which stated: "Inasmuch as the body develops no tolerance to benzene, and as there is a wide variation in individual susceptibility, it is generally considered that the only absolutely safe concentration for benzene is zero."

Though benzene is known to cause leukemia and other human blood disorders, its regulation has been stymied by a thirty-year-old disagreement over how much exposure it takes to produce cancer. The petrochemical industry, in hearings, petitions, and litigation, has persistently fought attempts by the federal Occupational Safety and Health Administration (OSHA) to lower benzene exposure levels. When the National Academy of Sciences concluded in the 1970s that occupational studies confirmed that benzene was a "suspect leukemogen," a request for an emergency temporary standard to regulate it in the workplace was filed, and OSHA issued a 1 ppm threshold. That standard was challenged in court by the American Petroleum Institute, and a deeply divided U.S. Supreme Court vacated the standard in 1980, siding with industry in its so-called benzene decision.

OSHA's presumption of "no safe level" was deemed inappropriate by the Court, which held that its rule placed too great a burden on employers and that the government had failed to prove definitively that benzene threatened workers' health. The high court's decision ushered in the current era of "quantitative risk assessments" for health standards, in which cost-benefit analyses would take precedence over public health considerations for the first time in our nation's history. In an impassioned dissent, Justice Thurgood Marshall wrote: "Today's decision flagrantly disregards . . . the plain meaning of the Occupational Safety and Health Act of 1970. The unfortunate consequence is that the Federal Government's efforts to protect American workers from cancer and other crippling diseases may be substantially impaired."

Since most health experts agreed that there was no safe exposure limit for cancer-causing chemicals, OSHA's policy was to set the standard at the lowest feasible level. The limit had to be technologically feasible, which meant technology had to exist to get the exposure down to a certain level, and it had to be economically feasible. But the Supreme Court said that feasibility wasn't an adequate measure to set an exposure limit. Instead, the Court declared, if OSHA was going to issue the standard, the agency also had to show a "significant risk" of developing cancer and that the risk could be "significantly reduced" by the new level. That decision, in other words, would profoundly change the way health agencies could set public health standards.

The day after the opinion was published, the *Washington Post* reported "industrial elation and regulatory panic." Essentially, it shifted the burden of proof; now, industry wouldn't need to prove its chemicals safe; instead, government regulators would need to prove a chemical harmful before action could be taken. Prior to the benzene decision, public agencies could act prudently on the basis of good qualitative evidence showing that a chemical could cause cancer in humans or animals. Now, agencies would need to adopt a more tedious, more comprehensive process that could take many years to complete, tracing in detail the relationship between a given level of exposure and a given level of disease. If chemicals were considered innocent until proven guilty, the Supreme Court made it much harder to prove a chemical guilty.

In 1987, after more than ten years of delay, OSHA tightened the standard for worker exposures to benzene by a factor of ten, bringing the allowable air exposure limit down to 1 part per million. The National Institute of Occupational Safety and Health (NIOSH), on the other hand, recommended an exposure limit of 0.1 part per million—ten times lower. According to Dr. Philip Landrigan, chairman of the Department of Community and Preventive Medicine at the Mount Sinai School of Medicine in New York and former director of the hazard evaluations for NIOSH, 492 workers died unnecessarily from leukemia caused by benzene exposure during those ten years.

The benzene standard was also one of the early examples of how far the industry would go to keep OSHA from issuing standards to protect workers. Dr. Peter Infante, a toxicologist with OSHA for more than two decades, recalled that scientists from Dow Chemical testified at the 1977 hearings but failed to reveal that their own study had shown chromosomal damage at low levels of exposure until after the hearing was over.

Whistle-blowers were also punished. In 1989, toxicologist Myron Mehlman had just been nominated to the National Academy of Sciences by his employer, Mobil Oil Corporation, when he abruptly lost his job. As director of toxicology and manager of the company's environmental health and science laboratory, he gave a presentation to corporate managers in Japan about the health effects of gasoline. When he learned during the presentation that gasoline sold by Mobil's Japanese subsidiary contained levels of benzene in excess of 5 percent, Mehlman warned the managers that the concentrations were too high and needed to be reduced, or the gasoline should not be sold. As soon as he returned to the United States, Mehlman was fired by Mobil, which accused him of misusing company personnel and supplies to promote his wife's scientific publishing business; according to court documents, Mobil subsequently attempted to "orchestrate a smear campaign" against him.

Mehlman successfully sued Mobil under New Jersey's employee protection act and recovered $7 million in damages in 1998. Still, he called his efforts to restore his reputation and to battle the smear campaign "nine years of hell."

I visited Mehlman at his home in Princeton, New Jersey, on a cold, rainy day in November 2004. He had just returned from Bologna, Italy, after the annual meeting of the Ramazzini Collegium, a group of some of the world's most prestigious environmental health researchers. In his den, atop his television set, he keeps a bronze bust of Ramazzini, which he was awarded by the group in 2002 for his "courageous service" and for "improving the lives of working men and women around the world."

Mehlman believes the current benzene standard in the United Sates is set far too high. He and Eula Bingham, a former director of OSHA, have been campaigning to lower the standard. He points out that in 1984, when a scientific review panel in California first listed benzene as a toxic air contaminant, it concluded that benzene "may act at all doses without any threshold level," meaning that there is no safe exposure level in the ambient air. The last thorough federal survey of exposure was released in 1987; the American Public Health Association recently urged Congress to provide the necessary funding to OSHA to conduct an up-to-date review.

Mehlman said that within the scientific community, there is no longer any question that benzene causes a wide variety of cancers, not just leukemia. The only disagreement, he said, has been caused by defense lawyers, whose job it is to manufacture uncertainty in the courtroom. "You've gotta be deaf, blind, or dead to deny all these positive studies," he told me. "You're not talking about something that's been occasionally studied. You're talking about tons of positive studies."

He added: "But you can create debate over anything. If you ask people who work in the field and who have no economic interest, you have no problem. The people who have economic interest, they get paid to generate debate. When attorneys go into court, it's wonderful—one scientist says this, another says this, so they disagree. It's for the purpose of litigation—that's why it's created. They're not real debates; they're manufactured."

"Junk science" and "good science," he said, are simply terms generated by industry. "Just listen very carefully," he said. "The minute somebody says 'good science,' you can almost be certain they'll start spinning. The definition of junk science is that the data doesn't agree with what they want it to."

If most people think of science as an objective discipline immune from market forces, the suppression of industry-sponsored research proves otherwise. One stunning example I uncovered in my research involves a 1992 epidemiology study commissioned by the Union Oil Company of California, now Chevron, which found increased cancer rates for its petroleum employees, but the study has never been published.

Entitled "A Case-Control Study of Leukemia, Non-Hodgkin's Lymphoma and Multiple Myeloma Among Employees of Union Oil Company of California," the study was written by Elizabeth Delzell, professor of epidemiology, and her colleagues at the University of Alabama's School of Public Health. They found elevated rates for all three forms of cancer at statistically significant levels, but published only the results about leukemia.

Delzell's positive findings for non-Hodgkin's lymphoma and multiple myeloma are especially crucial for scientists because the American petroleum industry has sponsored reviews of the published literature and consistently denied a causal connection between benzene and these two forms of cancer. In testimony from a 1998 lawsuit in Texas, Delzell said she couldn't remember why the data was never published; nor could she recall if anyone from the company told her not to publish it.

In September 2005, Raphael Metzger, a plaintiff's attorney from Long Beach, California, received the study in the course of discovery on another toxic tort case against Shell Oil, and forwarded it to the Confidential Business Information Center at the U.S. Environmental Protection Agency and to scientists at OSHA and NIOSH.

"This is a case of nonpublication bias—when industry gets the results they don't like, so they suppress it," Metzger charged. "This study would have upset the pretty picture industry was presenting that hydrocarbons don't cause multiple myeolma or non-Hodgkin's lymphoma."

I spoke to a Toxic Substances and Control Act specialist at the EPA, who said that Metzger had his facts wrong. He told me that Unocal did, in fact, submit Delzell's study to the agency back in 1992, though he wasn't sure if scientists at NIOSH or OSHA had received it. Why, then, had she not published the results of the study? My phone calls and e-mails to Elizabeth Delzell went unreturned. "The amazing thing," Metzger later said, "is EPA did nothing in response in 1992. The whole point of the reporting system is so our governmental authorities can gather information from industry for scientific review. And yet they apparently did absolutely nothing."

Days after her father's funeral, Jody Kleinman was supposed to be sitting shiva, the weeklong mourning period that Jews observe after the death of a parent or family member. She couldn't sit still, though, and drove to city hall one morning in early June 2003 for a "focus group" about the oil wells that was convened by the mayor, Tom Levyn. Like the other "public" meetings, this one would be conducted in secret.

Once there, Jody Kleinman became convinced that this was just another "divide-and-conquer" meeting. People spoke only of the pending litigation and how Erin Brockovich lacked credibility; it looked to them as if she was pursuing "junk science" to make a buck.

Without scientific evidence to warrant further investigations, the mayor said, the city was going to back off from its original plan to conduct more environmental testing, such as soil-gas tests. Instead, the city council had voted to use its legislative powers to subpoena information from Edward Masry. Publicly, the mayor claimed to be looking for specifics about Masry's data—when and where it was collected, how the chain of custody was preserved. In truth, the subpoena also sought documents from other defendants, including Sempra Energy, as well as insurance information from Venoco and Chevron.

The subpoena was a clever tactical end-run around the discovery process to get a head start on investigating the plaintiffs' experts. But Beverly Hills city attorney Larry Wiener labeled the subpoena "a health investigation" for parents, like Jody Kleinman, who were demanding information. It was his view that the plaintiffs' lawyers had done a great job at stirring up panic in the community, even though their evidence looked paltry.

"We got the Masry data, and it showed us, frankly, that his data doesn't support the conclusions that there's an air quality problem at Beverly Hills High School," Wiener said at the time. "We decided if we could get the rest of his information, it would be helpful. We came up with a way that works, and we approved those legislative subpoenas."

According to ambient air tests taken by experts for the city's defense law firm, the concentration of chemicals in ambient air at Beverly High was no different from air quality for the rest of Los Angeles. Data from the Masry law firm, on the other hand, showed that chemical concentrations of benzene at Beverly High were twenty-eight times higher than the average background concentration reported by the United States Environmental Protection Agency for Los Angeles.

Kleinman saw the subpoena as another delaying tactic. Walking out of the meeting, she called Piazza on her cell phone to nudge him about his report. She told him that the city was stalling her out with legal shenanigans.

We're being advised by attorneys, not scientists, she told him. They're worried about money and their lawsuit, not our kids.

"They don't need subpoenas to get the data," he told her. "All that stuff could have been collected by now. This is all for the love of attorneys giving bad advice. It just kills me. The hypocrisy kills me."

In a perfect world, of course, Bill Piazza was right: an independent investigation would help to address environmental problems at the high school for the sake of the children. Legally, though, it was an untenable position, since the school district and city were defendants in a lawsuit. As public entities, they were faced with the problem of setting a precedent if a settlement occurred. Getting legal advice and adhering to it would be a priority now, hypocritical or not. The search for truth was not the same as the search for justice.

By the time some of the defendants' lawyers realized something might truly be wrong, they could no longer admit it. The liability would be far too great. Limiting their clients' legal exposures, not their toxic exposures, had become the name of the game.

On a hot and smoggy July morning, trial lawyer Skip Miller appeared under the fluorescent lights in the downtown courtroom of superior court judge David P. Yaffe. The deadline for complying with the city's subpoena had come and gone, and the Masry law firm wouldn't budge from its position that the documents in question were protected by attorney-client privilege.

Known for his scorched-earth tactics, Miller was out for blood, or the legal equivalent—a contempt-of-court ruling. Better still would be to see Masry and Brockovich thrown in jail. "This," Miller told me, "is my only option."

Yaffe, a silver-haired and bespectacled jurist, was conducting an ex parte hearing on a motion filed by Masry & Vititoe for an emergency order to quash the city's subpoena.

Miller had represented the city of Beverly Hills in a racial-profiling case brought against it by several young black men. He had also represented the city of Los Angeles when it was a defendant in a civil lawsuit by Rodney King. He had a reputation for playing hardball, and for this, his opening salvo on behalf of the city of Beverly Hills, he would go all out. Since the plaintiffs made what Miller claimed were unsubstantiated allegations that the high school was unsafe, Miller wanted to force their hand. He also hoped to score some points in the press, leaving the impression that Masry's case was frivolous.

"What's the city's position relative to a stay?" Yaffe asked Miller.

Miller looked nervous; his skin was red and blotchy. "The city's position," he replied, "is we can't wait. It's vital for our environmental consultants to complete their analysis.

"These people have alarmed the community," he added. "They've scared the daylights out of everybody."

He raised his voice slightly. "We need to do it right now—no stays, no rigamarole of stalling or delays. We need the data right now. We're just asking for the raw data they claim they have. If there's any validity to anything Mr. Masry says, we have to know."

Judge Yaffe pursed his lips. "Let's suppose they won't produce—then what happens?" he asked Miller.

Miller smiled tightly. "A judge will have to issue an order and the police will go out and arrest these people. That's the appeal."

The judge wondered aloud about Brockovich, "a notorious paralegal," being arrested by the Beverly Hills Police Department and then hauled into jail for contempt of court. "Wow! I can just see the newspapers!" he enthused.

Nevertheless, he refused to insert himself into the fray and denied Masry's request for an emergency order.

In the weeks that followed, Masry's attorneys admitted in court that they had not yet conducted a formal epidemiological study, a process that could take years to complete correctly. Instead, his experts had relied upon American Cancer Society statistics to compare national incidence rates with cancer rates for Beverly Hills High alumni. That admission would be used by the defendants' lawyers to argue that Erin Brockovich and Masry were up to no good. The local newspaper intoned: "Masry's Attorney Admits in Court No Study Done by Them to Establish Cancer Rates at Beverly Hills High School."

The article, by Norma Zager, lampooned Brockovich's integrity. "Meanwhile," Zager wrote, "Erin Brockovich is taking time out from her battles with the city of Beverly Hills to star in Eve Ensler's *The Vagina Monologues*" at the Fred Kavli Theater in Thousand Oaks. Brockovich believed that the campaign to undermine her credibility was merely an attempt to distract the public from a far more grave fact: that the city and school district had put schoolchildren in harm's way and failed to do anything about it.

Meanwhile, Masry's partner, the Texas litigator Al Stewart, had begun to consult with Dr. Richard Clapp, professor of environmental health at Boston University's School of Public Health and a former director of the Massachusetts Cancer Registry. Among his findings, Clapp would conclude that the incidence of Hodgkin's disease among Beverly High graduates from 1976 to

2000 was *three times* what was expected for their age, race, and socioeconomic status. In the world of toxic torts, a doubling of the incidence is usually enough to prevail in court.

"I actually do think the numbers are elevated, but I don't think that's what the case will hang on," Clapp told me when I visited him in his office in Boston in January 2004.

What would the case hang on?

"The biological evidence that this exposure might have caused these cases," he said. "That's the medical question."

At city hall, Jody Kleinman happened to bump into a longtime resident named Judy Okun. "Keep going," Okun told Jody Kleinman, encouraging her to continue her fight. Okun believed that a lot of people worried more about being disloyal to the city or the school district than about the well-being of their children and the damages due them. She reminded Kleinman that it was courageous to take a stand. "It's a scary thing to think that people are so fearful."

The fight wasn't going to be easy, she warned Kleinman. People in Beverly Hills didn't want to acknowledge that they'd spent a lot of money to move to an imperfect place. Not only would it take a lot of effort to change things, it would require that she be willing to be socially ostracized, too.

If anyone in town understood the reason for the crushing silence of the community, it was Judy Okun. Some twenty-five years earlier, her husband, Erwin, the head of public relations for Disney, had written a letter to the local newspaper, questioning the wisdom of the city's real estate swap that paved the way for a developer to build condos at an industrial site—and he was promptly sued for $63 million by the developer. The six-year case went to the United States Supreme Court and landed back in California, where state law was rewritten to prohibit such harassment suits, known as strategic lawsuits against public participation, or SLAPPs.

Legal analysts would come to label the lawsuit "the most infamous California real estate SLAPP" and "southern California at its most flamboyant." California Chief Justice Rose Bird questioned whether people in Beverly Hills would have to consult a lawyer before writing a letter to a newspaper, and Justice Stanley Mosk wondered how such a suit might chill political activity.

Jody Kleinman thought she was experiencing that chill.

"This is a very social city," Okun reminded Kleinman. "The truth is resisted until enough people believe in the veracity of it. The emperor needs new clothes. Until it hits home, people don't understand a lot of things.

"People are unwilling to admit there's anything wrong," she added, "because they've made the commitment to move here. Once they're here, they think they can stop working. But they can't. They can't just hand it over to the maid."

Reviewing the Camp Dresser & McKee report, Piazza was distinctly unimpressed. The devil was in the details, he thought—and the CDM report made a mockery of all he believed in. "This," he later said sardonically, humming a tune from the musical *Chicago*, "is all about razzle-dazzle."

Not only was science being ignored, he believed, but worse, it was being manipulated to build a bogus rationale for avoiding an objective health risk determination. The report compared annual *average* ambient air concentrations compiled by the AQMD ten miles away in Burbank—a city with a sizable airport—to monitoring data on the athletic field for a few hours. That was like comparing apples to oranges. Here was a classic example of "junk science," Piazza believed, and it was being promulgated by defense lawyers and their experts.

"It borders on the pathetic," Piazza later said. "That doesn't tell you anything. You can't make chronic determinations based on two weeks' sampling: No can do."

The CDM report referred to elevated levels of the chemicals acetone and methyl ethyl ketone, which may not cause cancer but could be associated with acute problems, like headaches. But the analysis denied that oil well production could be the source of those chemicals.

In Piazza's view, the report also failed to examine all potential exposures, including releases from the power plant. Under the 1990 amendments to the Clean Air Act, 188 compounds are identified as hazardous air pollutants because of their potential to cause adverse health effects, such as cancer. For cancer risks, the margin of safety is defined as a lifetime cancer risk no greater than one in a million. Among the concern-causing pollutants being released from the plant were formaldehyde, acrolein, benzene, and dioxins.

"It's just smoke and mirrors," he later said of the CDM report. "To say there's no risk based on preliminary data—that's just crazy. They're saying it's safe because they don't want anyone hysterical. But it's not based on science, I can tell you that. It just gives them a war chest of information to fight exposures.

"Somehow, these people think they're exempt because they're Beverly Hills," he added. "The school is in the shadow of a derrick. It's pretty damn basic. They spend more time defending and deflecting than just going out and doing it right. This is the fleecing of America. The groundwork is there. The information is there. But it's all razzle-dazzle."

Piazza also issued a blistering attack on the AQMD. He said the accepted practice is to use air dispersion models of emission exposures that would include wind direction, velocity, and temperature. He pointed to a 1992 EPA citizen's guide that explains how to conduct community exposure assessments. For the local air district to suggest that health risks from chemicals in the air at the high school did not exceed standards, he noted in his report, "is contrary to the policies and procedures of the regulatory community.

"Clearly," his report added, "the assertion that basin-wide concentrations are indistinguishable from those identified at the high school is inappropriate and without merit. . . . Results of the air investigation are insufficient to allow for a safe use determination."

Perhaps most telling—and embarrassing to Beverly Hills—was Piazza's inclusion of another CDM report conducted just a block away in Century City at 2020 Avenue of the Stars. It detailed the need for methane gas monitors in underground parking structures, because the building was located on the old Beverly Hills oil field. Piazza pointed out that the city of Los Angeles had requirements to control methane gas seepage from geologic formations, whereas Beverly Hills did not.

Jody Kleinman immediately submitted his write-up to the city council and the school board. She was convinced that when they read his analysis, they would reconsider their course of action before school started that fall. But that is not what happened.

The real story in Beverly Hills, Kleinman would come to believe, was a cynical exercise in disinformation—neutralizing the opposition by paying experts to squelch dissent.

She expected Beverly Hills city attorney Larry Wiener to call that week, but Wiener didn't. She waited over the weekend, expecting to hear from Wiener at any moment, but he never called back. Neither did Mayor Tom Levyn. Or Barry Brucker, the school board president.

As it happened, Kleinman heard from no one—except Ed Masry. He called and left a message on her answering machine, wondering if she'd like to go on the *Today* show with Erin Brockovich in the coming weeks.

But she didn't call Masry back. She wasn't interested in going on TV, nor did she want to help promote his lawsuit. She just wanted answers about her kid's school now.

By the middle of July 2003, the oil wells were up and running again. The AQMD said it was satisfied that the company had made the requisite corrections to its pollution-control system. Owing to concerns over an excess cancer risk, though, regulators were requiring that the company submit a "health-risk assessment" in the coming months.

Discovering the whole truth of what had happened at Beverly Hills High School, Jody Kleinman realized, would be impossible. In the beginning, the truth had been obscured by a web of lies, evasions, and self-serving accounts from elected officials, government regulators, and corporate executives. In the end, it might remain hidden by death and the vagaries of memory. But for Kleinman's purposes, it really made little difference whether there had been six "upsets" or ten at Sempra and Venoco. She had uncovered more than enough to realize that a health-risk assessment would, finally, be meaningless.

"I hate them all," she said of the regulators, the lawyers, the company executives. "I fucking hate them all."

Not that her hatred propelled her to leave. Nor would she move her daughter to another school. Instead, she dug in.

When is a child safe enough? That question lay at the heart of Jody Kleinman's struggle to decide whether to take her daughter out of school in Beverly Hills. But what was happening in Beverly Hills was happening everywhere in America, from the asbestos poisoning of Libby, Montana, to the "cancer alley" of Diamond, Louisiana, to the chrome-plating plant in South Los Angeles. With the Bush administration dismantling environmental protections, from provisions of the Clean Air Act to research funds for children's health, was there any safe place to go?

Why hadn't Jody Kleinman acted the minute she suspected that the oil wells at the high school might be a source of environmental disease? Many viewed her as obstinate and self-defeating; others branded her "hysterical" and "alarmist" for simply asking questions. For Kleinman, though, weighing the risks involved a variety of considerations, many of them purely social. For one thing, her husband, Jeff, had moved with his family to Beverly Hills as a high school junior, and he had found the transition enormously difficult. He had promised his daughters they'd never be subjected to a similar trauma. Plus, there was Marisa herself: she wanted to play soccer and to edit the yearbook and to stay at Beverly with her friends. She begged her mother not to move her.

Jody believed that there was always a balancing act required of parents, but sometimes her instincts were just plain wrong. Her oldest daughter, Beth, had traveled to Israel her junior year of college. Convinced she had put her daughter in harm's way by allowing her to stay there, Jody had insisted that Beth return home early—and then her daughter had been hit by a car as she walked across the street in nearby Santa Monica.

There was also the scientific uncertainty over whether emissions from the industrial sites were responsible for illness. Given that she might be exposing Marisa to other dangers that could be worse if she moved her to another school, the options didn't seem great. A growing body of scientific evidence showed that living or going to school near roadways with heavy traffic was associated with a number of adverse health effects, including respiratory symptoms, increased risk of heart and lung disease, and elevated mortality rates. Other schools in the area, such as Santa Monica High School and Crossroads, were located next to a freeway. She learned that were she to put her daughter on a bus to go to school, vehicle pollution inside buses would be worse than levels found in roadway air.

She had all sorts of rationalizations, of course. She also believed that if everyone ran from the problem, the oil wells would never be closed. She felt a responsibility to stay and deal with the situation, not to run from it. "I really thought it would be closed that year and that science would get at the truth," she later said.

If there were no longer any watchdogs, then she'd simply take on that role for herself: she would be the watchdog of Beverly Hills. More like a pit bull, really. "Somebody's gotta be the prickly thorn in their side," she said. "That's my job. Unless you do it, it doesn't get done. The only thing I can do is be persistent. That's all I can do."

On a Sunday afternoon just a few weeks later, Jody and Jeff Kleinman attended a one-woman show at the Odyssey Theater in West Los Angeles. The comedic performance piece, *Jonna's Body, Please Hold,* tells the story of a woman's battle with cancer.

Before she took a seat, Kleinman bumped into a high school teacher, Susan Messenger. She told Messenger, a popular teacher who was famous for her flamenco dancing in class, that her daughter Marisa had just enrolled in her AP Spanish class that fall. "Maybe you've heard my name mentioned about the oil wells," she said, introducing herself. "I'm Jody Kleinman."

"Yes," Susan Messenger said. "You've been working on it. Thank you."

No one had thanked Jody for her work. This was new.

The teacher told Jody that she knew only what she was told at teachers' meetings at school. She hadn't been to any of the lawyers' meetings. She didn't have time. But she had had three different breast cancers, and now, at forty-seven, she just wanted to focus on her health, like the character in the play they were about to watch.

But here, at this small theater on a Sunday afternoon in August in West Los Angeles, she told Jody that the previous semester the administration had quietly moved a teacher out of her classroom and closed the room permanently because of environmental concerns. She was aware that a study of teachers in California had concluded that they had higher-than-normal rates of breast cancer, perhaps due to delayed childbearing. But she also knew she would soon sign papers to be part of the lawsuit.

Susan Messenger's fears and frustrations galvanized Jodi Kleinman. She knew she needed to figure out a way to join forces. But how? And with whom? "I think everyone's been pacified," Kleinman told her. "But not for long."

CHAPTER EIGHT

VELL MOALTALLI

Beverly Hills, birthplace of the $4 million "teardown"—a perfectly charming home that is demolished to make way for a Brobdingnagian one—is a place where people live in a world of fantasies, and earn their livings by promoting fantasies, and so all the world becomes a place obsessed with image. And excess. At Christmastime, Baccarat crystal chandeliers, encased in Plexiglas, are draped over the shopping district on Rodeo Drive. A silver-plated fire hydrant adorns the curb of the town's water-treatment plant. Behind gated estates protected by security cameras, residents stay walled off from the riffraff. "You will have 20 seconds to vacate this property if you have not been invited," reads a posted sign along the alley of North Foothill Drive. "Armed guards will respond immediately. Owner will not be responsible for trespassers' bodily safety."

Shutting out the real world, though, has its drawbacks. In the weeks prior to school's opening in the fall of 2003, parents in Beverly Hills received more notices from the school administration, assuring them that the high school was safe. Both air testing and soil samples taken by engineers who drilled holes in the dirt of the athletic fields indicated no problem. The superintendent, before she abruptly quit her post, also reported that an epidemiologist named Philip Cole, who had been hired by the city, had determined that there was not a higher-than-normal incidence of cancer among Beverly High's graduates. His report was not made public, however, nor was the fact that Cole had long worked as an expert witness for industry and was aligned with the libertarian think tank the Cato Institute, funded in part by energy conglomerates such as Chevron, ExxonMobil, and Shell, and their trade association, the American Petroleum Institute.

The residents of Beverly Hills fell broadly into two categories: those who paid little attention to such matters and those who believed what civic boosters told them, namely that Erin Brockovich was an ambulance-chasing floozy. Mahshid Soleimani, a member of the PTA safety committee, was part of the second camp—until she attended her son's lacrosse game on the football field at Beverly High and was overcome by fumes there. When she complained to state officials and to school board members, whose children were friends of her children, the response was the same: If you don't like it, leave.

But Soleimani, a beautiful woman with high cheekbones and a penchant for Prada shoes, wasn't going anywhere. Born in Tehran, she fled her homeland on the eve of the Islamic revolution and arrived in Los Angeles in 1979, like thousands of other expatriates. The Iranian community in Los Angeles is the largest in the world outside of Iran, and the population of Beverly Hills reflects that fact: one out of every five of its residents is of Iranian descent; as many as half of the students at the high school speak Farsi at home.

"For God's sake," Mahshid told her good friend Nelli Emrani, one evening. "We came thousands of miles from Tehran to Beverly Hills. This is our home now. Let Venoco leave."

The shiny black suburban assault vehicles, those oversized SUVs, Mercedes station wagons, and BMWs that transported housewives with cell phones and oversized coffee cups in hand, were lined up on the leafy street outside Mahshid Soleimani's home, signaling a gathering inside. It was a cloudless Thursday morning in early September 2003 on North Whittier Drive, across the street from the eucalyptus groves of the Los Angeles Country Club.

After six months of little more than talk, Soleimani, the forty-eight-year-old mother of three sons, was organizing the PTA for action. It was perhaps a bit odd that many of these women of privilege, who frequented Neiman Marcus, had their hair done at Frederic Fekkai, and greeted each other with double kisses on both cheeks, had come to view themselves as revolutionaries. But they felt it was time to take matters into their own hands. They had no choice.

One by one, the mothers from El Rodeo Elementary School buzzed an electronic gate to a Tudor-styled mansion with a semicircular drive and a basketball hoop out front. Inside, a housekeeper dressed in uniform ushered guests from a marble-tiled entrance to the family room, where white orchids and strawberries had been neatly arranged on the coffee table, and pastries and fruit were served on silver platters nearby.

As the elegantly attired PTA moms sipped coffee from china cups, Soleimani sat across from them and recited the now familiar litany of obstacles to getting rid of Venoco: a lack of evidence of harm to students and faculty, the school district's fear of being countersued by the company, and the CDM reports paid for by the city. Especially the CDM reports.

"This," she said, pointing to a poster-sized copy of the latest air-sampling data from CDM, propped up on a red silk-covered chair, "is the report that claims everything is okay." She had spent untold hours considering chemicals listed in the air, like benzene and acetone.

"Does anyone have the entire six-hundred-page report?" asked a parent named Marrina Waks, who had repeatedly testified before the school board about the use of radioactive iodine in the oil wells. She was convinced that the public was being purposely misinformed.

"No," the women said in unison.

The public was in the dark, Waks added. She believed that the community's silence had more to do with being misled by lawyers and government regulators than with apathy. Most people had no idea how much information was being withheld from them. "It's sad," she said. "It's not lack of interest. It's ignorance."

Jody Kleinman interrupted. "Mark Katchen has given us nothing—nothing," she said of the school district's environmental consultant, who had been monitoring the air for chemical concentrations inside classrooms and was retained by the school district's defense law firm as an expert witness. His data, he told Kleinman, "was with the lawyers."

Soleimani introduced the group to Kleinman, who apologized for sounding like "a bitter conspiracy person" but said she was tired of everyone in town putting their heads in the sand. She was glad these women were finally waking up. "Our municipal code says you can't drill for oil anywhere else in Beverly Hills—except our high school. How stupid can we be? Are we fucking nuts as a community?"

"Jody Kleinman has been an advocate from the beginning," Soleimani added. "We're just trying to join her and show them what it is we want. The city has presented its findings. They claim the school is safe—everything is safe.

"But Venoco has done illegal things. Basically, we do not have any guarantees they won't do it again."

She turned back to the CDM data. It was technical and difficult to understand, she knew, but she had spent the summer analyzing details. "ND" stood for "nondetect." There were six chemical compounds detected in the air, but only when the facility was producing oil. Anyone who took the time to review the data, she said, could see that the results were contrary to what school officials were saying. Not only were the levels of benzene three times higher in April, when the facility was in full production, than in July, when it was producing gas but not oil, but the data also showed increased levels of petroleum-related chemicals in the air above the football field—n-butane, isobutane, ethene, ethane, n-hexane, n-pentane, and propane.

"They knew they were being checked, so they brought the level of production down. We don't know exactly how much, though." She asked: Did you know it's not one well? There are eighteen wells? Did you know that production increased dramatically in the 1980s? Did you know that the school and city earn an annual combined income of nearly $1 million from the wells? Did you know that radioactive iodine is injected into the wells without giving notice to students and parents? Did you know that the AQMD never checked the oil wells until Erin Brockovich showed up?

Drawing a deep breath, Soleimani added: "You don't have to be crazy to be concerned." She acknowledged that the concentrations did not exceed state air-quality standards. But there were many unknowns. "They claim it's all safe," she said. "But safe, to me, is a relative thing. They've proven they pollute the air but they don't pollute it enough to make it illegal. I don't know how bad it is. I know it's not good. I like to believe it's not that bad. But no matter how bad it is, it has to go. That's how I see it: Over my dead body."

She sighed. "I say shame on these people on the school board, saying it's safe when they're not sure. Shame on them. We don't have to sit here and make our kids guinea pigs to wait ten years and find out if Brockovich was right or not."

Soleimani's words fell on the group like an anvil. For a moment, no one spoke. The subtext was clear: the PTA had been bamboozled, a charge many of these women resented. They also didn't want to ruffle feathers. They thought it important not to be antagonistic. After all, the school board members also had children in the school. Better to approach everyone without anger.

A petite blond woman named Myra Lurie spoke up. "I know how emotional this is," Lurie began, explaining that her son ran track and was on the cross-country team. A lawyer, her tone was conciliatory. She was campaigning for a seat on the school board that fall—and looking for compromise.

Like the school board, Lurie wanted additional monitoring by Venoco, but not to shut it down, which would cost the school district money when it could ill afford more cutbacks. California may once have been the "golden" state in terms of its public education system, but expenditures per pupil had fallen precipitously over the years. While New York, for instance, spent nearly $12,000 per public school student, California spent about $7,000, ranking next to last among the ten most populous states. Living in a well-to-do suburb no longer meant that property taxes could subsidize neighborhood schools; court rulings from the 1970s mandated that expenditures be equalized throughout the state for rich and poor school systems alike.

"We need to find things in common and not get sidelined," Lurie added. "I'm friends with Willie Brien and Barry Brucker on the board. I don't feel they're trying to hide anything. It's true they have a lawsuit to fight, and CDM has things to look for. But their kids' safety and health is as important to them as to us.

"If we come in angry and emotional, it will work against us. They don't want to be accused of putting their kids in jeopardy. We can do this calmly and reasonably."

But Lurie's call for calm had the opposite effect. It sounded patronizing to Nelli Emrani, for one, who was irate. She described how insulting it felt when she dared to speak out against the oil wells and was taunted by members of the PTA. "They say, 'For you Persians, we need to translate.' You Persians? No, I don't need translation. This embarrasses me. I become emotional.

"I hear kids saying they're throwing up on the track. There are so many kids complaining. I turn to my American friends for help. I'm a mother. I'm emotional. That's why we react this way. My daughter asks me, 'Mom, will I get sick too?' We don't want to be rude or barbarians. We just want answers."

This was Soleimani's cue. For her, the answer was to unify everyone by distancing themselves from Brockovich and the lawsuit. That was about cancer and the past; this was about educating the community and making the issues public at the next city council meeting.

"How many people have spoken out?" she asked. "Jody Kleinman? Marrina Waks? That's it. Twenty people won't make a difference. Two hundred people will.

"Bring your husband. Bring your mother. Bring your children. Bring two hundred people to the city council meeting."

Only half joking, Janet Morris, an attorney who worked at Jewish Legal Services in the Fairfax district and a 1979 Beverly High graduate, added: "Let's do it Reese Witherspoon's way: Go to your hair salon. Go to the nail salon. It's the absolute truth. With women, that's how you do it. Just drop a little bit of information. That's the best grassroots organizing."

"They're asking for us to rise up," Nelli added. "You need shrewd people in America."

"It's a first step," Janet agreed. "We can go further."

Jody Kleinman ducked out early. The meeting made her feel sick to her stomach because it didn't go far enough. "Instead of backpacks and AP exams, you've got twenty-five mothers talking about benzene levels at the school," she said. "It's fundamentally insane."

The activists' crusade was fraught with conflict from the start. The alliance was uneasy. Soleimani disapproved of Kleinman's in-your-face style and naive insistence that science could provide answers, when it was clear the data could be manipulated to suit political ends. "We have nothing—zilch—to do with Jody Kleinman," she later said. "I wanted this to be separate—a new voice." Kleinman didn't appreciate being excluded from Soleimani's conversations, conducted in Farsi, or her private meetings with Mayor Tom Levyn to discuss buying out Venoco from its lease.

Still, fueled by a shared fury and frustration, they needed each other. There was strength in numbers, Kleinman knew. Soleimani had an inside track to the PTA and the close-knit Iranian community; Kleinman was integral because she had already established herself as the local "toxic nutcase," who had doggedly begun to secure public records. And she was not Persian, important in light of the town's long-simmering culture wars.

"They think I'm the provocateur," Kleinman had said during a strategy session weeks earlier.

"We need you," Emrani said, "because you don't speak Farsi."

"We have Persian power!" Soleimani said.

"Good," Kleinman chimed in. "We have to show them there's a movement afoot."

The "movement" had begun in the car-pool line in front of the high school. Both Mahshid Soleimani and Janet Morris were picking up their sons from a school-sponsored trip to Yosemite National Park. Like everyone else, they assumed that the Tower of Hope couldn't be harmful if all the students at the school were involved in helping to paint it. But the more they learned, the less comfortable they felt. The wife of a cardiologist, Soleimani drew on her husband's medical expertise to help her understand. She took little comfort in the data presented in the USC epidemiology report, which said the cancer incidence of residents in Beverly Hills was normal but said nothing about graduates of the high school, or the CDM reports, which were overseen by the city's defense lawyers to control what tests were conducted at the high school.

She became especially angry after talking to Floyd Leeson, an engineer with the Divison of Oil, Gas and Geothermal Resources, the state agency responsible for the safety of oil wells.

When she called Leeson to complain about the fumes at the oil wells, she recalled, "he told me, 'Lady, if you don't feel comfortable, you should take your children elsewhere.'" When she called him back again, he refused to take her calls because he thought she was "loony" to be worried about the use of radioactive iodine. Only trace amounts were used, he insisted, and they were injected thousands of feet below the surface.

Mahshid Soleimani discovered that asking questions came with a price. Going before the school board one evening, she requested that the issue be placed on its agenda. She was told that the pending litigation made that impossible. One school board member, who was her son's baseball coach, suggested that she leave the school district if she didn't like it; another, who had approached her to host a coffee for her upcoming election campaign, suddenly changed her mind. "Right away, I knew it had to do with what I'm doing here," she later said. "I take it as a compliment."

She kept at it, working the inside. At a PTA Safety Committee meeting, she raised the issue and was told that Masry was a liar. "It's so hush-hush," she later recalled. "When I say it's taboo, that's really what it is. People believe what they're told. Now, all these PTA moms look at me like I'm a monster or I'm stupid."

She drafted long, sometimes raw letters to local officials, demanding answers about her sons' safety. And she studied and challenged PowerPoint presentations meant to explain how innocuous oil drilling was. At a breakfast meeting at the Beverly Wilshire Hotel, sponsored by Venoco and attended by about a dozen local businessmen and PTA parents, she dared to ask about the use of radioactive materials. Again, she felt like an interloper. "It was assumed that if you were against the oil wells," she later said, "you were on Masry's side."

She believed that what she was saying was different. "I'm saying there is not enough evidence to prove the cancers were caused by the oil wells," she said. "But even if there's a little bit of doubt, do not make guinea pigs out of our kids. I don't want to know if they do or don't cause cancer in twenty years. Just stop it right now."

The first step to organizing required that the parents be diligent about doing their homework. They researched state law and learned that a new school in California could not be sited next to an oil well; this one had been grandfathered in. They studied the city's municipal code and discovered that if the oil well operator violated the law, the lease could be terminated by the city. Weren't *six* notices of violation enough?

They pursued a three-pronged attack: a community petition directed at the AQMD to deny giving Venoco a permit for its amine unit; a second petition to the city council in Beverly Hills to shut down the oil wells; and a final push, through both the Los Angeles County district attorney's office and the state legislature, to protect their kids.

"People in Beverly Hills are used to paying the housekeeper to do things for them, to pay the pool man to clean for them," Nelli Emrani said. "They're not used to acting on their own behalf. But this is what we must do now, because we love our kids. That beautiful derrick reminded me of the concentration camps, and they used our children to paint over it? How dare they?"

It felt, to her, like déjà vu all over again.

"Back at home," she continued, remembering her days in Tehran, "we always talked about the politics around oil. Now, here in America, we're talking about oil again from morning to night in our house. We're stuck in the same situation again: oil politics.

"For God's sakes!" she added. "Americans are so forgiving, so naive, compared to Middle Easterners. The oil companies have cheated many nations and many people. Let's make sure our children are safe. Back in our country, we've seen so many changes in the government. It seems history is more open to us, to things that Americans don't see. Or don't want to see."

They grew accustomed to vacant stares and cold shoulders. They begged their friends and neighbors to accompany them to protest at city hall over the summer, but everyone was too busy or had other plans or was on vacation. The town's state of denial reminded Emrani of what it felt like to be a Jew in Tehran just before the revolution in 1979. "It's like that now," she said. "Here, we're trying to bring people to the city council in the middle of Beverly Hills, California—and we can't."

How could they get thousands of signatures in a hurry? They'd split up territories, go door-to-door and hit the Farmers' Market on Sundays. They divvied up the four elementary schools. Emrani would solicit signatures at her synagogue, Sinai Temple. Kleinman would bring petitions to her gym, At Your Side, on Robertson Boulevard.

They faced an uphill battle, though. Since so many of her clients had children at the high school, Kleinman's personal trainer encouraged her to leave a copy of the petition at the gym. After several weeks, though, no one would sign it; people said they were afraid of repercussions for their children at school.

"People think it's no big deal," Jody Kleinman said at the time, "and then I think maybe I'm the crazy one." In any case, she steeled herself with the knowledge that she wasn't alone. Now she had Mahshid and Nelli and Janet and Marrina on her side too.

As they fanned out into their neighborhoods, the dissidents' campaign gained momentum.

Jody Kleinman was having her hair shampooed and her scalp massaged when her cell phone trilled. She lifted her head out of the sink and flipped her phone open. It was Dan Wright, a prosecutor from the Los Angeles County district attorney's Environmental Unit, returning her phone call.

She was thrilled that someone, finally, agreed that something needed to be done.

But he warned her not to get her hopes up. This was not going to be an easy case for him to pursue.

Much as he wanted to file a criminal complaint against Venoco for illegally discharging its hazardous waste into the air, he didn't have the jurisdiction to do so. He told her that since the AQMD was already prosecuting the case as a civil violation, the laws of double jeopardy prevented him from filing a criminal case, too. Plus, he didn't have the backing of his supervisor, because the AQMD refused to refer the case for prosecution. Unless AQMD lawyers deferred to the DA, which was rare, there could be no criminal prosecution.

In the past few years, the forty-year-old deputy DA had been only referred three small-time asbestos-removal cases from the AQMD out of thousands of air pollution violation cases. If the state agency filed first, that precluded Wright's pursuing criminal sanctions.

"My supervisor is going the 'let's not create any waves' route, which they're known for," Wright told Kleinman. "These supervisors get to be supervisors because they don't create waves." He added: "I've warned them this could blow up in their face."

What Dan Wright didn't yet know was that Venoco's lead outside counsel was Robert Philobosian, the former district attorney of Los Angeles and a good friend of Wright's boss, District Attorney Steve Cooley.

That summer, hundreds of families signed petitions, wrote letters of protest, and made urgent phone calls to Barry Wallerstein, the head of the Air Quality Management District. E-mails were flying. Residents watched the developments with excitement and relief, exchanging detailed gossip about evidence on the Internet and calling into AM-radio talk shows.

They pointed out that neither the AQMD nor the city of Beverly Hills had ever regularly monitored the air quality at the high school in the decades that the oil wells had been operating.

And they reminded Wallerstein that the Venoco operation had been shut down twice, once in February for illegal venting of toxic gases and again in April because of a high level of toxic fumes caused by an amine scrubber unit. Since both shutdowns occurred after the AQMD began monitoring the site, and neither the city nor the state agency was willing to commit to monthly monitoring of the air at the high school, the parents questioned how allowing the facility to return to full production was good for their children.

"Why do we need another factor to pollute the air at a site with a population whose immune system is still developing?" one mother asked in her letter.

And why were the AQMD's air-testing results being compared to industrial areas of Los Angeles, such as the City of Industry or Burbank?

"Why can't we get air tests results from neighboring high schools, such as Fairfax or University High, in order to decide if Beverly Hills High School's air quality is normal?" another asked.

If California law forbids a new school from being sited within 1,500 feet of an oil production facility, why allow this facility to continue to exist? they wanted to know.

"Why do we need a lawsuit to prove to us there might be something wrong at Beverly Hills High School?" a parent named Debbi Rashti asked.

What none of the parents understood at the time was that Barry Wallerstein and his deputies were engaged in secret negotiations with Venoco that July. Indeed, after intensive lobbying by Venoco's lawyers, Wallerstein agreed to exempt the company from the California Environmental Quality Act, a state law that requires that a new environmental review be conducted by a company when a public controversy emerges.

"This facility has generated public controversy recently," AQMD engineer Hamilton Stoddard acknowledged in a twenty-eight-page report, "although the applicant indicated that there were no public controversy" concerning the amine unit. Thus, Wallerstein agreed, no controversy existed.

And so, despite the desperate pleas—the petition, the faxes, the barrage of phone calls—from parents in Beverly Hills and the daily influx of requests for media interviews, Wallerstein would once again rely on the word of the company, not the public. Even though his inspectors issued another notice of violation against Venoco—this time for hooking up its amine scrubber unit without a permit after being instructed by the AQMD not to do so—Wallerstein would excuse Venoco.

By narrowly interpreting the law and focusing on a single component of the operation, Venoco once again sidestepped further scrutiny. Wallerstein determined that because the amine unit was a "minor alteration to an existing facility," it would not create a "significant" impact on the school or neighborhood, since, technically, it did not increase production.

When Venoco's lawyer, Gisele Goetz, protested the notice of violation for hooking up a gas-treating unit without a permit, she claimed it was "an unintentional, technical violation by a well-intentioned employee," namely a nightshift operator who unknowingly hooked up a flex-hose to a carbon canister.

According to documents uncovered through a state public records act request, Goetz appealed to the AQMD in a September 16, 2003, letter. "We believe it is fair to comment," she wrote, "that this process is neither strictly legal, strictly regulatory nor strictly technical, but a non-intuitive combination of the three." Despite the tortured legalese, Wallerstein again let Venoco off the hook.

Like scores of other parents, Debbi Rashti quietly moved her daughter out of Beverly that summer.

No one, it seemed, could be held accountable. The AQMD denied it had the authority to shut down the facility, suggesting the issue was really about land use. School board members suggested privately that the city council was really in control.

That meant that the revolt of the PTA moms at city hall would be crucial.

City hall chambers on Rexford Drive in Beverly Hills resemble a film noir set. Golden deco chandeliers descend from a floral-painted ceiling with massive scalloped beams. Rows of mahogany-and-leather benches are framed by black-and-white photographs of former mayors. Behind the elevated dais on which the council members sit, there is a mauve wall and a stained-glass city seal, bearing the town's incorporation date of 1914. The majestic setting didn't quite translate for the handful of civic-minded denizens who faithfully watched the council meetings at home each week on TV, thanks to a local public access station.

On the evening of September 16, 2003, Jody Kleinman, Mahshid Soleimani, and Marrina Waks waited their turn to address the city council, though just about no one had shown up for the meeting. Members of the local crisis-response team from the Maple Counseling Center had come to receive recognition for their volunteer work. And the first-place winner of the local pie-baking contest was awarded a $275 check for her nectarine crumble, the largest cash prize for a pastry in the state of California.

As they did at each public meeting before taking their seats, the five city council members strode up the middle aisle, followed by the city attorney, Laurence S. Wiener, and greeted members of the audience as they passed by. There was a kind of pageantry to the proceedings, including the recitation of the Pledge of Allegiance, which was led by an unsuspecting member of the audience, who would be anointed by Mayor Tom Levyn.

"That number again," Levyn said, fielding calls for his telephone call-in quiz about Beverly Hills that would garner the winner a haircut at the famed Christofe Hair Salon, valued at $400, "is 285-1020."

Levyn loved to ham it up for the cameras. Holding a microphone and mugging for photo ops for the local throwaways allowed him to play the role of master of ceremonies. In recent months, however, his charm had worn thin as he continually recused himself from voting on the city's hotel business. He later admitted it was because of a real estate deal of his own: he had charged a $500,000 "finder's fee" to Merv Griffin, owner of the Beverly Hilton Hotel, for introducing the Hollywood mogul to a businessman who bought his hotel for $130 million—a transaction deemed perfectly legal by the state's Fair Political Practice Commission.

"That's 2-8-5-1-0-2-0," Levyn repeated. He appeared distracted, fiddling with his BlackBerry, when Jody Kleinman stood before him to discuss the oil wells at the high school during the public comment period.

She reminded the city council of Venoco's numerous air pollution violations. "Why aren't the city council and city attorney acting to enforce our municipal code?" she asked, pointing out that the lease agreement allowed for the contract to be terminated prior to its 2016 expiration if improprieties occurred.

"Is it our authority or the school board's authority?" Levyn asked the city attorney.

"The school board is the lessor," Wiener replied. "It's their authority." He said that the local ordinance provided standards for operating an oil well. "We could cite Venoco, it's true. But the lease is with the school district, not the city."

Kleinman, hands on hips, disputed the idea. "The ultimate power lies with the city council," she said, "and they've acknowledged they've illegally vented for twenty days."

Levyn asked again: "Do we have sufficient authority to shut them down?"

The city attorney replied that he did not believe "there is anything that has occurred to date" to do so. He was, in effect, punting.

Kleinman gasped. "How much more breaking of the law do they have to do?"

It was in that moment that Mahshid Soleimani came to believe that she was fighting a losing battle. She had believed that if something was morally wrong, it must be legally wrong, too. Now she knew better.

"None of them has what it takes to do the right thing," she later said. "They're so wrapped up in politics and image." To have any impact, she'd have to take her fight to the streets.

Mahshid Soleimani stood alone in the dark, waiting beneath a crescent moon. It was nearly 7:30 on Wednesday evening, September 24, 2003. She was stationed on South Elm Drive in front of Beverly Vista Elementary School.

Inside, it was Back to School Night at "BV," and the lights from the classrooms made sharp yellow rectangles on the sidewalk. The street was quiet, but in a few moments the parents now inside listening to their children's teachers tell them about the upcoming school year would pour out of the redbrick building. Soleimani waited stolidly behind a folding table she had lugged from her black Lexus SUV, the one with the personalized license plate in honor of her boys, Justin, Brandon, and Jonathan, that read "I ♥ JBJ." She clutched a clipboard and a Bic pen to gather signatures for a petition drive to shut down the oil wells at the high school. Her flashing green eyes were intent. She saw this as her last chance to keep the issue alive. Behind her, there were two signs tacked to a chain-link fence. One read RESPECT EACH OTHER. The other said RESPONSIBILITY STARTS WITH ME.

At last, parents began spilling out onto the sidewalk. "Parents' petition to shut the oil wells?" she asked politely. It was her mantra on this evening.

Sometimes she would pronounce her *w* as a vee, as in "oil vells" or "Vestvood." There was a slight Zsa Zsa–esque quality about her, by turns fetching and lit-tle-girlish, especially the voice. She had learned English by watching TV when she first arrived in America with a degree in management and accounting from Tehran University. She wore a black leather jacket, blue jeans, and stylish black suede boots.

Most hurried by without making eye contact; others stopped and con-versed in Farsi, their native tongue. Still others were confused; they thought the wells had been shut down already, and she informed them that they were back up and running again because the local government agencies had given the all-clear.

"Parents' petition to shut the oil vells?" she asked again. She had already secured more than one hundred names when people arrived two hours earlier. She was determined to present two thousand signatures to the city council, and she wouldn't stop until she got them.

"Get a life!" an angry father sniffed, walking away.

"Learn English!" another muttered.

The antagonism was palpable, not only because she was viewed as a dis-sident in a town that tended to avoid politics but because she was Iranian-born. The antipathy was mutual, especially when the American-born PTA president scrambled by.

"Those son-of-a-bitch PTA moms," Soleimani said under her breath. "They're afraid to sign it and have their names revealed. The fact that I'm a Persian woman makes me less intelligent in their eyes.

"I'll prove them wrong."

The divide between those who signed the petition and those who did not had everything to do with being of Persian descent. Since the Iranian Revolution in 1979 and the fall of the shah of Iran, the influx of Iranians to Beverly Hills had created deep rifts in the community. Never mind that most of the Persians, like Soleimani, were also Jewish, in a town that has long been predominantly Jewish. Beverly Hills, in fact, was originally settled by Euro-pean Jews in the 1920s in response to restrictive covenants that forbade them from buying property in nearby Hancock Park.

When Persians migrated to Beverly Hills, the wealthiest came with suit-cases full of cash and bought property. Some razed European-revival homes, built with Tuscan and Mediterranean influences and colors, and erected tow-ering white flat-front mansions with imposing columns that the locals dis-dainfully called "Persian palaces."

The town's changes have not come without tensions, and some resentment. In recent years, controversies have erupted at public meetings over the abundance of Persian palaces and whether it would be appropriate to have a taste czar dictating questions of architectural style. Some of the town's most progressive stalwarts admitted to their discriminatory attitudes. "I can't stand the brown lipstick," one of the locals sniffed. In mixed company, "Canadian" had become code for "Persian."

Longtime residents told me they didn't trust their Iranian neighbors, because they returned clothing to Saks Fifth Avenue after having worn it to an event. Stereotyping runs rampant: Persians are depicted as a shallow, overindulged, and insular group that distrusts public institutions and is plagued by language problems and apathy, refusing to assimilate. Perhaps in response to the criticism, a local businessman named Jimmy Delshad was elected to the city council in the spring of 2003, the first time an Iranian was voted into local office.

The most serious tempest erupted in March 2003, when a parent named Abraham Assil opposed the school board's plan to allow the city's consultant, CDM, to conduct environmental testing at the high school; he wanted an independent contractor instead. His pleas and those of other Persian families to the school board led some to brand the oil well imbroglio a "Persian issue."

The town's deep divide, though largely unspoken, helped to explain why the oil well crisis failed to gain political traction outside the community. Environmental justice in Beverly Hills was like a Rorschach on how one felt about Iran. "If this were a ghetto school," a longtime resident caustically observed, "the political implications would be too great [to ignore]. Here, we're only killing Persians, so it's okay."

Mahshid Soleimani was fighting that perception. She had met her husband, Touradge, on a blind date arranged by cousins. They first lived in Modesto when he started his cardiology practice, then moved to Beverly Hills in 1989. They spoke in Farsi at home to their sons, who answered in English. Her husband and boys had grown tired of her crusade and how it had taken her away from them.

She hated to think about the fact that Jonathan, now a sophomore at UC Berkeley, had been at the high school for four years and that Brandon, her middle son, had been there since sixth grade as part of a weekly program for gifted students. They had looked into other schools—Malibu High, Palisades High—and had applied to Harvard-Westlake, the private school over the hill where many doctors' children from Beverly Hills attended school. But Justin wasn't accepted.

She approached another parent for his signature.

"You don't believe the crap of the lawyers, do you?" he asked her.

Patiently, she explained how her position was different from Ed Masry's. She didn't think there was enough evidence to prove the cancers were caused by environmental factors. But as parents of current students, she and her friends didn't need to wait for their kids to become guinea pigs "ten or twenty years from now and, oh, by the way, they were right—the rate of cancer at this school is higher than anywhere else." Then she told him that the school district currently made about $350,000 a year from royalties on the wells.

"It can't be worth risking kids' lives for $350,000," he said, adding his name to the list. Another signature.

"*Salome*," she said to him. Like *shalom* in Hebrew, it means "peace."

She stood in the dark, waiting. She'd need massive patience to do what had to be done, again and again. Progress came in tiny steps. "In America," she said, "you're raised to believe this is a land of law: everything is regulated. It's a democracy. But in Iran, that is not how things work. We were born and raised in a country ruled by a dictator. If the son of a shah or his brother wanted to do anything, he could get away with it.

"In America, things are different. Am I naive to be so optimistic?"

By the time they returned to city hall, on Tuesday evening, October 21, 2003—this time with two thousand signatures on their petition to shut the oil well operations down—it was standing room only. Jody Kleinman couldn't believe her eyes: the chambers were packed with the families of high school students, scores of elementary school students and babies in strollers. She thought Soleimani had worked miracles to get all these people to show up.

Looking out at the restless crowd, Vice Mayor Mark Egerman appeared nervous. He had met earlier that day with parents and school officials, so it would be up to him to inform everyone about that meeting and CDM's most recent findings. He said he was very pleased to announce that the latest round of air testing by CDM showed that the high school had no problem whatsoever.

Kleinman and Soleimani rolled their eyes.

"We wish to ensure and maintain that the high school is, in fact, safe for the students," said Egerman, who was one of three lawyers on the council. He was reading from a prepared statement, and his face was beet red. "That is our first priority."

But the PTA moms were at the boiling point. "In story books," Mahshid Soleimani began, "the innocent and pure always prevail and evil is ultimately defeated. David overcomes Goliath.

"But in the real world, in the city of Beverly Hills, the innocent kids are losing to the evil empire of oil operators with their army of lawyers and scientists armed with their legal mumbo jumbo, questionable test result conclusions, and dollar sign as their shield."

The community, she told the council, wanted the oil wells shut down. Enough was enough.

Venoco had admitted to repeatedly "venting" its gases illegally. "That means," she explained, "that the oil company releases its unwanted potentially cancer-causing gasses into the air that our kids breathe."

The two thousand signatures on her petition to shut the operation down, she said, represented the views of parents, alumni, and residents of Beverly Hills—Persian Americans, African Americans, Asian Americans and the other ethnicities that made up the city today. "They might disagree on many different social, political, or religious beliefs," she said, "but they are in agreement that pumping eighteen oil wells on our only high school is wrong and has to come to an end.

"We say no to an industrial zone in the heart of a school zone."

Greeted by thunderous applause and a standing ovation, she pirouetted and curtsied.

Jody Kleinman went next. "I'm here tonight to say it's up to you to close them down," she said, standing before the council at a podium. "Forcing us to trust a repeat offender is ridiculous. This is not acceptable." Why is it okay to operate an oil and gas site so close to the school but nowhere else in the city? she asked. "Apparently," she said, "what's at issue is not the safety of our children but additional revenue for the city of Beverly Hills.

"Mayor Levyn," she said, "your child is a student at our school, like mine. How can you possibly justify a municipal code that prohibits any drilling in Beverly Hills due to health and safety issues—with the one exception being our students' school?"

For a moment, there was silence.

"Are you asking that question?" the mayor wanted to know.

"I'm asking that question," Kleinman replied, "and I want an answer."

The audience went wild with applause.

Levyn said everyone had to decide what was in the best interests of their child. "I have confidence in the science as the council has determined it," he said.

"I'm asking that question," she said again, hands on hips. "And I want an answer." She spoke in patient but insistent cadences, the kind you use in addressing a slightly dull child.

Levyn replied again: "I have confidence in the science as the council has determined it." The mayor didn't mention that night that his friend Skip Miller, the trial lawyer whose firm the city would pay $1 million for his work on the Venoco litigation, would soon become a colleague. In a move the editorial page of the *Beverly Hills Weekly* would describe as a "quid pro quo," Levyn would join Miller's law firm Christensen, Miller, Fink, Jacobs, Glaser, Weil & Shapiro as a partner once Miller signed off on the Beverly Hills case.

Jody asked yet again for the raw data of those tests—data which had never been made public.

"Our lawyers are in constant contact with the experts," the mayor said.

"That's the problem," Kleinman replied.

Even Nooshin Meshkaty, the PTA president of El Rodeo and a scientist at the California Institute of Technology's Jet Propulsion Laboratory, decided to speak before the council that night. She used no notes, no prepared text. She had grown too troubled to remain silent any longer.

"I tried to sit quiet among a lot of other community leaders, attend the meetings, look at the results," she began. Though the test results may appear to look good, she said, the CDM scientists admitted in a closed-door session at city hall that none of the test results took into consideration the age group in question, namely teens in high school.

She took a deep breath. Two of her brothers had died of cancer. "Twenty years from now," she said, "we may find out that this little bit of benzene may cause problems. Venoco has done enough. Many of you are attorneys on the council. If these children were your clients, I know you'd find a way to protect them. Just assume they're your clients."

Children were leaving the school district, she said. Some were attending community college and taking GED exams rather than deal with health risks. Others were fleeing for private schools as the district faced state budget cutbacks. Let's not let this be another reason for people leaving, she added. The city was well known for its fire department, police department. "Let's not forget its schools," she told the council.

Finally, she said aloud what everyone was thinking: "Real estate values will start coming down if people start looking elsewhere for schools."

Just when it seemed that the mothers' campaign was making some headway, the AQMD issued a news release announcing its settlement agreement with Venoco—a $10,000 fine and the promise of a monitoring system to be installed within the next six months, plus a health-risk assessment conducted by the company because of concerns that the facility exceeded a twenty-five-in-a-million cancer risk.

In fact, the air agency had no idea if the monitor would work. In an October 17, 2003, letter to Venoco, obtained through a California Freedom of Information Act request, Mohsen Nazemi, the AQMD assistant deputy executive officer, wrote: "The correlation between actual benzene measurements and total organics is yet to be developed and that data needs to be evaluated to make a final assessment of the efficacy of the warning device."

The warning monitor was little more than a public relations gimmick. According to Venoco's own documents, its monitor was "not an emissions monitor." It was, instead, "a software package installed in the Control Room Computer that utilizes a modem to allow wireless communication with the gas monitor."

Whether the gas monitor would be operational, however, was another question. According to inspection reports on file with the state Division of Oil, Gas and Geothermal Resources, which oversees oil and gas production sites in California, the gas-detection system at the oil wells at Beverly Hills High School had been plagued with problems since 1982, when the Southern California Gas Company first received a permit to run its dehydration plant there.

With expansion of drilling in the early 1980s came trouble, including ten tank-truck trips per day of wastewater disposal and gas monitors that didn't work properly.

In a confidential memo, dated January 15, 1982, a state inspector cautioned that the drilling of a "critical well," meaning one which was in close proximity to a vulnerable population, required that "[e]very precaution must be taken to keep the well under control at all times." But the gas-detection system (among other things) kept malfunctioning.

On August 5, 1986, the gas detectors and a high-level safety switch were not working when checked by state inspectors. On September 19, 1986, the gas-detection system was "not functioning properly" for hydrogen sulfide gas and combustible gas for the power fluid pit. On October 17, 1986, high- and low-level alarms were not functioning. Four months later, a state engineer named Kenneth Carlson refused to approve the system because "gas detectors Nos. 1, 2, 3 and 31 failed to function."

Carlson reported again, in May 1987, that Wainoco Oil Company employees had failed another safety inspection, this one concerning hydrogen sulfide gas in the well cellar. Despite efforts to complete his inspection, Carlson reported that the system could not be tested "due to maintenance repairs by Southern California Gas Company." But Wainoco reported that the equipment was tested "after regular working hours," and state regulators signed off on it.

Two months later, the system was "tested but not approved." The problem? All gas detectors. In July 1991, combustible gas detectors again failed approval by a DOGGR inspector, though he later noted that "all operations comply with CDOG (California Division of Oil and Gas) regulations." The following year, gas detectors in the well cellar and the deep production pit failed safety tests. After another safety inspection in April 1993, state officials wrote to Wainoco about its sloppy practice concerning gas leaks: "During the inspection, the engineer noted the gas detection sensors and monitors were not labeled correctly. The sensors and monitors must be labeled accurately to ensure correct identification of gas leaks."

After Wainoco sold the site to Venoco in 1995, more problems ensued. In April 1996, two combustible-gas detectors failed to be approved by a state engineer. On December 11, 1997, a nitrogen tank line was found leaking by a state oil and gas supervisor. On October 30, 2002, Venoco didn't pass its safety test because gas detectors in the production pit weren't working. The following month, around the same time that an editorial in the school newspaper opined that "THIS SCHOOL STINKS," a state inspector named Melvin Wells noted that three pit gas detectors were "BAD."

I spoke to Wells at the Division of Oil, Gas and Geothermal Resources offices in Cypress to find out what he had meant.

"It means it didn't work," he told me. "We tested it, and it didn't go off." He explained: "Gas detectors have a life span. Sometimes they quit working. You get oil on 'em. Somebody bumps into 'em with a wrench or a shoulder." Instead of tracing every problem, Wells said, he notes problems as "bad" and then the company follows up. For example, he said, Venoco passed its safety test soon after his last inspection when a contractor recalibrated the sensors on the gas detectors.

Wells told me he tried to conduct inspections quarterly or semiannually. But the forty-mile drive from Cypress to Beverly Hills made those safety checks impossible. "I don't get out there that often," he said.

With each passing day, Mahshid Soleimani grew increasingly radical. She pored over public documents that Jody Kleinman had secured from the AQMD and came to believe that the agency was playing fast and loose with its own data. The chemical acetone, for instance, didn't cause cancer, but it could cause headaches and asthma, and according to both CDM and the AQMD, the levels on campus exceeded ambient levels.

She looked up acetone on the Web site of the Agency for Toxic Substances and Disease Registry, part of the U.S. Department of Health and Human Services. "Breathing moderate-to-high levels of acetone for short periods of time," it stated, "can cause nose, throat, lung, and eye irritation; headaches; light-headedness; confusion; increased pulse rate; effects on blood; nausea; vomiting; unconsciousness and possibly coma; and shortening of the menstrual cycle in women."

Soleimani also found a 1988 article published in *Cancer Research* that was authored by two Swedish cancer researchers. Their research found that rats exposed to ethanol and acetone metabolized benzene at rates sixty-five times higher than rats not exposed to those compounds.

In its tests taken directly from Venoco's vent pipe, the AQMD found acetone in the range of five hundred parts per billion, according to a draft report. But in its final report, acetone was listed as "ND"—a nondetect. Soleimani charged that the agency was "manipulating the data."

Worse, she thought, was the AQMD's unwillingness to connect the dots. Even though the agency's own testing showed that acetone was abundant in Venoco's wastewater, AQMD inspectors had been sent on a wild-goose chase, looking for acetone at neighboring Fox Television. In public meetings, the AQMD's Barry Wallerstein dismissed the concerns over acetone. In fact, when he met with Soleimani in her living room, he brought a bottle of nail polish remover with him to illustrate how most people in Beverly Hills might be exposed to the chemical.

Saddened, Soleimani came to believe that nothing would change. "We are living in Beverly Hills," she said. "You think anyone feels sorry for us with our $4 million homes? We're these rich people who have it all." There was a growing sense of powerlessness in the face of all the riches.

What did financial security mean if she couldn't protect her sons? "It burns a hole in my heart," she said, "when I think of them running around that track."

When I asked her if she thought the city or school district would take heed of her efforts, she replied in Farsi: *"Vell Moaltalli."* Translation: "When hell freezes over."

The Gateway Corporate Center in Diamond Bar, California—a five-story glass-and-steel complex that houses government offices, including headquarters of the South Coast Air Quality Management District—is painted green and ivory and is situated on a hillside overlooking the Pomona Freeway, about forty miles east of Beverly Hills.

It was nothing but stubborn pride that led Mahshid Soleimani, Nelli Emrani, and Jody Kleinman there on Friday morning, January 9, 2004. They arrived in typical L.A. fashion—separately, in their own cars—to testify before the agency's governing board, a twelve-member panel of elected officials and political appointees who met in a cavernous high-tech auditorium with a giant television screen, a state-of-the-art sound system, and plush theater seats.

At issue was the agency's proposed new rule, 1148.1, billed as a precautionary measure to increase inspection and maintenance for the 3,600 oil wells in L.A. located near "sensitive receptors," regulatory vernacular for children and the elderly. The rule also provided for quicker cleanup if a liquid or gas leak was discovered. The idea was to reduce "fugitive emissions" from oil and gas facilities throughout southern California, by prohibiting well-gas venting.

A month earlier, the Beverly High soccer moms had testified in support of the new rule during a public-comment hearing. Soleimani and Kleinman were surprised to discover that they were the only members of the public to show up that day. To them, "public comment" was a misnomer; it was really "industry comment." They listened that day as a parade of about two dozen lobbyists and lawyers, working for oil and gas companies or their trade associations, the California Independent Petroleum Association and the Western States Petroleum Association, lined up to give their input on Rule 1148.1.

Soleimani shook her head. She had a bad feeling about what was about to happen that morning. Not to mention a crushing headache. Behind her sat DOGGR's Floyd Leeson, the man who refused her phone calls, and his boss, Richard Baker.

Leeson fingered the brim of his yellow trucker's hat. Baker strode to the podium to address the board.

He leaned into the microphone. "It seems astonishing to me," Baker said in a caustic tone, "that an organization proposing a rule that would have a profound effect on the oil industry would not want to work with the one regulatory agency that has eighty years of experience working with and regulating California's oil and gas industry."

An AQMD engineer disputed Baker's allegation, saying that DOGGR had, in fact, been consulted. This was a squabble between two warring government agencies, one that policed the air around oil wells and the other that policed the subsurface.

The rule, Baker continued, would create more deserted wells because of the added costs of regulation. "It raises very serious public and safety concerns: unattended wells, leakage due to lack of well maintenance, vandalism, spills, a loss of revenue to the state, and a loss of oil and gas production in California." Urging the board to postpone action on the new rule and to rewrite it with more input from the oil industry, he added: "In light of the recent election of Governor Schwarzenegger, who is currently working with all interested groups in California to make California more business-friendly, this is the only reasonable and fair approach to take in order to address the industry's concerns and protect the public."

Soleimani was livid—not because of Baker's tirade but because the new rule established a leak limit of five hundred parts per million of volatile organic chemicals at oil wells: how could the AQMD say that Beverly High students were safe when their own inspectors found leaks from rusted equipment that were as high as five hundred thousand parts per million?

"My most important question here," she said, "is how do you guarantee safety and the well-being of our children at that school with the oil operation back in full bloom without any of these cautionary rules in place?" She returned to her seat as AQMD chief Barry Wallerstein took over.

Venoco's violations, he said, were from leaks at the point of the equipment, not in the "breathing zone" on the athletic fields. Most of the gaseous emissions consisted of methane, which he viewed as harmless, and only a small percentage of benzene. Monitoring of air samples on the campus by AQMD staff, he added, did not show any significant abnormalities in air quality.

Soleimani raced back to the podium to dispute Wallerstein. Methane gas may not be toxic, but it is explosive. As for the amount of benzene in the vented gas, that was information denied to the public. Records Kleinman had received from the AQMD that detailed the content of the gas had been redacted by the agency because the company claimed it was a "trade secret."

William Burke, the head of the agency's governing board, cut her off before she could even speak. "You're through!" Burke shouted at her. "You're through!"

"Can I—"

"No, you're through," he interrupted. Then, to Wallerstein, he said: "Keep going."

Wallerstein explained that given the community's concerns, a fence-line monitor would be installed. If high levels were detected, an alarm would be triggered to give added assurance to families, faculty members, and residents—an approach recommended to him by the president of the Beverly Hills school board.

Outside the AQMD front entrance, with its logo of a dove, Baker was smoking a cigarette and conferring with Leeson. Before the hearing had ended, the governing board had voted to postpone action on its new rule—precisely the kind of delay that Baker had sought on behalf of the industry he regulated.

Leeson wagged his finger at Kleinman, as if she were a naughty child who needed to be disciplined.

"Look at them," Kleinman said, peering from the foyer through the front door at the guys from DOGGR. "They're so damned pleased with themselves."

Soleimani approached Leeson outside.

"You don't have to be so nasty," she said to him.

"Let's not even start," he said.

"You don't have to be rude to me. Why do you have to be rude?"

"Let's not even talk," he told her.

She turned to walk away. "I do this for my children," she said.

Baker joined in. "That's what makes this country so great—you do it for your children."

"Yeah, God bless America," Leeson said, laughing with derision.

Soleimani huffed off. What's the use of even talking to them? she thought.

Now it was Nelli Emrani's turn. "I left my country because of oil, and now it's oil again that's causing us problems," she said to Leeson.

"Are you with her?" Leeson wanted to know. "Whenever she calls the office, I say, 'If it's Mrs. Soleimani, I'm not here.'" He eyed Emrani. "Who are you?"

"I'm Nelli," she said.

Leeson tried to cajole her. "Nelli, like the rapper?" he asked.

"No, I'm not the rapper," she replied. "But I can think of something to wrap you in."

Leeson grinned. "I'm sure you can."

In the weeks that followed, the issue that had ignited the whole controversy in Beverly Hills, namely Venoco's venting its waste gas at the high school's athletic field, quietly reared its head again. Only this time, the implications were clear. So long as no one noticed or bothered to complain, the practice could continue indefinitely, thanks to legal loopholes.

Even though Venoco's settlement agreement with the AQMD expressly prohibited it from releasing oil field gas into the atmosphere at Beverly Hills High School, internal documents show that the agency's own inspectors thought otherwise. In a January 21, 2004, e-mail to her supervisor, an air quality inspector named Jeannette Holtzman wanted to know if venting was permissible.

She wrote: "It's my understanding that venting is okay if it is within the leak standards and time periods for repair. Is that correct? Also, Sally at Venoco wanted to know if sending the last bit of gas to the vent stack is preferable to venting at ground level. Let me know when we can meet to discuss this."

The problem of what constituted acceptable leak standards and time periods for repair was not limited to questions about venting toxic gas at Beverly Hills High School. In fact, during the administration of George W. Bush, the U.S. Environmental Protection Agency had issued a new rule that exempted 1,300 coal-fueled power plants and 17,000 factories, refineries, and chemical plants from having to comply with a provision of the federal Clean Air Act, known as New Source Review. The rule allowed for increased emissions during repairs or "routine maintenance." Even more astounding, the EPA excused companies from installing up-to-date pollution controls.

In March 2006, a federal appeals court in Washington, D.C., would rule that the regulation, which had been challenged by the states of California and New York and some environmental groups, was illegal. "Only in a Humpty-Dumpty world," the court noted, could the law be read otherwise.

But for now, in Beverly Hills, it was business as usual.

In a remarkable handwritten memo from Holtzman, obtained through a California Freedom of Information Act request, the air quality inspector apparently got her answer, and it had more to do with keeping the lid on public outrage than with taking precautions on behalf of sensitive receptors: "can vent up stack," she noted, "but possible PR *repercussions.*"

CHAPTER NINE

CHERNOBYL, 90212

Not all of the cancer victims in Beverly Hills were graduates of the high school. Many lived in the neighborhood nearby, which was largely made up of apartment buildings and condominiums. The locals called the area "Baja Beverly Hills" because it was on the south side of town. In fact, some even suggested that the dirty little secret of the oil wells was that had they been situated "north of the tracks," where the town's wealthy and powerful resided, they'd have been shut down long ago. Contrary to popular lore, the high school was in the 90212 zip code—less pricey and more middle class than the privileged 90210 enclave of television fame.

Lee Bova lived kitty-corner to the high school, on Spalding and Olympic. You could see the Tower of Hope and steam from the power plant from her living-room window. Her apartment, located in a charming two-story brick-and-stucco building fashioned around a courtyard and pool, was built in 1937 to service executives and employees of the 20th Century Fox studios nearby. The mineral rights to the oil that flowed beneath her home belonged to the building's original owners, John Wayne and Fred MacMurray.

A short, affable woman with red hair and wire-rimmed glasses, she had moved to Beverly Hills from New York in 1987 to see if she could, as she put it, "catch the caboose of nighttime television" after working as an actress on the TV soap operas *Guiding Light* and *One Life to Live.* She chose the area for its public schools, and her three children, all of whom were healthy, attended Beverly High in the 1980s and early 1990s.

Bova found work in a couple of episodics, what she called "middle-aged women parts: snoopy landladies, rich bitches, meddling mothers-in-law, or dying people." She recalled: "I once was a dead person coming back with their reported will so Dr. Kevorkian wouldn't go to jail." But the acting roles were hard to come by, and as her children went off to college, she returned to school too, and earned a master's degree in psychology and, later, a doctorate.

Just as she hung out a shingle to practice psychotherapy shortly after Christmas 2001, she was diagnosed with non-Hodgkin's lymphoma, stage IV, meaning it was in her bone marrow. She was surprised because no one in her family had ever had cancer. "I call it a real estate diagnosis," she quipped. "Unlike breast cancer, where if you're stage III, you're already writing a will. With this cancer, it's location, location. A little presence in the bone marrow, and that renders it stage IV." Hers was considered "low-grade" because she remained asymptomatic and had fewer than 15 tumors, the largest of which was only 2.1 centimeters in diameter.

Of course, she was curious how she got her cancer, especially in light of recent research from the Fred Hutchinson Cancer Research Center in Seattle which concluded that exposure to polychlorinated biphenyls (PCBs) and furans may increase the risk of non-Hodgkin's lymphoma. But she didn't have a clue if such a study was applicable to her case.

Bova felt that Beverly Hills was a closed community. After she clicked onto the Masry & Vititoe Web site, she tried calling city hall to ask if a committee could be formed to investigate allegations about the oil wells. She left a message for the city manager but never heard back. Meanwhile, her cat Bobo was diagnosed with lymphoma and died. In case anyone was interested, she kept a sample of his blood in her fridge. "I wouldn't be surprised if they keep denying, denying, denying—this is how cynical I am about the city—while pulling their kids out and sending them to Crossroads or Harvard-Westlake," she said.

Another resident, who had lived in Bova's building adjacent to Roxbury Park, was Tiffany Smith. A star hurdler from Springfield, Massachusetts, Smith attended UCLA on a track scholarship in the 1980s. During the time she lived across the street from Beverly High, she worked out at the track after work and on weekends to qualify for the Olympics. In October 2002, shortly after the birth of her son, Kyle, she noticed a lump on her neck and consulted a doctor, who asked if she was more tired than usual. She had a new baby with colic: who wouldn't be more tired? A biopsy proved inconclusive; she had half of her thyroid gland removed.

As it turned out, Smith was one of the lucky ones. She didn't have cancer, but she would need to take thyroid medication for the rest of her life.

"You could see the smokestacks from our living-room window," she recalled. "You never can conclude definitively if one caused the other, but it's worth trying to find out.

"My concern is five years from now—what may happen later, since I ran on that track every weekend. When I phoned Brockovich's office, they said the number of people with thyroid growths was incredible. I filled out the paperwork. It just seems too much of a coincidence."

Another thyroid cancer scare in Beverly Hills had preceded Erin Brockovich's arrival in town. In 1997, nine teenage girls—all members of the same soccer team who played at Roxbury Park—were diagnosed with thyroid cancer; all had surgery within two years of each other. All their doctors told them the same thing: it was a coincidence. Lisa Lewis, a 1999 graduate of the high school, was one of them. "I don't feel the need to bankrupt the city for what happened to me five years ago," she said. "I feel Masry is after the money—not what really caused it. If you sit down with a clear head and look at it, it's not abnormal. Three hundred cancers over a span of thirty years. People get cancer. It happens."

Privately, many doctors in town expressed concern about the existence of the oil wells at Beverly Hills High School. They agreed that it was absurd to have an industrial complex so close to a school, but they disputed that the medical literature was conclusive about increased rates of cancer from petroleum operations. One oncologist I spoke with said that to suggest a link between Hodgkin's disease and oil wells was "pure caca." Many who worked at Cedars-Sinai Medical Center would stand on the bridge between the hospital and the medical towers and observe another oil derrick, run by the Stocker Oil Company, next to the Beverly Center shopping mall. Publicly, though, few were willing to risk their standing in the community to speak out about either one.

One of those few was Dr. Abraham Waks. A professor of internal medicine at UCLA and staff physician at Cedars-Sinai, the sixty-seven-year-old Waks was born in Jerusalem and, after teaching at Tel Aviv Medical School, moved to the United States in 1975 for a sabbatical in hypertension and nephrology, and stayed. He and his Russian-born wife, Marrina, a concert pianist, and their two daughters had lived in Beverly Hills since 1989. With his thick Hebrew accent and slightly rumpled appearance, marked by oversized glasses, baggy suits, and a large mole on his upper lip, Abraham Waks could have been sent from central casting as the man most likely to offend the gussied-up sensibilities of Beverly Hills denizens.

Waks believed it wasn't surprising that the prevalence of some cancers would be greater among well-educated, higher-socioeconomic populations. The high incidence of breast cancer among women in Mill Valley was a perfect example. Better access to medical support and diagnoses could partly explain it. Still, he didn't see that as a reason to do nothing. He and his wife believed their only choice was to "make noise" about the need for continuous monitoring of the oil wells.

It was obvious to Waks why his fellow physicians kept quiet. "Of course, it's economics," he said, sitting with his wife in their small living room on a Sunday afternoon. "It's the money that Beverly Hills gets from it. It's the value of property. It's just to get their conscience quiet with what happens with the kids in all this. They try, with mixed results, to *not* look at the danger. Otherwise, why should you keep your kids there? They don't want to know. Or they don't want to say.

"If you could measure something really bad that happened there, everything would change. But it's almost impossible to prove something; the exposure is not permanent. That's why it makes it so hard to prove."

He added: "We have a lot of cancer in the neighborhood, and what we should try to do is not to say, 'Oh, it's nothing at the high school.' We should try to get the numbers down. Why are they high? There are multiple reasons, but mainly environmental factors. It can be radiation. It can be pollution. Everything contributes something. The approach for public health should be to try to lessen the exposure and pollutants. What happens here is the opposite—and I cannot understand it."

"When it comes to the children," added Marrina Waks, "this chapter will go down in history as 'The Silence of Beverly Hills.'"

For Abraham and Marrina Waks, the political was personal—starting with a lock of hair.

Even before there was any talk of a lawsuit, they were worried about their 13-year-old daughter, Shelly, who suffered from recurrent seizures and had been diagnosed with persistent development disorder (PDD), a form of autism. To rule out heavy-metal exposures as a cause, they had her hair analyzed. Unlike blood testing, hair analysis indicates long-term exposures. The results showed that both Shelly and her older sister, who had graduated from Beverly High in 2000, had high levels of uranium in their bodies. But where was it from?

Marrina vowed to find out. Late at night, after finishing her work as director of Children of the World, a children's choir which had performed at the Olympics and on *The Tonight Show,* she surfed the Web, tapping in key words, like "uranium danger"—and out popped sites about oil wells. The Waks family lived in a modest Spanish-style home on South Wetherly Drive, a block and a half from the BreitBurn oil-and-gas operation on Pico Boulevard, which had expanded its drilling program to operate twenty-four hours a day. Shelly's old nursery school was nearby.

Shortly after they made the link between oil wells and possible radiation exposure, the Wakses learned about Ed Masry and Erin Brockovich's allegations, connecting toxic chemicals at the oil wells at Beverly High to the illnesses of former teachers and students between about 1977 and 1996. But the Wakses suspected that Masry and Brockovich had it wrong. They believed that radioactive materials found naturally near oil wells or that are injected into wells as part of the extraction process might have done the damage, given the excess numbers of thyroid cancer, which is caused only by radiation exposure. (Thyroid cancer often does not manifest itself for several years after exposure but is usually very treatable, by surgery, chemotherapy, hormone treatment, or, ironically, radiotherapy.)

The Wakses, like Mahshid Soleimani, especially worried that radioactive iodine, which is regularly injected into oil wells to check for leaks in casings, might be a culprit, since it concentrates in the thyroid gland. Because the thyroid needs iodine to function normally, and cannot tell the difference between stable and radioactive isotopes, iodine-131 contributes to thyroid cancer more than to other types of cancer.

But the main danger from the oil fields, they believed, was not from iodine-131, which has a short life; it was from high levels of naturally occurring radioactive materials (NORMs), which have a half-life of millions of years and could potentially concentrate in soil and pipes running beneath the school and city.

It was not a far-fetched concern. In New Orleans, a pipe worker with leukemia discovered in 1996 that the land where he worked was contaminated with NORMs; the property had been used by ExxonMobil to clean pipes of radioactive material generated during oil production. Ten years later, ExxonMobil would appeal a $225 million verdict awarded to a judge who leased the land and discovered it had been polluted with radiation. The company had argued in court that the amount of contamination was not enough to be an immediate threat to public health—an argument rejected by the U.S. Supreme Court.

At some oil-field sites, the pipes and tanks that handle large volumes of "produced water" can become coated with scale deposits that contain radium. The accumulation of radium in oil-field equipment in the United States first became apparent in the 1980s, when scrap-metal dealers began to routinely detect unacceptable levels of radioactivity in shipments of oil-field pipe.

Looking at all the different kinds of cancer in the community—lymphomas, leukemia, and lung, testicular, and thyroid cancers—Abraham Waks believed that the only common causative mechanism was radiation. And there was also the epidemiological evidence: the USC Keck School of Medicine study by Wendy Cozen showed that there was a threefold excess of papillary thyroid cancer among young men in Beverly Hills, which could not be due to chance alone.

The first night that Marrina and Abraham Waks appeared before the school board, requesting an investigation to see if oil drilling had unleashed gamma radiation at the high school, they were broadcast live on KBEV, the student-run TV station that was aired on a local access station in Beverly Hills. It was Tuesday evening, April 29, 2003, and they were both quite nervous, especially Marrina, who was self-conscious about her accent, tinged with the inflections of both Russia and Israel, where she grew up.

"Our concerns have nothing to do with the motivation and intentions of Mrs. Erin Brockovich and her people," Marrina Waks said. "It should not be an excuse. This issue needs to be dealt with—for the sake of our children. We know you care about your children as much as we do. Please take the time to research this issue and not to rely only on people that their main worry is the lawsuit."

Since NORMs last for decades, she said, students might be needlessly exposed on the softball field when oil pipes were cleaned or removed just yards away. Oil companies use weights that contain depleted uranium to pull logging tools toward the bottom of wells and isotopes, such as I-131, to search for new sources and measure the amount of oil.

When Abraham Waks approached the podium that night, the school board members appeared agitated. Willie Brien, a well-respected physician on the board whose grandfather was the U.S. Supreme Court Justice Warren

Burger, looked especially annoyed. No other doctor in town had expressed any apprehension about the oil wells. Waks was the first to do so publicly.

Wearing a suit and tie, he had the disheveled look of an absentminded academic, his thinning hair askew and his voice reed thin. But his low-key manner belied his message. What he had to say was, in fact, alarming.

Waks compared the thyroid cancer rate in Beverly Hills to Chernobyl, the 1986 nuclear disaster which occurred when a reactor in the now-independent state of Ukraine melted down, throwing large quantities of radioactive isotopes into the atmosphere. One of these, radioactive iodine, is absorbed by the thyroid gland, particularly in very young children, where it can cause cancer, in some cases many years later. Medical studies about Chernobyl have shown that children are the most vulnerable group of people to thyroid injury due to radioactive fallout.

Referencing a 1999 study published in the *British Journal of Cancer,* Waks said that the incidence of thyroid cancer among young Ukrainian children after the Chernobyl accident was ten times greater than normal. But thyroid cancer rates among Beverly High alumni, he claimed, exceeded rates for Russian children by a factor of four. "It's even higher than Chernobyl," he said simply.

It was as if the air had been sucked out of the room.

Reminding the panel that children were once routinely radiated for head lice, for enlarged tonsils, for acne, and even for checking shoe sizes, Abraham Waks suggested it would now be prudent to distribute to students inexpensive radiation badges worn by medical technicians to monitor current exposures, since there was no way to reliably determine past ones.

He hadn't yet completed his presentation when he was chastised by school board president Barry Brucker for exceeding his three-minute time limit.

"He was so mad," Waks later recalled. "He just said, 'Your time's over. Your time's over.'"

The board, in accordance with state law that prohibits comment on items that are not on the agenda, said nothing in response. Then, in an odd moment of surreal pique, board member Myra Demeter congratulated a PTA president on her son's bar mitzvah. "A big mazel tov," she said, smiling.

"And the whole community is invited," Barry Brucker joked.

Abraham and Marrina Waks had now achieved persona non grata status in Beverly Hills. That fact was made amply clear when I later asked the superintendent what she thought of Dr. Waks's testimony that night. She said she had no memory of it.

Week after week, Marrina Waks returned to the school board to express her worries about the use of radioactive isotopes at the oil wells. She was becoming a standard fixture at public meetings—and a major headache for Beverly Hills.

One evening, she reminded school officials that the city's most recent water-quality report noted that local drinking water included radioactive contaminants "which can be naturally occurring or be the result of oil and gas production." If the amount of radioactive contaminants was large enough to be detected when testing a small water sample diluted in millions of gallons of water, she asked, shouldn't this fact be enough to establish independent testing and monitoring at the high school?

On another evening, she quoted from a Harvard School of Medicine study reporting that fatalities among workers in the oil- and gas-extraction process are higher than deaths for workers from all other U.S. industries combined. At a minimum, she said, since parents had never received notice about the use of radioactive materials at the oil well site, why not delay injecting iodine-131 into the wells until students were not there so as to minimize exposure?

Her campaign was unrelenting. She called the press. She contacted her elected officials. One senate staffer described her as "the most annoying person I've ever had to deal with in ten years on this job." But she was also effective.

As a result of her efforts, city, school, and Venoco officials secretly stipulated that "iodine-131 will not be used during the time when school is in session." According to documents uncovered through a state Freedom of Information Act request, Venoco further agreed—for the first time—"to coordinate with the District to conduct such testing on the first day of Spring Break next year to provide the maximum amount of time between the use of Iodine-131 and reopening of school following Spring Break."

Not long after the *Los Angeles Weekly* published a piece entitled "Radioactive High," Waks persuaded investigators from the radiological branch of the state Department of Health Services to take measurements for thorium, radium, and uranium on the Venoco site, the track, the baseball diamond, the tennis courts, and the athletic fields. Tests were also conducted to determine indoor radon concentrations.

The investigation concluded that radiation did not exceed normal levels at Beverly Hills High School. "There is no evidence," the report stated, "that the Venoco site has caused an increase in radioactive materials or radiation either on the high school campus, or at the Venoco site adjacent to the campus."

If most residents took that report as good news, the Wakses viewed it as a whitewash. The mapping survey to determine if there were elevated radiation levels was conducted on the top six to twelve inches of soil, but the report itself pointed out that the soil at the school "might have been brought in from locations other than the immediate area." Abraham Waks said it was like taking a culture after starting a patient on antibiotics.

They also questioned the wisdom of looking for I-131 a year after it had been injected into the wells, since it has a half-life of just eight days. To test for the presence of I-131 so long after its application, they felt, was "useless." The investigators also noted a high reading for thorium, but it was dismissed in the report because of its proximity to the concrete block wall separating Venoco from the softball field. Mysteriously, five of twelve field measurements for radioactive concentrations could not be quantified.

Marrina Waks asked: Why were the tests conducted after the oil pipes, which might have been contaminated, were removed and replaced with new ones? And there was one critical question that had been left unanswered: how often were radioactive materials used at the site? There were conflicting reports. While state oil and gas officials required the use of I-131 every other year to check for water leaks, the company admitted to applying it twice a year. Initially, the state Health Department report stated that Venoco "usually performs this I-131 logging procedure two times per year." But the words "twice a year" would be crossed out and later changed to "once every other year," with the notation: "Correction made 11/05/03."

The changes, Marrina Waks believed, provided further proof that the tests were "fake." The frequency of the use of the I-131 was not a trivial issue, since it reflected the amount of radioactive materials students might have been exposed to in the past. Even so, health officials insisted that the amount of radioactive iodine used was so tiny—less than the amount used to treat thyroid cancer in medical labs—that its accidental release would be too small to make any measurable difference to health.

The Wakses believed that even low doses of radiation raised long-term risks of cancer and birth defects and were not worth the benefits of their use at oil wells, especially those so close to children. The U.S. Committee on the Biological Effects of Ionizing Radiation, convened by the National Academy of Sciences, acknowledged in 2005 that "the smallest dose has the potential to cause a small increase in risk to humans."

"There are so many questions and nobody to answer them," Marrina Waks said. "We believe the parents have a right to know the truth."

The frustration of Marrina and Abraham Waks in securing basic information was understandable. After meeting with them, I set out to learn what radioactive materials are used at well sites, how often, and who regulates their use.

First I spoke with an inspector in the radiological health branch at the State Department of Health Services. He explained that even though his agency provides licenses to service companies to use radioactive materials, it does not conduct testing to oversee their use. He said the oil well site at Beverly High had probably *never* been inspected. Another health department employee agreed that the Wakses' concerns were justified: "We don't have to be nuking these kids' thyroids," the employee, requesting confidentiality, told me.

Robert Miller, a health department spokesman, offered the official response: "We follow Nuclear Regulatory Commission guidelines when we do licensing," he said. "We inspect periodically to make sure they're following regulations."

How often?

"I don't know," he said.

I was then referred to Kathleen Kaufman of the Los Angeles County Health Department's radiological branch, which theoretically oversees the use of radioactive isotopes. Since oil-well service companies may be based in one county but work in another, they receive statewide permits. As a result, Kaufman told me, they fall outside her purview.

Not only had she never inspected an oil well site in Los Angeles but she had no idea that radioisotopes were used to trace for leaks in wells until I asked her about it.

"I really don't know the process," she said. "Los Angeles County doesn't get involved." She told me she had neither jurisdiction nor authority on the use of I-131 at oil wells. Even so, it was her responsibility to inspect work sites, including medical facilities, to make sure that licensees complied with state and federal law.

Since the radioactive tracers are injected thousands of feet belowground, she added: "I don't see how this could be a risk on the track for the students." As for parents' outrage that they were not notified about the use of radioactive materials, Kaufman said posting requirements are enforceable only if the radiation area is accessible to individuals at a dose of five millirems per hour. Since Venoco's contractors used a fraction of that amount—less than three millicuries per application—notification was not required.

Kaufman then referred me back to the state's radiological health branch. This time, I was told that I'd need to gain clearance from a public health information officer before I could speak with a compliance officer.

I then formally filed a public records request, asking for documentation, notices of violation and all correspondences concerning the use of radioactive materials at the oil wells at Beverly High, including I-131, cobalt-60, americium-241, cesium-137, curium, radium, tritium, and thorium. My request was denied.

I tried a second time.

Again, my request was denied.

Both times, the stated reason for the denial was the same. I was told that the "release of information regarding current radioactive material licensees might jeopardize security and public safety in light of the events of September 11, 2001."

Homeland security, in other words, would trump the public's right to know.

I tried a third time through the agency's lawyers. This time, they admitted they had no records concerning the oil wells at Beverly Hills High School. More specifically, the agency "failed to identify any such records or documents in our possession." That could mean that no one bothered to look. Or that the records had been destroyed; the law requires they be kept only for up to three years.

What was becoming clear was that there was no evidence to indicate that health authorities had ever been to Beverly Hills High School to oversee the use of radioactive materials at its oil wells—a practice dating back thirty years. In the 1970s, the federal Safe Drinking Water Act codified oil field injection operations, and the EPA was charged with overseeing its implementation. In California, however, that responsibility had already fallen to the state's Division of Oil and Gas in the Department of Conservation.

"We were way ahead of them already," DOGGR engineer Floyd Leeson explained. "We were given primacy to oversee injection operations of oil fields. We've been in charge of the program for thirty-odd years." Historically, water injection to help produce oil dates back to the 1940s, when California's Department of Conservation began regulating oil company operations. There are no clear-cut standards for how often surveys are conducted. Each well is given a different time frame. Some steam wells are checked once every five years; wells that are considered "critical"—closer to sensitive populations, such as children and the elderly—are surveyed more frequently. Some oil companies even run them monthly.

"We continue to this day—until the lunatics there are trying to make a scene about it." The "lunatics" he referred to were Abraham and Marrina Waks and Jody Kleinman.

Leeson believed that since I-131 has a half-life of eight days, it's "gone in no time flat."

"Realistically," he added, once it's injected into the well, "it doesn't come up again."

In the months that followed, when the oil wells were injected with radioactive iodine again, health inspectors would monitor the air for radioactive emissions for the first time. Given the small amounts of isotopes used, no one thought that radiation could be detected.

They would be wrong.

On Monday morning, April 5, 2004, Kathleen Kaufman, the director of radiation management for the county health department who had no idea radioisotopes were used at oil wells, reluctantly arrived at Beverly Hills High School with Geiger counter in hand. In an e-mail the Friday before, she had warned her colleagues that some parents and the media might be present. She also provided last-minute advice about lugging heavy monitoring equipment there "in case I win the lottery and don't show up."

Kaufman was convinced that no problem existed at the high school. The amount of radiation energy absorbed by the body is measured in millirem. The average American gets about three hundred millirem a year from background radiation; the amount of radiation absorbed by the body from a chest x-ray is about 6 millirem. Health physicists agree on limiting a person's exposure beyond background radiation to about one hundred millirem per year from all sources. As Kaufman understood it, Venoco annually injected trace amounts of I-131 in liquid form to test for well leaks, thousands of feet belowground. How could that possibly get into the air?

It was the first day of spring vacation when, as agreed upon by lawyers for Venoco, the city, and the school district, the oil company would run a water-injection test, using radioactive tracers. Half a dozen lawyers would witness the procedure run by a contractor for Venoco, along with Kaufman and her colleague, Robert Greger, from the state radiological bureau, plus Venoco's PR front man, Mike Edwards, who had invited Jody Kleinman and Marrina and Abraham Waks too.

Edwards was proud of his operation and felt he had nothing to hide. He was certain that this tour would finally put to rest the worries of Kleinman and the Wakses. He had also invited *Beverly Hills Courier* editor Norma Zager. And, of course, Floyd Leeson, the engineer who believed Venoco should be "a low priority—low view—because they're one of the best-engineered facilities there is.

"But the crazies have the company so messed up, there's all kind of difficulties."

Leeson was a pragmatist. He viewed the use of I-131 for the water-injection survey in economic terms, not public health ones. "It's very expensive to pump this stuff down the hole," he later explained, referring to I-131. The job of the water is to push oil to the well. If the water comes right back, in a process called "breakthrough," it's a sign that the well is no longer economically viable and should be shut down.

Jody Kleinman shooed her black Lab, Riley, back onto the whitewashed living room floor, where the dog stood nearby her Andy Warhol painting of Richard Nixon, his face painted green like the Wicked Witch of the West. Then she clicked her red front door shut and hopped into her hybrid Honda. She backed down the brick driveway that Monday morning and eased onto Ambassador, a tree-lined cul-de-sac dotted with giant eucalyptus, until she reached Benedict Canyon Boulevard. She turned right on the road that served as a thoroughfare through northern Beverly Hills, and right again on Bedford Drive, passing the mansions that the tour buses drove by everyday.

The neighborhood's residential elegance melted into the commercial boutiques of downtown, along Santa Monica Boulevard. Ahead, the morning sun shone from the glittering towers that defined the architectural silhouette of the high school's skyline. It was Century City, the enclave of skyscrapers that served as headquarters to many of the most high-priced law firms and business interests in Los Angeles.

Kleinman glanced at the dashboard clock. Shortly after eight, early for her appointment. But already, she knew that this would not be a normal day. And she needed to be early to offset her anxiety about what lay ahead.

After more than a year of fighting, this would finally be her first chance to *see* the Venoco site. Not only was this the first day of spring break; sundown that evening would mark the beginning of Passover, and she had about twenty people coming over for a seder.

But she had promised Marrina Waks that she would come to act as a witness during the I-131 injection-test survey. Radiation and Exodus, she laughed to herself. Like the Hagaddah said—*dayenu,* enough already.

Kleinman parked on Spalding Drive, just east of the school. She hurried along Olympic Boulevard, the busy road by the football field that bordered Venoco. At the gate on Olympic she saw Mike Edwards, the Venoco spokesman, and noticed that the contractors and lawyers were already inside the property. Edwards led her to the Heath Avenue entrance to wait in the alley, next to the Century City Medical Building, until the Wakses arrived.

At 8:40 a.m., Edwards brought them inside the gate. He handed them goggles and helmets for protection and told them they would not be allowed to take photographs or videotape. Then he gave them a tour of the site.

Standing there, amid the clanging and banging and whirring and petrochemical fumes, they could barely believe their eyes—an industrial landscape of pipelines, wells, generators, compressors, and wastewater tanks sat just a few feet from the softball field and track. It was one thing to hear about it; it was quite another to see it and inhale the noxious odors.

They spotted a blue van, marked Welaco, and two unmarked white pickup trucks carrying the radioactive iodine in metal boxes, which were also unlabeled. Standing about five feet from the van, the parents were introduced to Kathleen Kaufman from the county health department. She handed Marrina Waks a portable dosimeter that looked like a small pager.

The blue van was equipped with a long arm that fed the iodine through a tube six thousand feet into the ground. Equipment in the van monitored the amounts of radiation on a graph as the iodine moved down into the well. They watched spikes on a computerized printout, each spike representing the release of I-131 as it proceeded deeper into the well bore. The spikes, they were told, meant there were no underground leaks.

Kleinman asked why the trucks didn't have radioactive warning labels, and she was told that each truck was carrying less than the limit required to display a warning by federal law. Kleinman asked if that meant two trucks side by side could exceed the limit, and she was told that might be possible. But one of the contractors told her he was healthy and had been doing this for years.

Marrina Waks noticed that in the next two hours, the dosimeter tracking levels of radiation kept rising. The readings on her monitoring device were twice background levels—0.04 millirem for two hours. In other words, the parents received about 1/100th of an x-ray during that two-hour period. To most people that sounded inconsequential.

But Abraham Waks, who had taken the morning off of work, was visibly shaken. He understood that the critical issues are inhalation of radioactive material not measured by Geiger counters—not direct exposure. He wondered why the children at Beverly Hills High School, who would be exposed for more than two hours, got less attention than the birds off the coast of Santa Barbara. "There was not supposed to be any reading at all [above background levels], because the containers were supposed to be completely sealed," he said. But the containers were not shielded in lead for protection.

Kaufman dismissed his concerns as unfounded. No one said there wouldn't be any exposure in the area, she said. "We were expecting low exposure rates, and that's what was found," she said. "No more than 0.02 millirem an hour."

She felt the readings they got were perfectly safe. "These are such low numbers, you've got to put this in context," she said, explaining that the public was allowed one hundred millirem per year of exposure and that nuclear industry workers were allowed as much as five thousand millirem annually.

Those assurances infuriated Daniel Hirsch, director of the Adlai Stevenson Program on Nuclear Policy and the Committee to Bridge the Gap, a Los Angeles–based nuclear watchdog group. "The explanation by Kaufman was bullshit," he later told me. "These Geiger counters are almost always used for public-relations purposes. The counter doesn't tell you what to worry about. I'm concerned by what she *couldn't* measure, not how much. What's important to consider is how much was breathed in.

"The problem with I-131 is when you breathe it in, it concentrates in your thyroid gland. This is why people take iodine salt. It irradiates thyroid tissue, because there's no distance.

"What she doesn't tell you is that one in eight workers receiving an 'acceptable' dose each year will die from cancer due to their radiation exposure, according to the Nuclear Regulatory Commission, the Department of Energy, the Government Accountability Office, and the National Academy of Sciences. The amount of radiation from background—330 millirem a year—will kill one in a hundred people from cancer. So 3 percent of us will get cancer from background radiation. They want you to think background radiation isn't harmful. But background radiation itself is killing lots of us. To say it's a fraction of background isn't very useful. The main risk of radiation is if the material gets into you—no shielding and no distance."

Greger noted in his report: "No radiation above background was detected at approximately 25 feet from the stored I-131." He didn't mention that the softball field is located just a few feet from the oil wells or that the track is less than ten feet away. The only "significant amounts of contamination" Greger found were detected on the injection tool itself, after it was raised out of the well, and on workers' gloves.

Greger told Kleinman and Marrina Waks that the radiation doses they received mostly came from the truck. When they left, both Marrina and Jody had sore throats; Jody attributed it to being "creeped out." She vowed to send her next royalty check from Breit Brevon, the oil company on Pico Blvd. that extracted oil from beneath a commercial property she inherited from her father, to Dan Hirsch's nonprofit group.

"Based on information today, we've not seen anything of radiological concern at that location," Kaufman added. Nonetheless, she and her associates had brought with them three heavy canisters filled with charcoal cartridges to test the air for radiation levels. They set up the canisters ten feet downwind from the oil wells in their effort, as she put it, "to do everything we could to assure the community that radiological issues are not an issue at Beverly Hills High School."

When I requested a copy of Kaufman's final report, the results suggested gaps in the data from outdoor radon canisters. One, on the southwest corner of the basketball court, the report stated, "couldn't be analyzed—too damp." And the canister on the northwest corner of the track, according to Kaufman, had been "removed by unknown person—no results."

In a final addendum, Kaufman noted that a state lab analysis of the three air samples taken near Venoco found that none exceeded "minimum detectable activity," and the radiation amounts were not statistically significant. She concluded: "Airborne iodine was not an issue during the testing."

But internal agency documents would tell a far different story.

In fact, despite their public assurances, e-mails between Greger and Kaufman revealed that there had been a leak of radioactive material that day that no one could account for. And it wasn't just contamination from the injection tools or from the truck, as Greger had told the parents. It was airborne. Iodine is very volatile and will turn into gas, even in liquid form.

Though the amount of I-131 detected in the air was quite small—less than 1 percent of EPA permissible levels, according to lab results—enough was getting out of the bore hole that the counter could measure it, prompting a rash of e-mails between Greger and Kaufman.

At 11:47 a.m. on April 23, Greger wrote to Kaufman:

> What the results say is that we detected some I-131, albeit at very low concentrations. I'm somewhat surprised that we were able to detect anything, but the numbers say we did.
>
> This raised a question in my mind as to how much time it takes for the I-131 released in the water injection wells to reach the production wells and be brought back to the surface. I would think that this would be a relatively long time (months), but maybe not. If not, could that account for the I-131 detected? I really don't think so, but this question may be asked, and it would be better for us to know the answer if it is.

On Monday, May 10, at 4:04 p.m., Kaufman replied:

> Do we have an answer to this yet? I'm telling the media that with the results we have thus far, we don't see anything that represents a concern for the H.S., or even Venoco—any problem with that?

Marrina Waks was sitting in the city hall chambers again, waiting her turn to speak after the Pledge of Allegiance. It was another Tuesday evening in April, and Jody Kleinman was at the podium, suggesting that all future city council meetings be held at the high school's oil and gas production site. Why should they be getting a positive reading for radioactive isotopes at all? she demanded. Why was Venoco using a radiological substance that didn't stay down in the hole? Why weren't they *preventing* additional exposures?

"You tell me who to trust," Marrina told an onlooker that night. "Find me one person who didn't at some point lie or change stories. So, let's see who does not want to know about it? We have the government. We have the oil companies. We have the school board. We have the city.

"Let's see who wants to find out the truth if there's something wrong: it's just us. Everybody else will be damaged. This is worse than being in Russia. In Russia, everybody knows they're screwed up. Here, they're living in a bubble and think their government is protecting them. People don't want to know. If they did, they would do something."

Then she stepped up to the podium. Her green eyes flashing, she reminded the city council that it had yet to provide radiation badges for the students at the high school. And, as he had before, the mayor told her that the city had no jurisdiction over the matter.

CHAPTER TEN

BUTT-ASS WRONG

O n most winter mornings, Phil Berman could be found across the street from his home in San Diego at the exclusive Hotel Del Coronado's pool, where he swam laps. At fifty-one, he was religious about getting exercise and eating well. Friends teasingly called him "fat-free Phil." A physician with entrepreneurial leanings, he played hard and worked harder. Berman had recently sold his multimillion-dollar business interests in a dot-com company that provided medical information to doctors online. He planned to open a new radiology practice not far from the brown-shingled home he and his wife, Judy, had built for their family of five, including their son, Skye, and daughters Spencer and Sloane. The trajectory of Berman's career seemed limitless, given his ambition and bona fides. After graduating from Beverly Hills High School in 1971, he attended Harvard University and then received a degree from the medical school at the University of Pennsylvania. Not that there weren't setbacks. One of the reasons Phil Berman became a radiologist was that, as a young man, he had survived testicular cancer.

But in January 2004, just two months before the California legislature would convene a public showdown in downtown Los Angeles over environmental problems at Beverly High thanks to the advocacy of Erin Brockovich and Jody Kleinman, Phil Berman could scarcely make it across the pool. He soon realized his life was about to radically change when the bad news came: a second cancer diagnosis, this one for advanced, non-small-cell lung cancer that had spread to his brain, liver, and bones.

After seven grueling rounds of chemotherapy—he likened the cisplatin-and-Taxotere combination to Drano—in addition to months of brain and neck radiation "just to make it entertaining," Berman still felt hopeful. He no longer had any detectable tumors. But the treatments took a toll, and he couldn't return to work. Trying to recover his physical strength, he devoted himself to life as a soccer dad—doing homework with his kids, driving car pool, and helping Sloane with college applications. Staying abreast of news about his alma mater was the last thing on his mind until he received a phone call from his sister, Claudia Resnikoff, who lived 150 miles north in Beverly Hills.

She wanted to know if he had heard about her friend Lisa Bloch, who was another Beverly graduate. Berman remembered that Lisa's sister, Amy, had died of leukemia many years earlier. Now Lisa, at forty-nine, had just been diagnosed with lung cancer too. Like Phil Berman, Lisa had never smoked.

That call led Berman to think. "For me to know three or four lung cancers of people in their fifties is remarkable," he said, given the incidence of the disease. There are only about twenty thousand lung cancer cases a year in the United States in which the disease strikes nonsmokers. Living in the San Diego area, Berman was barely plugged into the Beverly Hills grapevine. Yet, even at such a remove, the anecdotal evidence seemed compelling.

It was the same for testicular cancer, he thought. The incidence for the disease is rising in the United States, but it accounts for only 1 percent of all cancers in men. Scientists have postulated that the increased rates of testicular cancer and lower sperm counts may be due to endocrine-disrupting chemicals in the environment. The probability that an American white male will get testicular cancer in his lifetime is 0.2 percent. "I know a lot of people who had testicular cancer from Beverly Hills, and I'm starting to think, Yeah, it's too much—too many people," Berman said.

Even so, no one was more skeptical about the value of suing Beverly Hills and its school district than Berman. The son of an attorney, he was loath to jump on any litigation bandwagon. Perhaps out of self-protection, he viewed personal-injury lawsuits with contempt. "Deciding to join or not join this stupid class of money-scrounging lawyers and doctors is going to be a pretty hard decision," he told me. Still, if there was science that was reasonably convincing to show "I got poisoned and other people got poisoned," he believed it was a legitimate cause of action. He might consider getting involved.

"One of the great things you learn when you get cancer," he said, "is you don't have control over anything. You like to think you do, but you don't."

It was after six o'clock on a Tuesday evening in early February 2004, the light outside was fading, and Erin Brockovich was exhausted. It had been a lousy day. She had just learned that her TV show, *Final Justice,* had been canceled by Lifetime. And she had missed her appointment with her hairdresser to get her roots done. She picked up the phone to make sure her husband, Eric Ellis, was on his way to drive her thirteen-year-old daughter Beth home from cheerleading practice in Calabasas. Between a speech she had to write for the upcoming senate hearing and documents to decipher, it was going to be a long night.

Ever since the controversy in Beverly Hills first erupted a year earlier, Brockovich had been the recipient of hate mail. Thousands of e-mails had piled up in her inbox, telling her, as one correspondent suggested, that she was "old and had saggy boobs and should go away."

No doubt, she was an easy target. On this day, she was wearing another one of her come-hither getups: short gray pleated skirt, black T-shirt, black leather jacket, and thigh-high stiletto boots. It was your basic fetish attire; the only thing missing was a whip. "It's like, 'Oh, you know, I'm sick of Erin Brockovich,'" she said of the hate mail, "and 'Stop wearing your bustiers' and 'Quit trying to dress like you're eighteen! You look fifty-five!' And I was, 'Wow!' I was like, 'Really?' This isn't what this is about."

Indeed, what "this" was about for Brockovich was righting a wrong. For more than a year, she had been hounding the regulatory agencies—cajoling the Los Angeles district attorney's office, begging the federal Environmental Protection Agency, publicly flogging the AQMD—to take precautionary measures for students at Beverly Hills High School. Despite her celebrity status, or maybe because of it, the Beverly Hills case had not been an easy ride. She had never felt so defensive in her life.

Of course, she was used to the attacks—that she was a publicity whore, a stooge for the trial lawyers, a slut who should learn to dress appropriately. Over the years, she had especially grown accustomed to being smeared by industry front groups. There was, for example, Michael Fumento, the right-wing columnist and Hudson Institute writer, who accused her of pursuing "junk science" even after it was disclosed that he had lost his Scripps-Howard job for receiving payments from Monsanto while writing about the agribusiness company. And soon there would be the Civil Justice Association of California, a tort "reform" group funded by Chevron, Sempra, PG&E, and other corporations that would issue nasty press releases about her when she was honored for her advocacy work by the Harvard School of Public Health in the fall of 2005.

But the Beverly Hills stalwarts, who sent threatening e-mails advising her to dress her age and get the hell out of their fabled town, seemed especially malicious. Norma Zager, editor of the *Beverly Hills Courier,* the local throwaway that people in town skimmed for photographs of the latest plastic-surgery victims at black-tie events, led the charge to bring Brockovich down. If other journalists had been seduced by the paralegal's celebrity status, Zager maintained a skepticism that bordered on savagery. Her one-woman crusade to poke holes in Brockovich's case in Beverly Hills had earned her a Los Angeles Press Club award as well as a write-up in the *Columbia Journalism Review* that was subsequently picked up by the *Wall Street Journal.* Local pundits wondered if the press club award might have something to do with the fact that Zager sat on the club's board; the piece in the lofty journalism review was not as easy to explain. Written by Eric Umansky, the same writer who had pilloried Brockovich in the *New Republic* for her "weird science" at Beverly High, the article questioned the evidence upon which she based her claims of toxic exposure, without bothering to examine public agency records that showed repeated violations by both Venoco and the power plant, owned by Sempra.

She wouldn't be intimidated, though. She believed children's lives were at stake.

Brockovich rolled her eyes at the mention of Zager's name. A week earlier, Zager had taken issue in print with a TV news report that incorrectly referred to 700 cases of cancer in the Beverly Hills lawsuit. In fact, Zager pointed out, the plaintiffs' lawyers represented only 382 clients with cancer at the time; the rest suffered from other illnesses, including autoimmune diseases, skin rashes, and sinusitis.

"Only 382 cancers?" Brockovich snorted. "Hul-lo? Do I give a shit if it's 400 or 700?" The point, she said, was that hundreds of people had cancer, and she believed their illnesses could be linked to emissions from the industrial facilities at the school. "Even one cancer is one too many."

During the past six months, Brockovich had grown increasingly frustrated over what she perceived as the failure of regulatory agencies to intervene in Beverly Hills, so she initiated a lobbying campaign for a state legislative hearing. One key ally would be state senator Deborah Ortiz, a Democrat from Sacramento who had championed environmental bills in the legislature and chaired the senate's Committee on Health and Human Services.

The senator and paralegal had met the previous year when Ortiz asked Brockovich to testify at a highly charged public hearing. It exposed how a state-appointed panel of scientists, who issued a report that would have relaxed standards for hexavalent chromium in California's drinking water, had been manipulated to favor corporate interests—namely those of the utility giant PG&E, which had millions of dollars at stake in cleanup costs and legal liability. Hexavalent chromium, a lung carcinogen when its vapors are inhaled, was the chemical of concern in the film *Erin Brockovich,* which depicts how PG&E contaminated water in Hinkley. Increasing evidence had shown that more water wells throughout California were contaminated with the chemical, used as a rust inhibitor, but scientists disagreed over what constituted "safe" limits when it was ingested.

The panel's report, which included passages lifted word for word from previous industry-sponsored chromium studies, caused one of the scientists on the panel, UCLA professor John Froines, to quit over concerns about a conflict of interest by a fellow member, who had worked for PG&E as an expert witness in chromium-related lawsuits, earning $600 an hour. One of the findings of Ortiz's hearing was that a research company hired by PG&E helped rewrite a 1987 study by a Chinese scientist that concluded that chromium-6-tainted water was carcinogenic. The reworked 1997 version reversed the earlier claim, without acknowledging PG&E's role in financing it, but was subsequently included in the panel's report. As a result of the hearing, the report was scrapped. But for Ortiz, it exemplified how it's possible for bad science to influence public policy.

A lawyer, Ortiz understood how politically charged the web of law and science could be, especially in the area of linking toxic exposures with health effects. With new advances in "biomonitoring," for example, researchers around the country are able to detect very low levels of synthetic chemicals in blood, and Ortiz was interested in having Californians benefit from the new science, given the growing evidence linking environmental pollution to health problems. She believed citizens had a right to know what industrial pollutants were inside their bodies. As a result, she had repeatedly sponsored a biomonitoring bill to test for chemicals in the blood, urine, and breast milk of volunteers throughout the state. But her bill, which would have made California the first state to test for industrial chemicals inside its citizens' bodies, had been defeated three times by lobbying from the chemical industry and business interests. A biomonitoring law in California would ultimately be passed by the legislature and signed by the governor in September 2006. The obvious danger for industry was how that information might be used; Ortiz wanted to correlate levels of toxins with potentially hazardous sites, such as the Santa Susana Field Laboratory in the San Fernando Valley, where a recent study had found a higher cancer rate among residents of surrounding communities.

When they conferred, Brockovich told Ortiz that she viewed the senate hearings as a long-hoped-for opportunity. She told Ortiz that no matter what happened with the legal case, there were policy questions at hand, including glaring loopholes in California law. Not only was it impossible for the California EPA to address toxic contamination of existing schools, as opposed to new ones, there was also the anomaly in environmental law which barred criminal prosecution by district attorneys of air pollution violations if a civil penalty had already been imposed by the local air districts.

After Venoco received three air pollution violations and a minor penalty from the Air Quality Management District, Ortiz became concerned because the district attorney's office in Los Angeles was ready to go to court to bring criminal charges but couldn't. To Ortiz, it looked like the air pollution agency in Los Angeles was saying, in effect, You pay us money and you can buy two things—a penalty payment and protection from criminal prosecution. That policy offended Ortiz. She thought the situation was ripe for new legislation, and she conferred with some of her colleagues in the senate. Some of them had already received phone calls and letters from parents in Beverly Hills, frustrated by the AQMD's limited authority and the warring disinformation campaigns of attorneys.

Ortiz agreed to set a date for sometime after the Christmas holidays in 2003.

More than anything, Brockovich wanted to get the legislature to respond even if the judiciary wouldn't.

The legal case, after all, was going to be a long shot. And she knew it.

"This case is gonna be a bitch to crack," she said, meaning that the fight over the release of internal company documents that could reveal information about historical chemical exposures was going to be long and hard.

Years would pass before the litigation would be resolved.

She wanted action now.

Ed Masry was leaving for the night. He poked his head inside Brockovich's office. "You still here?" he asked, leaning against the doorway.

"Yeah," she said, yawning.

There were stacks of cardboard boxes full of thousands of pages of sub-poenaed documents from the South Coast Air Quality Management District, labeled "AQMD," on the floor beside her. In the nine months since they first filed claims for damages, the plaintiffs' lawyers had issued subpoenas to the agency to preserve many of these documents. Brockovich had to make sense of them before the state senate hearings in the coming weeks. Since she's dyslexic, she compensates by memorizing what she reads, a strategy that takes extra time, obviously, and more effort. She was also not pleased that the agency had stuffed twenty thousand pages of documents into boxes that looked to her like they had been thrown down a flight of stairs.

On a bookshelf, beneath a framed honeymoon photograph, she had taped up a page from a calendar: WELL-BEHAVED WOMEN RARELY MAKE HISTORY. The daughter of an engineer and journalist from Lawrence, Kansas, she had obviously come a long way from her original calling, namely to become a beauty queen.

Masry looked frail. The dialysis treatments for diabetes were wearing him down, but he didn't complain. People often speculated about his rela-tionship with Brockovich, but it was obvious that they shared a sort of father-daughter connection. When asked about the Beverly Hills case, Masry once said that it was entirely due to Brockovich's resourcefulness and intelligence. Though he publicly teased her, playing up the role of gruff old coot, he was, in truth, quite proud of what she'd accomplished.

"I'm going home, kid," Masry told her. He ambled down the hallway to the lobby staircase. Outside, the flowering plum trees that lined the drive to the law offices had begun to bloom, a cascade of pink and fuchsia. Dusk had fallen.

On her desk, she kept a four-inch-thick black binder, her "hot doc" book, with colored Xeroxes of the oil wells at Beverly Hills High School that she thought had made so many people sick and the documents to prove how the regulatory agencies had, time and again, failed to take charge.

"The AQMD is a shill for industry," she charged, rifling through a sheaf of papers that had been redacted with a Sharpie by an agency lawyer, who cited "trade secrets" as the reason for not revealing the chemical constituents of the natural gas at either Venoco or Sempra. What especially galled her was the privilege log the agency sent, claiming that Annual Emissions Reports are exempt from public review. "It needs to be abolished. It's profit over health.

"I am astonished that a public agency would allege that an Annual Emissions Report is not public information, especially since these reports provide information that's critical to the public health of adults and innocent children," she said.

She took a swig from a water bottle. She thought she was looking at a high-risk facility; it had "odor complaints up the yin yang and pipes that leak like a sieve." She questioned why no environmental impact report had ever been done on the clarifier pits, on the well cellar, on leaking pipelines under the school. Why had no one addressed the issue of a possible methane gas explosion? Even CDM, the city's environmental consultant, had found explosive levels of methane—227,000 parts per million—during soil-gas tests conducted on the athletic field.

"How far are we gonna have to go before someone steps in and says: *Stop*?" she asked. "As we sit here and more innocent people are exposed to toxic chemicals, are we supposed to wait for the bureaucrats a year from now?"

Appropriately revved up, she began to practice her speech for the state senators. She wanted to make somebody mad. She spoke of the need for the city of Beverly Hills "to stand down" and bring in the EPA or a state agency to make sure the environment at the high school was safe and clean.

"They need to follow the same rules and regulations the rest of us poor bastards have to live by," she said of Beverly Hills. "They sure as shit do." She crossed that one out.

Thinking of their clients with cancer, she wanted answers. "It just irks me—time and again—for the sake of money and the sake of greed that somebody suffers," she added. "And it's wrong. It's just butt-ass wrong."

That assessment was not exactly how Ortiz viewed the issue. For her, six air pollution violations had been issued against a company located on school property, and school authorities didn't view it as a problem. She saw that as reason enough to go forward with a hearing to, effectively, clear the air. Ortiz set a date for February, but after protests from lawyers for Beverly Hills, who argued that they needed more time to proceed, she agreed to reschedule the date to March. It was a delicate balancing act, given the litigation and everyone's agreement not to discuss it publicly.

In contrast to Brockovich's feelings of urgency, Ortiz preferred to conduct the public hearing more deliberately and, perhaps, use it a vehicle to gain publicity for new legislation to solve some of the lapses in protecting schoolkids from environmental assaults. Moving more slowly would also give Beverly Hills a better chance to present its side of the story to the public.

Perhaps the most acute reaction to the public announcement of a state senate hearing into the Beverly Hills fiasco was the relief that Jody Kleinman felt when Roger Dunstan, a state senate staffer, telephoned her at home in January to ask if she'd be willing to testify. It had been eleven months since the KCBS story aired, two months since she presented blown-up photographs of Venoco's leaking equipment at a city council meeting, one month since she heard back from the federal EPA that there was no case to pursue at Beverly High, and two weeks since she skulked around the Sempra site again, feeling vaguely silly. In all that time she had received no indication—formal or informal—that her initiative had produced any result. Therefore the news that state senator Deborah Ortiz was going to hold hearings on "the possible toxic contamination of Beverly Hills High School" came as a great relief, primarily because it indicated that enough people now knew of the seriousness of the situation to render any attempt to silence Kleinman or her "cabal" of complaining mothers futile and superfluous. They hungered for details of the district attorney's internal investigation and wondered what role, if any, the law-enforcement authorities had played in spurring the legislature to action. And it was with eagerness instead of trepidation that she looked forward to meeting Erin Brockovich for the first time at the public hearing, where she, Mahshid Soleimani, and Marrina Waks could finally be heard by people outside the city limits.

The hearing might be a camouflage for something not evident—a political fight within the legislature, perhaps? Or a chance for the plaintiffs' attorneys to expand their universe of clients? Such notions were inchoate at first, but they began circulating in limited Beverly Hills circles as early as January—the predictable reactions of an insular and insecure community.

By the time she arrived in downtown L.A. at one o'clock on Friday afternoon, March 12, 2004, Kleinman was a nervous wreck. Her black Labrador retriever, Riley, had eaten all the M&M's on the coffee table in the family room earlier that morning and gotten sick on the living-room couch. Then, as she headed south on Beverly Drive toward the freeway, the driver of a pickup truck without insurance rammed into the side of her little hybrid. Still, nothing was going to stop her from testifying that day.

Inside the pink granite Hall of Administration building, the stately auditorium's blue velvet curtains framed an inscription on the wall: "That government of the people, by the people and for the people shall not perish from the Earth." After a year of her protests, Kleinman had come to believe that democracy in Beverly Hills meant putting up or shutting up. Those who dared to ask questions, usually in three-minute blips prior to city council meetings, had either been effectively silenced or, like the student journalist Zack Anderson, driven underground. She was disappointed that Anderson couldn't be here; he was in Barstow, competing in a $1 million contest sponsored by the Defense Department to race robotic vehicles across the Mojave Desert.

Looking up at the dais, she saw how effectively the Beverly Hills city attorney, Larry Wiener, had influenced these hearings. In the preceding days, he and the city's lobbyists had fanned out across the state capitol in Sacramento to shore up support. The city had doled out tens of thousands of dollars to make that happen by hiring Rose and Kindell, a reputable lobbying firm that marketed itself as knowing how to pursue "tactics to help clients change or neutralize public opinion on issues of public concern." Mark Egerman, the vice mayor who would succeed Tom Levyn as Beverly Hills mayor the following month, was granted a special seat on the dais, along with the city's defense lawyer, Skip Miller. Jody Kleinman viewed this bit of staging as a sign that the panel had been "co-opted" and that the city had taken over the proceedings. But the state senators explained the seating arrangement as a simple courtesy extended to local government officials.

This, Kleinman believed, was the real story: how industry and government colluded to keep the truth from being told. But before she allowed her conspiracy brain to take over, she took comfort in the fact that her husband and daughters and sister had come to support her.

Still, the turnout was disappointing. There was the requisite number of cameramen and TV newspeople, and in addition to the state politicians and their aides, the hearing drew a sizable contingent of lawyers, paid consultants, experts and bureaucrats. But only a handful of parents and students from Beverly bothered to take the time to be there. This, she thought, was another lesson of Beverly Hills. The story was not just a tale of greed and corruption, as Erin Brockovich insisted. It was, in some ways, even more insidious. What the small turnout suggested was the complacency that affluence can bring.

Kleinman noticed how people congregated in the audience as if they were at a wedding: The plaintiffs' lawyers, Al Stewart from Texas and Ed Masry, were on the groom's side, and the bride's side of the aisle was all about Beverly Hills: its lawyers, PR handlers, lobbyists, and *Beverly Hills Courier* editor Norma Zager.

"I haven't had this much fun since my hysterectomy," Zager deadpanned. The mayor strolled up the aisle and greeted her warmly.

"Hi, sweetheart," she said brightly. "Everyone's so civil. Don't ya love it?" She guffawed. Sitting beside her was a thirty-eight-year-old Beverly High graduate named Ari Bussel, whose brother had a rare cancer and whose sister had an undiagnosed wasting disease.

Kleinman hesitantly introduced herself to Erin Brockovich, who was seated beside her husband, Eric, and not far from Masry. The exchange lasted no more than a minute, but the two women nodded at each other with a mutual respect and the realization that they were wearing identical black suits. Although Jody Kleinman had not personally experienced all the pain that had been suffered by Lori Moss and other plaintiffs, she had seen and felt very vividly the damage to the town and its people that had flowed from the oil and gas operations at the school.

Kleinman was surprised at Ed Masry's demeanor. Dressed casually in a yellow oxford shirt and slacks, he appeared physically weakened. He wasn't wearing socks, and his ankles were severely swollen. In contrast to her cynical reaction to Masry's announcement of his lawsuit some months earlier, she now felt compassion. To see the proud and normally bellicose attorney sitting meekly nearby was wrenching. Yet it was confusing as well, even disorienting. Could this be just another act? Another skilled performance? In the back of the auditorium, there were a couple of film producers from Universal Studios, who had a contract with Brockovich to develop a movie sequel, a fact that especially galled the Beverly Hills contingent.

Ortiz gaveled the meeting to order and introduced her colleagues.

California passed the Children's Environmental Health Act in 1999, the first state to pass such a law. The act required the state's Air Resources Board to identify which air toxics have the greatest impact on children and teenagers and to reassess air quality standards for children, a process that had yet to be completed. California's EPA is the nation's largest and best-funded state environmental agency, often adopting risk assessments for toxic chemicals that are more protective than standards set by the federal government. Even so, the author of that law, state senator Martha Escutia, who sat next to Ortiz on the dais, expressed her regret over it.

"Obviously," she said, "I would have to apologize, as the author of that bill, that it took me four years to pass it as a result of three vetoes that I sustained, and I also would have to apologize to the state of California and its residents that it's taken California this long to finally realize that children are exposed to these type of toxins at way different rates than adults." Escutia, a

Democrat whose district included a section of eastern Los Angeles where many industrial sites were located near schools, acknowledged that what happened at Beverly Hills High School was not unique: children were at peril in schools every day because of unnecessary toxic risks.

When the senate hearing was convened, it was appositely called "State and Local Governments' Role in Preventing and Mitigating Environmental Health Risks in California Schools." But there would be only one reference point of discussion, and that was the situation at Beverly High. The state senators cautioned that no one would answer the question of causality; that matter would best be resolved in court. As a result, the afternoon turned into a bitter if largely lopsided debate on whether Beverly Hills High School was safe.

And though the hearing purportedly had nothing to do with the litigation, it clearly had everything to do with it. Republican committee members attacked it as a reckless stunt that had no basis in fact, citing agency reports claiming that there was no problem. Lost in all the talk about the lawsuit, though, was the primary question as to whether the health of students and teachers was in jeopardy.

When Jody Kleinman sat before the panel, adjusting a microphone to read her prepared speech, she complained of being caught between dueling disinformation campaigns of lawyers. "My child is on that school campus right now while everyone argues with each other," she said, her voice quavering slightly as she began to speak. She demanded an independent panel to oversee environmental monitoring, since Venoco was allowed to self-report. "Government agencies act as though they really do have something to hide from us. They've not been held accountable." Kleinman recounted how a federal EPA scientist who reviewed the city's soil-testing data told her that it was "wrong" and "meaningless."

State senator Sam Aanestad, a silver-haired Republican from northern California, spoke up. "Your daughter is still there?"

"Right," Kleinman said, her hands trembling.

"So, the risk to you as a mother can't be as high as going to the point of, 'Hey, I'm taking my kid out of this school.'"

"Right," she replied. In that moment of cross-examination, Kleinman felt her face flush. It was a confusing and hurtful attack, the implication being that if you were truly concerned, you would take your child out of the school.

State senator Sheila Kuehl came to Kleinman's defense. "I don't like to see her testimony—I'll use the word—mischaracterized," Kuehl said. "I believe she was saying we have a right to know—and then we can make an informed decision." A former child actor, Kuehl had starred in the TV show *The Many Loves of Dobie Gillis* as Zelda Gilroy, the character who wrinkled her nose at Dobie and called him "Poopsie." Now she was better known as one of the most progressive members of the California legislature, respected by Democrats and Republicans alike as a representative of the Westside of Los Angeles. A Harvard Law School graduate, she was also the legislature's first openly gay politician, and had married her partner at city hall in San Francisco that year.

The fact that parents did not take their children out of Beverly High, she added, when there weren't necessarily a great many options, when doing so would be disruptive, and when there was no conclusive government study of the risk was understandable. Besides, there was only one high school in Beverly Hills. Many families simply couldn't afford private schools.

One parent who switched his son from a tony private school to Beverly High was Stephen Williams, and his testimony exemplified how divided emotions were in town. He was selected by Beverly Hills lawyers to testify, and his speech sounded as if they had written it. Williams, who said he had a Ph.D. in pharmacology and had studied toxicology, told the panel that he had received no compensation for his appearance. Then he launched into a blistering attack against the legal team that had produced "a few spurious results" that no one had been able to reproduce, putting the parents at the school in the impossible position of "either trying to prove a negative—that is, we're trying to prove that there's zero risk for our kids—or . . . chas[ing] ghosts of toxicity that we're told exist."

He lashed out at the plaintiffs' lawyers for creating "an opportunistic legal scam designed to be maximally sensationalistic with the promise of large legal settlements by tickling the most sensitive nerves of what I characterize as a rather liberal, very affluent, child-focused, environmentally conscious community that is by and large not technically savvy and is prone to react radically to the specter of anything that is labeled 'toxic.' Our community was cynically and strategically selected for maximum impact in the media. In fact, there is so laughably little historical or contemporary evidence of anything deleterious, it can be nothing else. I'm sure the screenplay for this one is already being written.

"Folks, the oil well is not the problem," Williams added, brushing a strand of his gray-flecked hair from his forehead with an air of arrogance. "The problem is that the legal system permits and encourages flushing away precious funds in the midst of ever-increasing budget constraints to feed the fortunes of the legal vultures to the detriment of the education of our children by raising the unrealistic hope and expectations among a few plaintiffs who are ill and who, of course, will seek remedy any way they can. The crime is this: we, the community, the state, the school board, and students already have lost by engaging, and there's no real way out."

Senator Ortiz wanted the record to reflect Williams's relationship with corporate chemical and oil companies. "You are a headhunter for corporate executives in the scientific community?" she asked him.

"Yes," Williams replied.

"So, do you place executives in Dow Chemical, Venoco—"

"Dow Chemical, Exxon Oil, Pfizer, all the major firms."

It was Erin Brockovich's turn. Accompanied by her consultant, Matt Hagemann, who had worked as a senior science policy adviser for the U.S. EPA, she sat before the panelists near a lineup of whirring television cameras.

She charged that the AQMD's own reports showed that there was a toxic cancer risk at Beverly Hills High School. The agency also confirmed that Venoco was leaking "fugitive" emissions at an alarming rate into the air as well as high levels of benzene and toluene in the open pits that volatilize into the air. There was no permit to vent natural gas, but Venoco did. There was no permit to operate the amine scrubber unit, but it did. CDM's findings of 227,000 parts per million of methane gas was a serious violation, since California law required that a new school could not be built on a site with methane levels higher than 50,000 parts per million of methane. She asked how long this would have gone on had she not come along. Where were the state agencies that were supposed to be overseeing these children and this facility? she asked. Where was the political will to address the problem?

Brockovich told the panel that money had corrupted the process. "I have seen numerous documents and city records showing the city of Beverly Hills and the Beverly Hills School District earn a 5 percent overriding royalty from this operation and could potentially earn $50 million combined," she said. "The city, who is the lead agency on this operation, and the school district were earning money from an oil production facility that sits right on top, not adjacent to, a school that they know might explode, might deteriorate the air, and might harm people.

"You can call me jaded. I think this is a serious conflict," she said. "No one here is saying the city and the school district are not entitled to earn money, but to do so from an operation that is dangerous to children, and to look the other way, is wrong.

"This isn't about whether we found benzene in the air on a given day, and the AQMD didn't. This is about a situation at a public school that has an oil and gas operation on its campus and is dangerous to the children," she said.

"I don't believe this is a safe operation to have on the campus of Beverly Hills High School or anywhere else. As a parent, I would be outraged. As a citizen, I am incensed to find out that for decades, children have been in danger and no precautions have been taken."

Aanestad was on the warpath.

"What reports are you talking about, except that report you based your lawsuit on, that the city of Beverly Hills had to subpoena to see?" he demanded.

"I'm not addressing litigation today," Brockovich replied. "This is about public policy."

Aanestad said, "I can tell you that ten different agencies all came up with a negative report. So there must be something that you have that says that, yes, there is a danger to these children—when all of these agencies are saying no, there isn't."

"Well," Brockovich said warily, "that's why I'm here. I think you have a problem, sir."

"Ten of them!" Aanestad interrupted, referring to government reports.

"I think it could be the AQMD," she said.

"Maybe we have a problem with the legal system!" he shouted back.

The mood of the hearing went downhill from there.

There was, of course, a yawn of testimony from agency bureaucrats from the Division of Oil, Gas, and Geothermal Resources, the state EPA, the city of Beverly Hills. Everyone was startled, though, when Barry Wallerstein, the head of the AQMD, was suddenly upstaged.

"We're not soft on business—," Wallersein insisted, boasting of an enforcement deal his agency had struck with the oil giant BP for $300 million, the largest air-quality violation in the country, a deal that had been seven years in the making.

"But with regard to this hearing," Senator Escutia interrupted, "I want to notify the members that your testimony will not deal with consultations you've had with the district attorney over Venoco's violations as a result of an active criminal investigation. Is that correct?"

"There is no active criminal investigation at this time," Wallerstein's chief prosecutor, Peter Mieras, told the panel.

"Excuse me—members of the dais," another man broke in. He hurried from his seat in the audience to the dais and introduced himself as Stanley Williams of the Los Angeles district attorney's office. He said: "We do, in fact, have a pending investigation."

Wallerstein and Mieras appeared dumbfounded by the surprise announcement. Oblivious of the district attorney's secret investigation, they generally controlled the prosecution of air polluters in L.A. The two agencies had to work in tandem, of course, but it was also true that once the air district issued a civil penalty, the DA's hands were tied. They viewed the move by Williams as a bald power play.

"So we have this now," Escutia said.

"That's correct," Williams said.

"If there is an active, pending investigation, then we cannot ask questions about that, and I would assume you cannot testify about that," Escutia added.

Cynics in the audience wondered whether the announcement was made simply to get Williams off the hook from having to testify about the neglect of his law-enforcement agency. As it turned out, an investigation had been launched well prior to the hearing. And subsequently, the district attorney did indeed conduct an investigation at Venoco. In fact, when Dan Wright of the DA's Environmental Unit visited the site with an AQMD inspector, they heard a giant valve leaking. Wright thought they had caught the company red-handed, and Venoco received yet another notice of violation. But there would be no criminal prosecution. A new AQMD rule, the one that Jody Kleinman had supported, precluded any prosecution for oil well operators if leaks were repaired within twenty-four hours, which Venoco had done.

Wright would have no case.

Wallerstein, a well-polished speaker, had brought with him his perfunctory show-and-tell visual aids, including PowerPoint bar graphs and a chrome Summa canister.

"This is what the Masry law firm used," he said of the air sampler, in slightly patronizing tones. "This is what we've used. This is what the city of Beverly Hills' consultant's using. It's a canister. It's clean, so it doesn't have any pollutants on the inside. It's put under a vacuum. We have a valve up here that slowly sucks the air in, in the case of most of our samples, over an eight-hour period. Then we bring the canister back to the lab and we analyze the sample."

All told, he said, his agency had visited the high school thirty-one times in 2003. "That is not normal when you have twenty-seven thousand facilities," he said. "We've received two odor complaints, although we were not able to confirm those."

On one of his charts, comparing the AQMD data to Masry's data, he referred to the state's "reference exposure levels" for health effects. But those levels were misleading. Most air toxics have no known safe levels. Some accumulate in the body from repeated exposures. As a result, ambient air quality standards are not set for toxic compounds. That is because there is generally no threshold concentration below which the air is considered healthy for air toxics.

Sheila Kuehl interrupted. "Would you go back to that slide for a minute?" she asked. He clicked the cursor on his computer and the slide reappeared on the screen.

Kuehl continued: "This says 'below which no adverse noncancer health effects are anticipated.'"

"Yes," Wallerstein said, bristling.

"Is there a different measurement for cancer-related health effects?"

"Typically, the noncancer health effects are at a lower level than the cancer health effects," he said

"So, if you're saying a lower level, do you mean you'd find it with fewer particles?" she asked.

Wallerstein felt trapped. He called on his health effects officer, who explained that the reference limits are set for noncancer effects because they are thought to have a threshold below which no effects occur. For cancer effects, however, it is assumed there is no threshold because, theoretically, only a few molecules can cause damage, resulting in a cell changing its metabolism and turning into a cancer cell. Given the long latency period of cancer, exposures are assumed to occur over a lifetime. While the average cancer risk in L.A. was 1,400 in a million, he said he believed the cancer risk in Beverly Hills was more like 1,000 in a million.

Under further questioning, Wallerstein made the first clear public acknowledgment that chemical concentrations in the air at the high school might be problematic and that his agency had known it, although a straightforward accounting of the situation had never been revealed until that moment. He pointed out that his most recent air sampling showed toluene measurements in the high school bleachers at seventeen parts per billion—higher than ambient levels but not high enough to be considered an "acute" problem. Toluene, which often contains benzene, is a neurotoxin.

Senator Martha Escutia interrupted. "Now, can you please repeat what you said?" she asked. "The data to the right, this is the first time you've shown it to the public. What exactly are you referring to again?"

Escutia immediately grasped the ramifications of Wallerstein's testimony. Seen in isolation, it appeared to be a serious matter, but it could be handled. Seen in the wake of the explosion of media attention, it was like a huge time bomb dropped suddenly in the midst of a battlefield where contending armies were already bloody and weary from protracted combat. Normal levels for toluene in the L.A. Basin were 2.45 parts per billion. CDM, the city's testing firm, would also detect higher levels of toluene—21 parts per billion—at the high school.

Still, Wallerstein said he didn't think the oil wells were the cause of the high levels of toluene, which is typically found in paints and solvents, nor was the use of paint in the area. The school's maintenance shop was about three hundred feet upwind of the bleachers, and the storage shed for paints and solvents was nearby, but "at this point we don't have a conclusive answer."

For the first time, the air district chief also made public mention of Central Plant, the power plant adjacent to the high school that was owned by Sempra, the Fortune 500 energy giant, which owned the Southern California Gas Company. Though he conceded that the facility was among the top 1 percent of industrial polluters in Los Angeles, he minimized its impact on the community. All the boilers and engines there added up to thirty-five megawatts, compared with one thousand megawatts for a standard-sized power plant.

He showed the politicians a slide that said the cancer risk from the plant was less than one in a million, but he glossed over details on how his staff had arrived at that assessment, namely by looking only at benzene and not other toxics from the plant. When the state reviews the potential for air toxics to affect health and property, it usually considers the impact of only one smokestack, boiler, or unit—not what the emissions of an entire plant, or multiple plants, can do to an area.

There was a great deal that afternoon that Wallerstein failed to mention about the power plant. For example, the facility had been "under review" for a federal permit to operate since 1996. One of the most important provisions of the Clean Air Act is its right-to-know section about industrial pollution, which requires facilities to provide "public notice" to local communities.

Under amendments to the law, which were enacted by Congress in 1990, citizens are given greater access to information about toxic releases from "major" sources of air pollution in their communities through a program called Title V. A key element of that program is a thirty-day notice period, in which anyone can weigh in on permits under consideration.

In the months following the senate hearings, Sempra would quietly give notice to the community about its operations. How was notice given? It was published in a Spanish-language paper called *La Opinion* and in a newspaper located in the San Fernando Valley, the *Los Angeles Daily News.* If Sempra wanted to notify the fewest people possible in Beverly Hills and Century City about a major source of pollution in their neighborhood but still adhere to the federal notice rules, this might be the way to do it. And that is precisely what Wallerstein signed off on for the plant. Notice like this explicitly follows the letter—not the spirit—of the law. "This facility generates steam for heating and cooling applications," the notice rather obliquely stated.

Not surprisingly, the AQMD received no comments from residents, students, teachers, or local businesses about Sempra. That is undoubtedly because no one had been informed about Sempra's annual release into the community, which the company estimated included 6.2 tons of hydrocarbons, 1.6 tons of reactive organic gases (excluding methane and acetone), 19.5 tons of carbon monoxide, 15.7 tons of nitrogen oxides, 0.1 tons of sulfur dioxides, 1.8 tons of particulate matter (the dust, mist, smoke, and acid fumes) and 1.8 tons of PM-10 and 1.8 tons of PM-2.5, the soot that is smaller than ten micrometers in diameter and penetrates in the lower respiratory tract. The facility also emitted 4.4 pounds a year of benzene, 3,500 pounds of chlorinated fluorocarbons, 25 pounds of the lung carcinogen formaldehyde, 1,460 pounds a year of ammonia, and less than a pound of naphthalene. One of the chemicals emitted by Sempra in sufficient volume that it was required to pay "pollution fees" is acrolein. It is a chemical to which children are considered especially vulnerable, according to a California scientific advisory panel. But government regulators had yet to develop methods for measuring acrolein in ambient air.

During his testimony that day, Wallerstein reasserted his belief that there was "nothing outside the norm" at the high school compared to ambient air quality in southern California. And, once again, he said that he would send his own children to the school, which was his alma mater.

Mahshid Soleimani sat behind him. She snickered and tittered during his testimony. When he spoke of his agency's transparency, she laughed aloud. So did the other mothers who were sitting in the audience that day.

Finally the floor was Larry Wiener's. After thirteen difficult months, during which he had overseen the hiring of a defense team for Beverly Hills and managed to avoid confrontations with the federal EPA and the state Department of Toxic Substances Control, the time for confrontation was at hand for the Beverly Hills city attorney.

He presented the panel with a thick stack of notebooks filled with data from his consultants—a symbol of the due diligence performed by the city and school district. More than two hundred samples of air, soil, and soil gas had been taken, he said, and they had come back "consistent" with AQMD tests. None of the results, he said, suggested "there were any conditions that were abnormal at the high school." All the data was available to "anyone who asks for it," and it was summarized on the school district's Web site.

Jody Kleinman shook her head. She had checked the district's Web site recently and found a blank page, entitled "Layperson's Report."

Wiener didn't mention that the soil-gas tests near the basketball courts revealed methane at explosive levels, but he admitted that methane sensors had been installed recently in bathrooms by the football field. Nor did he say that the city's test results showed arsenic in the soil on the playing fields that was eight times higher than background concentrations. Other "chemicals of potential concern" that exceeded background levels there included barium, cadmium, chromium, copper, lead, beryllium, and mercury, according to the city's tests—but Wiener cleverly alluded to none of these results in his testimony.

State senator Martha Escutia, who had practiced law in the same firm as Wiener and spoke of their friendship, asked what the city's consultants viewed as a baseline safety standard. "Mr. Wiener," she began, "what's the standard in terms of risk assessment in parts per million?"

The question was key to the proceedings. It underscored the elusive nature of what is deemed an "acceptable" risk—a political construct, not a scientific one.

"I'm not sure if I fully understand the question," Wiener said haltingly.

Standards for assessing health risks to children at schools are elusive at best. A one-in-a-million cancer risk is the level at which the U.S. Environmental Protection Agency decides to investigate a hazardous waste site. On the other hand, a twenty-five-in-a-million risk has been deemed "acceptable" for specific toxic "hot spots" in Los Angeles, even if they are located next to schools. Those relaxed standards, set by the local air agency, have evolved in recent years to accommodate industry.

"What I'm trying to get at here," Escutia continued, "is figures always lie and liars always figure. In this business of determining risk, the parts per million can vary as to, say, one part per million is considered a risk versus, say, somebody might say, no, twenty parts per million is considered risk. I just want to make sure that what CDM uses is the highest standard possible to protect the residents of Beverly Hills and the students of Beverly Hills High School."

Wiener said the approach of his consultants had nothing to do with an acceptable risk for children. He said they were trying to determine if conditions at the high school were different from the background air in Los Angeles. And the soil tests showed a risk of less than one in a million, he added.

"Now with regard to the contractual arrangement Beverly Hills has with the oil company," Escutia said, getting down to brass tacks. "You get a certain percentage of royalties?"

"I'm glad you asked that," Wiener replied. "As a parent of a child who will someday attend that high school, I find it hard to believe that someone would seriously believe that people whose children are in the high school now and people whose children will be attending the high school would have money influence this decision.

"I know there are people who do believe that. But let me tell you this. The city's annual budget is $258 million. Two hundred fifty thousand out of a $258 million budget—this is not a number that is a significant revenue source to the city of Beverly Hills.

"We have spent far more on testing than we do achieve in revenues, and we will continue to spend a lot of money on testing. I won't even tell you how much more in defense of litigation that we've had to spend compared to the revenue from that oil well. The revenue from that oil well is not influencing the actions of the city or the school board in this matter." The fact that the price of crude oil would soar from $30 a barrel to over $60 was not a subject that the politicians dared mention that day, though it surely engulfed the entire proceeding.

Brockovich's testimony dominated the television and newspaper reports that evening and the next morning. She felt upbeat about the hearing and was excited by the prospect of new legislation. However, the school safety bill quickly died because of lack of funds in the state coffers to support environmental testing at existing schools. And Ortiz's bill to allow for criminal prosecution of air pollution cases by district attorneys also quickly died in committee because of opposition from industry groups, including the California Council for Environmental and Economic Balance, the California Independent Petroleum Association, the California Independent Oil Marketers Association, the California Chamber of Commerce, and the Western States Petroleum Association. Ortiz, who took the long view on such matters, vowed to reintroduce the bill again the following year.

Before the hearing was adjourned at six o'clock, another man was finally summoned to speak. He had waited five hours to do so, because answers were still not forthcoming. As he strode to the dais, Ari Bussel could only think of his brother, Barach. The day before, Barach had gone back to the hospital, dealing with the residual effects of radiation treatments for nasopharyngeal cancer, a rare cancer of the upper throat. Ari was certain that lives were at stake.

"What is the real objective here?" Bussel asked the politicians, his voice rising with intensity. "And I will paraphrase what my brother said: *It should never happen again.* It should not happen to any parent that will have to face him- or herself in the mirror, that will have to face his or her daughter or son and say, 'Why did it happen?' We don't know the causality. We don't know that it's the oil drilling or the gas venting or Sempra or the close proximity to Olympic Boulevard, which is the major artery. We simply don't know, but we need to investigate, and the investigation must be impartial. Impartial meaning independent."

For Bussel, it was deeply unsettling that the people most impacted, namely the graduates with cancer and other illnesses, were not there. Of course, many of them, like Phil Berman, either lived far away or didn't know that the hearings were being conducted. Others, who had signed confidentiality agreements with plaintiffs' attorneys, were under strict orders by their attorneys to keep away from the press. Several months earlier, Masry had sent out a letter to his clients, advising them to steer clear of the media. Controlling information in the press was crucial for both plaintiffs and defendants.

Lori Moss, the thirty-year-old graduate who was in remission for both Hodgkin's disease and thyroid cancer, had a good excuse for avoiding the limelight: just a month earlier, she had given birth to a seven-pound baby.

She was, of course, ecstatic. But no sooner were Lori and Randy Moss celebrating the arrival of their baby daughter than a routine ultrasound would reveal yet another tumor in Lori's neck. The bad news was that the tumor was attached to her carotid artery, requiring extensive surgery. The good news was that the recurrence was isolated in a single node. Living with the anxiety, though, was a perpetual reality.

No amount of money, Bussel told the legislators, could reverse what his family had been through. He recounted how his family had moved from Israel to Beverly Hills in 1982, when he was a junior in high school. He, his brother, and his sister graduated from Beverly in the 1980s and then went on to Stanford, Harvard, and UCLA. "We have five different advanced degrees," he said proudly. But then: "My brother is a cancer survivor, and my sister— both are part of the litigation."

He took issue with the city attorney's suggestion that the money the town received from oil revenues was a mere pittance. He remembered quite clearly how, in response to statewide legislation in the 1970s that equalized school spending, salaries were cut, teachers were laid off, and the school district faced major budget cuts. In fact, every dollar was crucial, especially from oil revenues. When oil drilling expanded in the 1980s, he said, "half a million dollars per year was a very substantial amount of money to the school district, because we suddenly found ourselves, even in a very affluent community, without the money."

Cancer has a long latency period, he reminded the senators. "We're not talking about people in their late thirties, like I am," he said. "We're talking about people in their late twenties, in their early thirties—beautiful people that suddenly have autoimmune disease, that have things that are too horrible even to mention." And yet, no one had bothered to conduct an epidemiological study. He had contacted the president of the school's alumni association for help, and been told, "I don't want to hear this ever again."

"I believe it is our obligation," he said, "to find out.

"You can come up with all these excuses until it hits you," he said. "When it hits you, suddenly you see you're not as smart as you thought you were, because you can't play with fate. Now, you are the one on the line. It's a course you should not reckon with."

Tears streamed down the face of Mahshid Soleimani as Ari Bussel spoke, and other eyes in the room were moist as well. The only people not visibly moved by Bussel's words were the senators who had already departed for the evening.

But questions of causality were not for this panel. Nor had it been convened to determine who was right or who was wrong. That would require a
day in court, or, more precisely, three years in court. Lori Moss's original
complaint had been filed for 21 people with Hodgkin's disease; Al Stewart's
client roster would soon include a total of 1,065 claims. Of those, there were
417 people with cancer—70 of them with multiple cancers. Phil Berman
would be one of them.

A year after the hearings, I received another e-mail from him:

> From: Phillip Berman MD [mailto:pberman@pacbell.net]
> Sent: Tuesday, April 19, 2005 5:20 PM
> To: 'Joy Horowitz'
> Subject: club of litigants
>
> Okay, I just joined the club of litigants (God save me if this is bullshit,
> please!). There are, at this point, no summary documents on the evil
> humors in the air, land & water of BH; but I'm assured they will be created
> following discovery and before trial of the first 12 unlucky graduates,
> teachers & employees. Stay tuned.

PART 3

Tort 1. A civil wrong for which a remedy may be obtained, usu. in the form of damages, a breach of duty that the law imposes on everyone in the same relation to one another as those involved in a given transaction. 2 (pl.) The branch of law dealing with such wrongs. Mass tort— many people. Negligent tort: failure to observe standard of care.

—*Black's Law Dictionary*, Eighth Edition

Courts should be extremely cautious in concluding that reasonable minds cannot differ about factual causation.

—*Restatement (Third) of Torts, Tentative Draft No. 3*

CHAPTER ELEVEN

CASE MANAGEMENT ORDER

T he Central Civil West courthouse of Los Angeles Superior Court, built in the 1970s of granite and tinted glass, is situated in a converted office building in the Mid-Wilshire district. It is the only courthouse in America that is privately owned, having once served as headquarters for CNA, a Chicago-based insurance company. Sandwiched between the palm trees and playing fields of Lafayette Park and a Gothic-style church on Commonwealth Avenue, the eighteen-story building occupies one-fourth of a city block and towers over a neighborhood of low-slung strip malls, Salvadoran restaurants, and a billboard for the Spearmint Rhino Gentleman's Club, featuring exotic dancers. From a distance, the structure's mirrored windows refract light in such a way as to create the appearance of a gleaming green edifice; emblazoned on the outside in huge block letters are the words SUPERIOR COURT. Thanks to its reputation for granting huge awards in product liability cases, the courthouse is also known simply as "the Bank."

Friday morning, January 23, 2004, was a brisk day, the mountains clearly visible to the north and topped with snow. Under the sunny winter sky, the building looked shiny to the plaintiffs' attorney, Allen M. Stewart. His palms were damp, and his cheeks were marked by patches of redness, probably from lack of sleep. He'd lain awake the night before, thinking about how much work lay ahead in this case, the flight home to Dallas that afternoon, his young children's needs through the weekend at church and Sunday school.

When he arrived upstairs on the fourteenth floor in Department 307, inside Judge Wendell Mortimer Jr.'s courtroom, Stewart and his bearded law partner, James D. Piel, with whom he had worked since both had graduated from law school fifteen years earlier, took their seats at the counsel table, bypassing a gaggle of opposing counsel who gathered at a nearby lounge in the corridor. It was just past 8:30 a.m.

The son of a cop, Stewart was an optimist at heart. He believed if he could get this case before a jury, the defendants would be held liable for his clients' illnesses. "I wouldn't want my kid at that school, because it looks really dangerous," he later said. "And the only reason it doesn't look really dangerous to people in Beverly Hills—and there's only one reason—is because they're numb to it."

Still, he faced many hurdles, not the least of which was a veritable army of extremely able corporate defense lawyers from some of the biggest firms in the country, including litigators from Latham & Watkins for Chevron and from Morgan, Lewis & Bockius for Sempra Energy, the corporate parent of the power plant operating adjacent to Beverly High.

In recent months, the defense lawyers had filed a raft of demurrers, claiming that Stewart had failed to shoulder even the minimum legal burden required to sustain a toxic tort action in California's state court system. Though California's rules are generally more liberal than those of federal courts in such cases, recent appellate rulings had made it more difficult for plaintiffs to present expert testimony to support their claims of injury. At issue was the same line of defense raised in most mass tort cases: the question of causation.

In any tort action, two elements must be shown—causation and liability. In other words, a plaintiff must prove that something the defendant did caused the plaintiff's alleged injury. Toxic torts are no different, but they are marked by the difficulty of linking causation, a herculean task for plaintiffs, since many diseases don't manifest until years after exposure to a chemical. The basic premise of the defense is that to prove liability, the plaintiff must first identify the defendants' chemicals and show that he or she was exposed to them in sufficient amounts to cause disease.

Under California law, Al Stewart would need to prove that his clients had been exposed to the defendants' emissions, that their injuries were "more likely than not" the result of the defendants' behavior, and that each toxin was "a substantial factor" in causing or aggravating their cancer. Establishing a causal connection between a particular injury and a specific exposure, then, was the biggest obstacle Al Stewart would face.

Technically, the pre-trial conference on this morning had been scheduled for two reasons. One was for the judge to hear oral arguments on the defendants' demurrers, which offered their first crack at knocking the case out of court; the other was to discuss a proposed "case management order" to provide a sort of road map on rules for pretrial procedures. Contrary to press reports, this was not a "class-action" lawsuit; it was, instead, eight separate cases that would ultimately involve 1,065 claims for 419 people with cancer (70 with multiple cancers) and 318 individuals with noncancer illnesses. The eight cases, filed over a period of two years as cancer victims continued to contact plaintiffs' lawyers, were then "consolidated" by the court for the sake of efficiency.

The lawsuits alleged twelve causes of action, including negligence, malice and oppression, strict liability, fraud, intentional infliction of emotional distress, negligent infliction of emotional distress, battery, alter ego/piercing the corporate veil, loss of consortium, and wrongful death.

Monetary damages had yet to be specified in court filings. Those would be determined later, by insurance carriers and the testimony of plaintiffs and medical experts and, finally, by a jury.

On this morning, the judge assigned to the case could dismiss the action entirely.

Clearly, he understood, if this case went to trial, the stakes could be enormous: a school district could go bankrupt; a city known the world over for its glamour could have its image forever tarnished; the Fortune 500 companies Chevron and Sempra Energy, which stood accused of causing the deaths of many graduates of Beverly High, might be looking at damage awards amounting to hundreds of millions of dollars, or even billions. Already, legal pundits had begun to take bets on the outcome; the vast majority of these cases sidestep jury deliberations by way of secret settlements, despite the possibility of ongoing environmental hazards. Still, Al Stewart was determined to bring the case before a jury, even though the odds were stacked against him. Less than two percent of civil cases ever get to trial.

His foot nervously tapping beneath the table, Stewart calmed himself with water. He unfastened a white plastic thermos, took a Dixie cup from the stack the clerk had left on the table, and poured a drink. He and Piel sat on the left side of the courtroom. The defendants' counsel were on the right.

Ernest Getto, the wavy-haired partner from Latham & Watkins, one of the nation's premiere corporate environmental defense law firms, extended his hand to Stewart. "Good morning," Getto said. He was defending the oil giant Chevron in this case and had flown down to Los Angeles from San

Francisco the day before. In recent days, Latham & Watkins, which represented the utility industry, had garnered media attention when two memos prepared by the firm's attorneys were incorporated verbatim by the EPA into its rules relaxing mercury pollution standards for power plants. The head of EPA's air policy office had worked for Latham & Watkins before joining the EPA.

Stewart grasped Getto's hand firmly and nodded, avoiding eye contact.

Getto also greeted Piel. "Jim, nice to see you," he said, nodding.

The forced civility was nothing new for these trial lawyers, who, one by one, were signing in with the clerk and taking their seats. Many sat in the purple-cushioned seats of the jury box. Others took a swivel seat at one of the two long counsel tables and began to furiously thumb-punch messages into their hand-held BlackBerry devices.

In the gallery, the Beverly Hills city attorney, Larry Wiener, sat behind the Beverly Hills defense counsel, Skip Miller, from the leading Hollywood entertainment firm Christensen, Miller, Fink, Jacobs, Glaser, Weil & Shapiro. Also representing Beverly Hills was Christopher P. Bisgaard, a senior partner from Lewis Brisbois Bisgaard & Smith, who sat at the back counsel table. Getto took the lead position in front.

When the judge entered the courtroom from his chambers, his clerk ordered everyone to be seated, even though no one had bothered to stand, a gaffe that didn't seem to bother the judge in the slightest. Deeply tanned with graying temples and a large, round face, Wendell "Mort" Mortimer Jr. had the relaxed air of a man who seemed constantly amused by life. Tall and friendly, he bore the demeanor of a former football jock, at once affable and eager to please but stern when necessary, too. The posted sign at the back gallery bespoke his no-nonsense manner: "No Talking, Gum Chewing, Eating. Please Turn Off Your Cell Phone and Pager."

On the bench, Mortimer sat beside a computer and beneath a bronze replica of the seal of California. It featured Minerva, the Roman goddess of wisdom, gazing upon a miner at work near the Sacramento River, with a grizzly bear at her feet and the Sierra Nevada mountains rising in the background under the state motto: Eureka, the Greek word for "I found it."

He quickly scanned his courtroom and smiled. "All right, with *Moss* and related cases," he began, "we won't have everyone introduce themselves for the record."

There were at least twenty attorneys before him now, and Mortimer wanted to make efficient use of everyone's time. He was a well-liked jurist, both because he conferred respect on the attorneys who appeared in his courtroom and because he understood the practical realities of their caseloads.

Mortimer, who had been named after Oliver Wendell Holmes, knew from the time he started law school at the University of Southern California in the early 1960s that he would be a judge. It took him thirty years to get there; in 1995, the Republican lawyer from Alhambra was appointed to the bench by then-governor Pete Wilson. Some judges simply didn't believe in toxic tort cases; others allowed them to get to a jury. Mortimer was neither liberal nor afraid to rule on summary judgment motions that would knock the case out of court, depending on the facts.

For the moment, though, with so many lawyers present, the billable hours were steadily mounting. Piel did the math in his head: twenty lawyers times roughly $500 an hour—$10,000 just for showing up in court that morning. Not bad for a drive on the freeway and the $8 cost of parking in the lot across the street.

For the plaintiffs' lawyers, working on a 40 percent contingency basis, the payday wouldn't come for years. If at all. Not that Baron & Budd was exactly impoverished. The Texas-based firm, which boasted a fleet of Gulfstream jets, had offices across the country and appeared to some more like a defense law firm, given its cadre of eighty attorneys, large support staff, and huge suite of offices atop the pink granite Centrum building in downtown Dallas. In the 2004 presidential election, the firm contributed $1 million to federal candidates, more than any single oil company, according to *Forbes.*

But even a legal payday could spell future headaches. In recent months, two of Stewart and Piel's law partners had successfully represented the city of Santa Monica in a landmark lawsuit against a dozen oil companies for contaminating that town's drinking-water supply from leaking underground fuel tanks with the additive MTBE, a carcinogen banned in California. The 2003 settlement agreement included a $300 million payout to Santa Monica, but the city turned around and sued Baron & Budd for "unreasonably" interpreting the agreement to boost their take—a charge that founding partner Fred Baron had called "silly."

Stewart rose to ask a question. "Your Honor," he began, "is the court taking defendants' position that *Bockrath* is requiring us to plead with specificity what chemical is producing what ailment?"

At issue on this morning was the judge's interpretation of a 1999 California Supreme Court case, *Bockrath v. Aldrich Chemical Co.,* in which pleading requirements were established for toxic tort cases. In that case, several Hughes Aircraft engineers who had developed multiple myeloma claimed that their blood-borne cancers were caused by chemical exposures. California's pleading requirements may be less strict than other states', but the *Bockrath* case established the requirement that plaintiffs identify what toxin caused or contributed to the development of disease. Stewart's complaint had listed more than 180 toxic chemicals—a "blunderbuss" of allegations, according to defense counsel.

Mortimer said he had read the *Bockrath* case more than once. "The case is different," he said. "In the Beverly Hills case, you have byproducts, not products. If you allege a multiple of chemicals in the pleading state, I guess that's adequate." So long as Stewart agreed to narrow the number of chemicals at issue by amending his complaint a third time, the judge would overrule the motion to dismiss the case. "That," the judge said, smiling, "will be the ruling."

Stewart looked visibly relieved. He had survived the first round of attack. The job of defense counsel, as he saw it, was to delay, delay, delay. His mission was to speed up the process as much as possible—to get to trial.

Clearly, Mortimer was intent on moving the case in that direction.

Al Stewart was pleased but not surprised. He wasn't tilting at windmills. If he didn't think he could win this case, he would never have taken it in the first place. "I'm an expert in toxic tort cases," he liked to say. "And I'm pretty doggone good at it."

Bravado aside, the forty-year-old attorney, who had been named one of the best young litigators in America by both the *National Law Journal* and *American Lawyer,* was on a mission. A Dallas Cowboys fan, he was fond of quoting the words of head coach Bill Parcells: "Performance is everything, potential is nothing."

No doubt, he was also on a winning streak. The previous year, he had secured more than $130 million in settlements for his clients. In Lake Charles, Louisiana, he was co-counsel for more than 850 plaintiffs who had alleged that their cancers and neuropsychological problems were the result of a pipeline leak. In another environmental pollution case in Mississippi, he represented more than 2,000 plaintiffs who said they had been injured from the nearby DuPont chemical plant, the largest generator of dioxin in the state. He saw the Beverly Hills litigation as part of that continuum, though of course the ironies weren't lost on him—from "Cancer Alley" in the industrial south to the wealthy confines of 90210.

The grandson of a West Virginia coal miner who had died from black lung disease, Stewart grew up on a cotton farm outside of Phoenix. After graduating from the University of Arizona, he followed his brother, a Baptist minister, to Fort Worth, and found work there as a chemist. But he soon grew restless and moved back to Tucson to attend law school at the University of Arizona, where he was editor in chief of the law review. It was during his years in law school that he met his wife, Chris, in church when she was a student in pharmacy school. "I tell my wife everything," he'd say, often sharing details of his caseloads with her as she offered her expertise on toxicology.

Stewart's first job was for Gibson Dunn & Crutcher in Dallas, where he handled commercial litigation. He was assigned the "shop and flop" docket of the Wal-Mart account, the slip-and-fall cases in grocery stores that most young lawyers avoid. Stewart, though, grabbed the assignment because it gave him the opportunity to do trial work. But it didn't take long before he realized that his heart was on the other side of the docket. In short order, he began to specialize in toxic tort work, particularly asbestos cases, for Baron & Budd.

Since he dealt with only a few cases at a time, it was important to him that each one "mattered." Just as he believed that his grandfather was one of thousands of Americans who worked in unsafe conditions that could be remedied through reasonable corporate care, he viewed his line of work as his "greatest honor" – a calling. Beverly Hills was part of that mission, and it offered proof that cancer is an equal opportunity offender. Stewart's job would be to create a narrative for a jury that would tell that story.

"You can live in one of the richest places in the world," he would later say, "and that does not mean that the people around you care more about you, are not infected by the same sorts of tendencies and greed that will kill you just as dead as they kill a poor man down south. Your zip code can't protect you. That's the story.

"You'd think with all that education and success and power, people could figure out you don't put oil and gas operations on a high school and you don't build power plants right next to a school. These are not dumb bubbas from the South. These are highly educated and sophisticated people. And they were just lulled into sleep."

It was, for him, a commonsense case. That's why he loved it so much. All he had to do was get a jury to tour the Venoco site and Sempra, as he had. "These are scary places," he said. "Very, very scary. They're large industrial operations and you're on them and you get where you can see the school. All you see is kids. It's all you see. Can't miss them. Just can't miss 'em."

Despite how obvious the case seemed to Al Stewart, signing on to it wasn't always a no-brainer for potential plaintiffs, even those in some of the hardest-hit families, like the Greenwalds. The family lived on the 400 block of South Rodeo Drive, just around the corner from where I had grown up.

John, a physician who had run track at Beverly and graduated in 1966, died of lymphoma—"the bad one," according to his brother, Eddie—after receiving a diagnosis of non-Hodgkin's lymphoma when he was forty-eight years old. John's college roommate, who also attended Beverly, died of testicular cancer; John's wife had breast cancer, as did her sister, both of whom had graduated from Beverly.

"Maybe it's coincidental crap," Eddie, who owned the Mexican restaurant Eduardo's Border Grill on Westwood Boulevard, told me during an interview in early 2004. "My brother would dismiss this all as garbage."

The "this" to which he referred was the litigation claiming that a variety of cancers had been caused by toxic exposures at the high school. "He'd say 'I got unlucky.' It took five years for him to die. It was pretty painful. He did the City of Hope thing—a bone marrow transplant that didn't work. Slowly, he got worse and worse."

A year later, when I called Eddie back, he told me his sister was still alive.

Your *sister*?

Not long after we spoke, he told me, his sister Ann had been diagnosed with brain cancer on her forty-eighth birthday. She had had three brain surgeries and was doing "fair," trying to raise two teenagers. He was convinced she was going to die too.

Then Eddie was diagnosed with prostate cancer and scheduled surgery the following month. His younger brother, Bruce, was told by his doctor that he now had a five times greater chance of also getting prostate cancer, since Eddie had it. Ashkenazi Jews have poor cancer "repair cells," which might help to explain a genetic link to the cancer in the Greenwald family. Or there could be a particular genetic-environmental interaction, in which environmental factors weaken an already vulnerable constitution. The lawsuit, whether they joined it or not, would surely zero in on such pivotal questions.

For a brief moment, Eddie Greenwald considered suing. But he wasn't interested in money. "If there was money involved, we'd want it to go to can- cer research," he said. "We'd sue to help other people."

"My parents are still alive, and they don't have cancer," Eddie said of his parents, now in their eighties. "I don't know what that means." He re- flected on the fact that parents are not meant to outlive their children: "It just about killed my father, to see his son die."

As it happened, none of the Greenwalds joined the lawsuit. Bruce Green- wald, a gastroenterologist who now lives in Ventura and who graduated from Beverly in 1971, explained: "When I first heard about it, I thought it was bullshit. The thing is, these things are really hard to prove. From an epi- demiological point of view, it took years to prove smoking caused lung can- cer. With the oil wells, you have to find out if there really is a bigger incidence of disease among those exposed. What is the data? For what years? To tell you the truth, I try not to think about it."

For Al Stewart, this reluctance to join the suit was not uncommon. In ev- ery toxic exposure case he'd ever litigated, the number of people who filed claims was less than half of those actually affected.

Now that Judge Mortimer had decided that there was, indeed, a legitimate case at hand, he'd have to let everyone know how to proceed. It was not a trivial issue. One of the key factors in adjudicating environmental pollution cases is the administration of hundreds of related cases—bringing justice to a large group of people. It may sound like legal rigamarole. But procedure can define substantive issues concerning evidence: Do you try cases by fo- cusing on one form of cancer at a time and thereby shorten discovery? Or do you take a sampling of different illnesses as a bellwether of the pool of litigants?

In the weeks prior to this January 2004 court hearing, opposing counsel had briefed the judge on which cases they felt should go to trial first. Al Stew- art argued that the case should focus on one cancer at a time, beginning with the twenty-one young graduates of Beverly High with Hodgkin's disease—the *Moss* case. He reasoned that since it was his "hardest" case to prove—the de- fendants insisted that the medical literature showed that Hodgkin's disease was caused by the Epstein-Barr virus, not from carcinogens in the air at Beverly High—it would provide the clearest signal of what would follow.

Stewart never mentioned it in court, but twenty-one cases of the same type of cancer would clearly have more impact on a jury than several unrelated cancers. But even more important was the fact that he had convincing epidemiological evidence from Dr. Richard Clapp, professor of environmental health at Boston University's School of Public Health and the former head of Massachusetts's cancer registry. Clapp's statistical analysis showed that graduates of Beverly High had an incidence of Hodgkin's disease that was three times greater than the national average. Since Clapp's study was based only on people who had contacted attorneys in this case, Stewart felt certain that the cancer numbers they were looking at were really just the tip of the iceberg.

The defendants' lawyers needed to prevent a trial of only Hodgkin's cases. They wanted a cross section of sixteen plaintiffs with a variety of cancers to go to trial first, reasoning that with fewer plaintiffs the trial would move more swiftly. The strategy was important to the defense counsel for several reasons. It would require more medical experts and, thus, be more costly to the plaintiffs. It would also prolong discovery, possibly making the plaintiffs more likely to settle. Not only would the plaintiffs need experts on "general causation"—which chemical exposures experienced by plaintiffs are capable of causing the specific types of cancer that those plaintiffs ultimately developed—but also experts on "specific causation," namely whether the exposures at issue were a substantial factor to each plaintiff's development of cancer that could be proved with "reasonable medical probability."

At first, Judge Mortimer announced to the lawyers assembled in his courtroom on that Friday morning in January 2004 that he had "tentatively" decided to proceed with the *Moss* case—the twenty-one former students with Hodgkin's disease. He was, in effect, adopting Stewart's proposal.

"Something's gotta go first," the judge said. The case "may or may not be typical," he explained, "but it will at least give everyone an idea of how the other cases will go.

"There's never an ideal cross section of cases," he added.

Chevron's counsel Ernest Getto (pronounced Jet-toe) rose to address the court. The sixty-year-old trial lawyer and senior member of the defense team needed to change the judge's mind. He was very distinguished-looking and had a studied air of confidence, the posture and calm of someone used to giving orders and having them obeyed instantly.

"Your Honor," Getto said, smoothing back his graying hair, "we have a sheet here we'd like to distribute." He handed out copies of a tally of litigants in the case to the assembled lawyers and the judge. Getto had been litigating these kinds of cases for the past twenty years and had never tried one where the court ordered a trial of only one type of cancer.

Getto had authored several articles about the need to keep "junk science" out of the courtroom, a crusade of defense counsel that resulted in the U.S. Supreme Court's 1993 *Daubert* decision that turned federal judges into "gate-keepers" of scientific evidence in court, thereby preventing many environmental cases from ever being heard by a jury—a key victory for the business community.

In 1997, Getto had represented the Southern California Gas Company in a case involving its storage facility in the tony L.A. neighborhood Playa del Rey, where a physician claimed that she had contracted lupus and aplastic anemia due to benzene leaking from the site into her cliffside home nearby. The trial judge dismissed that case on summary judgment because the plaintiff's experts had failed to present admissible evidence that the plaintiff had been exposed to benzene in an amount sufficient to cause her illness. Getto felt certain the same would occur in the Beverly Hills case because Stewart faced an uphill struggle to build an exposure case.

Getto didn't think there was an exposure scenario that would cause a health problem at Beverly High. For example, he was certain that benzene from cars on Olympic Boulevard exceeded whatever small amounts of benzene were being emitted by the oil wells. He believed you got more exposures pumping your own gas at a Mobil station. One of Getto's corporate clients was Erin Brockovich's nemesis, Pacific Gas and Electric, which he had come to represent after its settlement in that well-known case. Getto had also negotiated a secret settlement in the 1990s on behalf of Mobil after it was sued by more than six hundred residents living nearby its sprawling refinery in Torrance, California; the plaintiffs in that case had claimed that their sooty homes, nausea, and respiratory problems were caused by the facility, which admitted no wrongdoing.

Now, Getto reminded Mortimer that the purpose of complex civil litigation is to bring about a just resolution of a dispute as speedily and economically as possible. He argued that trying only the Hodgkin's disease cases would not shed light on the other cancers. Though the twenty-one plaintiffs with Hodgkin's disease would be grouped together in one case, each of their stories would still need to be told, detailing family history, exposure scenarios, and medical information. "We'll know nothing about breast cancer or lymphoma or the others," he said.

"Everyone knows each cancer has its own etiology."

To prove his point that proceeding with one cancer at a time would be unwieldy and not representative of the cases at hand, he held up his chart, entitled "Preliminary Data on BHHS Litigation Plaintiffs." It showed that the 905 plaintiffs currently in the litigation included 376 cancer claims, 316 non-cancer medical claims, and 205 plaintiffs who did not allege any medical claims. Among the top ten types of primary cancers alleged were 60 cases of Hodgkin's lymphoma, 57 cases of thyroid cancer, 50 cases of breast cancer, 45 cases of non-Hodgkin's lymphoma, 36 cases of skin cancer and melanoma, 29 cases of testicular cancer, 24 cases of leukemia, 14 lung cancers, 12 colon cancers, and 9 prostate cancers. Most of these involved former students.

Getto also told the judge that, like other toxic tort cases, this one would be "expert-intensive." Ultimately, he said, it would depend upon two types of experts: experts trying to reconstruct exposures and experts opining on medical causation and whether environmental exposures were a significant contributing factor of disease.

At the counsel table, Getto peered at the judge over his black-framed glasses. "Any meaningful mediation," he added, would require information about more than just one form of cancer. Many complex civil cases are referred to mediation early in the process, giving lawyers an opportunity to explore settlement options with the assistance of a trained mediator and possibly avoid a lengthy trial. In recent days, Al Stewart had proposed just such a mediation session thirty days after the conclusion of expert testimony. Getto was suggesting that the defendants wouldn't have enough information to settle anything other than the *Moss* case if the judge adopted Stewart's proposal.

Low-key and laconic, Getto was quite persuasive. "Where we disagree," he told the judge, finally, "is on the economics. It may be more cancers, but the trial will be shorter." Obviously, what Getto did not mention that day was his belief that the defendants had stronger cases with other kinds of cancers than Hodgkin's disease.

This was as much about psychological warfare—the posing and posturing and maneuvering—as about the brass tacks of lawyering.

One of the oil company lawyers sitting in the jury box passed a note to Getto, who glanced at it, then added, "More than half the plaintiffs don't even have cancer. I submit that after discovery, many of these cases will fall out." He was implying that it would become clear through an analysis of medical histories during discovery that many of Al Stewart's clients would have developed their illnesses anyway, whether they had attended Beverly Hills High School or not.

Getto also knew that the sheer volume of Stewart's client roster could work against him over time. Already, many of Stewart's clients had begun to make noise about pulling out of the case. They had received some form letters and Christmas cards from the firm, but little else. "No one ever returned my calls," a classmate of mine with Graves' disease, Madeline Cantillon Fries, complained to me after she dropped out of the case. "I sent an e-mail and no one ever responded. I said, 'Take me off your client list.' I just don't see how they can make the connection."

Christopher Bisgaard, the hired gun for the city of Beverly Hills, rose to address the court. The heart of the city's defense was that the entire case was frivolous, especially for those plaintiffs whose connection to Beverly Hills was attenuated. He pointed out that one plaintiff simply drove through town; another happened to visit relatives one summer. "The plaintiffs made serious allegations at and around Beverly Hills High School," Bisgaard said, his face turning red. "They caused a serious response in the community in their efforts to promote the litigation. The city is anxious we resolve this as quickly as possible so this fallacy can be eliminated."

Getto and Bisgaard were both well-respected defense lawyers on environmental matters. They had worked together on the 1989 Stringfellow waste-disposal site case, one of the largest cases in the nation's history involving toxic substances. In that case, most of the 3,800 plaintiffs living nearby claimed their immune systems had been damaged because of toxic chemical exposure from the site, which taxpayers rather than the site's owner, represented by Bisgaard, or Montrose Chemical, represented by Getto, ultimately paid to clean up.

"The poster child for how not to try" these cases, Bisgaard said, was the Burbank-Lockheed litigation, a water-contamination case in Burbank which had dragged on for decades and involved many trials by thousands of residents who claimed that the defense contractor illegally disposed toxic chemicals that caused their cancers. The company reportedly paid $60 million to 1,350 residents in 1996 and $5 million to 400 residents in 2000 in out-of-court settlements related to cancer-causing chemicals first found in 1980. "That seems to be the path we're going down," he warned the judge.

Judge Mortimer, who had been listening attentively, was polite but terse. "I'll take this under submission," he said slowly. In any event, he would issue his final order in the coming months.

Right from the start, the *Moss* case was teeming with vitriol. Even before the complaint was formally filed in court in August 2003, the big guns had been drawn. Skip Miller, one of the lawyers hired by the city of Beverly Hills and whose Century City law firm was known for its scorched-earth tactics, would see to that.

Unconvinced that the plaintiffs' evidence showed safety problems at the high school, Miller wanted his experts to get their hands on the plaintiffs' raw data and chain of custody—the procedures used to account for the integrity of each chemical sample by tracking its handling, storage and laboratory testing—and any other proof of environmental problems to poke holes in their case. By filing a legislative subpoena on the plaintiff law firms Masry & Vititoe and Baron & Budd in July 2003—just after administrative claims against the city and school district had been filed—Miller could get a headstart on discovery and plan the city's attack by reviewing his opponents' documentary evidence.

But there was one glaring problem with his strategy: plaintiffs' counsel was less than eager to comply with it. In response to the subpoena that summer, they turned over some data but not all of it, claiming the rest was protected by the attorney "work-product" doctrine under the rules of evidence. The attorney work-product doctrine is a rule that protects materials prepared by a lawyer in preparation for trial from being seen and used by an adversary during discovery or trial. The rationale is that an attorney's strategic and tactical thinking regarding litigation needs to be protected.

Now Miller was livid. In Santa Monica, he asked Superior Court judge Valerie Baker to levy sanctions against Stewart for failing to comply with the subpoenas. The judge wouldn't go that far, but on January 26, 2004, Judge Baker ruled that Stewart's work-product doctrine was outweighed by the city's interest in obtaining evidence of environmental problems. She ordered Stewart to turn over a "privilege log," indexing which documents he withheld because he believed they were exempt from disclosure.

For Stewart, Baker's decision violated one of the core principles of a democracy—how a dispute is litigated—and smacked of Big Brotherism. He believed it was "a legal fiction" that the city of Beverly Hills wanted his notes to see if it had a public health problem. In fact, he believed the only reason for the city's subpoena was to gain a tactical advantage over him in the litigation. It was, he said, a "gross miscarriage of justice."

Baron & Budd lawyers appealed to the state court of appeal and then the California Supreme Court on the grounds that the privilege to protect work product is absolute and not provisional. As Stewart grew more outspoken, he drew more fire. Before long, Miller launched a second blistering attack. This time, he set his sights on Stewart himself—to have him tossed off the case.

Pro hac vice is a Latin term meaning "for this one particular occasion." The phrase usually refers to an out-of-state lawyer, such as Stewart, who has been granted special permission to participate in a lawsuit, even though he is not licensed to practice in the state where the case is being tried.

On February 10, 2004, less than a month after Judge Mortimer's hearing on the proposed case management order, Miller demanded that the judge revoke Stewart's *pro hac vice* status in the case. Miller wanted the hearing before Judge Baker in Santa Monica, whereas Stewart deemed Mortimer's courtroom the appropriate venue. As a result, Miller accused his opponent of "judge shopping."

To observers, the bickering bordered on the absurd. After Judge Mortimer denied the motion by Beverly Hills to have the Texas trial lawyer removed from the case, Stewart accused Miller of "shooting blanks." Stewart believed that Miller's repeated requests for sanctions established a pattern in the case. "What defendants say," Stewart would later accuse his adversaries, "is *never* the truth.

"It was a shot across our bow. It was their way of saying, 'Welcome to California.'" It was, in short, all part of the power and positioning and chess game of litigation.

But finally, Stewart believed, the diversionary tactics of the defense were really "just a sideshow. The real show is a bunch of people from Beverly Hills High School who have cancer."

Still, the sideshow seemed to be overtaking the main event. After collecting $1 million for his efforts on behalf of the city of Beverly Hills six months later, Skip Miller was off the case. In order to avoid the appearance of any conflict of interest, the firm of Christensen, Miller, Fink, Jacobs, Glaser, Weil & Shapiro withdrew from representing Beverly Hills because its mayor and Miller's friend, Tom Levyn, joined the firm that fall.

As it later turned out, Levyn's move couldn't have come at a worse time. In the spring of 2006, the law firm would be in a state of chaos. Skip Miller left the firm he helped to found because his partner, Terry Christensen, was indicted by a federal grand jury for paying a notorious private investigator $100,000 for wiretapping his client's ex-wife—a charge Christensen denied.

By late February 2004, word arrived from the California Supreme Court that the plaintiffs' motion for relief from the legislative subpoena was denied. In lawsuits as in poker, strategy is everything: you never reveal your hand before you have to.

For now, Stewart's bluffing game was over. The plaintiffs' lawyers would need to show their hand, or at least part of it. With access to some of the plaintiffs' research materials, the defense now had a tactical advantage, namely more time to mount its assault, especially on the crucial issue of historical chemical exposures from both the oil wells on campus and the power plant next door.

Since they could no longer withhold the subpoenaed documents, Stewart and Masry made the release of them as unpleasant as possible. They dumped nearly everything they had up to that point on the defense—thirty-five boxes containing eighty-five thousand pages of material that included old aerial photographs, old maps, and documentation about the history of both the Sempra site and the oil operations on the high school campus.

"I hope they have fun reading them," Masry quipped. He had made no secret of his disgust with the whole exercise. "It's the biggest red herring I ever heard of," he said at the time. He believed that the school district and city were "risking the health of their kids to protect themselves from a lawsuit.

"That's the situation," he added. "It's pathetic."

The paper trail, it turned out, included many of the historical records that Erin Brockovich had secured through her Freedom of Information Act searches from a variety of government agencies. Those documents, many of which were already in the possession of defense counsel, provided a startling glimpse into the inner workings of both Sempra's Central Plant operation and the oil-and-gas site on the high school's football field—two industrial sites with a hidden, forty-year record of trouble, including repeated fires and explosions. The internal reports uncovered by Brockovich showed that it wasn't just that things were going wrong at these sites. It was the frequency of "upsets" and the pattern of denial by government agencies supposedly protecting the public's safety that was most troublesome.

Fires and explosions, of course, affected what was being emitted into the air and could be important to the plaintiffs to establish theories about toxic exposures and negligence. For the defense, though, the question was whether those historical emissions could be quantified in any meaningful way, or were simply best-guess estimates.

Still, the evidence was powerful, even if incomplete. In the fall of 1963, a transformer at the oil wells behind the football bleachers caught fire. After the local fire marshal reprimanded the Beverly Hills Oil Company for violating state fire codes, including the use of heaters that were "improperly installed and connected to well gas," the superintendent of schools complained that the emergency phone number did not work and no employee could be found on site. Nonetheless, as the price of oil skyrocketed, operations expanded at the school decade after decade.

Next door at the Central Plant, according to engineering reports, a 7,500-ton compressor was installed in 1974 that was "the largest of its kind in existence." With the expansion of Century City, including a new hospital, there were added demands for heating and air-conditioning, so more giant boilers, compressors, steam generators, and cooling towers were installed.

But in May 1996, records show, the plant suffered "a catastrophic failure," according to Sempra's environmental compliance director. Firefighters from Station 92 of the Los Angeles Fire Department were called to the scene to respond to "a structure fire." The firefighters noted in their log that, together with the police, they "handled an explosion involving the boilers."

Two months later, an AQMD inspector named Jim Molde issued a "notice of violation" to the plant for exceeding its pollution limits and for unplugging its emissions monitors on Boiler 3, the same boiler that had exploded. That meant that precise records of toxic emissions during that "upset" simply did not exist.

In 1997, the AQMD received a complaint from a Beverly Hills resident who lived across the street from the high school on Spalding Drive. There was, according to the AQMD report, a "strong burning odor causing respiratory problems. Goes on daily." Just two weeks later, a second boiler exploded. Again, the emissions monitors had been disconnected. This time, though, the facility was granted an exemption for its release of air toxics by the AQMD. If strict compliance with pollution limits was enforced, the agency determined, the result to the plant would be "economic harm."

As for Venoco, public records show in 1998, for example, that its oil wells at Beverly High had been permitted by the local air district to release 2.17 tons of organic gases and methane gas, but its nonpermitted emissions summary was three times that amount.

How those emissions summaries might be incorporated into a workable scenario by Al Stewart's air-modeling experts was unclear. Defense lawyers could only second-guess how an exposure case might be built around a number of incriminating documents, including one written in July 2002 by Venoco's foreman: "Pumped down the slop tank. Hunted down soccer ball for BHHS kid—found in well cellar trough—soaking in oil."

The fact is that most of Stewart's clients claimed their injuries occurred long before any of these records even existed. Plus, there was a twenty-year gap of information about emissions from Sempra. If anything, defense lawyers for the city of Beverly Hills, Chevron, and Sempra could rest assured that these documents did nothing but reveal the weakness of Al Stewart's case.

It was also possible, of course, that none of the documents turned over to the defense prior to discovery would be incorporated by the plaintiffs at trial.

At this point, it was really just a guessing game.

When he began to formulate notions of negligence that would come into play in the Beverly Hills case, Al Stewart might as well have been invoking the words of U.S. federal district court judge Jack B. Weinstein in the 1984 Agent Orange case. "Benign neglect is as illegal as malign intent," he wrote in that decision. "Both are unconstitutional."

After considering dozens of different tactics, Stewart knew he needed to hit the sweet spot: not just seeking to prove that the corporate defendants' day-to-day operations neglected to consider the health of the neighboring community but identifying each defendant's liability by matching it to what carcinogens it released into the environment at the high school.

But when it came down to it, Al Stewart viewed his case in extremely simple terms: you're either a bad guy or you're not. "To see it more technically than that," he would say, "is not to see it for what it is."

So, of all the records he released to his opponents prior to discovery, perhaps the most important one for him was unearthed from the files of the Beverly Hills Unified School District. In 1956, the school district invited oil companies to bid on an oil and gas lease on the high school property. In response, the Universal Consolidated Oil Company offered a bid in which the drill site would not be placed near the school campus but, instead, within the 20th Century Fox studios nearby. This was proof to Stewart that the school district was given notice in 1956 that putting an oil-and-gas drill site on the high school property was not reasonable and a simple alternative existed.

But there was more to it than that.

Ironically, neither the city nor the school district wanted oil drilling at the high school. After Standard Oil, which would later become Chevron, scooped up mineral rights in Los Angeles in the late 1960s, the company set its sights on Beverly Hills. Since 1968, Standard had been extracting oil and gas within the city limits from nearby drill sites in Los Angeles. But some property owners, who had leased to the company, believed oil was being taken without compensation for royalties. The city's properties at La Cienega Park and Roxbury Park were also subject to extraction. In response, the city council created the Oil Committee and enacted an ordinance prohibiting drilling within the city.

Standard Oil persisted. Drilling within Beverly Hills was considered "essential," and the company offered millions of dollars to the city and residents in royalty payments if it was permitted to create a drill site in the city's industrial area a few blocks east of city hall. The problem, though, was that by 1973 Standard Oil of California—the first company to strike oil in Saudi Arabia, an event that reshaped the world's economy and politics—had become persona non grata in Beverly Hills, a predominantly Jewish community. As the largest member of the Arabian American Oil Company, Aramco, (which also included Texaco, Standard Oil of New Jersey, and Socony Mobil), Standard's business interests were not allied with Israel in the days preceding the Yom Kippur War.

At the behest of King Faisal of Saudi Arabia, Standard chairman Otto N. Miller sent a letter in July 1973 to stockholders and employees to support "the aspirations of the Arab people" and "their efforts toward peace in the Middle East." Miller warned: "There is now a growing feeling in much of the Arab world that the United States has turned its back on the Arab people."

His letter set off a firestorm of criticism. Some saw it as an attempt to "exchange Jewish blood for Arab oil." In Beverly Hills, the response was especially vitriolic. The mayor, Phyllis Seaton, wrote to Miller on August 10, 1973. "All the members of the City Council are greatly distressed over the fact that Standard Oil would issue such a letter calling for a drastic change in our foreign policy," she wrote. "Changes of this nature are a matter for governments to consider and not the economic dictates of private industry."

Nine months later, the city's Oil Committee had come to a conclusion: "An oil drill site within the city of BH, no matter how housed, masked or disguised is not compatible with the character of the city." However, in an *unzoned* area, such as the high school, a drill site would be permissible—especially given the promise by Standard of $50 million in royalties—and thus, the city's municipal code would be rewritten for it.

At the time, it was determined that 10 million to 30 million barrels of oil would be extracted from the site, and a lease was signed by the school district, the city, and the Beverly Hills Oil Company in 1978—the same year that

California voters approved Proposition 13, the tax initiative that was good for homeowners and horrid for public schools. It was the schools that would benefit most from the expanded drilling. Or so everyone said. According to public hearings of May 3, 1978, the pipeline part of the project would be covered by a blanket franchise by the Standard Oil Company.

Based on its lease with the city, the Beverly Hills Oil Company paid about $6 million in royalties in 1983, including $1.2 million to the school district, a slightly smaller amount to the city, and the rest to about five hundred property owners living above the reserves. The royalties represented slightly more than a quarter of the company's gross sales. The lease also contained more than fifty-one conditions regulating noise levels, vibrations, dust, odor, and other potentially harmful effects. In addition, the lease promised new technical improvements as they evolved.

So even though the archives of the city of Beverly Hills offered ample evidence of secret backroom talks with Standard Oil of California during the 1973 Arab oil embargo, the question was whether Stewart planned on using those documents as evidence of the town's greed and the corporation's avarice—proof of negligence, perhaps, but not of medical causation.

Not long after Al Stewart and his partners at Baron & Budd were forced to release a cache of evidence that could help the case they were trying to build, I obtained a memorandum during the course of my own research that seemed to offer more clues about historical chemical exposures at the high school. I wasn't convinced I understood what it meant, though. So I contacted a structural engineer named Jack Bruce to help unravel its meaning.

On Monday afternoon, October 25, 2004, I met with Bruce, who directs the Los Angeles section of the Division of the State Architect, the agency responsible for reviewing construction plans for California's public schools and certifying projects for safety upon their completion. His corner office, located on the thirteenth floor across the street from the Ronald Reagan Building on South Hill Street, is part of the old bank district in downtown Los Angeles and has a sweeping view of the San Gabriel Mountains to the north.

Back in 1967, plans were under way to create a new building at Beverly Hills High School. The school district had hired the noted architect Rowland H. Crawford, who had designed the Los Angeles Times Building downtown, the Brown Derby restaurant, and the streamlined modern edifice for the

Santa Monica Sears-Roebuck store, since designated a historic landmark building.

On March 3, 1970, in a letter to his contractor, Crawford requested that the planned plumbing on the girls' athletic field be changed. At the time, the girls' field was located between the oil wells on campus and the power plant, which was just a few hundred feet east of Gulf Oil's twenty-five oil wells that were operating next door in Century City. Under the heading "description," Crawford wrote: "Furnish and install new water connection to the drinking fountain in the Girls' Athletic Field as instructed on the site." Crawford noted this change would cost an additional $242.95 for the school district.

Under the heading "REASON," he explained:

> The original water connection that had been installed by the [school] District, which the new fountain was to be connected to, was found to be hooked up to the industrial water used for sprinkling the Athletic Field. This was illegal and dangerous water to drink.

"Illegal and dangerous water" sounded alarming. I asked Jack Bruce to evaluate the letter for me: What does "industrial" water refer to? Could it have been waste water from the oil wells, or from the adjacent Century City power plant that was built in 1965? How long had there been a "cross connection"? When was it changed?

The notation, Bruce told me, was highly unusual. "In my twenty-five years here," he said about the architect's reference to "illegal and dangerous water," "I've never seen a statement like that." Bruce said he had no idea what "industrial" water meant, except "obviously it was not the potable water it should have been."

Was the situation corrected at Beverly High? According to public records on file, Crawford's proposal was forwarded to Sacramento and greenlighted in December 1970. But at the top of the Beverly High file was a startling notation, written in longhand, from 1971: *"Closed without approval."*

What does that mean? I asked Bruce.

"Beats me," he said. "It doesn't make sense."

For $80, the cost of shipping, Bruce offered to have several boxloads of thirty-five-year-old files sent to L.A., where I could review them. If the piping had been changed, there would be an approval to the change order on record, he said. "If it's not here," he added, "it means it never came through here."

When the boxes arrived a few weeks later, I spent several hours digging through the musty files. There was no approval to the change order.

Had I uncovered a smoking gun? If so, Bruce was nonplussed. He suggested that the file in question could have been lost or misplaced over the years. He also questioned whether an overzealous lawyer or hapless bureaucrat might have removed it.

In any case, the paper trail I was following on my own left no doubt that the school district had been made aware of health hazards from contaminated water on campus three decades earlier: not only was "dangerous" water sprayed on the football and baseball fields then, but students were drinking it, too. For how long was unclear.

Rowland Crawford's memo offered compelling evidence, I thought, about the chronic poisoning of Beverly High athletes. It showed that the students could have been dosed with contaminants by drinking the water, by breathing the vapor, and by absorbing the molecules through their skin while playing on the athletic fields.

When I contacted the school district about the memo, an official told me that the pending litigation prevented him from responding. Kenneth Peters, who was superintendent of schools in 1970, told me in an interview that he had no recollection of the memo.

When I asked Al Stewart about it, he said he was aware of Crawford's memo but wasn't sure if a document about drinking water would be helpful to the case he was building about air emissions.

Strategy was everything for him, but he had more pressing needs to focus on at the moment, like keeping his case alive.

No doubt, the paper trail would help the defendants to better understand the plaintiffs' case; the documents could help to support theories of negligence and failure to warn. But they said little about causation. In toxic tort cases, if you can't prove causation, usually a doubling of the incidence of cancer, you often don't even get to the question of negligence.

For Al Stewart, that would mean relying on at least three of his causation experts: Dr. Max Costa, a chromium researcher who was chair of the Department of Environmental Medicine at NYU's School of Medicine; Dr. Nachman Brautbar, a physician and toxicologist at the University of Southern California who had worked with Erin Brockovich on her case in Hinkley, and would conduct a medical exam of each of the trial plaintiffs; and Dr. William P. Sawyer, a toxicologist who believed that past high exposures to the types of chemicals at Beverly High would equal high rates of cancer in the future. And, of course, there was the critical piece of his causation case from his epidemiologist in Boston, Richard Clapp.

Stewart still needed to get his hands on emissions records from the oil and gas companies to build up his exposure case. What did they report and what did they, in fact, emit? To obtain those, he had already filed motions in court to compel the oil companies Chevron, Wainoco, Frontier, and Venoco in addition to Sempra's Central Plant to turn over their documents. He had also filed subpoenas on the AQMD to produce key reports.

After being forced to release tens of thousands of subpoenaed pages to the defense, it seemed to Stewart that they had all of his information, and he had none of theirs. He would need to provide any documents he could uncover to his air-modeling experts, whom he had hired to determine historical exposures through meteorological records, aerial photographs, engineering reports, and computer models. They already knew from AQMD records that at least two carcinogens were leaking out of the oil wells and power plant. There was, of course, benzene. And, documents showed, the plant had used hexavalent chromium to clean out its cooling towers until the early 1990s. Even tiny amounts of that chemical could be deadly when inhaled.

Once the preparations for trial were officially under way, the expert testimony on exposures and causation would be of utmost importance.

By the time Judge Mortimer signed the case management order in March 2004, he had cobbled together a compromise: The case would proceed with twelve bellwether plaintiffs with the six types of cancer that were most prevalent—thyroid cancer, non-Hodgkin's lymphoma, Hodgkin's disease, breast cancer, testicular cancer, and melanoma. Six of the plaintiffs would be selected by the defense team and six by Stewart and his colleagues. They would notify each other of their selections by e-mail. Plaintiffs suffering from other diseases would need to be especially patient. Their cases were now on the proverbial back burner, a spot that seemed particularly painful to families whose loved ones had died or were now suffering from a second or third form of cancer.

The case management order, then, would be at the heart of the proceedings. A trial date of July 25, 2005, was set, with a mediation session a month beforehand. But mediation would be impossible without knowing the strengths and weaknesses of each other's cases through discovery.

That gave everyone eighteen months to get ready for trial—a ridiculously short amount of time for a case as complex as this one. As it happened, the case management order would be amended five more times to reflect those complications, just as the actual trial date would be rescheduled and delayed another sixteen months.

"You go with the flow," Getto said at the time. "It'll be fun."

Stewart was less sanguine. "We'll be working night and day," he said. In the coming days, he'd need to confer with experts on wind direction and on a host of other contamination issues. Epidemiology, the study of disease occurring in human populations, is not the sole method of establishing causation. Stewart could rely on biomarkers of exposure and of susceptibility that were on the cutting edge of molecular toxicology and biology. Also important would be blood tests for toxins that persist in the bloodstream longer than benzene. And once the bellwether plaintiffs were selected, there would be hundreds of depositions to take.

Still, Stewart was grateful for small victories, like the setting of a trial date and, especially, the proposed mediation, which could benefit everyone if conducted properly. "There will be a sit-down in this case," Stewart later said. "That's when they'll say what these cases are worth." Stewart knew as well as anyone that if he was successful, this case could be extremely profitable for his law firm.

The legal wrangling had just begun.

CHAPTER TWELVE

DISCOVERY

The Watchtower at Beverly, pre–Century City (courtesy Seaver
Center for Western History Research, Los Angeles County Museum
of Natural History).

E rin Brockovich stood on the fifty-yard line of the football field at Beverly Hills High School and snapped another photograph. *Click.*

It was Friday afternoon, September 17, 2004, the day after Rosh Hashanah, and no one was in school. Everyone had the day off for the Jewish New Year. The sun was exceptionally bright.

Brockovich looked miserable. She was sunburned from the day before when she didn't get home until nine o'clock. "I was here all day yesterday, and I'll be here tomorrow," she said. "I canceled my trip to Vegas. Now I'm gonna miss the fight."

She had planned on a weekend of fun in Las Vegas before hitting the road again for more speaking engagements in Georgia, Arkansas, Texas, and Nebraska. She was especially looking forward to seeing Oscar de la Hoya fight Bernard "the Executioner" Hopkins. Instead, she would be here all weekend, helping to document the soil-gas and indoor air testing that was part of the discovery process.

When I asked her for details about the testing process, she apologized and handed me a written statement that had been prepared by both sides in the litigation. "There are lawsuits pending in which claims have been made by a number of Plaintiffs contending that they have suffered injuries as a result of historical conditions at Beverly Hills High School," the statement said. "While those claims are disputed by the Beverly Hills Unified School District, the cases are currently in the discovery phase. As part of discovery, the Plaintiffs are entitled to perform an inspection of the soil and air at Beverly Hills High School, and are doing so." She said that Al Stewart had taped it to her windshield earlier that day. He didn't want her blabbing about their evidence. He left nothing to chance in preparing a case. He had worked too hard to get to this point to allow Brockovich to screw things up for him. Plus, testing in 2004 might not necessarily reflect exposures from years ago.

Bill Ireland, one of the school district's lawyers in the litigation, sat nearby in a baseball cap. He glowered at her and then flipped his cell phone open. *Click.* She glowered back and snapped another picture of the sampling process: A white pickup truck backed up to the middle of the football field beside a tiny orange flag. Then, a twenty-foot hydraulic lift began to drill a hole into the perimeter of the field. A soil-gas probe would sample for volatile organic compounds from one to twenty feet below the field. *Click.*

As they unloaded their equipment from golf carts, engineers in khaki baseball caps, gray T-shirts, and blue jeans, from the plaintiffs' environmental testing firm, H&P Mobile Geochemistry, were shadowed by the defendants' environmental engineering firm, CDM, whose orange-vested employees took copious notes in little yellow notebooks marked "Beverly Hills High School."

She took more photographs as an H&P technician wearing blue latex gloves used a plastic syringe to suck in fifty cubic centimeters of air. The contents of the syringe would be analyzed at a mobile lab parked up in the lot by the redbrick Business Education Building. Other samples would be sent to an off-site laboratory for analysis. Would the chemicals found in the soil gas also be found inside classrooms?

The issue of migration or "vapor intrusion" of toxic gases could be critical: students spend more time indoors than out, and if outdoor air containing toxins were to migrate indoors, students would be exposed at higher levels. According to the school district's testing, chemicals found inside classrooms were no different from those in the ambient air. Those sampling results showed that the indoor air quality at Beverly Hills High School was precisely what would be expected of a facility using products containing common volatile chemicals such as inks, markers, cleaning products, and art supplies. "Results of soil-gas sampling provide no evidence that significant migration to indoor air is occurring or that the chemicals found beneath the High School are likely to represent a future health threat to students and staff," CDM's report concluded.

Click. Brockovich snapped another photograph as a technician uncoiled the one-eighth-inch plastic tubing and extracted a long piece of metal piping from the ground. They still needed to run tests near the old abandoned oil wells, known as Rodeo 106 and 107, on the upper field and between the main building and bungalows. These were the bungalow classrooms tested back in 1999 by an environmental consultant, who found high levels of benzene and formaldehyde inside. Those tests were prompted by parents' concerns about bungalow classrooms at Beverly Vista Elementary School, where some children had fallen ill and parents blamed toxic mold and chemical contamination inside the classrooms. At the time, school officials claimed the chemicals came from the off-gassing of materials *inside* the portable classrooms; teachers were assured that if they opened their windows, the problem would disappear.

But by the time the plaintiffs' environmental engineers and Brockovich arrived inside classrooms to take air samples on that Friday in September 2004, all the windows had been popped wide open. When they tried to take soil samples in the middle of the softball field, where CDM had found its highest readings of benzene in soil samples, they were forbidden from doing so and told it might create a "trip hazard." Other locations had been covered up with Dumpsters.

Brockovich scanned the field. She claimed that the defendants' soil gas testing showed benzene readings as high as four thousand parts per billion of benzene in the soil gas near the field, but that result never made it onto the data sheets given to the public by the city. She accused the defendants of concealing important evidence about contamination. *Click.*

"It's the deceit behind it that drives me," she said, looking at the "steam" rising from Sempra's plant, not far from the flowered Tower of Hope. "I just can't believe that four hundred cancers is a co-ink-ee-dink." She sounded like a modern-day Cassandra with a silly accent.

The next day, though, I picked up the phone and Brockovich was on the other end. She sounded upset. The call came as a surprise because she rarely called, and whenever I tried to reach her by phone it could take weeks to hear back. "They got their panties in a bunch because I talked to ya," she said of the lawyers on the case, who assumed she had informed me about the gathering of evidence on the football field. (I learned about it from another source.) The school district lawyer, Ireland, had complained to Stewart, who threatened Brockovich with a gag order if she didn't stop talking to the press, meaning me. "Al and Jim [Piel] jumped my ass," she said. "They immediately took the side of the defendants."

She was frustrated that Stewart and his co-counsel Piel, who intended to honor their discovery agreement with defense counsel, had muzzled her.

They refused to let her talk to the press at all and were concerned, she said, about the ramifications of her movie deal with Universal. She didn't care if there was a movie or not, she said. She cared that industry was operating so close to a public school. "I really don't give a shit anymore," she said. "My job is to create an awareness of what's going on."

I called Bill Ireland, the school district's hired gun, to find out why he had been so indignant when I introduced myself to him on the football field. "I expect people to live up to agreements and they didn't," he said, referring to Brockovich and the pact between the parties to not speak to the press. When I asked him about the lab results of the field tests, he said he wouldn't discuss the merits of the case. "I'm a lawyer in a lawsuit," he said.

As if I didn't know.

Masry, who normally loved talking to reporters, was equally skittish when I reached him. "I've got my own problems," he barked at me.

Like what?

"Like keeping control of Brockovich."

Discovery is an exhausting phase of litigation. It is invisible to the public but the place where trial lawyers spend the bulk of their time on a case, a time when they go to war to extract information to build evidence, always seeking tactical advantage.

In addition to formal site inspections of the high school, such as the Rosh Hashanah soil-gas testing on the football field, the first part of discovery—the "fact discovery phase"—allowed the plaintiffs' experts to conduct environmental tests at both Sempra's Central Plant and Venoco, just as the defendants' experts had. No independent testing group was ever brought in, such as the federal Agency for Toxic Substances and Disease Registry or the state EPA, which had been prevented from overseeing soil samples by the school district.

During this initial part of discovery, each of the twelve trial plaintiffs was also deposed for two days by defense counsel, as were their treating physicians, family, and friends. The plaintiffs were also required to undergo medical exams by physicians hired by defense counsel.

In turn, the defendants released about 1 million pages of documents to opposing counsel. They also asked the plaintiffs for eight hundred "fact" questionnaires to determine theories of liability, viewed by the plaintiffs' lawyers as an attempt to overwhelm them with tedious and largely repetitive discovery requests.

And then, according to the terms of the case management order, experts were deposed. First, defendants had the opportunity to question the plaintiffs' exposure experts about their opinions of the types of chemicals emitted by the defendants' facilities, how those chemicals were emitted, and amounts emitted over time. Then the defendants' exposure experts were deposed. Finally, there were the depositions of causation experts to take; they would testify under oath about the toxicity and carcinogenicity of the chemicals found at the site and the relationship between those chemicals and the plaintiffs' injuries.

Each step of the way, of course, there would be squabbles over the production of documents, over delays, over the number of vials of blood that needed to be taken, over the amount of time the defendants' medical experts could examine the plaintiffs.

But it was the testimony of the first twelve litigants and their families that could make or break the case for defense counsel. Every memory, every recollection, every bit of information conveyed, would be used to refute their claims that their cancers were the result of the defendants' actions. It would be the job of defense counsel to tease apart the facts of each plaintiff's story so that the defense could suggest to a jury that the plaintiffs' cancer risks could be attributed to factors that had nothing to do with Beverly Hills High.

At nine o'clock on the morning of August 2, 2004, retired social worker Geneva Day drove with her daughter, Janine, from their three-bedroom bungalow in the working-class neighborhood of Inglewood on West Seventy-sixth Street to the sleek law offices of Latham & Watkins on West Fifth Street, along the high-rise corridor of the financial district of downtown Los Angeles. The building, known as the Crown Building for the large glass "crown" at its top that is lit with purple and gold when the Los Angeles Lakers play in the NBA playoffs, is the seventh-tallest high-rise in the United States. According to the 9/11 Commission, the original plan for the September 11 attacks called for the hijacking of ten planes, one of which was to be crashed into the skyscraper that houses Latham & Watkins.

Just past the security guard, they stood on the ornate gray-and-black marble-tiled floor, waiting for one of the elevators with its own flat-screen TV to whisk them upstairs. Geneva Day typically wore blue jeans and a T-shirt at home. But on this day, the seventy-five-year-old grandmother wanted to engender the respect of the corporate lawyers who would take her deposition in the *Moss* case. So, she made a point of looking her best and wore a dark pantsuit, the one she regularly wore to church on Sundays.

Having never been part of a court case, Geneva Day was a bit nervous. She had no idea what to expect. She had spoken with her minister at St. John's United Methodist Church in Watts, where she was an active member and volunteer organist. In fact, it was from other church members, who had seen TV news reports, that she first learned of a possible connection between the oil drilling at Beverly Hills High School and elevated rates of cancer, particularly lymphomas. Her friends at church knew that Geneva had sent four of her five children to Beverly and that her thirty-six-year-old daughter Janet, a school teacher and Janine's twin, had died just a few days after Thanksgiving in 2002 due to complications arising from Hodgkin's disease.

When she asked her minister for advice prior to her deposition, he counseled her to "tell them what you know." As one of the first plaintiffs to provide testimony in the case that summer, Geneva Day vowed to do just that. "I thought it was necessary," she later recalled. "I thought to myself, 'I'm a Christian woman,' and that gives me the strength I need for this."

Upstairs in a glass-walled conference room on the thirty-seventh floor, Geneva Day was greeted by ten corporate lawyers representing Chevron, the Wainoco Oil Company, the city of Beverly Hills, the insurance company for the Beverly Hills Unified School District, and Sempra Energy, the parent company of the Southern California Gas Company. Her two lawyers from Baron & Budd, the partner Jim Piel and his young associate with longish hair named Scott Frieling, were there too. There was also a videographer, who clipped a microphone to her lapel and pointed a camera in her direction, and a shorthand reporter who created a transcript of Geneva Day's testimony over the next two days.

Moss v. Venoco had been filed a year earlier, but Lori Moss, the lead plaintiff, was not among those who had been selected to proceed to trial first. This was how the wheels of justice ground on, halting and imperfect, but steady just the same, particularly in mass tort actions. That the litigation, which now included more than one thousand plaintiffs in eight separate civil actions, would boil down to the testimony of eleven people with cancer and one whose daughter had died, namely Geneva Day, was no fluke.

In fact, about six months earlier, the attorneys representing both sides in the dispute had stipulated a case management order by choosing, with the simultaneous push of a Send button on their e-mails, twelve cancer cases. Not surprisingly, the defendants selected six cases in which chemical exposures seemed least likely, and the plaintiffs chose those six that would most tug on a jury's heartstrings. This was psychological warfare, potentially involving huge sums of money.

Most of the trial plaintiffs had been students at Beverly Hills High School. Two had not: a nurse with basal cell carcinoma, Christine Busch, who worked part-time in 1994 at Century City Hospital next door, and a thyroid cancer victim, John Laurie, who had attended programs at the nearby YMCA and played sports at the high school from 1976 to 1984. Gary Davidson, who had Hodgkin's lymphoma, had attended Beverly for only one year, from 1981 to 1982. Interestingly, the one signature disease of benzene exposure—leukemia—was not reflected in the cases selected to go to trial, even though twenty-four people in the lawsuit believed their leukemia had been caused by industrial emissions at the high school. Their cases would either be prosecuted after the first trial or be considered as part of a settlement, should that occur.

Not a bellwether plaintiff, Lori Moss remained upbeat. She had begun taking her daughter to baby group in the San Fernando Valley and wasn't as plugged into the lawsuit as she had been the year before. Her case would be factored into settlement talks that were scheduled just prior to trial, if indeed the case survived the defense team's planned summary judgment motions.

For the moment, her interests as a survivor with Hodgkin's lymphoma and thyroid cancer were in some very crucial ways being represented by the mother of another graduate of Beverly Hills High School whom she had never met, Janet Day.

Geneva Day defied the stereotypes of Beverly Hills. She was African American and a resident of Inglewood. A UCLA graduate who sent her children to UES, the laboratory teaching school at UCLA, she tended to keep to herself. "I didn't talk to many of the mothers or too many of the parents at Beverly Hills High," she testified during her deposition. With the exception of back-to-school nights, open houses, and her daughters' athletic competitions, she said, "I was just going and coming."

If anything, her case was emblematic of the divide that seemed to exist between those who pursued the litigation and those who did not: Beverly Hills residents who weren't part of the case saw the legal proceedings as an affront, and damaging to the image of the town. Most of the plaintiffs, on the other hand, either had moved away long ago or, like Geneva and Janine Day, were looking for answers as to why their loved ones who had been so healthy could grow so ill and, in the case of Janet, suddenly die.

Like other out-of-district parents who received special permits for their children to attend Beverly, Geneva Day had sent her twin daughters, Janet and Janine, to school there because of its fine reputation. Her older daughters, Caroll and Rachel, had been cheerleaders at the high school, and she had often attended Friday night football and basketball games to watch them shake it up on the sidelines.

By the time Janet and Janine arrived in 1980, they excelled at the cello and violin and regularly played in church. Janet spent more time than most students on the athletic fields, since she was on the drill team and varsity basketball team and threw shot put for the track team at Beverly, where practices were held less than one hundred feet from the oil wells and even closer to the power plant next door.

After graduation in 1984, Janet attended the University of California at Santa Barbara and later earned a teaching credential to become a first-grade teacher of students with disabilities. In April 1997, after she discovered a lump on her neck, her treating doctor noted: "Janet Day is a delightful 30-year-old woman who presents with Stage II-A nodular sclerosing Hodgkin's disease."

But not wanting her mother to worry, Janet shielded her mother from her illness and treatment—a heartbreaking point Geneva made to the lawyers that day. "She was trying not to worry me," she recalled during her deposition. "She did not want to upset me; so she didn't tell me a lot, but she told her sister, she told Janine much more than she'd tell me.

"I had just retired, and she was trying to relieve me of the burden of her sickness. She was very independent, very strong and she wanted to do it alone."

Geneva Day cleared her throat. "After she got better, she told me the details. She would tell me how miserable that chemo and radiation was and how sometimes she cried herself to sleep at night.

"And so I would tell her, 'You should have told me, I would have been there.'"

In remission from Hodgkin's disease by November 2002, Janet Day seemed to be in such good health that she entered a triathlon on Catalina Island. But later that month, after conducting parent-teacher conferences, she returned home to Los Angeles for Thanksgiving break. She felt feverish and exhausted on Wednesday night. By Saturday, she was rushed to the hospital and died. The cause of death was a viral infection, listed as (GAS) disease/streptococcal toxic shock syndrome (STSS).

In her claim against the defendants, Geneva Day alleged that Janet suffered Hodgkin's disease, a thyroid condition as a result of the radiation to treat her cancer, shortness of breath, chronic cough, numbness of extremities, dental conditions, recurrent back or neck pain, respiratory-system injury, immune-system injury, and low white-blood-cell count.

Christopher Bisgaard, the lawyer representing the city of Beverly Hills, handed her a document, Exhibit 105, marked "death claim." The cause of death was listed as toxic shock syndrome. "Do you see that, ma'am?" he asked her.

"Yes, I do."

"So Janet became sick on what day?"

"The Wednesday. She came home for the Thanksgiving vacation. It was Wednesday before Thanksgiving, the last week of November. She said, 'You know, I don't feel well. I'm going to stay in bed the whole weekend to get ready to go back to work.'"

Her mother remembered that Janet "was agonizing, trying to figure what caused her to get so sick." One of her students had scarlet fever. There were the back-to-back parent conferences. Early Sunday morning, her family took her to the hospital.

Bisgaard began: "And then late—"

"And then at noon," Geneva Day quietly told the lawyers assembled at the conference-room table.

"She died?" Bisgaard asked.

"She died about noon."

Geneva Day testified under oath that her daughter had 70 percent lung function.

"Wow," Bisgaard said, "and she did the marathon and triathlon with that, wow."

"That's right," her mother said proudly. "That's what I say, too."

Bisgaard continued. "Okay," he said. "The next item that's checked 'yes' in both columns is immune-system injury. What can you tell us about that?"

"Immune system?"

"Yes."

"The doctor told me that her T cells were damaged and that's why she couldn't fight this infection she had. The T cells or the white blood cells were damaged. She had Hodgkin's and treatment. The doctors said, 'You're okay.' Then, all of a sudden, she got sick and died."

"That must have been a shock," Bisgaard said.

"Yes," Geneva Day agreed. "It was a shock. A terrible shock."

The art of deposing a plaintiff in a lawsuit requires some finesse.

Christopher Bisgaard, the fifty-seven-year-old partner at Lewis Brisbois Bisgaard & Smith representing the city of Beverly Hills, was adept at projecting a sort of just-folks demeanor despite his corporate bona fides. Active in Republican circles and on the board of the exclusive Flintridge Prep School in Pasadena, Bisgaard was considered one of the most prominent business attorneys in Los Angeles. The landmark case of *Cottle v. Superior Court* arose out of another trial of Bisgaard's, involving homeowners who bought property built over a landfill in Ventura County. It is the leading reported appellate case in California requiring plaintiffs to establish a prima facie case of medical causation before they can proceed to trial in toxic tort cases.

A graduate of USC and the UCLA Law School, Bisgaard specialized in representing business interests in environmental and toxic tort cases. Among both colleagues and adversaries, he was known as a gentleman. Penny Newman, the environmental activist from Riverside, California, who opposed him in the Stringfellow acid pits case, believed he was "always civil, always kind." Indeed, he was at once courteous and a bit of a geek, the kind of man who was so deeply enmeshed in his work that he had little regard for pop-culture references. He once absently confided to a colleague that he had no idea who the pop music star Gwen Stefani was.

With Geneva Day, he needed to be respectful of her loss but also to charm his way into her good graces. It wasn't easy. A burly man, his face reddened easily and he could come off as aloof and arrogant.

Part of Bisgaard's style was to ingratiate himself with his deponents by identifying with them. He told Geneva Day, for example, that he had grown up in a neighborhood not far from hers, and that his mother-in-law shared her birthday and also subscribed to *Prevention* magazine, as she did. He told her that he was born in 1947, the year she arrived in California from Louisiana, that he drank too much Diet Coke, that he was a USC Trojan fan (whereas she was a UCLA Bruin), and that one of his children had once eaten poisonous mushrooms and had to be rushed to the hospital as a result.

When he needed to be, Bisgaard could be downright folksy. "I'll bet you dollars to doughnuts you didn't allow any tattooing, right?" he asked after inquiring about any home-care products, shampoos, hair straighteners, chemicals, or body piercings that might have increased Janet's chemical exposure.

"No indeedy," Geneva replied, "and thank God that wasn't the thing at that time. This is a modern-day thing, the tattooing."

But Bisgaard could be cutthroat, too.

At one point, he asked her if anyone smoked in the house. Did Janet have accidents as a child? Broken bones? Sprains? He asked: "She never was poisoned accidentally?" The implication was that Geneva Day was an uninvolved mother. His job, after all, was to create gaps in her testimony that could be used later to impeach her credibility. So he tried to mine the inconsistencies between what she said under oath and the evidence his investigators had accumulated.

What amazed her about the process was how much the defendants' lawyers knew about Janet. They knew how much she weighed at birth, when she had a drippy nose, her medical records—every last detail. "It's amazing how they can get a whole history of you," she later recalled. "Every single thing that happened to her. Her whole life. Everything can be investigated. It was somewhat intimidating. I was surprised you have no privacy."

By the time she completed her first day of testimony and six hours of questioning, she recalled, "I was drenched."

Bisgaard needed to sort out Janet Day's life story relative to chemical exposures—what she ate, where she lived, how often she exercised. Like the other plaintiffs in the lawsuit, Geneva Day would be asked a range of questions that the defense lawyers could use to poke holes in their exposure scenarios. There was, of course, the boilerplate list of confounders: Hair colorings? Shoe polish? Pesticides? Air travel?

He asked about nearby freeways, time spent driving, whether her home was in the flight pattern of the airport or had an attached garage. Was she a junk-food lover? A chocoholic? Since her father had worked for the Los Angeles coroner's office, what about his use of formaldehyde? Did he wear clothes from work home? Did she visit him at the office? And so on.

On occasion, Bisgaard's interrogation techniques backfired.

During the second day of her deposition, he pulled out a medical record, dated April 14, 1967, from a medical clinic visit when Janet was five months old. Geneva Day had testified the day before that, in general, Janet had been a very healthy and happy child who loved the outdoors—bicycling, skateboarding—and was "very athletic, very sturdy and very strong."

Reading from the medical records, Bisgaard said: "It appears to me to say 'Baby gets frequent colds,' and I can't read—and it may say—and I'm kind of guessing here, work along with me if you would, 'has got a very,' perhaps 'ill cough.' Do you see where I'm trying to read there, Mrs. Day?"

"It looks like 'mild,'" she said, reading from the old medical file. "M-i-l, yes. That's mild."

"I think that's a better reading, Mrs. Day."

"Uh-huh."

"Anyway, this—"

Geneva Day kept reading from the file. "'Healthy looking,'" she read. "'Healthy looking fatty child.'"

Scott Frieling, the young lawyer, read over her shoulder. "'Sits up.'"

"The reason I pulled this document," Bisgaard said, sounding annoyed, "is because of the reference to frequent colds, and that's a little inconsistent with what you were talking about yesterday."

"Uh-huh."

"And I'm just wondering whether this refreshes your recollection or you disagree with this, this statement in here, that Janet in the first five months of her life got frequent colds. Do you remember that at all?"

"No, I don't."

Scott Frieling interrupted, objecting to the form of the question.

Geneva Day continued reading. "Did you finish reading that farther down?" she asked Bisgaard. "'Lungs clear.' Did you finish reading? Oh, you don't want to read it. 'Development is normal.'"

"I think he's done," Frieling advised his client.

"He's finished." Geneva Day nodded. "Okay."

A week earlier in downtown Phoenix, the same corporate lawyers had convened to depose another plaintiff, a thirty-three-year-old Beverly Hills High graduate named Jeffrey Frankel, whose testicular cancer had resulted in a stroke, among other things.

Jeffrey Frankel's father was the president of Wilshire Boulevard Temple, one of the oldest synagogues in Los Angeles, and his grandfather was the *hazen,* or cantor, there. His oncologist, Dr. Barry Rosenbloom, was also a member of the synagogue. The Frankel family had had its share of cancer: Jeffrey's cousin Rachel, who grew up on South Roxbury Drive just a few blocks from the high school, had childhood leukemia.

As an undergraduate at the University of California at Santa Barbara, Frankel was diagnosed with mononucleosis in early 1994. When he returned home to Beverly Hills one weekend, as he often did, he wasn't feeling right.

Rushed to the emergency room at Cedars-Sinai Medical Center, he wound up in the ICU in a coma but had no memory of it for eleven days. When he woke up, his parents told him that he had had a stroke, that he had testicular cancer, and that he had already begun a round of chemotherapy for it. He was twenty-three years old.

For his deposition, Frankel had brought with him a photocopy of a booklet he had written, entitled "Imagine There's No Heaven; a Look at a Person's Values Systems Under a Disability," and a diary called "The First Journey of My Second Life." He also turned over a voluminous record of his medical history and a spate of photographs, including from his 1989 graduation.

The attorney Martin Refkin of Gallagher & Gallagher, representing the Wainoco Oil Company and the Frontier Oil Corporation, reviewed the photographs' captions and asked: "Whose handwriting is that?"

"That is my wife's handwriting," Jeffrey Frankel said, "and the reason I instructed her what to write is because of the stroke that came subsequent or due to the cancer, my hemi-paralysis has a—." Jeffrey Frankel was shaking.

"Try and stay still for the camera," Frieling advised.

"I apologize," Frankel replied. "My hemi-paralysis has me with a shaking right hand and my writing would not be legible to all parties."

Refkin interrupted. "I will move to strike everything after 'my wife,'" he advised the stenographer.

During discovery, plaintiffs quickly learn that nothing is off-limits. During his deposition of Jeffrey Frankel, for instance, Martin Refkin apologized to Frankel before launching into his line of questioning. "This is probably the last question I'm going to ask in the area, and I apologize for getting into the area," Refkin said, "but we just have to do what we have to do." Then he initiated a series of questions about Frankel's sex life with his wife, Rachel, prior to his cancer diagnosis.

"In that time frame, October to February, did having sex with Rachel include her having oral sex with you?" Refkin asked.

"Hold on," Scott Frieling interrupted. "Hold on. I'm going to object to the form of that question and I'm not going to have him answer that question; so—"

"I think—"

"I think it's harassing. If there's some reason that you feel like you need to have that question answered, we can somehow do it in a written interrogatory or something else but—or a written deposition question later on if the judge says that that is something that you need to know. I don't think it's something you need to know."

"It is something that we need to know," Refkin insisted.

"Tell me why."

"It's going to go to the issue of when and how he should have or did notice the mass in his testicle and who else might have noticed it and when care was given."

"So ask him that question," Frieling said, indignant now. "Ask him that question."

"Well, that's not the question I want to ask him," Refkin said.

"Well, then forget it." He turned to his client. "Don't answer that question. That's inappropriate and it's harassing."

Based on their depositions, some of the plaintiffs' cases would be more difficult to prove than others. Karen Lee, a fifty-seven-year-old realtor who had been treated for breast cancer, testified that she was a former smoker; her mother had breast cancer and so did her father's sister, though her physician told her that he didn't believe the cause of her illness was genetic.

The defense attorney Cindy Cwik from Latham & Watkins asked if she remembered ever getting drunk in college.

"I remember only one time ever getting drunk in college," Lee replied.

"And what do you remember?" Cwik queried.

"That it was rum punch." Presumably Cwik, a graduate of the Yale Law School, where she still returned to recruit students for her firm, was trying to establish that Lee had an increased risk of breast cancer from alcohol consumption. After years of research, one of the few known risk factors for a cluster of women with breast cancer in Marin County, California, was drinking two glasses of wine a day.

When Karen Lee, once a Beverly homecoming princess, told the lawyer that she now drank maybe one or two glasses of red wine per week, Cwik abruptly changed her line of questioning. Why had she not been in contact with her brother for twenty years? The question seemed out of left field and suggested that Cwik would stop at nothing to put Karen Lee's life under as harsh a light as possible.

And then: "Do you believe that you were exposed to chemicals while attending Beverly Hills High School?" Cwik asked.

"I don't know," Lee answered. "I guess that's where this case is going."

Many questions bordered on the absurd. Monica Revel, a twenty-nine-year-old veterinarian with metastatic melanoma, was asked by a defense lawyer why she failed to follow her orthodontist's instructions as a teenager—as if she were responsible for her cancer because she hadn't worn headgear.

If they wanted to keep their trial date of July 2005, Stewart and Piel had to let the defense counsel begin deposing their clients' physicians. The plaintiff Melissa Gross, a thirty-one-year-old mother of four who lived in Orange County and was married to a neurosurgeon, was being treated by a well respected breast cancer specialist named Dr. John Link.

For two hours, Link was deposed in his Long Beach office in December 2004. Link estimated that he had testified in about two hundred medical malpractice cases in the past decades—for both plaintiff and defense lawyers. The number one payout for medical malpractice lawsuits in California is missing a breast cancer diagnosis. He explained: "That's when a woman comes in with a lump and her doctor says, 'Don't worry.'"

Link understood that it's one thing to treat cancer; it's quite another to opine on its causes. He could talk about the severity of Melissa Gross's disease: It was Stage II. Advanced. Five positive lymph nodes. "She has a very bad cancer," he said. "She's in real trouble."

And he could talk about her treatment and why it was so aggressive: she received preoperative chemotherapy and radiation, then a double mastectomy. It was highly unusual, in his experience, for a thirty-one-year-old with no family history of breast cancer to be diagnosed so young.

But toxicology, the study of poisons, and etiology, the study of the onset of disease, were not his specialties. "They tried to ask me," he said. "I pleaded ignorance. The truth is, I just don't know."

Link was also asked about the cause of breast cancer, in general. From known risk factors, he said, a strong family genetic history researchers had discovered was most important. Link said that since Melissa Gross was Jewish, she was tested for the genetic markers on the Ashkenazi panel. They were all negative, meaning she didn't have the BrCA gene for breast cancer. "That's important for plaintiffs to show there are not other major potential causes of her cancer," he said.

He added: "The problem with a lawsuit is they want a number to assign for damages. They want hard numbers. The lawyer asked me, 'What is this woman's chance of survival?' I gave her very aggressive therapy. I think she's right at fifty-fifty.

"She's really on the cusp of survivability. It's a $250,000 award for lost chance of a cure in California. You can't be compensated for loss of life unless it's more likely than not you'd survive. I'd say she's got a fifty-fifty chance of survival forever."

John Link's testimony was not unique. Dr. Michael Van Skoy-Mosher, Karen Lee's oncologist, for example, also testified that the most important risk factor for breast cancer is a genetic history. But despite Karen Lee's mother's history of breast cancer and her Ashkenazi heritage, genetic testing eliminated those factors as contributing to the development of her particular cancer, because her genetic test results were negative for the BrCA gene. That testimony would be important for Lee's case because it meant that other risk factors, such as exposures to carcinogenic substances, may have played a bigger role in the development of her breast cancer than her genetic history.

Even so, it was the consensus among the treating physicians that they didn't *really* know what caused their patients' illnesses. They could discuss specific treatments and known risk factors for a variety of cancers, in a general way, but anything beyond that was pure speculation from the standpoint of medical science. In fact, course offerings in occupational health have declined in recent years as many medical school curricula no longer include courses in environmental medicine, or the study of the health effects of environmental pollution. Few doctors specialize in the field, which requires a multidisciplinary understanding of toxicology, biology, oncology, and epidemiology.

So the value of testimony from treating physicians would be limited. Just as the litigants themselves couldn't help their own cause, beyond agreeing to have blood tests done and medical records retrieved, it was unclear whether their depositions would help or hurt them. No matter how clearly they remembered events in their lives, they still had no knowledge when, or if, any of them coincided with toxic chemical exposures. When defense counsel asked Jeffrey Frankel if he remembered March 23, 1994, Frankel said that was the day Wayne Gretzky broke Gordie Howe's record as all-time leading goal scorer. But Frankel had no idea what happened on that date relative to operations at Sempra's Central Plants and its introduction of low-NOX burners.

That information would have to be pulled together by Al Stewart and his team of experts.

During her deposition, Karen Lee remembered exactly when she first got her period, because it was the day that Buddy Holly and the Big Bopper died. She had no idea, however, that when she moved into an apartment across the street from the high school's tennis courts in 1965, Sempra's Central Plant had just begun its operations.

What really mattered was how closely opposing counsel analyzed their testimony.

Both of Monica Revel's parents had melanoma, which meant that she could be predisposed to developing it too. She believed that both of her parents' having the same disease suggested an environmental link, since they were not blood relatives.

Gary Davidson worked as a gas station attendant for three years, which meant that his occupational exposure from benzene could have exceeded his exposures to that chemical during the year he attended Beverly High. The defense lawyers would undoubtedly argue that his contraction of mononucleosis and infection with the Epstein-Barr virus contributed substantially to his developing Hodgkin's lymphoma. But the plaintiffs' lawyers believed that those additional risk factors didn't eliminate the probability that his chemical exposures at Beverly High *also* played a substantial role in the development of his Hodgkin's disease.

Each case would need to be reviewed with great care by the medical-causation experts, whose work wouldn't be revealed to opposing counsel for another year. Only then could the lawyers in the dispute hammer home their cases to a jury.

Though he was relying on his partner Jim Piel to handle the details of discovery, Al Stewart remained at the helm. Ed Masry had been undergoing dialysis for the last several years and needed to be hospitalized that spring. After bypass surgery, he threw a blood clot, and needed a second surgery when he lost all blood flow to his feet. Now, he'd have to relearn how to walk.

But his rehabilitation went poorly. A second blood clot soon followed, and then the amputation of his left leg. Transferred to the intensive care unit at Los Robles Regional Medical Center in Thousand Oaks, he died on December 5, 2005. At his memorial service in city hall, where he once held forth as mayor, colleagues invoked his favorite Harry Truman quote: "I never gave anyone hell. I just told people the truth—and they thought it was hell."

But even after his death, Masry was back in the news.

In a sweeping criminal investigation that implicated some of the biggest names in Hollywood, a federal grand jury indicted a private investigator named Anthony Pellicano for illegally wiretapping the phone lines of his clients' enemies. Many of his clients, including Ed Masry, were big-time lawyers.

The lawyer Kissandra Cohen, a former Masry & Vititoe employee, had claimed in court that the law firm bugged her telephone while she was litigating a sexual discrimination and slander case against Masry. Before he died, Masry was questioned by the FBI about the case. He denied that he had ever authorized Pellicano's wiretapping, though he did admit to employing him. Cohen's lawsuit against Masry and Brockovich was ultimately settled out of court, and the terms of the settlement were kept confidential.

In a case of spy versus spy, it turned out that Pellicano was also working for Masry's adversaries, including Christensen, Miller, Fink, Jacobs, Glaser, Weil & Shapiro, one of the law firms representing the city of Beverly Hills. In fact, the only lawyer who was indicted by the federal grand jury in the criminal case was Terry Christensen, Louis "Skip" Miller's partner. Christensen pled not guilty to charges of conspiracy and wiretapping, but he was caught on tape talking to Pellicano about the detective's wiretapped recordings of Christensen's legal adversaries, who were planning legal strategy.

In the dog-eat-dog world of toxic tort litigation, where the mantra is "Win at any cost," beating one's opponent was the name of the game. Sometimes, to prevail, that meant digging up dirt—both literally and figuratively.

CHAPTER THIRTEEN

TRADE SECRETS AND OTHER
PRIVILEGES

O n Friday, August 26, 2005, just days before Hurricane Katrina destroyed
the Gulf Coast, a jury in Gulfport, Mississippi, voted 9–3 to award
$14 million in compensatory damages to an oyster fisherman named
Glen Strong, who claimed that his multiple myeloma was caused by emissions of
dioxin from Du Pont's titanium dioxide plant, five miles from his home. Du Pont's
lawyers vowed to appeal the decision, but they were also facing two thousand
other plaintiffs whose cases hadn't yet been heard. Their lawyer was Al Stewart.

Every day he was in trial on Glen Strong's case, Al Stewart couldn't help
but notice that the gallery of spectators included many of the defense lawyers in the Beverly Hills case. They were closely observing his every move in
court. "They were taking copious notes," Stewart recalled. The guys representing the Wainoco Oil Company from Gallagher & Gallagher were there;
Marty Refkin sent his daughter. And the school district's attorney, Jeffrey
Vinnick from Haight Brown & Bonesteel, was also there.

No doubt, the defense lawyers wanted to watch Stewart in action. But they
were just as interested in the expert testimony of both a chemistry professor
from Baton Rouge, Barry Dellinger, and an environmental engineer from Los
Angeles, Jim Tarr, whom Stewart had also enlisted as expert witnesses in the
Beverly Hills litigation. The willingness of the defendants to settle claims
against them would be based, in part, on their estimate of the persuasiveness
of the witnesses against them and their guesses about a jury.

When he first spotted them in the courthouse, Stewart said: "I know
y'all don't have the kind of practice that brings you to Laurel, Mississippi."

Without hesitating, Refkin replied: "*You're* our business."

As discovery proceeded, the problems of proof confronting the plaintiffs' lawyers became increasingly apparent. Their clients couldn't help them prove their case. The clients didn't know what had happened to them or when. They only knew that something had gone wrong and they'd got sick. The causation case, therefore, had to be proved almost entirely from documents in the defendants' files and from existing court records of related cases that could offer clues about the defendants' behavior in terms of historical emissions and toxic releases.

As a result, the focus would shift to the operations of Sempra's Central Plant in Century City, directly next door to Beverly Hills High: what releases were emitted there and how did they disperse?

A published opinion by the Second District of the California Court of Appeals from June 17, 1996, would prove crucial to Stewart in building his evidence of exposure. In that case, *Transwestern Pipeline Company v. Monsanto Company,* some of the historical facts about gas lines near Beverly Hills came into focus, revealing shocking information about just what was coming through the pipelines. The case detailed the twenty-year saga that began with the 1981 discovery that natural gas pipelines throughout the United States were contaminated with polychlorinated biphenyls, or PCBs. A group of toxic chemicals once used widely in industry as coolants and lubricants, PCBs were banned by Congress in 1976 because of evidence that they accumulate in the environment and present health hazards to humans. Under the Toxic Substances Control Act, the EPA regulates the limited use of PCBs to protect the public.

When the Southern California Gas Company, or SoCalGas, tested its lines, it found that they were indeed contaminated at the point where they connected with Transwestern's pipeline in Needles, California. It is believed that the chemicals' most serious danger could be that PCBs mimic natural hormones, such as estrogen, and can severely disrupt the body's endocrine system, resulting in birth defects and sterility as well as cancer.

PCBs and their even more toxic by-products, dioxins and dibenzofurans, are fat-soluble, meaning that they bio-accumulate. Potentially dangerous levels of PCBs have been reported in the fatty tissues of seals, whales, eagles, fish, and human beings. PCBs have been implicated in breast cancer, brain cancer, malignant melanoma, non-Hodgkin's lymphoma, and soft-tissue sarcomas. Even at current background levels, the EPA has found that PCBs can damage the body's immune and reproductive systems.

Purchased by Enron in 1996, the Transwestern Pipeline Company transports natural gas from Texas and Oklahoma to California, where its pipes connect with pipes belonging to the Southern California Gas Company. On the way to California, the gas passes through stations which compress it, allowing more gas to be transported through the pipeline. In 1968, a Transwestern compressing station in New Mexico was destroyed in a gas explosion. In the process of rebuilding the station, Transwestern installed a new turbine-driven gas compressor. The compressor used a lubricant manufactured by the Monsanto Company known as Turbinol. Turbinol is a synthetic, fire-resistant lubricant consisting mostly of PCBs.

Because the condensate in its pipelines contained detectable levels of PCBs (at least fifty parts per million), federal regulations required SoCalGas to take special precautions to monitor the PCB levels in the condensate and to specially train its employees to remove condensate from the pipelines. This special handling and cleanup effort cost SoCalGas more than $1 million a year. In 1990, court records show, a settlement was finally reached in an arbitration proceeding in which Transwestern paid SoCalGas about $10 million for costs associated with the PCB removal, since the entire distribution system was contaminated. Two years later, Transwestern paid SoCalGas an additional $2 million; testimony from the people who ran the PCB program at SoCalGas indicated that the costs to the company would continue for the next two decades.

According to the appellate court, the problem had lasting impact:

If the PCBs remained confined inside the SoCalGas pipelines they would pose no danger. But PCBs cannot be confined inside the pipes. The PCBs mix with pipeline condensate, liquids which form naturally inside the pipes. This pipeline condensate must be removed on a regular basis or else it will clog up the pipes and impede the flow of gas. The PCBs enter the outside world when the condensate is removed from the pipes. Even though Transwestern stopped using Turbinol in 1972, once the PCBs entered the SoCalGas pipelines, they coated and clung to the pipe walls and thus continued to infect the pipeline condensate more than 20 years later. No technique exists for removing PCBs once they have entered a pipeline. As one expert testified, once the PCBs entered its pipeline system, "SoCal was done for."

Documents from the *Transwestern* case would be critical for Al Stewart in helping establish his theory of chemical exposures, but only to a point.

The time frame of contamination of the pipelines fit perfectly with the time many of his clients had attended Beverly Hills High School. But he still needed to find out how those contaminated lines impacted Beverly Hills High School, if at all. For that, he would need specifics about gas content and testimony from the arbitration to see if the PCB-laced condensate made its way to Sempra's Central Plant or a nearby compressor station in West Los Angeles.

From his work on Glen Strong's dioxin case in Mississippi, Stewart understood that PCBs come from the same chemical family as dioxins. Structurally, they're separated by only a single oxygen molecule; when PCBs combust, they convert to dioxinlike chemicals. If he could prove that Central Plant was burning natural gas laced with PCBs to fuel its boilers, he might just win this case. It was a huge gamble, he knew. But for the moment, it was his best shot.

The deadline for fact discovery had come and gone. In the days before Christmas 2004, the lawyers at Baron & Budd still hadn't secured the evidence they needed from the Southern California Gas Company, the company that Venoco was selling its natural gas to and that was owned by Sempra, the operator of the power plant. SoCalGas was not a defendant in the Beverly Hills lawsuit, but its parent company, Sempra Energy, was.

On November 29, 2004, plaintiffs' counsel had issued a subpoena to the custodian of records of Southern California Gas, seeking data on gas content and "documents without redactions." As Erin Brockovich knew so well, public-records searches of government agencies could go only so far. The Beverly High soccer mom Jody Kleinman also learned that lesson the hard way. More than a year after filing a Freedom of Information Act request on the South Coast Air Quality Management District, Kleinman finally received a thick packet in the mail. Inside a legal-sized envelope were Venoco's records, detailing gas volume from the Southern California Gas Company's measurement collections systems. All the papers were stamped "CONFIDENTIAL—TRADE SECRET."

Those records, which included flow rates, flow temperatures, carbon dioxide content, nitrogen content, BTU ratings, and other specific information about gas content sent by the facility through the gas company pipeline, had been completely redacted by the government agency. The AQMD lawyers had deferred to the company, deleting what it claimed was proprietary information.

Until the company complied with the subpoena, the contents of the natural gas would stay secret.

In addition to the emissions information that Stewart and Piel had been requesting from the defendants for nearly a year and still did not have, they would need to serve more subpoenas on the Southern California Gas Company for its business records and confidential documents from arbitration proceedings concerning PCB contamination of its natural gas pipelines. The gas company's lawyer refused to comply with the first subpoena, blaming the Baron & Budd attorneys for failing to provide enough time to gather the documents in question, as required by California's Code of Civil Procedure.

On December 14, 2004, the plaintiffs tried again, but this time they were facing a December 22 cutoff date for discovery, an even shorter time frame for the company to respond. Nonetheless, SoCalGas agreed to produce the requested documents on January 11, 2005. In response, lawyers for Sempra filed a motion in court to quash the subpoena, claiming they had not received sufficient notice, given discovery deadlines.

At 8:30 a.m. on Tuesday, February 15, 2005, Judge Mortimer would be asked to settle the matter in another pretrial hearing. And on this day, it was Sempra's attorney, V. Thomas Meador III, a partner at Morgan, Lewis & Bockius, who would face off against James Piel, Al Stewart's partner at Baron & Budd.

Meador rose to address the court. He argued against extending discovery "to get who-knows-what records." Besides, he told the judge, his voice rising, "the emissions are known. *None* related to PCBs. It's not in our waste stream."

Meador was usually unflappable in court. A graduate of UCLA and UCLA Law School, he had an easygoing manner. On this case, he liked to joke about his prescience in having authored an article years earlier about a theoretical scenario in which a lawyer receives a complaint that reads like the sequel to the film *Erin Brockovich.* But on this day, the irony was lost on him, and he was growing increasingly agitated.

"How does some contaminated gas in Texas relate to any issue in this case?" he asked the judge. "The plaintiffs haven't articulated any theory." Meador complained that opposing counsel wasn't playing by the rules. "If they have this new theory that contaminated gas in Texas went to users in L.A. and somehow got into the pipelines and exposed the plaintiffs, they're under an obligation to articulate that theory."

Finally, he said, "there is *no* relationship between PCBs and my client."

Jim Piel countered that the defendants had known since the beginning of the lawsuit that dioxins, toxic by-products of PCBs, were at issue in the case. "Sempra's own documents show they had contaminated lines," Piel said. "They've known about this contamination for years and years."

"We asked the defendants time and time again: What are your emissions? We sought this stuff back in October."

Piel referred the judge to Sempra's Web site, which included links to the Southern California Gas Company. There, customers could read warnings about "high-pressure" gas, defined as one hundred pounds per square inch and greater, and the presence of PCBs in natural gas lines. According to the Web site:

> High pressure customers are warned about pipeline liquids and possible harmful constituents, such as PCBs and benzene, because pressure reductions of the gas result in cooling, which is likely to cause pipeline liquids to form by condensation.

> People exposed to PCBs who are concerned about the exposure should be advised to see their physicians.

Meador looked worried. "This is a can of worms," he told the judge, his voice rising. "Why should we not be allowed to do discovery if they can?"

The judge was unimpressed. He found Sempra's responses ambiguous and decided that the documents at issue were "calculated to lead to the discovery of admissible evidence." He overruled Sempra's motion to quash the business-records subpoena and gave Meador ten days to turn over the documents in question, unless they were privileged attorney-client communications.

A month later, Piel would finally see what the gas company had—but not before agreeing to keep the records secret. On April 21, 2005, Judge Mortimer signed a protective order. "These documents," the order read, "must be kept confidential to protect the privacy rights for Southern California Gas customers, to protect SoCalGas facilities from terrorist attack, and to protect SoCalGas trade secrets from its competitors."

Despite his willingness to reopen discovery for plaintiffs' counsel, Judge Mortimer was nonetheless growing impatient with them. On November 23, 2004, in response to a motion by the city of Beverly Hills to compel them to answer a set of special interrogatories, the judge ordered the Baron & Budd attorneys to identify what specific chemicals they believed caused their clients' injuries. After all, more than eight months had passed since Stewart and Piel were served with the interrogatories, and they had hired experts who presumably could help clarify what carcinogens were at issue in the case.

A month later, in response to the judge's order and through discussions with their experts, they narrowed their list of "chemicals of interest" from more than 180 chemicals to 8: Chromium, nickel, arsenic, benzene, PCBs, polycyclic aromatic hydrocarbons (PAHs), formaldehyde, and chlorinated dioxins and dioxinlike compounds, including furans.

But the defense lawyers for Beverly Hills continued to object. PCBs, PAHs, and dioxins were "broad categories" of chemicals that included hundreds of specific chemicals. In e-mails, they advised the Baron & Budd lawyers there were more than one hundred different polychlorinated aromatic hydrocarbons, more than two hundred polychlorinated biphenyls, and about seventy-five compounds referred to as dioxins.

Scott Frieling, the associate from Baron & Budd, was unfazed: "Although I have repeatedly asked for the chemical constituents of their emissions, your defendant brethren are either unwilling or unable to provide this information to plaintiffs, but I surmise that you may be able to obtain it more easily than I," he said in a fax.

The judge then issued a second order on March 25, 2005. "These cases have been pending for quite some time and are set for trial," he said. The trial date had now been set back to March of 2006. "Plaintiffs should be able to be specific and defendants are entitled to the information. . . . Plaintiffs are again ordered to identify specific chemicals alleged to have caused plaintiffs' injuries."

"Just because I moved the trial date doesn't mean the pressure isn't still on," the judge warned them during a conference in his courtroom.

The judge didn't levy sanctions against them, but Jim Piel and Al Stewart were faced with a dilemma: they had to specify what chemicals their clients had been exposed to, but they still hadn't received many of the key documents they needed to prove their case. And the sooner they showed their hand, the more time the defense had to prepare its attack against them. The rules of discovery clearly required that the defense lawyers be informed precisely what chemicals allegedly caused what illness; otherwise the plaintiffs needed to remove them from consideration in the case. And from the defendants' point of view, the plaintiffs weren't providing specifics because they had essentially conceded that they had no case. It was that simple.

By the summer of 2005, two years had come and gone on the Beverly Hills case, and Al Stewart had already spent upwards of $5 million for his experts to conduct a complete assessment of chemical contamination at Beverly Hills High School. One of his environmental firms submitted a bill for $343,261.95 for two years' worth of work. His wind-tunnel experts from Colorado received $250,000 for the first phase of their work, which included the creation of a precise physical model of the high school and surrounding neighborhood; they were on to the second, calculating air flow, using meteorological data.

Knowledge about the toxic effects of chemicals is a relentlessly dynamic process, driven not only by human curiosity but by lawsuits, publicity, politics, and economics. In court cases, disputes often revolve around questions like how "safe" is safe enough—questions that science can pose and perhaps narrow but can never answer authoritatively. There are those who believe that although science can't accurately assess how a level of contamination causes cancer in kids, that is no reason to do nothing. It is, finally, a political issue, not a scientific or engineering one.

Indeed, the role of scientists in the litigation would not be primarily about environmental health or the search for truth. Rather, the experts represented a power struggle. Truth and justice played a part, but only a part. It was, instead, largely a behind-the-scenes contest for control over the debate. At times high-minded, at other times brutal and raw, those forces vying for control offered two competing narratives: one was that exposures to industrial and synthetic chemicals represent negligible cancer risks, and animal studies have little or no scientific value for assessing human risk; the other was that even the smallest exposure—a single molecule, for example—is enough to do harm and that in the absence of human data, animal studies are the most definitive for assessing human cancer risks.

So it would be science—or expert opinions—that mattered most in determining causation in court. And, ultimately, the scientists would be used to persuade a jury one way or the other.

A former chemist himself, Stewart had put together an impressive team of air-dispersion modelers to analyze both industrial gas emissions and deposits from Sempra's eight cooling towers and four boilers. He had also enlisted geologists to interpret aerial photographs, historical oil field records, and soil-gas tests. By the time he toured the Sempra plant with his air-modeling experts in April 2005, Stewart would notice the steel beams near the cooling towers on one side of the facility closest to the Century City Medical Building. They had holes in them the size of silver dollars. Some appeared to be corroded completely through. Stewart wondered if the acid and heavy metals emitted in the water vapor from the cooling towers had caused the corrosion. Hexavalent chromium, a corrosion inhibitor, was used to clean the cooling towers for nearly twenty-five years before the state of California banned its use for that purpose in 1989.

He would need his experts to piece together the puzzle of precisely what emissions, if any, had caused the corrosion. "You think that's good for people?" one of his engineers asked him. "How could this be good for kids?"

One of his experts specialized in air flow around buildings. Another created a model of deposits coming out of Sempra's cooling towers. It was their opinion that water vapor and water droplets created drift, or what fell on the campus; the droplets were contaminated with chemicals from the cooling tower, such as hexavalent chromium. Gases such as formaldehyde and dioxins passed through campus like fog—a "toxic chemical fog," as one of the experts described it.

In terms of potency, Stewart knew that there was a critical equation: one pound of hexavalent chromium equaled five thousand pounds of benzene. Because of his Du Pont case in Mississippi, he had also been reading up on dioxin, a highly potent carcinogen that causes neuro-developmental, immune, reproductive, and endocrine disorders at very low levels of exposures. Tiny doses in the range of nanograms (one-billionth of a gram) to micrograms (one-millionth of a gram) per kilogram of body weight of dioxin can cause harm.

In the months that followed, he'd need his dioxin expert, Barry Dellinger, to analyze data about PCBs in the gas lines from the Southern California Gas Company to calculate chemical emissions from Sempra's Central Plant.

Modeling is a shorthand—a description of what happened—intended to address historical questions, which were at the heart of the legal case. One of Stewart's experts believed that the boiler stacks of the plant were unusually short, possibly for aesthetic reasons. Had they been taller, would the plume have bypassed the high school? "Only a damn fool can argue there's not harm from this facility," he told Stewart. "The question is the degree and nature of the harm being done. It's silly to talk about a single entity, because people aren't being exposed to one thing. They're exposed to this toxic chemical cloud."

Robert N. Meroney, a professor of environmental engineering at Colorado State University in Fort Collins, Colorado, who helped to oversee the wind engineering lab there, presented a report to the court, "Prediction of the Impact of Cooling Tower Drift Near Beverly Hills High School." He concluded that the twin towers in Century City, built in 1969, strongly affected wind patterns in the area: the forty-four-story buildings increased drift deposits by a factor of ten at distances from five hundred to one thousand feet. "Because such fog and drift contain the minerals of the makeup water and often contain water treatment chemicals, contact of these chemicals with plants, buildings, surfaces and human activity can be hazardous," Meroney wrote. "The presence of tall, upwind buildings and terrain elevation changes will accelerate droplet deposition downwind of Sempra."

Meroney and one of his Ph.D. students, David Neff, had constructed a precise model of Beverly Hills High School, which they placed inside a wind tunnel. They found that at a wind direction of 160 degrees, particles were trapped on the grounds and buildings of the entire campus. "For a shift in wind direction of only 20 degrees, significant differences in dispersion and deposition occur," Meroney wrote. "Wind approaches the cooling tower complex from upwind passing between the Century Medical Plaza buildings and Century Plaza 2. Although moisture from the cooling towers still spreads upward and laterally, the initial trajectory of the plume is not over the main BHHS complex but more toward the BHHS athletic facilities."

From the wind tunnel model, David Neff created a dramatic videotape, which illustrated how billows of gas vapors traveled on the high school campus. Using meteorological data, such as temperature and wind flow, he created an animated depiction of how toxic dispersion occurred on the campus. He would submit "Cooling Tower Plume Visualization Pictures" to the court. There were also pictures to depict air dispersion for the boiler stacks and for the oil well drill sites.

Another expert hired by the plaintiffs was a professor of environmental engineering at Pennsylvania State University, Jack Matson. Based on his review of internal company reports from Sempra's Central Plant facility, Matson believed that the power plant failed "to take the necessary steps to prevent exposure to the nearby school and community from its hexavalent chromium emissions." In his report, Matson said that it was known as early as 1957 that the corrosion inhibitor, when used in cooling-tower water treatment chemicals, was toxic. And even though the plant had the opportunity to convert to the use of other, less harmful water treatments, it failed to do so until 1989—the year that the state banned hexavalent chromium's use for that purpose.

In early March 2005, just prior to his deposition, the plaintiffs' air-modeling expert Steven Hanna had traveled from his home in Kennebunk-port, Maine, to New York City to join a team of about fifty scientists to release a tracer gas next to Madison Square Garden. They were conducting a study to determine how air flows through the city, in case of a terrorist attack or an accident involving toxic chemicals. The study was part of the "Urban Dispersion Program," a $10 million project sponsored by the U.S. Department of Homeland Security, Department of Defense, and Department of Energy.

Hanna, a professor of environmental health at Harvard's School of Public Health, had developed "applied diffusion models" to study plumes from cooling towers for the U.S. Department of Energy and was the author of a book, *Wind Flow and Vapor Cloud Dispersion at Industrial and Urban Sites*, published by the American Institute of Chemical Engineers. Part of his research, supported by the Department of Defense, was to evaluate meteorological models for releases of chemical and biological agents.

Hanna's work on the Beverly Hills case resulted in a report, "Deposition of Chromate Released to the Atmosphere in Drift Water from Cooling Towers Adjacent to BHHS." He had determined that the model normally used by regulatory agencies to calculate air dispersion was inappropriate in this case because it failed to account for the effects of other buildings around Sempra's cooling towers, such as the soaring twin towers of Century City.

When I contacted him in late June 2005 to discuss his testimony, he apologized and then said: "I really don't think I should be saying anything. They seem to be keeping things confidential on both sides."

Back in Texas, Al Stewart worried that he might be losing ground on another front. His clients with testicular cancer, such as Jeffrey Frankel, could prove to be especially valuable, since testicular cancer is a relatively rare form of cancer. Each year, it accounts for less than 1 percent of all cancers in men. At the same time, the medical literature has documented a link between cancer of the testes and employment in natural gas and petroleum industries.

But even more crucial was the finding of his well respected epidemiology expert, Dr. Richard Clapp of the Boston University School of Public Health. Former director of the cancer registry for the state of Massachusetts, Clapp had conducted dozens of evaluations of cancer in communities on workers, veterans, and school employees. He was also an expert on the health effects of nuclear weapons production, military toxic exposures, and electro-magnetic radiation.

On the Beverly Hills case, Clapp had been hired by Stewart to analyze statistics from the Surveillance Epidemiology End Results program of the National Cancer Institute and compare them to information gathered from Beverly Hills High School yearbooks and from pathology reports, to confirm cancer diagnoses. Contrary to media reports from the previous year, when the plaintiffs' counsel were flogged in the press for not having proof of a public health problem at Beverly High, Clapp's epidemiological study sug-gested otherwise.

In his report, Clapp found a statistically significant increase in Hodgkin's disease, thyroid cancer, and testicular cancer among Beverly High graduates from 1975 to 2001. An increase in three types of cancer in the world of epide-miology is a remarkable finding. For testicular cancer, he concluded, the rate was *twice* as high as the national average. In toxic tort cases, a doubling of the incidence is often all that is needed to prove causation.

Clapp's testimony, therefore, would be essential in providing evidence that attending Beverly Hills High School was associated with higher rates of some cancers. So the defense attorneys needed to attack him at every turn to discredit his report; to do so they would launch an all-out assault on Clapp's arsenal of scientific inquiry.

When Clapp had requested (through the plaintiffs' lawyers) access to Cali-fornia's cancer registry to compare the population of students from Beverly High to state cancer statistics, he was flatly refused—despite a promise of con-fidentiality through a court order. A lawyer for USC, which housed the state cancer registry, determined that California law provided "absolute protection" of its database. Lawyers for the school district pursued the same tactic. Citing California's education code, they refused to release personal information—date of birth, Social Security number, married name—of 33,256 former students for an epidemiological study without prior written approval. To do so would not only be "unduly burdensome and harassing," it would also be a breach of students' constitutional privacy rights and jeopardize federal education funding.

"Given the great number of highly successful Beverly Hills High School graduates in the film and other industries," lawyers for the school district ar-gued in court, "keeping personal information private is of paramount con-cern." Yet, in December 1994, when it had not been faced with a lawsuit, the school district had readily complied with requests to release confidential medical information, some of which was redacted. At the time, a county health department epidemiologist asked for information for a breast cancer study of teachers at Horace Mann Elementary School, where the incidence of breast cancer was found to be "at the upper end" of the expected statistical range.

If there was a turning point in the litigation, this was it. Privacy rights would trump the public's right to know. At a moment when the truth might finally be revealed, it would, instead, be obscured by more legal finagling and a vituperative exchange of e-mails.

In a January 19, 2005, e-mail to the school district's counsel, William Ireland, Baron & Budd lawyer Jim Piel wrote:

> Bill,
>
> I am sorry that you and your client have refused to join us in seeking the Court's guidance and assistance in putting together a confidentiality order to permit Plaintiffs access, under rigid protections, to extremely valuable information necessary to make a true analysis of the epidemiology related to this case. I would have thought you would readily have joined in a request that the information be provided in order that the public and the students, faculty and staff at your client's Beverly Hills High School campus would have the benefit of a true epidemiological analysis to get to the bottom of what Plaintiffs obviously believe is a serious public health issue.

Ireland wrote back:

> Jim: I realize that you are merely posturing for perceived advantage and that I should not be offended by your e-mail but I find it hard not to be.
>
> The remedy you propose of a confidentiality order does not authorize the violation of the student's statutory and constitutional rights to privacy. You know that. . . . You also know that the cancer registry is not willing to turn over information that it contends is privileged to you. Without that information and even with it, you still would have to contact all the former students and no one has the information needed to do that.
>
> As for dedication to finding the truth, I would refer you both to the history of the City's legislative subpena [sic] and to the District's website. The

District has been dedicated to public safety and to keeping the public informed. The steps the City had to take to investigate and disclose the lack of support for the claims that were made at the commencement of this controversy speaks volumes.

I realize that the purpose of the posturing . . . is just a litigation tactic hoping for advantage. Its [sic] still hard not to be offended by your email which is why I have responded at such length, albeit after a day so my response would be more tempered.

Stewart believed this was a pivotal moment in the case because it was when he lost all respect for the school district and its lawyers. "The pretense that the law just doesn't allow us to do that is a false pretense," he said bitterly. "This is from the people who supposedly care about children."

"They could have answered the question, once and for all, what's going on at Beverly Hills High School. When they did not do that and then gave the reason that they'd love to help us but couldn't, I could see they feign care and concern for the children. It's a lie."

Stewart believed that the real reason the school district wouldn't conduct an epidemiology study of its own was because it didn't want to know the truth.

Trials aren't about broad issues. They're about specifics. And for all the broad concerns, the specifics of this case still favored the defendants. It wouldn't be enough for Al Stewart simply to show emissions coming from the oil wells and power plant. Nor would his epidemiology report prove causation. With the help of his experts, he would have to prove that from these emissions, people were being exposed to dangerous levels of carcinogens; that is, that these specific emissions poisoned his clients.

What were the "pathways of exposure"? Inhalation? Absorption by skin? Ingestion? When Stewart had walked around the high school campus, he had observed not just where the students' lockers were located but where they ate lunch: at a rooftop cafeteria and on the front lawn—precisely where his air modelers said the fog moved on campus.

During the spring of 2005, the defense counsel continued to take depositions of the plaintiffs' experts. One of them was the unassuming Professor Barry Dellinger, who chaired the Chemistry Department at Louisiana State University in Baton Rouge. Dellinger was a member of the U.S. Environmental

Protection Agency's science advisory board on environmental engineering. A world-renowned expert on PCBs and dioxins, he had received a $1.3 million grant from the National Science Foundation the previous year for a proposal entitled "Combustion-Generated Nanoparticles: The Role of Transition Metals in Nanoparticle and Pollutant Formation." His research was on the cutting edge of the science of air pollution prevention and control.

Dellinger's team of U.S. EPA scientists was working to develop air monitors for dioxins, which were on the plaintiffs' short list of "chemicals of interest." Resonance Enhanced Multi-Photon Ionization (REMPI) was an apparatus to analyze for benzene and chlorobenzene and minuscule concentrations of dioxin compounds. According to the government scientists: "Relevant concentrations of these compounds are often in the parts per quadrillion levels."

For the past two decades, the regulation of dioxin in the United States has been a political hot potato. Since 1985, the Environmental Protection Agency has been working on publishing a study of the health problems associated with dioxin. Twenty years later, the report has yet to be completed, its delay due largely to pressure by industry.

In 1997, the International Agency for Research on Cancer, part of the World Health Organization, announced its finding that the most potent dioxin, 2,3,7,8-TCDD, is a "known human carcinogen." In January 2001, the U.S. National Toxicology Program upgraded TCDD from being "reasonably anticipated to be a human carcinogen" to "known to be a human carcinogen." In 2003, a reanalysis of the cancer risk from dioxin reaffirmed that there is no known "safe dose" or "threshold" below which dioxin will not cause cancer, despite efforts by industry to suggest otherwise.

On April 28, 2005, in a hotel conference room in Baton Rouge, Louisiana, another chapter in the annals of dioxin would unfold during the deposition of Barry Dellinger. He testified that PCBs inside natural-gas transmission lines were fed into Sempra's boilers for energy production. The burning of PCBs, he said, created a chemical conversion to furans and dioxins, a family of some of the most poisonous man-made chemicals on the planet. Dellinger's testimony could be the linchpin of the plaintiffs' case and the undoing of the defense.

According to California's Office of Environmental Health Hazards Assessment, dioxins in particulate matter are the most potent carcinogens known to man. They are also the most worrisome chemicals for susceptibility in children, according to a state scientific panel. The average amount of dioxinlike substances in the body is nine nanograms per kilogram (ng/kg), although burdens vary depending on diet, workplace exposure, and proximity to hazardous waste sites. At 13 ng/kg, sex hormones are diminished in men; at 47 ng/kg, decreased growth is observed in children.

Scientific understanding about the dangers of PCBs dates back to 1936, when workers at the Halowax Corporation in New York City exposed to PCBs and related chemicals called chlorinated naphthalenes started coming down with chloracne, a painful, disfiguring skin disease. Three workers died. Harvard University researcher Cecil K. Drinker was asked to investigate. Drinker's results, presented to the U.S. Public Health Service and company executives, left "no doubt as to the possibility of systemic effects from the chlorinated naphthalenes and chlorinated diphenyls." Nearly seven decades later, Ukrainian opposition leader Viktor Yushchenko's face was disfigured by an illness caused by dioxin poisoning.

In his deposition for the Beverly Hills case, Dellinger's testimony was often quite technical. He explained how the basic structure of all dioxins consists of two benzene rings joined by two oxygen atoms. A closely related family of compounds are the polychlorinated dibenzofurans. They have structures similar to dioxins and are often found in association with them. The potency of dioxins and dibenzofurans depends on the chemical structure of the individual compound.

Dellinger's calculations focused primarily on past toxic emissions from the Century City plant. When he analyzed data about PCBs in the Southern California Gas Company's transmission lines from the 1980s and 1990s, using records that Stewart had subpoenaed and that were sealed by the judge, he found "extremely high levels" of furans and dioxins coming out of the smokestacks at Sempra—"more than enough to make it dangerous."

Dioxin is produced by every municipal solid waste incinerator ever tested; it is produced by hazardous waste incinerators, cement kilns, and boilers and industrial furnaces that burn chlorinated wastes. Recent testing in California has also revealed dioxin air emissions from refineries. According to a 2003 report by California's Department of Health Services, "many other types of industrial point sources identified nationally have not been adequately tested anywhere else in the U.S."

Dellinger testified that the scientific community has been trying for years to do a "dioxin material balance," meaning that all the sources of dioxin in the environment haven't been accounted for. The U.S. EPA's most recent dioxin reassessment report, for example, stated: "Source characterization is an ongoing effort, and if new major sources are identified, they will be factored into future inventories."

"Now," Dellinger testified, "I think I've found it!"

During his deposition, Dellinger later recalled, one of the lawyers at the conference table asked him if all power plants in the United States could have been emitting furans and dioxins.

"I said 'Yeah,'" he later said, "and they turned white."

Even Dellinger was astonished by his own findings. "I was surprised to find PCBs were in the gas line," he later said of the documents that Stewart had unearthed from the gas company through discovery. "I never heard of that in my life. I've told my colleagues about this case. They never heard of PCBs being burned in boilers either. It's been kept quiet for thirty years."

Dellinger's explosive testimony so unnerved Tom Meador, the defense counsel for Sempra, that he asked Judge Mortimer to allow him to designate an additional expert to rebut Dellinger's findings.

Had Dellinger revealed a thirty-year-old secret?

If so, I wanted to understand how it was possible for no one to know about it. Things got curiouser and curiouser when I called Sara McGurk, a chemist in charge of regulating PCBs in natural gas pipelines at the Environmental Protection Agency's Office of Prevention, Pesticides and Toxic Substances. Even though PCBs were banned by the federal government in 1977, they remain ubiquitous in window caulking and rubber products, and in schools built in the 1960s. Natural gas pipelines, though, were another story.

Ever since 1983, the EPA has promised not to take enforcement action against companies for the improper use of PCBs as long as they monitored their own systems. Not every company followed the rules, though. In February 2002, for example, the United States Justice Department announced a settlement agreement with the Transcontinental Gas Pipe Line Corporation (Transco) to clean up and test for PCBs along its ten-thousand-mile pipeline that crossed twelve states, from Texas to New York.

"It's sort of a Catch-22," McGurk told me. "There's no requirement to monitor. The regulations say you don't have to test for PCBs. But if someone from EPA were to inspect a facility from our enforcement office and found PCBs, then the company would be out of compliance."

Does that mean PCBs are no longer in natural gas lines? "Theoretically," she said, "they shouldn't be. I'm not saying they couldn't be in there. Historically, we don't know a lot about how systems work. We rely on industry and their trade associations to tell us how they work. The presumption is PCBs are not getting into the gas."

She added: "We write our regulations based on what Southern California Gas Company tells us. But they shouldn't be burning PCBs."

What if they are? I asked.

"I don't know," she said. "I don't know if they've done any work to see if anyone's gotten sick."

While litigants and scientists were being deposed and evidence was being gathered, defending parties were continuing to take action to keep from going to trial. On April 5, 2005, Sempra had filed a motion for summary judgment, claiming it had been improperly sued.

It was Friday morning, July 8, 2005. Al Stewart sat silently in the jury box, waiting for the judge to arrive from chambers. Judge Mortimer had already issued a "tentative" ruling on summary judgment for Sempra, which the court clerk had distributed to the lawyers as they arrived in the courtroom. It was bad news for Stewart.

Stewart hadn't been inside this courtroom for more than a year, since he had been preoccupied with his Mississippi dioxin case. He wore a charcoal gray suit and a maroon-and-blue striped tie. He sat in front of opposing counsel but didn't look at them. His head was bent, his gaze fixed on his yellow legal pad resting on his lap. He flipped through his papers again, preparing his thoughts for oral argument.

Written in longhand, the judge's ruling granted Sempra's motion for summary judgment. With headquarters in San Diego, California, Sempra Energy is a Fortune 500 corporation with eight subsidiaries. The company has more than $7 billion in annual revenues and twelve thousand employees. It serves 21 million consumers, the largest customer base of any energy service company in the United States. Sempra owns two utilities, the Southern California Gas Company in the Los Angeles area and San Diego Gas and Electric. Sempra is derived from the Latin word *semper,* meaning "always."

Lawyers representing the giant energy company had argued in their briefs that the corporation had nothing to do with the day-to-day operations of its power plant in Century City. Just because it was the parent company did not mean that it was liable for its subsidiaries. In his tentative ruling, the judge agreed. "Mere existence of a parent-subsidiary relationship is insufficient to establish alter ego liability," he wrote.

Sitting behind Stewart in the jury box, the lawyers for Sempra Energy appeared elated. Stewart would have to persuade the judge that he had erred.

In the days before this court appearance, he and Jim Piel had gone out to lunch at their favorite barbecue place in downtown Dallas, Fat Ted's. Stewart ordered his regular—a burger and onion rings—and Piel got the barbecued chicken salad. They remembered deposing the plant foreman.

"He doesn't have the power to go to the bathroom without asking upstairs," Stewart said.

"They moved the shell around so much, even their own employees are confused," Piel agreed.

As Judge Mortimer, who bore a certain resemblance to the *Wizard of Oz* actor Bert Lahr, took the bench, he nodded warmly at Stewart. It wasn't clear whether the gesture was his way of welcoming the lawyer back to his courtroom or of apologizing for his decision. In any case, Stewart assumed the judge hadn't had enough time to read the papers his law firm had filed on this motion.

"Good morning," the judge announced to the dozen lawyers before him.

"Good morning, Your Honor," the lawyers replied in unison. On "court call"—his voice projected from a telephone speaker box—was the city of Beverly Hills' counsel, Chris Bisgaard, who said he had just returned home from the hospital for knee-replacement surgery.

"He's playing the sympathy card," Wainoco Oil's lawyer Marty Refkin joked.

When Stewart rose to address the judge, he spoke quietly but forcefully.

"You ask the president of Central Plant, Inc. who's your boss?" Stewart said. "He went up the subsidiary chain and named the chief shareholder that held the subsidiary.

"For the last two years," he said, "a big thing has happened to this plant. Nine hundred people showed up in court and four hundred of them have said, 'You've given me cancer.' But for those two years, there's no board meeting?

"If they're handling this, it should be on the mind of the boards. There should be meetings about whom they're paying. Whom they hire. They don't control those decisions. The absence of those meetings for two years is evidence of control by those above them.

"Someone else is taking care of it. The parents and subsidiaries are represented by the same lawyers. They're sued by nine hundred people, and he has to go up the chain to get permission to do anything.

"I respect your tentative," Stewart added, sounding deferential. He said he hoped his arguments might help the judge to "flesh out" a decision.

Thomas Meador rose. He told the judge that the burden shifted to the plaintiffs to show fraud. "It's their burden to show bad faith conduct, and they haven't done that," he said. He reminded the judge that in his deposition, the plant foreman stated he was in charge of every operation there. "He said, 'The buck stops with me,'" Meador said. "He didn't have to meet with the board of directors. . . . He made all the operational decisions."

In the days that followed, the judge issued his final order. And, just as he had shown these lawyers a year earlier when he reversed himself on the case management order, he was open to having his mind changed. Now he sided with the plaintiffs' counsel. "This Court finds that the parent companies *did* exercise control over the environmental issues relating to the plant in question," he wrote. "There are triable issues of fact as to the nature and extent of that control. Further, if this motion were granted, it would create an injustice." Therefore, he concluded, Sempra's motion for summary judgment "is denied."

Now Stewart could look to Sempra's parent corporation for compensation for his clients; a jury could assess damages against the parent corporation, Sempra Energy Solutions, valued at $7.89 billion. That would be another consideration for the company's defense lawyers and insurance company in deciding future settlements.

With nine months until the new trial date of March 27, 2006, there was lots of work to do, including an appeal by Sempra's lawyers of Judge Mortimer's latest ruling—an appeal that would be denied.

When Sempra's designated expert, an engineer from Vernon Hills, Illinois, named John Woodyard, was deposed by Al Stewart on Thursday morning, February 16, 2006, it appeared that any hope of obtaining information about the Southern California Gas Company's PCB-removal program had vanished.

Woodyard, an industry consultant who had written extensively about PCBs in natural gas, worked for a variety of utilities, including SoCalGas. In a "white paper" for the Northern Natural Gas Company, which operated interstate natural gas pipelines for seventy-five utilities, Woodyard had presented a view that was diametrically opposed to the one expressed by Barry Dellinger. He had been enlisted by the defense for this very purpose.

"Although often erroneously reported," Woodyard wrote, "the creation of dioxin compounds from the incomplete combustion of PCBs is chemically impossible. Incomplete combustion of the PCBs can occur at lower temperatures and residence times, but only to a limited extent, and under certain circumstances can create dibenzofurans (a dioxin-like chemical but 10 to 10,000 times less toxic)."

Now, seated beside Sempra's attorney Tom Meador, Woodyard was asked by Al Stewart if he had ever tested for PCBs in boilers.

"I've never encountered an issue where PCBs in boilers were a concern until this issue came up," he said.

"You mean this case?" Stewart asked.

"Whatever. Yeah. It's unusual because it's not been an issue for people."

"How do you know it's not been an issue for people if you haven't done the research?"

"I'm not going to start going around testing boilers for anything and everything just because I feel like it. There's no reason to believe that PCBs are going into boilers, gas-fired boilers."

Now Stewart dug in. "So, PCBs being in the gas that feeds the boilers is not a sufficient reason to test a boiler to see if PCBs are coming out of the boiler or furans are coming out of the boiler?"

"Well, you're misstating my testimony. I didn't say PCBs were in the gas. They aren't in the gas. They're in the liquid and it's being collected in all of these collectors."

"Oh, I understand your testimony."

"And so it's not making it to boilers and so there's no reason to test boilers for PCB."

"Well, why not test to be sure?"

"Because there's no reason to believe it's there. These things cost money. Why would you do that?"

"To test a theory to see if it's right. That would be a reason, wouldn't it?"

"Well, but it's not my theory; so why would I want to test the boiler?"

"Well, actually it is your theory. Your theory is PCBs don't go into the boiler, that's your theory. You're saying that PCBs can't get into the gas to get into a boiler to be burned. That's your theory, right?"

"Exactly."

"Okay. So—"

"So why would I want to test the boiler?"

"To see if your theory is correct. Why wouldn't you want to do that?"

"Well, because PCBs, in every other gas system where there are PCBs, have been used in boilers, and it's never been a concern of anyone else's, including EPA's."

"So is it your testimony that EPA doesn't have any concern about PCBs being burned in boilers?"

"Oh, I—I'm sure they would if they had evidence that there was PCB being burned in boilers. What's at issue here is whether or not PCBs are being burned in the boilers, and I—I'm—I'm telling you in my opinion that I don't believe they are. My theory is that there are no PCBs reaching the boiler; so why test for it?"

Stewart asked when Southern California Gas began testing for PCB in its lines.

"I don't know," Woodyard answered.

"I thought you said it was in the 1980s," Stewart said.

"Objection," Meador interrupted. "Misstates his testimony."

"I said it could be as early as the 1980s, but I don't know."

"You looked at this material, yes?" Stewart asked.

"What is 'this material'?" Woodyard replied. "I'm sorry."

"The test material, these tests that you said you had looked at. You looked at these right—"

"I—" Woodyard began.

"Objection," Meador said. "Vague and ambiguous."

"—for PCBs from the SoCalGas lines?" Stewart finished.

"The test data I looked at in relation to this case was just what Dr. Dellinger set forth based on this review of the database," Woodyard said, referring to Dellinger's analysis.

"That's all you looked at?" Stewart asked.

"That's correct."

"You didn't look at the materials yourself?"

"Not for this case, no."

"Well," Stewart continued, "have you looked at it for some other reason?"

Woodyard replied: "I have looked at some of it in the past."

"What for?"

"For another project for the gas company."

"What was that?" Stewart asked.

"It's confidential," Woodyard said.

"Well, I'd like to hear about it," Stewart said.

"Well, I can't tell you about it," Woodyard said.

"Why not?"

"Because it was for Southern California Gas Company."

"Okay."

"And it's—it was for their attorneys and it's privileged."

"Uh-huh. Did it have to do with PCBs?"

"I can't tell you about it."

"You can't tell me whether or not it has to do with an issue in this case, is that right?"

"I can't tell you about it."

"Uh-huh. You understand this is a case about polychlorinated biphenyls in SoCalGas's lines in part; you understand that, correct?"

"Yes, I do," Woodyard replied.

Stewart persisted. "And what I hear you saying is SoCalGas hired you to take a look at something that had to do with data that's been used in this case; isn't that correct?"

"Objection," Meador said. "Misstates his testimony."

"I just told you I can't talk about it," Woodyard said again.

"Uh-huh. When were you hired by them to look at this data?"

"I can't talk about it."

Stewart turned to Meador. "You're taking the position that he can't talk about this, Tom?"

"Just ask your questions, Al," Meador said, sounding miffed.

"No," Stewart insisted. "I'm asking what your position is."

"I'll give it due thought," Meador said.

"What?"

"I'll give it due thought and we can discuss it sometime."

Stewart wanted an answer now. "No," he said. "I kind of need to know what it is now. Are you instructing him not to answer the question?"

"I don't hear anything, Al—"

"Okay."

"—coming out of my mouth."

"Okay. Good." Stewart resumed his questioning. "So, sir, I need you to answer my question about what work you performed for SoCalGas in the past."

"It's argumentative," Meador said.

"That's not argumentative. You're not instructing him not to answer my question."

"That's not—"

Woodyard interrupted. "It's privileged information. I can't answer the question."

"Well, sir, I hate to tell you, you're not the person who can invoke the privilege; so because you're not the person who can invoke the privilege, you need to answer my question."

Meador had a different spin on the privilege question. "I would not rely on Mr. Stewart for legal advice, because my interpretation, if you dealt with other lawyers, would be they'd ask you not to waive the privilege."

Stewart said: "And unless this lawyer sitting beside you is instructing you not to answer the question, you need to answer my question."

"I can't answer the question," Woodyard said. "It's privileged information."

"So," Stewart said, "you believe when Southern California Gas hired you previously is privileged information; is that right?"

"I believe everything about that project is privileged," Woodyard said.

"Okay," Stewart said. "And why do you believe that?"

"Because I was hired by the attorneys with the understanding that all the work would be privileged."

"Okay. Did you write a report for Southern Cal Gas?"

"I can't tell you. It's privileged."

"Did you meet with anyone besides SoCalGas's lawyers in your previous work for them?" Stewart asked.

"And just so you know," Meador said, "if the lawyers instructed you to meet with somebody else, that's privileged, too."

"That's not true," Stewart said.

"I—I can't tell you anything about the project. It's privileged."

Stewart was starting to lose his cool. "Tell him to go meet with the press. That's not privileged."

He had a few more questions.

"How many times have you been hired by SoCalGas in the past?"

"Once, I believe," Woodyard replied.

"How much did you charge SoCalGas for that consultation?"

"I'm sorry," Woodyard said. "That's privileged."

The legal shenanigans had become commonplace. Stewart would need to file yet another motion before the judge to compel Woodyard to testify under oath. In California, the attorney-client privilege, which is statutory and not part of common law, cannot be invoked by an expert hired by a law firm. Woodyard was neither a lawyer nor a client in this case. But that didn't stop him from giving it his best shot anyway.

Woodyard had already testified that no PCBs had contaminated the pipelines leading into Sempra's facility near the high school. But after

Stewart filed a motion on April 28, 2006, to force him to testify, he produced a December 2003 report he had done for Sempra and SoCalGas that proved the existence of PCBs in the SoCalGas pipelines. The report stated: "Sempra Energy Utilities' Southern California Gas Company (Sempra) has historically found PCBs in pipeline liquids above the 50 ppm regulated level in several locations." He had prepared the report, stamped "Attorney Work Product Attorney-Client Privileged Material," for the Sempra Energy Law Department; it was entitled "Development of a Self-Determination Exit Strategy from Federal PCB Use Authorization Requirements." Yet, Woodyard testified that he had never tested for it.

Confidentiality—or the claim of attorney-client privilege—had become a central theme of the litigation. It was used as a legal ploy on more than one occasion by both sides to block the release of pertinent information to opposing counsel.

The deposition of the plaintiffs' expert witness, Randy Horsak, was one such occasion. Horsak ran an environmental engineering company called 3TM International, and Al Stewart had put him in charge of overseeing the plaintiffs' soil-gas testing at Beverly Hills High School. Horsak had also been hired to do residential testing in Beverly Hills by Lundy & Davis, a law firm in Louisiana, for a separate property damage case. Horsak refused to answer questions about residential test results during his deposition, citing client confidentiality. "They're two different clients," he testified, sitting in a conference room at the Hilton Hotel in Houston, Texas, on the morning of March 21, 2005. "Two different cases."

That response infuriated Bill Ireland, the school district's lawyer. "He's blocked by the point that information from Lundy & Davis is somehow confidential against disclosure of his deposition, even though he's leaving an open door to go into stuff at trial that's not in his report," Ireland fumed. The defense lawyer was worried that Stewart could gain an advantage over him at trial if Horsak had test results showing high levels of benzene, for example, in soil-gas samples from households in the neighborhood or from samples taken along the sidewalk on Moreno, near the high school tennis courts.

Chris Bisgaard, the lawyer for the city of Beverly Hills, was equally inflamed. "We do have a real problem here," he told Horsak, "and we'll reserve our right to reconvene the deposition to be able to ask questions about the off-site testing."

Ireland added: "He can't hide behind some confidentiality agreement between him and Lundy & Davis, block us from asking questions about communications or information he received regarding that work—that's just not the way it's done."

Then Bisgaard turned on Horsak. "I saw somewhere that you hired felons in your business," he said.

"Objection," Jim Piel said. "Form. Object to the sidebar. What does that mean?"

"I saw it somewhere," Bisgaard replied. "I'm just curious. Is that wrong?"

"What are you referring to?" Horsak asked.

"I thought you're doing a good deed for other people—that you hire people that have been incarcerated as part of your hiring program."

"It has nothing to do with anything," Horsak said. "I mean, it has to do with a personal ministry that I'm involved in." On behalf of his church, Horsak worked with prisoners in Texas.

"None of these people are working on the case?" Bisgaard wanted to know.

"No."

"I'm not being critical in any way," Bisgaard said, softening.

"It's better to have them employed than robbing your house," Horsak said. Still, Bisgaard had made his point; if Horsak was called as a witness in the case, the defense lawyer could call into question his reliability by implying that his business was populated with crooks.

When opposing counsel returned to the courthouse on Friday morning, March 10, 2006, a month after Woodyard's deposition, the defense attorney Tom Meador complained to the judge. "Your Honor," Meador began, "I was cranky before Christmas." Since the case against his client alleged that all eight so-called chemicals of interest (chromium, nickel, arsenic, benzene, PCBs, polycyclic aromatic hydrocarbons [PAHs], formaldehyde, and chlorinated dioxins and dioxinlike compounds, including furans) had come from Sempra's plant, Meador had been working like a dog to depose the plaintiffs' experts. He had flown to Florida and Baton Rouge and had missed the Rose Bowl as a result.

"Did that make you cranky too?" the judge asked, smiling.

"I'm fifty-two years old," Meador said. "I've never missed a Rose Bowl. I live above the Rose Bowl. On January 4, it took me eighteen hours to get to my house from Baton Rouge."

"It was great," Baron & Budd's Scott Frieling said of the football game. Frieling was a University of Texas alum, and his school had been victorious over Meador's alma mater in that game.

"I missed the game," Meador whined.

"But we digress," the judge interrupted.

Meador said that when he spoke to Woodyard after his deposition, his expert had advised him to conduct tests of Sempra's boiler stacks. Woodyard was responding to Barry Dellinger's calculations that predicted high levels of furans coming out of Sempra's boiler stacks because of the combustion of natural gas contaminated with PCBs.

"There are no furans in them," Meador told the judge. "The plaintiffs have come up with figures that are incredible!" Meador said, referring to the calculations Dellinger had arrived at back in April 2005, when he received the subpoenaed data from the Southern California Gas Company about PCB condensate in gas lines. "They find furans that are fifty-two thousand times higher than what's in the standards! Nobody in the United States tests for furans and dioxins in boiler stacks. That's because either they don't exist or they don't exist in any meaningful concentration. They've had scientists *create* chemicals that do not exist in our boiler stacks," Meador charged.

How could two experts come up with such wildly different results? After Dellinger recalibrated his results, using the new source test information from Meador's experts, he was deposed a second time. This time, he testified, it was obvious that there were fewer PCBs in the gas lines in 2006 than in the early 1980s because there was an exponential decay as PCBs were removed from the line. In 2006, there were 0.03 parts per million of PCB, compared to 200 parts per million PCBs in 1981. Though the amount of furans diminished over time, there were spikes in 1984 and 1985, for example, which probably related to "events," in Dellinger's view, when PCBs got into the gas lines.

In other words, Dellinger testified, Sempra's "field data" from 2006 served to confirm his model.

On Friday, April 14, 2006, the defense lawyer for Beverly Hills, Chris Bisgaard, turned up the heat by announcing that he would file a motion for summary judgment in the coming months. But rather than attack Dellinger, as Meador had, he zeroed in on another of the plaintiffs' expert witnesses: Jim Tarr, who was president of a private environmental consulting firm in California and had worked as an engineer at the Texas Air Control Board.

Bisgaard said: "We're really looking at the testimony of an expert by the name of Tarr. Jim Tarr. And he has provided the fundamental premise for the entire plaintiffs' exposure case. And he has made certain assumptions which we believe are completely—I know the word 'fabricated' is offensive to the plaintiffs, so I won't use that word."

"You just did," the judge reminded him.

"But the fact of the matter is—"

"Thanks for your consideration," Stewart said.

"You're welcome," Bisgaard said sarcastically. "The fact of the matter is, if you measure the actual amount of benzene that's in the oil that's coming out of these oil wells at the Olympic site, there would have to be spilled some seventeen hundred barrels per day to get the numbers that Mr. Tarr has ginned up. Seventeen hundred barrels a day! Now, that's an interesting number, because it's about three times more than the wells actually produce."

He continued: "There's a serious, serious disconnect here. And if we are successful in convincing this court that Mr. Tarr has no basis, in fact or fiction, for his opinions, then the plaintiffs' oil and gas case just completely collapses and it's gone. Let's tee that up. Let's get a decision on that and go from there."

Not to be outdone, Al Stewart had returned to the courtroom to accuse the defendants' lawyers of misconduct. Not only had they sought to obstruct the search for truth by using courtroom tactics designed to upset the presentation of the plaintiffs' case, he charged; the defense had done worse—by actively concealing evidence.

At issue was an e-mail sent by an attorney at Haight Brown & Bonesteel, the law firm for the school district. After speaking to the judge in chambers, the lawyers resumed their discussion in open court. School district lawyer Peter Ezzell asked that all copies of the e-mail be returned and no further mention of it be allowed in the case, claiming it to be a privileged document. He said it was a simple oversight in which a DVD had been corrupted and was not produced.

Al Stewart said: "Our view of what has happened in this case is there has been an improper act, and the improper act wasn't a mistake. And it wasn't anything other than there was an instruction by someone to someone else— a boss to a subordinate—to withhold evidence and violate the rules of this court and of this state."

The e-mail had to do with DVDs containing evidence. Stewart said that the "DVDs were never posted until we got hold of this e-mail and asked for them. And then, when we got them, they had no Bates stamp number on them"—showing that the defense had not intended to turn them over as evidence to the plaintiffs. "For us to not be able to use that e-mail," he added, "would mean to me that an injustice to our clients would have been done."

"Well, how would you intend to use the e-mail?" Judge Mortimer asked. "I mean, other than for inflammatory purposes, how would you use the e-mail?"

"I would use the e-mail to support a motion for sanctions," Stewart said. "Your Honor, please keep in mind, to us it's about a course and scope of activity of the defendant counsel who's in charge of all the information from the other defendants' counsel going through, making determinations about what we get and what we don't get.

"And what that e-mail says to us is, there's some things that if they determine they don't like how they look, we just don't get them. And I'm very interested in knowing how many other times that has happened.

"Justice requires us to know, how deep does this go?"

Ezzell cut in. He was worried about anyone in the courtroom who wasn't a lawyer. "I'm sorry, Your Honor. All of this was supposed to have been sealed. I really have a great deal of difficulty with Mr. Stewart in open court. If we have somebody in here who is a nonlawyer, I'd ask the court to inquire."

"Well, so far, he hasn't talked about the actual content of the e-mail," Mortimer replied. For the judge, the one issue left was what to do with the e-mail in question: "Do we seal it in a lockbox or do we allow plaintiffs to use it?"

The judge chose the lockbox. He issued a protective order, requiring that the e-mail be returned to the law firm. Then his order was redacted—expunged from the record so that no one would ever know precisely what was in it.

When the trial, which was just six months away, got under way, all these accusations of misconduct, fabricating evidence, hiding evidence, and stonewalling would seem like ancient history.

Judge Mortimer acknowledged receipt of documents lodged with the court by plaintiffs' counsel on Thursday morning, April 27, 2006. Technically, the "successor-in-interest" papers filed with the court clerk that day included declarations by the daughter, the son, the sister, the husband, and the mother of plaintiffs who had died. They would, once again, remind the judge what was at stake: people's lives.

No matter what happened inside his courtroom, the death toll continued to mount outside of it. Included among the court papers were copies of six death certificates, one for a thirty-eight-year-old Beverly High graduate with leukemia.

I was especially struck by the death certificate of an English teacher from Beverly Hills High School named Susan Srere. She had devoted thirty-seven years of her life to the school district. She had created the conflict-resolution program there and volunteered as a friend of the public library. No sooner had she retired than her cancer, a melanoma that had metasta-sized to her liver, was diagnosed. Nine months later, she would be dead.

"It's really unfair that she doesn't get to enjoy her retirement," her good friend and chair of the English Department, Gail Shafran, told a student reporter for the school newspaper, *Highlights,* at the time. Shafran, too, would retire. And sooner than expected, because of advanced lung cancer—the same cancer that had struck my classmate Phil Berman.

As opposing counsel argued over e-mails and plotted new strategy, I wondered: How many more bodies would have to be counted before all the legal maneuvering would stop and preventive action might begin?

CHAPTER FOURTEEN

ACCEPTABLE RISKS

The movie version of this story would end with the triumph of Lady Justice. Or a jury trial in which documents stamped "confidential" might finally see the light of day. Anything's possible, of course. But for many, the real story, like real life, is murkier, messier, more mundane, more ambiguous, than the movie version. That fact became abundantly clear to me when I visited my Beverly High classmate Phil Berman at his home outside of San Diego in June 2005.

Like other plaintiffs in the lawsuit, he was now battling his second cancer, and I wanted to find out what he was thinking. We had corresponded by e-mail and talked on the phone, but I hadn't seen Phil for more than thirty years. So I was nervous and excited about interviewing him. I had looked him up in the twenty-fifth reunion book from the Harvard class of 1975 and was intrigued by the photos: there he was, with his giant Afro, or Jew-fro, and aviator glasses in 1975; twenty-five years later, he appeared gaunt. His write-up on himself included this:

During my last twenty-five years I trained and practiced as a physician in rural and urban America during a time of profound technological and social change in American medicine. I have enjoyed life in Boston, Philadelphia, San Diego, northern New York State, Tucson and now, Coronado, California. While I enjoyed my fifteen years of practice very much, I was fortunate enough to launch a career in medically related hi-tech and now enjoy the enormous challenge of building both medical manufacturing and Internet portal businesses under the same corporate umbrella (Lumisys, Inc.) in Silicon Valley. On a daily basis, I am surrounded by enormous intellectual capital and voracious drives for success. I have had the privilege of seventeen years of a fantastic marriage to my wonderful wife, Judy, who regularly provides the humor and love when I need it most. I have suffered and survived a cancer and still been fortunate enough to enjoy the miracle of three births—our children, Sloane, Spencer and Skye. It astounds me that twenty-five years have passed, for it is a long time to have disappeared in the blink of an eye.

Now, since his lung cancer had been diagnosed and had metastasized to his brain, he had begun a Web site, "One Red Toenail, my fight against cancer." It included breezy entries and pictures of his children and wife, Judy, whom he referred to as St. Jude. The entries were sometimes hilarious, as when the family suddenly took off in response to a tsunami warning that never materialized. And they were sad, too. He had given the site its name because he had painted one of his toenails red in honor of having survived the lung cancer diagnosis for one year; each year he was alive meant another red toenail.

On a warm, breezy Sunday morning, I drove across the giant bridge that connects San Diego to the island of Coronado, a historic town across the bay where naval ships are stationed. The waves of the Pacific Ocean were breaking phosphorescent green.

Phil answered the door wearing khaki shorts, a black T-shirt, sneakers, Tibetan prayer beads from his Yoga teacher, and a little peace sign on a cord around his neck. He gave me a tour through the shingled three-story home he and Judy had built, replete with an elevator, jazzy TiVo hookups, and a screening room. He appeared tanned and fit, with a gray goatee and shaven head. "I will tell you that if you looked at me the day I had my diagnosis of cancer, you'd say, 'You look fucking fabulous,' 'cause I looked a lot better then than I do now," he said.

"I feel pretty good for someone who sleeps twelve, thirteen hours a day," he added. "I'm Sleepy now, like one of the dwarfs." He lifted up his shirt to show me his abdomen, where twice daily he gave himself an injection of Lovinox, a low-molecular-weight heparin. He pointed to his right side. "That's my testicular cancer scar," he said. "All this black-and-blue shit and fat is from those injections twice a day. Pretty gross. Then I take Tarceva, which is a pill, $1,000 a bottle. I'm only paying half. The insurance company pays the other. I take one of those a day. Those scramble my brain pretty badly for about five or six hours. So I take them before I go to sleep. I don't sleep so good, but I sleep a lot—volume makes up for the quality of sleep."

We were sitting upstairs in a room he called "the theater," with a giant movie screen, theater chairs, and black curtains. He had become a soccer dad, dropping the kids off at school, helping out with homework, doing what he could when his energy didn't wane. "The rest is errands, food. I don't do shit. I take care of little things."

Five-year survival for advanced lung cancer at the time of diagnosis is less than 1 percent. On the other hand, 170,000 people receive the diagnosis every year in the U.S., and 1 percent turns out to be 1,700 people. "It's not zero," he said of the odds against him. "It's pretty damn close. So, I don't know. There's a pretty bad chance that I'll survive. The numbers are godawful terrible."

He told me he harbored no illusions about joining the lawsuit. It was simply a practical decision. The statute of limitations—two years from the time he discovered his illness might have been caused by toxic exposures—had run out since he first heard Katie Couric report the story on the *Today* show in early May 2003. He wanted in to find out whatever he could. And, he was impressed by the Baron & Budd partner Jim Piel when they spoke about the case by phone. "I think he had a short list of cancers that he was willing to take, and I had them both," Phil said.

"The way the legal process is working here is actually a little backward," he said, taking a swig from a bottle of water. "I have very little information. In order to get information, I have to become a plaintiff. And if I don't become a plaintiff by the time the information is available, I'll have forfeited my right to be a plaintiff because of statutes. So I'm a plaintiff because I fit in a category, but it doesn't necessarily mean I know what I need to know to decide if there's liability in my view of the school district and other defendants."

He was a thoughtful man who exuded wry detachment, perhaps to defend against feeling too much. Mostly, he thought like a doctor—rational and controlled, wanting evidence, peer-reviewed research to be certain. Trying to fit science into legal precepts, he knew, didn't work. "Even if you have computer modeling, it's still best-guessing. No one's plunked down this mixture of poison in a community and measured the outcome against a control group. It just doesn't happen that way in real life.

"We don't know what the exact brew of poison is or was. When, exactly, it was there. How much exposure it took to generate a cancer. There's less definable events and circumstances than proof or near certainty would demand."

Still, if the best guess and the best judgment were that the cause of his cancers was based at Beverly Hills High School, he wanted to see his family compensated. "It's a real and true loss to them," he said of his being taken out of the workforce, having earned more than $1 million a year in his tech businesses. How does one compute such things? His testicular cancer, he believed, resulted in loss that was "more modest—tangible but less quantifiable. You lose a testicle. There's pain and suffering involved. But you get over that. There's the inability to conceive. The in-vitro fertilization runs that don't work. Two kids adopted; middle one is frozen sperm of mine. But that was sheer luck. The numbers shouldn't have happened. There are two failed adoptions. One of the failed adoptions was the death of a kid. Those are harder to quantify than Phil gets taken out of the workforce."

After we talked for a couple of hours, his tone changed. "Look, life is full of shit," he said. "I got mine. Where I got it from doesn't really matter—I got it. I'm not really angry. But if the poisons at the high school are the cause, then the score has to be evened for my family. Nobody can give me my life back, if that's the price."

A breeze wafted into the room, and we sat side by side in the theater seats for a few moments, saying nothing. "You gotta do what you gotta do," he said finally. "I may be dead and gone by the time this case is settled."

He felt he could write the script for the lawsuit's denouement. "My dad's a lawyer and it's a movie I've seen a hundred times. At some point, there's enough concern and enough evidence accumulated through experts and discovery that they sit down and figure out a settlement. Does that mean it's really been settled that that's the cause? No. It just means the defendants are sufficiently worried that they need to do a settlement and the plaintiffs are sufficiently satisfied that they'll take it. It doesn't mean the science has proven anything. The case will be settled but the truth won't be."

Whatever the outcome of the Beverly Hills lawsuit, many of those most intimately involved in the case understood that they might never have a chance to discover the truth, because records were being sealed and evidence was being concealed. At Beverly Hills High School, the decades-long hazardous discharges into the air and water from the Sempra plant and the Beverly Hills Oil Company—later bought by Frontier and Venoco—subjected thousands to potentially grave risks, the full nature of which might never be resolved.

The vast majority of toxic tort cases, if they're not dismissed on summary judgment, wind up being settled, and the terms of those settlements are rarely made public. Without the litigation, the environmental issues at

Beverly High would never have been brought to light, nor would it be possible to hold anyone accountable. The paradox is that a settlement will neither reveal useful public health information nor act as a deterrent from future harm. Only one thing was obvious: opposing counsel, who now exhibited a kind of begrudging respect for each other, were in a dogfight. Defendants' lawyers pushed ahead with their planned motions for summary judgment, and plaintiffs' counsel insisted that a trial was in the offing.

The lawsuit, in other words, was really a mirror of the ferocious ambivalence that exists in America regarding how to address environmental pollution—a challenge to the legal structure and the regulatory structure that haven't been updated for three decades.

Is it sufficient to have risk to regulate? Or do we need to prove harm first? In the courtroom, of course, plaintiffs must bear the burden of proof, regardless.

Still, the most crucial questions had yet to be addressed: What risks are acceptable for children? When is regulatory oversight required for children in schools? How are we doing in protecting our children from chemicals in the environment? These were policy questions that no lawsuit could resolve.

A few years ago, in a journal of the National Institute of Environmental Health Sciences called *Environmental Health Perspectives,* a team of scientists at UCLA's School of Medicine published a groundbreaking study on air pollution that detailed the biological basis for how ultrafine-particle pollution promotes illness. The research, which was the first to show a direct link between ultrafine particulates and destruction of a specific entity in a human cell, demonstrated how tiny particles of soot or acid invade a cell wall and then penetrate the mitochondrion, which is like a cell's battery, causing the cell to die. What that means is that every time you take a breath, you have ultrafine particles in the mitochondria in the cells in your lung and in your heart and in your brain, bypassing the body's defense mechanisms.

One of the members of that research team is a friendly, bespectacled man named John Froines, who directs UCLA's Center for Occupational and Environmental Health. A former director of the National Institute of Occupational Safety and Health during the Carter administration, Froines now oversees the Southern California Particle Center and Supersite, one of five federally funded programs dedicated to better understanding the health effects of toxic air contaminants. His office on the second floor of UCLA's School of Public Health is an unremarkable one, save for the keepsake he's hung on the wall above his computer—an artist's sketch from the Chicago Seven conspiracy trial of 1969. For his role in having made stink bombs to disrupt the 1968 Democratic National Convention, Froines, then a Yale Ph.D. in chemistry, was tried and acquitted of charges of conspiring to cause a riot.

Froines specializes in understanding the carcinogenic effects of chemicals, such as chromium and arsenic, as well the health effects of air pollution. These days, the radicals he seems most fascinated by are "free radicals," or highly reactive molecules, that damage brain tissue. He is a member of the scientific panel that advises the California Air Resources Board, and he has served on the U.S. Public Health Service's National Toxicology Program, which identifies carcinogens. Scientists like Froines have been called upon to list compounds that have toxicological evidence of a problem. But he told me: "The follow-up regulation is either slow or nonexistent."

Part of the problem is tied to risk assessment. Since available data is often based on animal studies, there is considerable uncertainty in the underlying science and methods for extrapolation. "But we can't allow uncertainty to be an excuse for inaction," he added.

In the past five years, scientists like John Froines have been responsible for a veritable explosion of research linking environmental factors to public health "endpoints"—asthma, autism, sudden infant death syndrome, inflammation of the brain, and cancer. To ignore the scientific evidence is to knowingly permit tens of thousands of unnecessary illnesses and deaths each year. In California alone, 9,600 people die annually from cancer and respiratory problems caused by air pollution. The highest cancer rates in Los Angeles are found near the ports, where as many as one of every two hundred residents—many of them children—are expected to get a pollution-related cancer during their lifetime. As is the case with so many public health issues, a disproportionate number of those affected are the poorest of the poor, who live in the shadows of hulking refineries and power plants. That doesn't mean, however, that the comparatively wealthy will escape harm. The story in Beverly Hills is ample proof of that.

As a nation, though, we've failed to heed the lessons of science. In September 2006, for example, every member of a twelve-member panel of scientists convened at the request of the White House Office of Management and Budget and the National Academy of Sciences found that twenty-four thousand lives could be saved annually in the United States—and savings in healthcare would outweigh costs—if the Environmental Protection Agency tightened annual soot standards for particulate matter by one microgram per cubic meter. The agency refused, saying that "reasonable minds can disagree."

In terms of air pollution, scientific investigation often sidesteps the obvious. Monitoring programs are not based on the knowledge of where chemicals are used. And most EPA regulations stem from the study of single chemicals. In the workplace, workers tend to be exposed to individual chemicals. But it's not true in the environment, because people are most often exposed to chemical mixtures, such as those at Beverly Hills High School, although no programs exist to test for complex mixtures.

Decisions regarding how to regulate single chemicals have often been delayed for decades by litigation or the search for stronger evidence. Arsenic, radon, lead, DDT, and hundreds of other air and water pollutants and food contaminants provide examples of protracted regulation processes. Occasionally, Congress becomes so impatient with EPA delays that it demands action on lists of chemicals by specified deadlines, as has occurred with air pollution and pesticide laws. But the single-chemical focus, in addition to routine delays in regulation, has left the government's capacity to protect children's health from environmental hazards in serious question.

Froines, of course, is not the only public health advocate who speaks about these matters with a growing sense of urgency. Across town, at the University of Southern California's Keck School of Medicine, Dr. John Peters has spent the past two decades tracking the effects of air pollution on children's health. As director of the Children's Health Study, a long-term analysis of children's lung development and air toxics, Peters, with his colleagues, has discovered, for example, that athletes suffer more from air pollution than others because of their greater exposure to pollutants. But when I asked him about the wisdom of operating oil wells at a high school campus, it was not science he invoked so much as common sense. "Why take chances?" he asked simply. "Why do things like this? Why put schools near freeways? Why put schools on waste dumps? It doesn't make sense, whether you've got the studies to prove there's a problem. You're asking for trouble."

So far, the federal Environmental Protection Agency has ignored its own science advisers, who have pointed out that modern science demands that it set tougher standards on everything from soot in particulate matter to synthetic chemicals in order to protect people's health, particularly of those most vulnerable to disease. New scientific data on blood tests of newborns, for instance, has shown that the developing reproductive, hormonal, and neurological systems of infants are being disrupted by synthetic chemicals that we are exposed to every day. Babies are born with fire retardants, pesticides, mercury, dioxins, and a chemical used in the production of Teflon, PFOA, in their blood.

Study after study has documented the need to take action. In 1994, the Government Accountability Office (formerly the General Accounting Office) released a report on environmental health which revealed that the federal government collected very little data on human exposure to chemicals in the environment. Six years later, the GAO released another report finding that the EPA was failing to protect the public from thousands of toxic compounds because it had not gathered data on the health risks of the majority of industrial chemicals. U.S. industries manufacture and import some seventy-five thousand chemicals. The current regulatory system, according to yet another GAO report, from 2005, does not require comprehensive testing of chemicals before they are put into products, and it does not provide authority to the EPA to prevent harmful chemicals from being used in products and released into the environment. The agency has reviewed human health risks of only 2 percent of the sixty-two thousand chemicals that were in use in 1976, the year Congress passed the Toxic Substances Control Act (TSCA).

Over the years, government safety standards have consistently shifted downward—for lead, for mercury, for benzene. But each chemical requires years of study, and more years before action is finally taken. While the European Union, invoking its "precautionary principle," has banned more than 450 chemicals, the U.S. has banned or restricted the use of only 5 chemical substances in the thirty years since the TSCA was enacted. The system, which relies on voluntary steps from industries rather than regulation, allows chemicals with known hazards and clear health impacts to remain on the market, even when safer alternatives are available.

Environmental diseases *are* preventable. As a result of taking lead out of gasoline, for instance, children average three IQ points higher than their parents. But the EPA hasn't eliminated any industrial compounds since it sought unsuccessfully to ban asbestos eighteen years ago. U.S. law requires the EPA to prove that a toxic substance "presents an unreasonable risk of injury to health or the environment," to consider the costs of restricting its use, and to choose "the least burdensome" approach to regulate industry. As a result, environmental science has turned into a kind of warfare—a tug-of-war between those adhering to public health and those adhering to the bottom line.

"We're sort of like the tip of the missile," a toxicologist named Melanie Marty explained to me of her work at California's EPA, where she heads the

Office of Environmental Health Hazard Assessment's branch on air toxicology and epidemiology. A tiny woman with wire-rimmed glasses and a pixie haircut flecked with gray, Dr. Marty chairs the federal EPA's Children's Health Protection Advisory Committee. "There's always this push-pull—a tension between being cautious and regulating based on limited data versus industry scientists who say you don't have enough data to regulate."

The frustration for Marty and other public health officials is that science is still in its infancy with respect to understanding how chemicals in the environment impact children, because there is a huge lack of data on most chemicals used in consumer products and manufacturing. The DDT du jour is polybrominated diphenyl ethers, or PBDEs, the flame retardants. California women have the highest levels of PBDEs in the world, and the state legislature banned the chemicals in 2003 because they accumulate in the blood of babies and nursing mothers. The flame retardants also appear to be traveling widely around the globe, showing up in polar bears, dolphins, and sperm whales.

There is presently a voluntary children's chemical evaluation program that the EPA and manufacturers created to test for risks to children of high-volume chemicals. "The pilot is going extremely slowly," Marty said, sighing. "The system is set up for failure right now."

All manner of scientific questions have yet to be addressed. For example, human sperm counts have been decreasing for three or four decades. Nobody can explain why, though many researchers suspect environmental influences. An explosion of new studies on "endocrine disrupters"—substances that may, at tiny doses, interfere with hormonal signals regulating human organ development, metabolism, and other functions—has shown that tiny amounts of toxic chemicals can have large effects on health, especially for babies in the womb and young children. The new science is challenging old notions that low doses are always safe. Instead, scientists now believe that small amounts of chemicals, at critical times in development, can have life-long health impacts.

Of particular concern are the estrogen-mimic chemicals, like bisphenol-A (BPA), which is used in polycarbonate baby bottles and in resins that line food cans, and phthalates (pronounced tha-lates) found in children's plastic toys and cosmetics. In more than one hundred animal studies, government scientists have found that very low doses can cause fertility problems, hyperactivity, altered immune function, and early sexual maturation. By contrast, eleven of eleven studies sponsored by industry found no health effects from exposures. But the teeniest exposures can have profound consequences, and the Centers for Disease Control has found traces of BPA in 95 percent of urine samples tested. In a study of fetuses exposed to phthalates in the womb, researchers found a strong relationship between phthalates and changes in the size and anatomy of the genitalia of male babies and toddlers, suggesting that phthalates may "undervirilize" boys. Another study found that low doses of bisphenol-A could be a contributing factor to the development of breast cancer. A Japanese study found that women with a history of miscarriages had higher levels of bisphenol-A in their bodies.

This new research has created a paradigm shift in one of the basic tenets of toxicology—the poison is in the dose—because levels of bisphenol-A that create health impacts are in the parts-per-trillion range. That is one-millionth of the smallest traces even *measurable* three decades ago, when most of to-day's environmental laws were written. The same is true for the dioxinlike chemicals at issue in the Beverly Hills case.

The connection to certain human diseases, such as asthma, autism, and breast cancer, is just beginning to be understood. Research has shown that there are windows of susceptibility during development to chemicals that influence disease later in life. Animal studies have offered clues about the profound impact of early-life exposures on breast cancer. When a class of chemicals, the polycyclic aromatic hydrocarbons, is given to rodents in the pubescent period, more tumors develop when the animals are old. "That shows you that kids' risk is frontloaded to the earlier years of life," Marty said. It was a finding with obvious implications for teenagers at Beverly High, though defense lawyers had already engaged a team of industry scientists to dispute even that idea. "When one is talking about adolescents it is possible that they are more susceptible, less susceptible, or as susceptible as adults," one toxicologist stated.

In her role as chair of the Children's Health Protection Advisory Committee, Marty has written countless letters to the EPA, urging more protective standards for mercury; for particulate pollution; and for the rocket fuel perchlorate, which has been found to disrupt thyroid function and has been detected in drinking-water supplies in thirty-five states, as well as in fruits, vegetables, and breast milk. She's also lobbied for the release of rules for determining cancer risk from early-life exposures to carcinogens—rules the EPA has delayed for years.

Under the leadership of John D. Graham, who oversees the Office of Information and Regulatory Affairs at the White House Office of Management and Budget, the Bush administration has proposed funding cuts for EPA research on suspected endocrine disrupters and a host of other industrial chemicals whose regulation might result in greater costs for the corporations that fund the Harvard Center for Risk Analysis, the industry-backed program begun by Graham. The center's corporate backers include Amoco, Bethlehem Steel, British Petroleum, Chevron, Coca-Cola, Dow Chemical, Eastman Kodak, ExxonMobil, General Electric, General Motors, Inland Steel, Merck, and Monsanto.

When it comes to enacting policy of any kind, delays are commonplace. In the case of environmental regulation, the real scientific issues have been compounded by disinformation campaigns spawned by public relations firms and lawyers representing the economic interests of those who stand to profit from keeping matters unresolved. In 1997, for example, the EPA, relying on years of rigorous study by Harvard researchers, decided to extend its regulations to control ultrafine particles of 2.5 microns or less in diameter. In response, the American Petroleum Institute, the electric utility industry, and other groups charged that federal regulators were relying on "junk science"—the old phrase developed by lawyers wanting to discredit ideas with which they disagreed. Industry even hired unemployed actors, dressed in white lab coats, to picket Harvard's School of Public Health with placards that read "Give us your data." More delays followed.

What, exactly, is an "acceptable" risk? What can we live with? After some debate forty years ago, the one-in-a-million risk for cancers was considered a kind of gold standard by regulators because it's fairly small. But as the years progressed, one-in-a-million was not always feasible through regulation. As a result, acceptable risk has fluctuated.

Acceptable risk is a social construct that stems from economic imperatives, not public health ones. Typically, it's been believed that non-cancer health impacts have a threshold of safety, and if you get below the threshold you're not going to see a risk. "That's sort of fallen apart now, too," Marty told me. The most basic tenets of risk assessment are being challenged by science. "Lead is a good example. We can't see a threshold. More recent examples are airborne particulate matter. You can't have no cars, no industry, no human activity, to get below that threshold. So there are these factors that are pushing and pulling the level of acceptable risk that's floated around."

The San Francisco offices of the Natural Resources Defense Council are located on Sutter Street in a lovely old downtown building overlooking the bay. Gina Solomon is a senior scientist at the NRDC and an assistant clinical professor of medicine at the University of California, San Francisco. She is tall and thin, with short brown hair and a gentle manner. Waiting for an elevator at Harvard's School of Public Health ten years ago, when she had just completed a postgraduate program in medicine and public health, she spotted an ad on the bulletin board for a job opening at the NRDC, one of the country's leading nonprofit environmental organizations. She's been there ever since.

"I used to like to think the best about people, and assume I might have valid scientific disagreements with folks from industry in terms of our interpretation of data or in terms of our assessment of the results," she told me on a warm Wednesday afternoon in February 2006. "But I've actually gotten more cynical with time, because the stuff these guys did was beyond smarmy."

Solomon was referring to the secret campaign waged by tobacco company executives and their front companies, revealed in internal memoranda filed in court proceedings, to cast doubt on evidence that secondhand smoke and other environmental toxins cause disease. By promoting "sound science" and "good epidemiological practices"—buzz phrases coined by a public relations company hired by Philip Morris lawyers—Philip Morris could manipulate the standards of scientific proof to serve its corporate interests and to create the illusion of scientific controversy. It was a slick effort, and it continues to this day in other arenas.

The PR firm APCO and Associates first hired scientists who would look independent and created an organization they called The Advancement of Sound Science Coalition (TASSC). Not wanting to look like hired guns for the cigarette industry, TASSC then broadened its issues to talk about other purportedly questionable science, such as global warming and the health effects of dioxin and other chemical hazards. TASSC had a broad agenda to attack independent science showing any link between these issues and health effects. The campaign was extraordinarily successful. By recruiting other industries, the tobacco companies were able to obscure their role in fighting smoking restrictions around the world. And the themes that the tobacco industry came up with were then picked up by other industries and by the Bush administration. In the name of "sound science" corporate lawyers have launched elaborate strategies to question studies documenting adverse health effects of exposure to lead, mercury, benzene, vinyl chloride, chromium, benzidine, and nickel, among others.

TASSC has been disbanded, but references to "sound science" abound. It has become a catchphrase that has more to do with antiregulatory lobbying than with laboratory results. As Donald Kennedy, the former head of the

Food and Drug Administration and now the editor in chief of the influential magazine *Science,* has explained: "Sound science is essentially a politically useful term, but it doesn't have any normative meaning whatsoever. My science is sound science, and the science of my enemies is junk science." In fact, the head of TASSC, a lawyer named Steven Milloy—a commentator for Fox News—would later publish the junkscience.com Web site, financed by ExxonMobil and devoted to debunking environmental health effects.

By "manufacturing uncertainty," as David Michaels, professor at George Washington University's School of Public Health, has called it, lawyers and front groups working for industry profit from keeping matters unresolved. In a memo from an official at Brown & Williamson, the cigarette maker now owned by R.J. Reynolds, the game plan was laid out years ago: "Doubt is our product," he wrote, "since it is the best means of competing with the 'body of fact' that exists in the mind of the general public." From 1989 to 1992, a consulting firm called the Weinberg Group became the recruiting agency for Phillip Morris. Its motto? "We'll get you where you want to go, no matter where you are."

According to journalist Paul Thacker, the Weinberg Group's strategy of setting up a network of scientists and experts to give lectures, show up at public hearings, and publish articles on behalf of corporate clients continues, particularly in the bellwether state of California, where bills modeled on the precautionary approach popular in Europe have been introduced. The Weinberg Group authored the American Chemistry Council's 2005 position paper on endocrine disrupters. The ACC is the lobbying group for chemical manufacturers. One of the two coauthors of the report, James Lamb, had also worked for industry on other chemicals, such as perchlorate. That same year, Europeans permanently banned six phthalates from baby toys, and the California legislature tried to replicate the ban. When the state held hearings in January 2006 to debate the health risks and possible use restrictions for six phthalates and bisphenol-A, the suspected endocrine disrupters in baby toys, Lamb testified that the chemicals are safe.

The Weinberg Group also sponsored an attack against Dr. Frederick vom Saal, professor of biology at the University of Missouri and an expert on endocrine disrupters. In January 2006, a letter criticizing vom Saal's research was published in *Environmental Health Perspectives,* signed by a consultant for the Weinberg Group.

"It's not 'sound science' if it's something they don't like," Solomon told me. "It's been appalling. The other thing that's been incredible is trying to

follow the money, and see these folks that end up on scientific advisory panels that are supposed to be independent." For example, a special scientific
panel for the state of California on chromium-6 included some scientists
who were paid by industry to dispute the need for tighter controls of
chromium in drinking water.

According to documents filed in state court proceedings and testimony
from a state senate hearing, one of those consultants is a prominent toxicologist, Dennis Paustenbach, who once soaked in a Jacuzzi filled with chromium
to bolster his argument that the stuff is harmless. Dr. Paustenbach's company, ChemRisk, received $1.5 million for litigation support work for PG&E
on chromium cases brought by Erin Brockovich and Ed Masry on behalf of
residents of Hinkley, California, and neighboring towns.

One third of California's groundwater is contaminated with chromium,
primarily from aerospace and utility companies such as PG&E. So the issue
of setting stricter limits on chromium exposures is critical to those businesses in terms of liability and clean-up costs.

In 1999 state officials had proposed a new public health goal of limiting
chromium-6 in drinking water to no more than 2.5 parts per billion; industry
lobbyists considered that level far too strict since California's standard of 50
ppb was already twice as strict as the federal standard. The state convened a
blue-ribbon panel on chromium—a special board of supposedly impartial
scientists—to establish protective drinking water standards and issued a report in 2001, concluding that there was no evidence suggesting chromium-6
in drinking water causes cancer. As a result, the state withdrew the stricter
standard. Dr. Paustenbach was the lead author of that report. Delighted, he
sent off an e-mail to a colleague: "Buy a good bottle of wine, pull up a
chair . . . and then read this. Then, say to yourself 'Yep, I really finally did
something good for society.'"

When Dr. Paustenbach's role as a PG&E consultant was revealed, however,
he resigned from the panel because of a perceived conflict of interest. Neither
the University of California, which oversaw the panel, nor the California Environmental Protection Agency required the scientists on the panel to declare
potential conflicts of interest. When the issue was raised by his fellow committee members, Paustenbach quit—a move he later said he regretted. As one
state senator said: "If being on the payroll and receiving thousands of dollars
does not constitute a conflict of interest, I don't know what does."

The most controversial aspect of Dr. Paustenbach's consulting work for
PG&E, though, goes even further. Court records show that his company, in

the course of providing legal support to PG&E's lawyers—the same attorneys from Latham & Watkins now representing Chevron in the Beverly Hills case—persuaded a respected Chinese scientist to participate in an update of his 1987 study that found that chromium-contaminated water in rural China was linked to an increase in villagers' cancer. The new study, ghostwritten by Dr. Paustenbach, found no such link between chromium-6 and cancer.

The revised study's co-author was listed as the now-deceased Zhang Jiandong, whose own paper misspelled his name three times. Even so, the 1997 "reanalysis" of Dr. Zhang's data concluded that the higher cancers rates in China could be attributed to "lifestyle" choices, not chromium exposures.

That finding, published in the influential *Journal of Occupational and Environmental Medicine,* would have an even greater impact on regulatory assessments of the chemical. In 2000 the U.S. Agency for Toxic Substances and Disease Registry updated its chromium profile with a paragraph about the 1997 study. Then, both the Environmental Protection Agency and the California Department of Health Services cited it as evidence that greater restrictions of the carcinogen were unnecessary. After Dr. Paustenbach resigned from the California blue-ribbon panel on chromium, whose report lifted entire passages from one of his industry-funded epidemiology reviews, he became a Bush appointee to a U.S. Centers for Disease Control panel on toxic chemicals.

But the story didn't end there. Not long after *Wall Street Journal* reporter Peter Waldman published a detailed account of it in December 2005, chronicling how PG&E's consultants blurred the line between legal advocacy and scientific inquiry, the *Journal of Occupational and Environmental Medicine* would retract the Paustenbach reanalysis. The journal's editor said it was not a case of scientific fraud but of financial nondisclosure. By February 2006 PG&E agreed to settle the rest of its Hinkley cases, known as Erin Brockovich II, for $315 million, issuing an apology but no admission of wrongdoing.

"All of these examples have been terrible," Solomon told me. "They've confused the public about what science really is, what science can do, and what it says. They have caused people to become cynical about science and to begin to think about scientists in the way they think about lawyers, which is they'll work for whoever is paying them. It has also meant that necessary public health protections have been picked away at and delayed and tied up in confusion, because there really is this focused agenda that manufactures science to cast doubt on links between environmental hazards and health effects.

"It's horrendous for those of us pushing for public health protections. It's also personally offensive as a scientist, that science has become trashy because of the fact that scientists have agreed to be misused in this way. So, basically, it's awful all around." In the summer of 2005, a bill called the Child, Worker, and Consumer Safe Chemicals Act was introduced in Congress to enhance protections for Americans from toxic chemicals. As of this writing, that legislation was stalled in committee and denounced as unnecessary by the American Chemistry Council, whose motto is "Good chemistry makes it possible." More recently, EPA officials announced that in order to relieve businesses of the burden of reporting requirements, the government wanted to stop forcing companies to report small releases of toxic pollutants and allow them to submit pollution reports less frequently.

Not surprisingly, the "sound science" banner would be waved in the Beverly Hills litigation. In March 2006, Dr. Max Costa, chairman of the Department of Environmental Medicine at NYU's School of Medicine and a preeminent researcher on chromium, testified during his deposition that hexavalent chromium, which had been used from 1965 to 1989 to clean out the Sempra plant's cooling towers and allegedly wound up in drift and vaporous droplets on the high school campus, could cause the skin cancer, breast cancer, thyroid cancer, Hodgkin's disease, testicular cancer, and non-Hodgkin's lymphoma suffered by the plaintiffs in the lawsuit.

Dr. Costa testified that epidemiological studies of chromium exposures are limited because they lack the statistical "power" required to uncover causal effects that may exist. So, using the classic criteria of Sir Austin Bradford Hill for inferring causation, he relied on biological evidence from animal studies to render his opinion, since humans and animals metabolize chromate in identical ways. Chromate will, he said, "penetrate every cell in the body." As a result, he added, hexavalent chromium compounds "have the potential to injure many different organs depending on the levels of chromate reaching these organs."

In response, the defendants' lawyers lashed out in a ninety-three-page reply motion, arguing in favor of summary judgment and urging "only that sound judgment is required" to understand that Dr. Costa had "no reasonable basis" for his opinion. His testimony, they said, was "riddled with inaccuracies, speculation and unsubstantiated hypothesis that render his opinions inadmissible." As proof, they pointed to the findings of a monograph by the International Agency for Research on Cancer, which concluded that only lung and sinonasal cancers were caused by chromium exposures among workers.

One of the peer reviewers of that monograph, however, was Max Costa. "Just because there isn't a human study available," he testified, "doesn't make it impossible for you to reach that conclusion." Costa, in other words, believed in taking the "weight of the evidence" approach, as opposed to waiting for the evidence.

Dr. Steven Patierno, one of Costa's former graduate students, was hired by defense counsel to refute his testimony. Dr. Patierno directs the George Washington University Cancer Institute and is a professor of environmental and occupational health. He testified that one of Max Costa's 1997 research articles, "Toxicity and Carcinogenicity of Hexavalent Cr in Animal Models and Humans," was not accepted by the general scientific community. He also took issue with Dr. Costa's choice of strain of hairless mice on which to conduct research about the effects of chromium exposure on skin cancer. Dr. Patierno also testified under oath that his research had been financed by the Pharmaceutical Manufacturers Association Foundation, the Motorola Corporation, and the Nickel Producers Environmental Research Association.

In the months after I met with him, Phil Berman was thrilled to paint another of his toenails red—a symbol of reaching the two-year mark from his diagnosis. But the side effects of Tarceva, after sixteen months, were becoming intolerable. "Rash, diarrhea, runny nose, dry eyes, dry mouth, achy joints, etc.," he wrote on his blog one day in April 2006. "Maybe even my persistent exhaustion, muscle weakness, new loss of appetite.

"Just getting long in the tooth." But he wasn't fatalistic. In fact, he felt hopeful. "I'm fighting as hard as I can. I consider it miraculous I'm doing as well as I am two years out. The hill continues to be steep. And it's not going to get any less steep."

On September 26, 2006, he would write: "I am here. Struggling. But here."

Back in Judge Mortimer's courtroom, the mudslinging continued. On Friday, September 29, 2006, defense lawyers accused the plaintiffs' expert, Dr. Barry Dellinger, of creating scientific "fabrications"; they said his evidence about dioxinlike chemicals from the Sempra plant was "junk science," and therefore inadmissible.

But the judge denied their motion to exclude his testimony, saying it was "reasonable" and should be heard by a jury. That cleared the way for Al Stewart to present a particularly compelling piece of evidence for the jury, namely the blood serum levels of eight of ten plaintiffs. They revealed high levels of a particular type of furans—the same type that Dellinger's model predicted would be emitted in large quantities from the plant.

Two weeks later, on Friday, October 13, another round of evidentiary hearings were convened by the judge. This time, Chevron's lawyers from Latham & Watkins had filed a motion *in limine* to exclude the testimony of the plaintiffs' air modeling expert, Jim Tarr. A motion *in limine* is a request of the judge to exclude certain evidence because the mere mention of it would confuse a jury. The strategy of defense counsel for the oil companies was to target Tarr as a linchpin in the plaintiffs' case: since the plaintiffs' medical causation experts had relied on his work to render their opinions, the defense wanted Tarr out. With his analysis defeated, the rest of the plaintiffs' case would fall too. It was like a house of cards, they reasoned, and they wanted to see Tarr topple first.

Latham & Watkins attorney Kirk Wilkinson accused Tarr, a chemical engineer, of creating "pure fiction" with his estimates of benzene emissions from the oil wells at Beverly High. According to defense expert Mary Jane Wilson, a petroleum engineer who graduated from Stanford University and ran a consulting business in Bakersfield, California, Tarr found "impossibly high" concentrations that he never measured at the sites by using "fictional assumptions" about oil wells. Wilson, who was paid nearly $1 million by the defense for her work, said Tarr exaggerated his emission estimates by over 1,000 times regulatory estimates. Indeed, she said he found that there was 1,200 times more benzene than what is actually measured in crude oil.

During the evidentiary hearing, Tarr, a tall Texan with a mustache and laconic style, was sworn in by the court clerk. He told the judge that he based his benzene calculations on a 1983 California Air Resources Board report on "emissions factors" at oil wells and a 1978 study for the Air Pollution Control Association with input from the oil industry. He found that 38 per cent of the 127 parts per million of hydrocarbons coming from the drill site well cellars consisted of benzene, or less than 1 percent of the total of a gas sample. One year, that meant a total of 127 tons of benzene was pouring into the air from the drill sites.

Tarr testified for two days. Under a withering cross-examination by Wilkinson, he blasted Mary Jane Wilson for her incompetence and withstood the defense lawyer's questioning about sumps, about "mass balance" equations, about gravity ratings of crude oil in Beverly Hills.

On November 7, 2006, after conducting pretrial hearings in his courtroom on three successive Fridays, Judge Mortimer would issue his order. The attorneys had been told to expect his decision the previous day. But by the end of the workday, neither side heard a thing.

The court clerk, who had been sending the judge's minute orders to the attorneys by fax, changed the routine that day. Now, he explained, the order would be sent by snail mail on Tuesday.

Waiting was not an option for Al Stewart. If the judge granted the defendants' motion, his case against Chevron, Wainoco, and Venoco would essentially be over. Planning an appeal would be critical. From Dallas, he called a courier service in Los Angeles to get a copy of the judge's decision and fax it to him.

When it finally arrived over the transom that afternoon, Stewart was elated. The judge's order would deliver a fatal blow to the defense's attempt to prevent a jury from hearing the case.

To exclude Tarr's analysis, the judge wrote, "would be to take evidence from the jury which this Court is unwilling to do."

"Motion for defendants is denied."

The judge's decision may have been swayed by a startling footnote that Tarr attached to his written declaration. The footnote included a listing, spanning fifteen years, of "mishaps" at the oil drill site, as documented in the logbook that lawyers for Venoco turned over to plaintiffs' counsel during discovery. Tarr said his emissions calculations did not quantify any of these events:

1987: "cleaned up well cellar"
1988: "cleaned up deep cellar"
1989: "cleaning sump in Well Cellar—Very full and disgusting"
1990: "Dan clean up well cellar and pit"
1991: "Cleaning well cellar per instructions"
      "Cleaning well cellar"
      "cleaned well cellar floor"
      "Cleaned cellar floor"
      "Pump oil—some sludge out of well cellar sump"
      "oil on ground—can't see where or if it's leaking"
      "cleanup more of deep cellar"

1994: "Please note that there is a pool of oil forming in trench around
         bottom pump"
         "oil, oil everywhere!"
1997: "Use taraway and clean up oil"
1998: "Holding fluid coming out & oil MAKING A MESS IN CELLAR!!"
         "went to cellar to see where oil is coming from—check BH-15 for
         sample lots of oil!"
1999: "Oil everywhere!"
2000: "started pumping well cellar not working very good 'cellar pump'"
         "Raining all day, dumped cellar out"
         "got oil out finally at 7:00 p.m., got well cellar almost all out at
         7:30 . . . oil leak in Century Park East"
         "OS-6 still bleeding in cellar"
         "Dale had a f****d day and I had a f****d night. My short story, oil
         everywhere"
         "pump out well cellar"
         "clean up all the oil mess around transformer again"
         "Clean some of the oil spilled around the deep pit"
         "Oil spilling on to floor again"
         "found OS-10 flooding in the cellar fast (packer blew). S**t really
         hitting the fan."
         "clean well cellar most of the day"
         "pump out well cellar"
         "Pump out well cellar"
         "oil spillage . . . cleaned around 500BBL"
2001: "tk overflowing! What a mess!"
         "had to roll up pant legs to shut valve off a little (lot) —pumping
         out well cellar"
2002: "cleaned well cellar pump pit of more s**t"
         "Cleaning up oil all day"
         "scrub down Prod Pit grating to get sticky oil off shoes!!!"
         "Fixed the biggest oil leak on this lease . . . oil pouring out"
         "Pumped out well cellar (got oil on floor!) Hosed down cellar"

In the war to protect children's health, the conflict at Beverly Hills High
School is one battle. But it reflects a far broader problem. At the Suva Elementary School in the southeast Los Angeles community of Bell Gardens,

parents still worry that their kids have rare cancers and teachers have high miscarriage rates because of two chrome-plating plants next door, one of which recently agreed to close down. In the San Fernando Valley's western suburb of Calabasas, there are fourteen children in a three-mile radius with retinoblastoma, cancer of the eye, which their parents attribute to a radioactive meltdown in 1959 at the Rocketdyne nuclear weapons plant—a cancer cluster the local health department disputes was caused by environmental pollution. Even so, two studies paid for by the federal government show elevated cancer rates among people living within two miles of the facility. In Eldorado Hills near Sacramento in northern California, playing baseball or other sports at the high school may expose people to high levels of asbestos, according to a recent EPA report.

Increasingly, schools strapped for much-needed funds are being constructed on cheap, contaminated property. Mostly, the practice is perfectly legal. According to figures compiled by the Center for Health Environment and Justice, the nonprofit environmental group founded by the activist Lois Gibbs after the Love Canal disaster, more than six hundred thousand students attend classes in 1,100 public schools built within a half-mile radius of known contaminated waste sites. Only five states in the country prohibit locating schools near hazardous waste sites. And twenty-four states have no policies that require sponsors of new school projects to assess environmental hazards at potential school sites.

Schools are just one part of the picture. Even more children are at risk when you consider where they live, according to the Agency for Toxic Substances and Disease Registry. More than 3 million children live within one mile of at least one of the 1,300 hazardous waste sites on the national priority list. Yet, most pediatricians are not trained to recognize how exposures to environmental contaminants can cause, trigger, or exacerbate pediatric diseases.

What are the effects of these chemicals on developing children? Recent research has suggested that one of every two hundred children in the United States now suffers from a developmental or neurological disability which was caused by an environmental toxin. Forty to fifty years ago, when many of today's public schools were built, school boards did not understand the seriousness of the threat that chemical exposures pose to human health. Nor was there any understanding of the special vulnerabilities that children have to chemical exposures. Now, after the Love Canal dump site crisis in Niagara Falls, New York; the discovery of the clusters of childhood leukemia in

Woburn, Massachusetts, Toms River, New Jersey, and Fallon, Nevada; and other, similar cases across the nation, we know better.

In community after community across America, science can go only so far in helping to answer questions. Scientists either try to assess the "weight of the evidence" or, thanks to political realities, they "wait for the evidence." So we are left wondering. "Other than stupid land use," the NRDC's Gina Solomon told me, "where we're putting schools next to industrial sites and industrial sites next to schools, you end up hitting that brick wall of the limits of science. What people are seeing with their own eyes and experiencing in their own communities is often something that science either cannot verify or refute effectively.

"So, people walk away, still wondering."

Still wondering, indeed.

I have to go back for one last look at Beverly Hills High School.

Amid the clank, clatter, and whir of the giant boilers next door, I park my car on the southern edge of campus, near the Sempra plant and a few hundred feet from the oil wells in a parking lot that overlooks a piece of contaminated property in Century City, where Standard Oil once drilled twenty-five wells, then abandoned them in the early 1990s. Now the property is being developed as a parking lot.

On this day in early October 2006, the air has a metallic odor. You can see the vaporous clouds of emissions from the plant. And you can hear the students at play—on the soccer field, on the tennis courts, and down on the football field. To them, the whole episode with Erin Brockovich had become a nonissue, a distant memory, another scam by yet another publicity hound intent on sullying their hometown's image.

Looking at the football field, my mind wanders back in time. Suddenly, I'm watching my brother getting pounded on the turf in his orange-and-white football uniform. There are fleeting images of my days here, too. Cheerleaders; pom-poms. Track meets; cleats. My sense memory that associates starting blocks with petrochemical fumes. The pump jacks that morphed into nineteen wells, three of them high-pressure water injection wells where toxic sludge gets redistributed underground and washed into rock beneath Rodeo Drive.

Sitting in the bleachers now, I wonder: which is more powerful—human greed or the human impulse to protect one's children? I assumed it was the latter until I began my reporting for this book. My research has shown the truth to be otherwise. It is a depressing revelation, of course, one that I resisted as long as I could. It occurs to me that the real tragedy of this story is that no one has ever bothered to conduct the appropriate studies to determine the full extent of contamination and what effects it has had on the health of the people—except for a plaintiffs' law firm looking to win its case. I think about the cost to the community to figure out the science as best as it can be determined and then put the facts in a forum where *everyone* has access to it. Who's paying for that? At the moment, a Dallas law firm is footing the bill. In the long term, though, we all pay.

I think about complacency, and I am reminded of W. H. Auden's poem, "Musée des Beaux Arts," in which the tragedy of Icarus falling from the sky is accompanied by life simply refusing to be disrupted. A plowman goes about his work, a ship "sailed calmly on," dogs keep on with "their doggy life." At Beverly High, where tiny soccer players gather on Saturday afternoons in the shadow of the power plant's "steam" and the oil well's flowered derrick, Auden's poem plays out in a modern rewrite.

I can't help but think of the mud man who helped drill these wells and then became a "dog man." Of the air pollution regulators who refused to see a "controversy," despite repeated protests by the locals. Of the backroom deals and secret agreements among lawyers. Of the sick teachers and dead graduates whose illnesses may have been preventable. The promises of safety unfulfilled. In fact, the school district's own documents show that officials knew dangerous emissions were seeping onto the school grounds as early as 1970. Yet it would take more than three decades before they would be required to tell anyone what they knew. And even then, they would refuse to allow the one state agency that could properly assess contamination to do so. A perfectly legal strategy, clever even, but one that makes me wonder if this community is too smart for its own good.

Tentatively, I make my way down the steps in the bleachers to the track and watch the students run. They do sprints. They do hurdles. They pass the baton, just as we did so many years before. I'm slowly coming to understand that the only thing I can do is hold on to my hope and believe in a future.

I think of my own children, two of whom have played soccer on this field. Fifty years from now, will they be smarter than we are? Will their children be asking: What were they thinking? But they, too, will face that deal we must constantly make and remake in our daily lives—how much risk are we willing to trade for our children's health?

Science has taught us that it's not parts per million that matter any longer. It's parts per trillion—staggeringly tiny amounts of chemicals that can have profound effects on hormones for the rest of one's life, less than a trillionth of a gram in a milliliter of blood. My own medical history could be instructive. My thyroid is enlarged, so I need to have it biopsied on a regular basis. In addition to giving birth to three beautiful children, I had two miscarriages and two stillborn babies. Might their deaths have been caused by chemical releases here? We'll never know for sure.

What is truly remarkable, though, is that on a high school campus in one of the wealthiest towns in America, not one but two industrial facilities can operate with impunity for decades, and that is acceptable.

I just stand there, listening to the dull roar of the power plant, its humming and clanging an incessant reminder of the cost of progress. Documents uncovered during discovery showed that the chromium in the mist from Sempra's cooling towers back in 1984 damaged the cars of doctors in the Century City Medical Plaza by the high school. After threats of litigation, Sempra, which had installed "drift eliminators" for the release of white chromate powder, paid $75,000 to repair the damage. What an L.A. story: it's about paying for the polishing and waxing of fancy cars and cleaning pitted windows, not about caring for schoolchildren.

I walk over to the oil derrick with its aqua, peach, and purple covering, the so-called Tower of Hope. Standing before it, I can do nothing. Seeing its posted warnings about reproductive hazards and inhaling the putrid petrochemical smells, I can only shudder and feel, along with fright and disgust, appeasement and complicity. These sources of energy have become our country's pride. To survive in their midst, one had to believe in their safety. Or pretend they weren't even there. I could do neither any longer.

Forty years has elapsed since Rachel Carson wrote the stunning environmental primer *Silent Spring*. She died of breast cancer, as did my mother and my track coach. In their honor, I could no sooner pretend that nothing was wrong here than erase these remarkable women from memory. They were my heroes; they were the ones who taught me to question, to love, to jump hurdles. All I could think about was what a wonderful thing it had been that they had inspired me to open my eyes to the bigger story here—and the possibility of change.

And so, finally, I lace up my sneakers. But rather than make my way around the track for old times' sake, as I planned to do, I take stock. I watch everyone running in circles. Breathing in and out. One foot in front of the other. A step at a time. It all seems too absurd. And then, I do what any journalist would feel compelled to do. I hightail it home to write this story—minus its ending.

For that, I would have to wait for a jury of twelve men and women to reach a verdict.

During the three and a half years that I had been following this story, the media had lost interest in it. But with jury selection scheduled to begin in the days before Thanksgiving, it was certain to cause a ruckus again in the press. Judge Mortimer had already announced to opposing counsel that because his courtroom was relatively small, he had been thinking about conducting the trial elsewhere, possibly in a downtown courtroom to accommodate the dozens of attorneys, paralegals, plaintiffs, and their families. It was guaranteed to be quite a spectacle.

After three and a half years, Al Stewart was eager to have his day in court. Ever the optimist, the trial lawyer from Dallas still believed in the American system of justice. "Our deal," he said, "is to get our clients their constitutional right—a trial by jury."

But all the high-mindedness would mean nothing if he couldn't prove his medical causation case. Everything else, said Cindy Cwik, the Latham & Watkins partner defending Chevron, was simply "a parade of distractions."

The trial of the first twelve plaintiffs ended before it even began.

On Wednesday afternoon, November 22, 2006—the day before Thanksgiving—Judge Mortimer unexpectedly issued his decision in the Beverly Hills High School case. In a stunning reversal, he dismissed all twelve cases on summary judgment.

The judge's sudden turnaround, which was all the more remarkable given his recent rulings against the defense on the admissibility of expert testimony, coupled with his announcement that he might allow the trial to be televised, was a defense lawyer's dream scenario. And, no doubt, it was influenced by a devastating, two-day attack inside his courtroom against the plaintiffs' medical causation case by the seasoned Chevron trial lawyers Ernest J. Getto and Cynthia H. Cwik from Latham & Watkins.

Sitting in O'Hare Airport the day after that hearing, Getto was waiting to catch a connecting flight to visit his ninety-seven-year-old mother in Pennsylvania for the holidays when his BlackBerry showed an incoming fax from the judge's clerk. He couldn't open it, so he called his secretary in San Francisco for help. She said: "Oh my God, he granted your motions! All of them!"

Indeed, by the time Judge Mortimer finished hearing arguments on the defendants' summary judgment motions, the only question seemed to be how far he would go to get rid of the cases against the oil companies, the power plant, the city of Beverly Hills, and the school district. Would he dismiss a handful of Al Stewart's weaker cases, the ones selected by the defense? Or would the judge go further and, as Getto had urged, rule as a matter of law that the plaintiffs had failed to provide enough evidence for a jury to hear the case?

At its most profound, the debate in the courtroom was over what scientific evidence should be considered in the first place and by whom—a judge or a jury? As it turned out, it would not be enough for Al Stewart to produce a statistical report to the court, showing an elevated incidence of three types of cancer—thyroid, testicular, and Hodgkin's lymphoma—among Beverly High graduates from 1975 to 2001. Nor would the blood tests of nine of twelve plaintiffs revealing an "unusual prevalence" of two of the same dioxinlike chemicals emitted by the Central Plant, prove useful to show causation.

Since the plaintiffs' experts had theorized that benzene from the oil wells had "promoted" cancers by suppressing the immune systems of an already vulnerable population, namely high school students, while the chromium and dioxinlike chemicals from the power plant "initiated" genetic damage at the cellular level, the defense demanded hard evidence: where were the medical records showing frequent infections or colds? Or peer-reviewed studies showing what level of exposure to this precise mix of chemicals was required to cause harm?

Without them, Getto and Cwik insisted, the expert opinions were nothing more than "pure, naked speculation."

Getto argued that the plaintiffs' claimed benzene exposures were "vanishingly small"—hundreds of times lower than those causally associated with cancer. He accused the Baron & Budd lawyers of engaging in "an extended subterfuge" intended to draw attention from those miniscule exposures. The critical concentration of benzene needed to cause acute myelogenous leukemia (AML) is twenty to sixty parts per million over a period of years. By comparison, he told the judge, the plaintiffs' own experts claimed exposures that are a fraction of that—"no more than infinitesimal exposures," Getto said, in the range of parts per *billion*. One of the plaintiffs' toxicologists even admitted under oath that such exposures were "very, very, very miniscule."

"With exposures this low and without any support in the scientific literature," Getto warned the judge, "to take this case to the jury will swallow the tort system."

But the question of *how* the cancers developed was one that mainstream science couldn't answer definitively. From the plaintiffs' perspective, the mere presence of these cancers was proof enough of compromised immune systems: every cancer is a failure of the immune surveillance to detect growth in abnormal cells. Medical records would not necessarily show a suppressed immune system over time, because physicians don't routinely screen for it unless their patients have undergone organ transplants or have AIDS or immune-modulated diseases such as lupus. Some particularly attentive doctors might screen for immunoglobulin or T-cell function, but deciphering immune deficiencies can be far more complex than those screening tests alone.

Even so, without clinical evidence of his clients' compromised immune systems, Al Stewart's case appeared sunk. On that score, at least, he had come up empty-handed.

The moment that may have changed the course of the Beverly Hills High School case came in a packed courtroom the Monday before Thanksgiving, November 20.

"Okay, I've done some reading, and I think I'm up to speed," the judge said of the voluminous motions and reply briefs he had spent the weekend reading while not tuned in to the USC-Cal football game. "Good to go."

He nodded to Getto. "So, Mr. Getto," the judge continued, "are you taking the laboring oar first?"

"I am," Getto replied. Tall and lanky with hooded eyes, Getto had clearly put in late nights for this court appearance and his voice crackled with anticipation. "I'm leading off, your honor."

From the moment he launched his assault, it was obvious why the oil giant Chevron, which had reported record profits of more than $14 billion that year, entrusted Getto to oversee this case: his command of the courtroom seemed limitless, especially with his forty-two-year-old partner, Cindy Cwik, at the ready. She was equally formidable in a prim teal suit and pointy black pumps, her step-by-step dismantling of Al Stewart's medical causation case a study in discipline and focus. Cwik, who seemed to relish her role as Getto's eager-to-please acolyte, was, in truth, the mastermind behind the defense team's savvy attack.

Standing before a screen that projected computerized images of their argument and portions of the medical experts' videotaped depositions, Getto told the judge that exposures that cause one type of cancer don't necessarily cause all types of cancer. He lashed out at the sworn affidavits of two of Al Stewart's toxicologists, which contained ninety paragraphs that were identical, implying that they had been authored by the plaintiffs' lawyers, not their experts.

"Yeah, I noticed that too," the judge said, sounding annoyed.

Like a well-oiled machine, the defense team's performance couldn't have been more carefully choreographed. They delivered a one-two punch, with Getto sounding the theme that the benzene exposures were so miniscule as to be negligible and Cwik following up with specifics about each case, particularly in light of scientific studies cited by the plaintiffs' medical experts which she argued were purely hypothetical and couldn't provide solid proof of cause and effect. But their most savage attack was reserved for the plaintiffs' expert who was hired to assess the incidence of cancer among graduates of Beverly Hills High School.

On the screen in a videotaped deposition was Dr. Richard Clapp, the plaintiffs' distinguished epidemiologist from Boston University whose "draft report" was being dissected by defense counsel. Dr. Clapp's report had found elevated rates of three types of cancer among Beverly High graduates.

"Let me stop you there," the judge said, interrupting. "This draft report was done specifically for this case; is that correct?"

"Yes, it was, your honor," Getto replied. It was unusual for plaintiffs' lawyers to finance such a study; most occupational studies and epidemiological reviews are supported by corporate interests.

"Okay. Thank you," Judge Mortimer said. "I just wanted to be sure we were referring to the same thing."

"It's this little, four-page report, your honor," Getto said dismissively. "The plaintiffs rely so heavily on this study that they call it the single most powerful piece of causation evidence available in this case."

But, Getto continued, Clapp's report said nothing about breast cancer, non-Hodgkin's lymphoma or melanoma. Nor could it account for two of the plaintiffs who had never graduated from Beverly High, or played on the athletic fields but didn't attend the school. And Clapp didn't adjust his study for socioeconomic status, a common practice in the field, especially in light of Hodgkin's disease's being associated with higher social class.

It was an awkward omission that Dr. Clapp didn't bother to explain. At one point, he was forced to admit that he had done nothing more than "eyeball" yearbooks to determine the race of students at the school.

Finally, on the videotape, he was asked how he chose to study the three cancers in his report. A hush descended on the courtroom, packed to standing-room capacity with corporate defense lawyers in the jury box and insurance company lawyers in the wooden pews of the gallery.

"I had no way to make that decision," Dr. Clapp replied. "That was his— Al Stewart's—decision."

At the counsel table, Stewart bristled. He sat beside his partner Steve Baughman Jensen, Baron & Budd's young appellate specialist, who would provide the plaintiffs' arguments for this hearing.

"Now, your honor," Getto continued, "that's not the stuff, not the type of material upon which an expert can rely to form an opinion in the state of California. It was done by counsel. It was designed by counsel.

"Your honor, that is really only the tip of the iceberg because Dr. Clapp's study cannot form the basis for an opinion here. It doesn't even mention causation." Of course, what Getto failed to mention was that epidemiologists rarely determine causation. Inferences can be made, but not from a single study. And no defense expert criticized Dr. Clapp's actual calculations. Still, it seemed obvious that if Dr. Clapp believed the chemicals caused the cancers, he would have said so.

Getto also insisted that summary judgment should be granted because Dr. Clapp's unpublished report was not peer reviewed, just as his study for another lawsuit in California had been rejected on evidentiary grounds. Getto, however, didn't bother to explain *why* that previous study had been thrown out by the trial judge. It was a salient omission.

In 2004 Dr. Clapp worked as an expert witness on a case in which IBM was sued by a number of its workers with cancer at a semiconductor plant in San Jose. In that lawsuit, Dr. Clapp's statistical study found abnormally high rates of cancer deaths among IBM's 32,000 employees. But his report was barred by the trial judge after IBM attorneys argued it was "junk science" because it was not peer reviewed and misused the company's data; an IBM-funded study found that its workers had a lower cancer incidence than the general population, though Dr. Clapp argued that IBM's study failed to adjust for the fact that employed people tend to be healthier than nonworkers, the so-called healthy worker effect. After several plaintiffs lost their first round of lawsuits, the IBM case ended in a settlement for an undisclosed sum. But when the lawsuit had ended, IBM continued to fight Dr. Clapp over the release of his study. It showed higher rates of mortality from brain, breast, kidney, lymphatic, and hematopoietic cancers, and melanoma among the workers when compared to the general public. Arguing that his use of its Corporate Mortality File was a breach of confidentiality, IBM sued him over his right to publish. Dr. Clapp's paper, which had been scheduled for publication in a special issue of *Clinics in Occupational and Environmental Medicine*, was then rejected. The journal's publisher claimed his paper was revoked because it was original research, not an assessment of prior research. But other contributors withheld their work in protest, at the request of the issue's guest editor, Joseph LaDou of the University of California School of Medicine in San Francisco.

After a New York judge ruled that its publication was in the public interest, Dr. Clapp's long-suppressed study would finally appear in the online scientific journal *Environmental Health* in October 2006, just weeks before the Beverly Hills case was scheduled to go to trial. Vindicated, the Boston University professor had nonetheless been subjected to every scientist's worst nightmare: an attack on his science and his integrity. Moreover, the IBM case demonstrated how original research that is lawyer driven can be useful to science, because research on an issue might not even begin until it works its way into court.

At his deposition in the Beverly Hills High School case, Dr. Clapp testified that he had considered publishing his findings about elevated cancer rates among graduates. But when I contacted him in late November 2006, he said he had no plans of doing so, because he had "too much on my plate already."

The search for the truth in science and the truth in the courtroom are two completely different endeavors, defined by different standards of proof. Scientists don't accept a finding unless, statistically, the odds are less than one in twenty that it occurred by chance. It is a higher standard than the typical standard of proof in a civil case, namely the preponderance of the evidence.

But in toxic tort litigation, the two standards are sometimes melded together in a strange sort of evidentiary mishmash. What happens, for example, when an epidemiological study shows an elevated rate of cancer that doesn't reach the 95 percent certainty threshold, but instead, is 94 percent certain? Should such a study lacking statistical power be considered when weighing evidence on causation, along with other studies, as recommended by a panel of the National Academy of Sciences in 1991? Or should that evidence be discarded entirely, as the defense lawyers insisted, because it is "scientifically unreliable" and would mislead a jury?

When Steve Baughman Jensen got his chance that afternoon to explain why low levels of chemical exposures were nonetheless "substantial factors" in causing the plaintiffs' cancers, he said that research consistently showed that there was no "safe" threshold of the carcinogens in question. As a result, every molecule of exposure counts. What may be a safe dose for one person could be a lethal dose for another. Even very small exposures to carcinogens should be considered risk factors, he argued, especially when evaluating childhood exposures.

Drawing on the analogy proffered by one of his experts, he said it was like a glass of water filled with grapes, each grape being a molecule of benzene or chromium or PCBs from background exposures. "If you keep adding a grape, eventually the water will overflow, just as one extra molecule will eventually result in cancer," he said.

Furthermore, he said that exposures at Beverly High for hexavalent chromium and benzene were as much as thirty times higher than the EPA's public health goals for cleaning up hazardous waste sites. Getto countered that these public health goals were "default assumptions" to calculate risk, not to determine causation, and were overprotective.

One of the underlying issues was the question of who financed the science invoked by the lawyers and, just as important, how it was interpreted.

Cindy Cwik argued that the plaintiffs' experts had cherry-picked peer-reviewed studies, particularly about Hodgkin's disease and chemical exposures. One by one, she discounted each study with her own spin of the science. A National Cancer Institute study about benzene, she said, couldn't provide foundation for an expert's opinion because it was a research paper, not clinical evidence. Even so, that tightly controlled study found that Chinese workers who inhaled less than one part per million of benzene—an exposure considered safe under U.S. occupational guidelines—had fewer white blood cells than unexposed workers. The research, published in *Science* magazine in 2004, offered the first direct evidence in humans that benzene harms the progenitor cells that give rise to blood cells. It was not surprising, therefore, that the defense lawyers would try to bar it from being considered, especially since the data provided evidence that benzene causes blood changes below 1 ppm, "particularly among susceptible subpopulations."

Cwik went on with her attack. "In the Yin study, there is not a single case of Hodgkin's disease," she said of a 1989 retrospective cohort study of 28,460 chemical factory workers that found an association between benzene and a wide spectrum of blood cancers. "The Bernard study doesn't mention benzene. And Wilkinson only shows 'weak evidence' of an increased risk of Hodgkin's disease. Garland is a mixed-exposure study in the navy.

"None of these studies," she added, "provides a foundation for the expert opinions." Thus, she said, the judge needed to strike them from the record and rule for summary judgment.

Steve Baughman Jensen rose to address the court. He reminded the judge that his medical experts analyzed the data itself, not the interpretation of the data by the study's author.

"If you look at the Bond study," Jensen countered, referring to a 1986 study of 956 male chemical workers in Michigan, "it was written by Dr. Bond, who is an employee of Dow Chemical USA. Now, does Dow Chemical have a vested interest in interpreting this data? They do. And that vested interest shows why this court should not be judging which side is right in this credibility battle about interpreting that data. The data is what it is. And it supports the expert opinions."

In response to another study, which found a statistically elevated risk of eleven times with respect to Hodgkin's disease and benzene exposure, even though the study's authors discounted their own findings, Jensen asked: "Who were the authors? Three of them are employees of BASF Corporation, your honor. Again, a corporation that emits chemicals, pollutes the environment, and has a highly vested interest."

Jensen cited case law in California that prohibits a trial judge from acting as an "uber-scientist," second-guessing the foundation of testimony. He warned the judge: "You're not allowed to determine that they're right and our experts are wrong about what that data means."

But that is precisely what Judge Mortimer chose to do.

In his nine-page opinion, the judge found that "none of the twelve plaintiffs here at issue, by plaintiffs' own experts' admission, were exposed to significant levels of the chemicals in question.

"These trivial levels of exposure," he continued, "do not support a finding of specific causation, or raise a triable issue of fact."

He added: "They are based upon an assumed twenty-four-hour per day exposure which does not reflect reality. The figures are, at best, inflated."

In order to arrive at his decision, the judge had to exclude any evidence that was favorable to the plaintiffs' case. And that is precisely what he did. He sustained every one of the eighty-one evidentiary objections raised by the defendants.

That meant he threw out such evidence as the EPA's "Supplemental Guidance for Assessing Susceptibility From Early-Life Exposure to Carcinogens," which set standards in 2005 for acceptable chemical exposures for children and adolescents in air or at waste cleanup sites. He rejected the experts' use of peer-reviewed studies about dioxins, because he said PCBs were not the same as dioxins. He rejected the plaintiffs' mention of a 2006 NIOSH study that suggested a "no-safe" threshold for hexavalent chromium and lung cancer, since lung cancer was not an issue for the first twelve plaintiffs. Also stricken from the record by the judge were the EPA's reassessment of dioxin, which determined that the chemical is "non-threshold" and, even more important, the U.S. National Toxicology Program's eleventh annual report on carcinogens, which made clear that "dioxin-like chemicals," such as furans and PCBs, are not as potent as some forms of dioxin, but they bind to protein receptors that can trigger the mechanism that causes cancer in precisely the same manner.

Having wiped out the experts' evidence, the judge concluded: "None of the plaintiffs' experts can name any authoritative textbooks, peer-reviewed articles, regulatory organizations or scientific bodies that say that benzene causes any of the diseases involved in this case. Their opinions on causation are without support and speculative."

Though he methodically analyzed exposures for benzene, the judge sidestepped mention of biological evidence, such as the blood tests of the plaintiffs. As a matter of law, Judge Mortimer decreed, "there is no evidence that PCBs or that furans cause any of the cancers in humans that are in issue here."

In that regard, the judge's legal finding ran counter to the available science: one of the plaintiffs' experts, for example, provided a peer-reviewed study on how PCBs cause thyroid cancer. The EPA's peer-reviewed cancer reassessment concluded that PCBs are "probable" human carcinogens. The International Agency for Research on Cancer has said that PCBs are "probably" carcinogenic to humans. The National Toxicology Program has stated that it is reasonable to conclude that PCBs are carcinogenic in humans, based on animal studies. The National Institute for Occupational Safety and Health has determined that PCBs are a "potential" occupational carcinogen. And, according to California's proposition 65, PCBs are listed as a "recognized carcinogen and developmental toxicant"—ranked as "one of the most hazardous compounds [worst 10 percent] to ecosystems and human health," according to Scorecard, a national tracking system of chemicals.

I approached this story as a journalist, trying to gather facts and withhold opinion. But after three years I realized that the truth demanded more. If most reporters fight against restrictive deadlines, I had the luxury of time despite editors demanding that I reveal myself. Simply put, I knew that anything less would be an abdication of responsibility.

It seems clear to me that the lesson of Beverly Hills High School is that something has gone terribly wrong—with our regulatory system, our legal system, and our political will. They have all, in some important ways, been poisoned.

The defense in the lawsuit may have won the first round, but the case is hardly over. The defense motions involved only the first twelve of more than one thousand plaintiffs. Just because the judge knocked out the first twelve cases for evidentiary reasons does not mean that there is no evidence that children are at risk.

In fact, the case management order, which was structured so that the most prevalent cases of cancer would be tried first, didn't necessarily reflect Al Stewart's "best" cases in which his burden of showing "general" causation would be easier. In other words, the leukemia cases or the lung cancer cases of nonsmokers such as Phil Berman.

To me, the case exemplifies the vagaries of the adversary process, where the rules of law and rituals of the courtroom obfuscate reality. It shows how the worlds of science and law can be used to protect corporations from accountability, and school boards and city councils from taking responsibility for their children.

Despite evidence that both Venoco and Sempra exceeded emissions permits, it remains extremely difficult to prove that people are being made ill as a result of exposure to toxic chemicals. There is the difficulty of proving that a specific chemical released from a facility caused a specific disease. And there is a dearth of air-monitoring data from the community: the closest air monitor to Beverly Hills is located in Burbank, ten miles north.

No one denies that these facilities are creating an increased health risk. The question is how much. Who measures it? Who is accountable? Venoco itself conducted a health risk assessment and concluded its operations posed less than a one in a million cancer risk measured over seventy years. On the other hand, the Air Quality Management District found the cancer risk at the site from benzene exceeded the risk for the rest of Los Angeles, though that risk magically disappeared just a few feet away on the school's baseball diamond and track.

The corporate polluters don't deny they emit hazardous substances at the high school. They insist, however, that they are so tiny as to be inconsequential. In the eyes of the law, those chemical exposures are "trivial." But risk, no matter how small, is additive. I believe we ignore the signposts of each additional exposure at our peril: the "curse of the English Department" is one such sign, as are the anecdotal stories of teachers who have attended too many funerals of their contemporaries and students. Not to mention the mounting cases of young graduates with fatal brain tumors and lymphomas.

No matter what the legal outcome, the situation at Beverly Hills High School shows how the environmental regulatory process in the United States is not stringent enough in its emission standards, in its enforcement of existing regulations, or in the scope of its monitoring programs to protect the health of those who live or work or attend school next door to "hot spots" of pollution, especially children.

At the heart of the problem, there is a lack of political will to provide lasting protections. Politicians and regulators are more worried about attracting and keeping large industry than they are with protecting citizens from fallout from industry. Why do we protect the polluters? Industries are permitted to emit huge volumes of toxic chemicals, but they do not have to prove that the air in the adjacent community is safe to breathe.

As a society, we wait for proof of harm rather than insist on proof of safety. So something has to be proved dangerous before anything is done. In the end, then, the poisoning of the high school turns into a political question about who is conducting research, who pays for it and what evidence, inevitably, will be ignored.

The cold hard facts are these:

- State law prohibits *new* schools from being sited next to an oil well. Ironically, the only place in Beverly Hills where oil drilling is permitted, according to a 1979 ordinance, is at the high school. That ordinance was enacted so that the school district and city could reap royalties from oil production there. At the time, Standard Oil promised the city council as much as $50 million. Though the high school sits atop an oil field that has been worked over for the past fifty years, no one has been monitoring for toxic exposures to students or faculty on a consistent basis. There is no independent third party because scientific judgment has been clouded by economic incentive. The one state agency that exists to investigate toxic contamination of schools was barred from conducting an independent inquiry at Beverly High. The watchdogs are gone.
- Under the Clean Air Act, a "major" source of pollution is defined as any facility that emits ten tons a year of a single hazardous air pollutant or twenty-five tons a year of two or more hazardous pollutants. There are two such facilities at Beverly High: Central Plant and Venoco. In 2002, after AQMD identified the oil production site as a major source, loopholes in the law exempted it from having to report releases of "fugitive" emissions, thereby cutting its releases in half—at least on paper. The following year, the facility was shut down for excessive emissions of benzene, a carcinogen that causes leukemia. One source test taken in April 2003 by the agency showed emissions in the

range of nine hundred parts per million—more than nine hundred times the "safe" level for workers. It is supposed to be a "closed-loop" system. It is not. If it were, there would be no need for methane sensors in the boys' bathroom, gas alarms, or toxic hot spot reporting requirements. The Central Plant in Century City, next door to the high school, continues to pay emissions fees for its release of toxic chemicals, including acrolein, which was identified by a state scientific advisory panel as a chemical to which children are especially vulnerable, especially as a cause of asthma.

- The Central Plant used the carcinogen hexavalent chromium to clean out its cooling towers from 1965 until 1989, when it was banned for that use by the state of California. When inhaled in large enough doses, that form of chromium causes lung cancer and sinonasal cancers in humans. Judge Mortimer decreed that the plaintiffs' exposure to chromium was in the range of 45 to 125 nanograms per cubic meter, well below established risk levels. Still, many of the plaintiffs whose cases have yet to go to trial suffer from lung cancer, as did veteran teachers who are not part of the lawsuit. At the same time, chromium risk levels are in flux. In 2006 the Occupational Safety and Health Administration lowered the chromium standard for workers by a factor of ten, from fifty-two to five micrograms per cubic meter.

- Epidemiology studies are an important way to assess cancer causation, but they are not the only assessment tool. Since some chemicals don't necessarily persist in the environment, one way to determine exposure is through blood tests of chemicals that don't break down in the body. From 1981 to 2003, according to testimony in court, natural gas pipelines operated by the Southern California Gas Company were contaminated with PCBs, which cause cancer in animals and are considered "probable" human carcinogens by the National Toxicology Program; PCBs were banned by Congress in 1977 because they persist in the environment. One of the by-products of PCB combustion is furans. As recently as February 2006, PCBs were detected coming out of the Central Plant. According to papers filed in court, blood serum tests of nine of twelve plaintiffs revealed high levels of a particular type of polychlorinated biphenyl, PCB-126, and a type of furans. Initially, Sempra's lawyers insisted that PCBs had nothing to do with the plant; later they conceded that PCBs were emitted by the plant but claimed they were so infinitesimal as to be harmless.

■ Thyroid cancer rates among high school graduates from 1990 to 2001 were more than double the national average, according to Dr. Clapp's report. The local cancer registry, using census tract data, also reported an elevated incidence of thyroid cancer among young men in Beverly Hills; officials said those results were a statistical fluke. The only known cause of thyroid cancer is exposure to ionizing radiation. Radioactive iodine-131 (I-131) is used to check for leaks in casings at the oil wells on the high school property. In April 2004 a report by state and local health officials found that the underground injection of the radioactive material resulted in a doubling of background radiation in the ambient air at the site. Public health officials could not determine how the I-131 got out of the well bore and into the air.

■ In 1970 a high school contractor warned that students were drinking "illegal and dangerous" water on the girls' athletic field, located next to the oil operations and close to the Central Plant. Common sense and the principle of precaution suggest that students and teachers should not be at a school so close to industrial operations that handle large volumes of highly toxic, flammable, and explosive products and by-products.

Most people believe government agencies are protecting them from harmful chemicals in the environment. This is simply not the case. Chemical mixtures are not even studied, and regulations protecting trade secrets keep communities in the dark. The burden of proof has been shifted from industry to government. And loopholes in federal laws, like the Toxic Substances Control Act, prevent the EPA from taking action on problematic chemicals.

As scientists debate what constitutes a "safe" level of chemical exposures, particularly at low doses, risks accumulate. The tendency is to throw up our hands and assume that everything—the air we breathe, the water we drink, the plastics our babies suck on—is toxic. But the real question is: what is preventable?

Back in Dallas the afternoon before Thanksgiving, Al Stewart was shopping for groceries with his mother when his cell phone buzzed. It was Jim Piel, calling with news of Judge Mortimer's order.

The call lasted no more than five minutes. Both lawyers, to put it mildly, were in shock. It was difficult for them to square the judge's previous rulings with this one. After years of work and millions of dollars, they were not about to give up now. The judge's decision, they felt, was a colossal mistake. Contacted by the press, Stewart spoke of his respect for Judge Mortimer and of his conviction that the judge was flat-out wrong.

Ever the optimist, Stewart wondered if the judge decided to pull the plug now, rather than waste everyone's time in a four-month trial, because the California Supreme Court had scheduled oral arguments on a case that could preclude everything here. In that case, known as *Lockheed II,* the court would have to decide how much discretion a trial judge has in reviewing the scientific evidence supporting an expert's opinion.

Trial judges in California have broad authority to withhold unreliable expert testimony from jurors if they believe it is lacking in scientific foundation. The question is how limited the judge's role should be in screening the evidence and the grounds for doing so. Stewart, of course, believes that jurors should be the final arbiters of the value of expert testimony.

For Stewart, it was clear as day that the evidence in this case supported his experts' opinions. He felt certain that his partner, Baughman Jensen, had done a superb job of presenting their case in court. "Looks like we have an intermission, don't we?" he asked Piel. "Yup, it's intermission time."

During the next three agonizing weeks, they awaited the judge's more fully explicated ruling, which his clerk sent by e-mail. With rising indignation, Stewart read the opinion and was flooded with disbelief. "He takes away all my evidence and then says, 'now you have no evidence!' It's like he took a big meat cleaver and said, 'I don't like that—chop. Clapp report. Chop.

"We're in this Alice-in-Wonderland world where the judge thinks the epidemiologist has conceded a lot by saying he doesn't know what caused the increased cancer at the school. So nobody gets to use that report. It's crazy talk. Just *crazy* talk! It's the equivalent of saying a masked gunman went to the high school. Your witness says someone shot one hundred kids. Are you saying who shot them? No. Then you're speculating they were shot.

"He's saying the underlying opinion is speculative. He clearly doesn't understand what epidemiologists do and don't do. In this context, there are three kinds of cancers that are elevated. You can't get the California registry to open up their registry. Here's a fact, an uncontroverted fact, that he threw out on speculative grounds."

In effect, Stewart thought, Judge Mortimer struck the evidence he either didn't like or understand, turning himself into a scientist. "The guy threw out math!" he said incredulously.

I asked Stewart if he regretted not providing more evidence to bolster his belief that his clients' immune systems had been suppressed by the mixture of chemicals at Beverly High. "The road to cancer is a road, not a one-day event," he said. "No person who ever got cancer wasn't immunosuppressed. If we [had] had something on that, they would have had something else.

"Why do you think PCBs have been banned in the United States? It's because exposures to PCBs cause cancer, and there is medical and scientific evidence to back that up. We presented a study on PCBs and thyroid cancer at a PCB plant. We produced medical and scientific opinions that showed dioxin and dioxinlike compounds produced *all* those cancers. We've got the leading chromium expert in the world explaining the mechanism of how that works.

"So *Doctor* Mortimer disagrees with Dr. Costa?" he said with some bitterness. "The last twenty years there's been a wholesale effort by corporate America to butcher science, and it has been successful."

If the case had become a potential disaster for Baron & Budd, as one of its experts suggested to me, Stewart refused to say so. Some insiders believe the law firm has spent as much as $10 million on the case, but Stewart said the real question was how much the defense team has spent. Given the number of lawyers involved—more than two dozen by my last head count in court—it was an amount that exceeded my math abilities.

Only one in five cases are reversed on appeal in California, but Stewart felt his odds were better than that. He asked a colleague at his firm to research Judge Mortimer's record and discovered that the judge had a reversal rate of fifty-fifty. That, for Stewart, was cause for hope. Everything now depended on the Court of Appeals.

But even within his own camp, there were rumblings about how Stewart had botched the case. What Jim Tarr, the plaintiffs' air modeling expert, had liked most about Stewart when they first met ten years earlier was the way the lawyer got all his experts together at the same time. "In this case," Tarr told me, "he didn't do that. I don't know why—either money or he didn't want people talking to each other. The whole thing has been weird."

Tarr was buoyed by the fact that the use of chromium by the Central Plant ended seventeen years ago. Still, he remained shaken by what he had seen at the high school. "Why are you going to expose these kids to these things if you don't have to?" he asked. "The facts we've got are meager. It's just not possible to quantify, because there's no certainty involved in our computations. Just as there's no certainty with regard to what government regulatory agencies do to protect public health.

"You need to keep people away from dangerous chemicals—particularly kids. I want these kids to be safe, and they're not safe the way that school is operated. It takes a real moron to do what they did there."

Among the litigants themselves, there was a split reaction to Judge Mortimer's ruling. In San Diego, Phil Berman had just discovered that his cancer had spread to his cervical spine, the top vertebrae that reach into the neck. He was getting ready to begin twenty days of radiation to his spinal cord. As for the lawsuit, he said: "Sounds like it'll be a lot longer road. But hell, that's what these guys do. So we'll watch 'em do it. Hopefully I'll still be around at the denouement."

Other plaintiffs were less sanguine. In Marina Del Rey, my former English teacher Lou Versace viewed the legal shenanigans in Shakespearean terms.

"What strikes me as entirely tragic and irresponsible," he said of the school district and city of Beverly Hills, "is that they are spending their ill-gotten gains on lawyers whose goal is transparent to anyone with an ounce of reality-sense—for the sole purpose of wearing out the plaintiffs in time and in who has the most money to outlast the other.

"Now, when someone happens to ask me where I have taught, I hesitate a little and, then, I feel ashamed that I ever worked there."

Lori Moss, whose chance meeting with Erin Brockovich four years earlier set the whole thing in motion, no longer stayed abreast of the legal case. She and her husband, Randy, had recently moved to a bigger home in the San Fernando Valley to accommodate their growing family. In addition to their two year-old daughter, they also had a new member of the family, a six-month-old son, Ryan.

By happenstance that fall, I met the mother of another young Beverly Hills High School graduate, Jack Malony, who had died from a fatal form of brain cancer a year earlier. A football player at Beverly who also played flute in the marching band at halftime, Jack was featured in a July 2003 segment about Beverly High athletes who had fallen ill on the HBO program *Real Sports with Bryant Gumbel,* while Jack was undergoing radiation treatments.

It took Carol Malony a couple of days to get herself together just to call the lawyers at Baron & Budd after the judge dismissed the case of the first twelve plaintiffs. She had spent Thanksgiving marking the year anniversary of her son's death at the age of twenty-seven. "I don't know what I was expecting to happen," she said of the case. "It wouldn't bring Jack back, but it did seem like it could help me cope."

In recent days, she had met others who were not even aware of the lawsuit. "To have the oil drilling stop and the area made safe for everyone is my priority," she added.

With enough time, the local activists simply gave up. They no longer stayed involved. No one was there to keep the pressure up.

When word arrived about the dismissal of the first twelve cases, Mahshid Soleimani was incensed that school board members were claiming victory. "They always were hiding behind the lawyers," she said. "Now, they're pushing it to the point of saying this is good for our kids. The extent of the deception is what bothers me." She believed it was ridiculous to say that the oil production on the school grounds was not a problem. "It *is* a problem."

Nonetheless, Soleimani was done fighting. She had opened a little business of her own, a Laundromat, that kept her busy. All she could do now was hope that the defense was right and that the operations there weren't causing the type of harm claimed in court. "That was a chapter in my life, and now I can say it's pretty much effectively over."

In Cambridge, Massachusetts, Zack Anderson was a sophomore at MIT. He rarely gave much thought to the oil wells at Beverly High. He had left his underground newspaper in the hands of a Beverly senior. But during the summer, there was a mix-up with his credit card expiration date, and the Web site's domain expired too. "Immediately, someone bought it and then offered to sell it back to me for $40,000," Anderson said. "After explaining that we don't have such funds, they came down to $10,000, which is still totally outrageous. I'm still working out the kinks."

Jody Kleinman thought it was sad that people got worn down. Now that her daughter Marisa had graduated from Beverly, she was less plugged in. But she hadn't given up entirely. No doubt, she had grown cynical in a way she could never have predicted. If she originally believed that regulatory agencies protect people from hazardous chemicals, she no longer thought so. Now, she was convinced that the AQMD and DOGGR had been corrupted by the industries they were supposed to be overseeing.

She noticed that the cast of characters had changed over time. Not only had the school principal and superintendent departed, so had many other key players. The city manager. The city clerk. The engineer at the oil wells.

The fire chief. Even the corporate ownership of the power plant had changed hands: Sempra had sold its Central Plant operation to a Boston-based company, Thermal Western Holdings, and its subsidiary Trigen.

This, she believed, was precisely how the status quo stayed the same: bureaucrats switched jobs, new people had to be reeducated and the populace didn't care to bother itself with details. "That's why changes are so damn little and so damn slow," she said. "It really is baffling how money corrupts common sense."

But she hadn't lost her fire, especially when the news of the dismissal of the first twelve cases was accompanied by news reports of city officials who claimed vindication. "Did they have lobotomies over the past three years?" she asked of the city council. "These problems are real. They haven't gone away, whether the lawsuit is gone or not. There's some bad shit coming out of these facilities. Whether it's enough to cause cancer, I don't know. But it's additional risk in this air in L.A., which is the worst in the country. We know the scientific proof is weak, because the studies haven't been done. I feel like now the whole thing has been whitewashed into a nonissue."

Peeved that the *Los Angeles Times*'s story about the judge's ruling included a dismissive quote from Wendy Cozen, the epidemiologist who runs the local cancer registry and whose husband consulted for defense counsel as she issued a report about cancer rates in Beverly Hills, Jody Kleinman sent off a letter to the editor criticizing what she saw as Cozen's conflict of interest, and chastising the newspaper for not mentioning it. The letter was never published.

But she wasn't about to give up. Not now. She was encouraged to read how members of the European Parliament had voted for new controls on thousands of toxic chemicals. "Call me hysterical and foolish, but no child should be exposed to additional risk. I've got zero tolerance for added risks. It's a dirty business and it doesn't belong on a school campus. It just all adds up to total nonsense as far as I'm concerned. Shit happens. That's why it shouldn't be there. Refineries have it much worse, but that still doesn't make this okay. I may lose. But I'm gonna go out fighting.

"This is about baby steps." There was an upcoming city hall meeting she needed to calendar on her BlackBerry about more oil drilling beneath Beverly Hills. For Kleinman, taking one step at a time was nothing short of an act of faith.

With Judge Mortimer's ruling, Tom Meador, the lawyer for Sempra Energy, had much to celebrate. It was as if he had won the trifecta: Meador expected to be in trial over the holidays, but he scheduled a Tahitian vacation for his family instead; plus, it was his birthday *and* his beloved UCLA Bruins beat their crosstown rivals, USC, in that weekend's football showdown.

For Meador, this lawsuit was the most interesting one he'd ever worked on. What distinguished it, he later said, was not only the respect he had for Al Stewart and Steve Baughman Jensen, the Baron & Budd attorneys, but also the amount of money they had invested in it. Still, despite Meador's relief, he knew this case could go on for quite some time. The Lockheed toxic tort case, which he began working on back in 1987, was proof of that. "That's twelve down," he said of the Beverly Hills High School lawsuits. "Nine hundred and eight-eight to go."

One might have expected Ernest Getto to exult in his victory. But it didn't exactly turn out that way. Getto was pleased, of course, but reluctant to get ahead of himself; there was simply no way to predict the outcome of Al Stewart's appeal of Judge Mortimer's ruling. And there were the chronic physical maladies that were catching up with him. Getto was an avid golfer, but nagging back problems had intensified for him during this case. Plus, there was his ankle surgery from a year earlier. Over Thanksgiving, there was another back flare-up, so golf wouldn't be on his itinerary as he planned a little getaway to his second home in Santa Barbara after Christmas.

From her home in San Diego, Cindy Cwik also spoke of vacation plans for New Year's. She had been taking malaria pills for an upcoming trek in Peru with her family. "I'm off to the jungle," she said with excitement.

Erin Brockovich was no longer employed full-time by Masry & Vititoe. For the last several years, she had worked for the firm on a consulting basis only as her involvement with the case tapered off, except for occasional press interviews and a brief visit to court for an evidentiary hearing. Most of her time now was spent on the lecture circuit, giving inspirational talks about overcoming fears and believing in oneself. She had plans to travel to Australia and Asia the following year. She also had become a producer on a new TV series, *Class Action,* for NBC. The show follows a team of high-powered lawyers, not all of whom have the most altruistic intentions, "in the morally vague world of class-action lawsuits," according to one write-up.

"For me, the biggest victory in Beverly Hills wouldn't be a $322 million settlement," she told me. "It would be to have that school moved to another location or have that thing shut down and the laws about industry being so close to schools changed. That would be the victory for me." She had hired a public relations firm, Levick Strategic Communications in Washington, D.C., which, according to its Web site, specialized in "high-stakes PR and crisis management." She said she wanted to put out a Web log with information about the case; now that it seemed to be collapsing, she would almost certainly need some help revamping her image as a crusader.

Still, Brockovich felt proud of her role in the lawsuit. She had no intention of backing down, even though she still had her differences with Al Stewart. "I'll never be ashamed of taking the side of the public health and safety. It's just the right thing to do. If you lay down your sword and retreat now, the fight will have been for nothing."

She missed Ed Masry, but she also felt his presence from time to time. "It's a comfort," she said. "It guides me. You don't change your morals and values because you lose once in a while. Something was taken away from these families in Beverly Hills, and it bothers me. Hinkley was about all of us. Beverly Hills High is about all of us. I don't care if you're rich or poor, black or white. We value our families, our love for them, and our health. I just don't think the situation at Beverly Hills High is right at all.

"Even if we lost, I won't change."

In Beverly Hills, Thanksgiving was a day of much gratitude. It appeared that this whole nightmare might soon end. The new mayor, a lawyer named Steve Webb, chastised Erin Brockovich in the press for generating fear and anxiety with her baseless allegations, all for her self-promotion. He said the judge's decision made it clear, once and for all, that there was no health or safety issue with respect to the oil wells. The whole thing, he believed, was a ridiculous charade.

For his part, Webb used his royalty money from BreitBurn, the oil and gas company on Pico Boulevard that drilled below the streets of Beverly Hills, to buy his cigars. BreitBurn had a permit pending with the city to re-drill an old well under Rodeo Drive and Olympic Boulevard. The City Council had been postponing hearing the matter for more than a year. Maybe now, a decision would be forthcoming. And the lawyer consulting for Breit-Burn on that permit would be none other than Mark Egerman, the city's former mayor. It was business as usual in Beverly Hills.

Myra Lurie, the petite school board president, believed that Judge Mortimer's dismissal of the first twelve cases was "courageous and wise." Asked for a comment from the local paper, she said: "This is a victory for our children and our community." It was as if the whole thing had never happened.

In the weeks that followed, Judge Mortimer had more surprises for the lawyers. On January 9, 2007, the sixty-nine-year-old jurist dismissed the remaining cases against the city of Beverly Hills. Despite its 1978 lease agreement, which guaranteed the city a 5 percent royalty interest from oil production at the high school, the judge determined that the city neither controlled the operations there nor the air emissions. And, without notice to the city of a dangerous condition at either the oil well or Central Plant, the judge said, it could not be held liable.

The judge set a hearing date for oral arguments in March 2007 on the school district's motion to be dismissed from the case too. That still left the deep-pocketed oil and energy companies to duke it out with Stewart over the remaining one thousand cases or so. Judge Mortimer stayed those cases, pending the plaintiffs' appeals.

The spinmeisters for Beverly Hills, meanwhile, were cranking out press releases so that its leaders could take a victory lap. City Attorney Larry Wiener no longer relied on the services of Steve Sugerman, the city's former crisis communications expert, who had faced a crisis of his own. In June 2005 Sugerman pled guilty in federal court to participating in a scheme to bilk the city of Los Angeles through phony billings. His plea was made in exchange for testifying against his old boss at the PR firm Fleishman-Hillard. Sugerman admitted he was involved in the overbilling of more than $120,000. In September 2006, he was sentenced to three years probation and community service.

Now Wiener counted on the services of PR specialist Tom Goff, who worked in the Los Angeles offices of Edelman, a crisis communication company that represented the American Petroleum Institute, to convince the public that the industry is facing "challenges" as it pulls in record profits. Goff himself has managed oil-spill communication for the Atlantic Richfield Company and has helped to promote the defense contractor Lockheed.

"Needless to say," Wiener said in his statement issued by Goff, "we are very gratified by this result as many years have been spent battling claims that were made loudly in the media, but never supported by reliable data or credible science."

Standing outside the courthouse, Al Stewart insisted the war was far from over. Stewart said: "I've still got 988 cases to get it right. In the life cycle of a lawsuit, it's far from over.

"Even if we go down in flames," he added, leaning on his rolling brief-case, "I'll be proud of the work we've done on this case. I've said it before and

I'll say it again: I'd never send my children to Beverly Hills High School, because there's evidence that you're at an increased risk for getting cancer if you graduate from that school." But the game for Stewart was effectively over; in the following weeks, he abruptly resigned from his law firm over a dispute with his partners that he wouldn't discuss publicly—a move that made Erin Brockovich extremely happy.

NOTES

The narrative of this book is based on primary sources: hundreds of thousands of pages of public records, historical documents, and interviews with two hundred people, conducted primarily between February 2003 and December 2006. Many subjects were interviewed several times; they are usually listed by date of the first interview. Quotations used in reconstructed conversations at which the author was obviously not present are derived from author interviews of at least one of the direct participants in the quoted conversations and are noted throughout. The vast majority of documents were filed in Los Angeles Superior Court in case number BC297083, *Lori Lynn Moss et al. v. Venoco, Inc. et al.* (hereafter *Moss v. Venoco*), though many documents were culled from public-records requests of several government agencies.

INTRODUCTION: WAKING UP

Page

xiv *with a 5 percent:* City of Beverly Hills Response to Freedom of Information Act Request: Letter from J. E. Brooks, Standard Oil Company of California, Division Land Manager, to Beverly Hills Oil Committee members George Slaff and J. M. Stuchen, March 18, 1974 (minimum case at $4.75 per barrel: $26,650,000; maximum case at $9 per barrel: $50,550,000).

xv *One caught fire:* Internal memo of Beverly Hills Public Works Department, "Re: Oil Operations on Beverly Hills High School Property," from Peter Gardett, geologist, to Beverly Hills City Councilman George Slaff, November 26, 1973.

xvi *The local CBS station:* http://cbs2.com/specialassign/local_story_041191240. html.

xvi *Soon after:* Martha Groves, "Cancer Cluster in Beverly Hills Alleged," *Los Angeles Times,* February 22, 2003.

xvii *Not only had she:* Army Archerd, "Brockovich, Masry Head to Beverly Hills," *Daily Variety,* February 19, 2003.

xvii *The fact is:* Interviews Barry Rosenbloom, Thomas Mack, Wendy Cozen, April 2003. See also National Cancer Institute, www.cancer.gov, or Lynn A. Gloeckler Ries, "Cancer Survival and Incidence from the Surveillance, Epidemiology, and End Results (SEER) Program," *Oncologist* 8 (2003): 541–52.

xvii *But mostly, the e-mails:* Yahoo! Groups: BHHS 1971 Messages: Message 471 of 473, retrieved February 18, 2003.

xviii *Worried that the city:* Lee Bova, Letter to the Editor, "Cancer in Beverly Hills," *Los Angeles Times,* March 1, 2003.

xviii *When I tried:* Letter from Roxanne Diaz, City of Beverly Hills assistant city attorney, Richards, Watson, Gershon, "Re: Joy Horowitz Public Records Act Request," January 26, 2004.

xviii *Months after:* Interview Sam Atwood, AQMD, August 2003.

xviii *Other reports:* AQMD, "Southern California Gas Company Measurement Collections System Gas Volume Detail Report," March 6, 2003, Venoco Inc., CONFIDENTIAL—TRADE SECRET.

xix *But this time:* Letter from Ken August, deputy director, Department of Health Services, "Re: Public Records Act Request," August 6, 2003.

xix *My first book:* Joy Horowitz, *Tessie and Pearlie: A Granddaughter's Story* (New York: Scribner, 1996).

xxi *In the well-known case:* Interview Richard Clapp, Boston, Massachusetts, January 2004. See also Kevin Costas, Robert S. Knorr, and Suzanne K. Condin, "A Case/Control Study of Childhood Leukemia in Woburn, Massachusetts: The Relationship Between Leukemia Incidences and Exposure to Public Drinking Water," *Science of the Total Environment* 300, issues 1–3 (December 2, 2002): 23–35.

xxi *Despite rosy pronouncements:* American Cancer Society News Center, "Nature Versus Nurture: The Debate; Twin Study Finds Nurture More Important Than Nature in Causing Some Cancers," 2004; Cancer Prevention Coalition, "U.S. National Cancer Institute Manipulates Cancer Statistics," http://www.prevent cancer.com/losing/nci/manipulates.htm, retrieved November 22, 2004; P. Lichtenstein et al., "Environmental and Heritable Factors in the Causation of Cancer," *New England Journal of Medicine* 343, no. 2 (July 12, 2000); 78–85; Sharon Begley, "New Statistics Show Increase, Not Decline, in Cancer Rates," *Wall Street Journal,* October 16, 2002. National Cancer Institute, "Cancer and the Environment: What You Need to Know, What You Can Do," U.S. Department of Health and Human Services, 2004. www.nei.nih.gov/newscenter/benchmarks.vol4.issues3.

xxi *We don't hear more:* Howard Hu, "Introduction to Environmental Health Concepts," Center for Health and Global Environment, Harvard Medical

School, www.med.harvard.edu/chge/course/introduction/hazards/transcript. htm, retrieved March 11, 2003.

xxi *It wasn't until:* Interview Dale Hattis, Boston, Massachusetts, January 2004; Jane Kay, "EPA Report Details How Toxics Harm Kids' Health: Additional Risks to California Children Are Listed," *San Francisco Chronicle,* February 25, 2003; "EPA: Cancer Risk May Be Higher in Children; Tougher Assessment Guidelines Proposed," Associated Press, March 4, 2003; Jennifer 8. Lee, "Agency Says Children's Risk is Higher for Some Cancers," *New York Times,* March 4, 2003.

CHAPTER ONE: FROM CEDARS-SINAI TO THE BEVERLY HILLS HOTEL

Page

3 The scene in the doctor's waiting room was reconstructed from interviews with Lori Moss (March 2003), Judy Lewinson (February 2004), Erin Brockovich-Ellis (March 2003), Randy Moss (March 2004) and Stephanie Meyers (October 2003), and drew on information reported by Drew Griffin's KCBS broadcast, "Toxic School?" on February 10, 2003.

4 *Some doctors:* Interviews Barry Rosenbloom, December 2003, Thomas Mack, March 2003, Wendy Cozen, March 2003; American Cancer Society, Cancer Progress Report—2003 Update, National Cancer Institute, NIH, DHHS, February 2004.

4 *Lori Moss knew:* Interview Lori Moss, March 2003.

5 *In recent years:* Interview Myra Lurie, April 2003.

6 *"The big joke":* Interview Lori Moss, March 2003.

6 *Thanks to life-saving treatments:* Denise Grady, "Childhood Cancer Survivors Face Increased Risks Later," *New York Times,* October 12, 2006. See also Kevin Oeffinger, "Chronic Health Conditions in Adult Survivors of Childhood Cancer," *The New England Journal of Medicine* 355, no. 15 (October 12, 2006): 1572–82.

7 *After placing:* Interview Sam Atwood, AQMD spokesman; AQMD e-mails.

7 *Keeler wasn't scheduled:* Phone interview Katsumi Keeler, February 2004.

7 *Thanks to cars:* AQMD, "Multiple Air Toxics Exposure Study in the South Coast Basin," MATES II, 1999, www.aqmd.gov/matesiidf/matestoc.htm; see also Scorecard: The Pollution Information Site; "Who Is Polluting?" http://www. scorecard.org/community/who.tcl?fips_county_code=06037&name=LOS%20. The Federal Toxic Release Inventory for Los Angeles County lists ExxonMobil Oil Corporation in Torrance, Chevron USA Inc. in El Segundo, and the Cono-coPhillips Company refinery in Wilmington as the top toxic stationary sources. See also "Oil Refineries Fail to Report Millions of Pounds of Harmful Emissions," Government Reform Committee report, Special Investigations

Division, U.S. House of Representatives, 1999; Lisa Getter, "Cancer Risk from Air Pollution Still High, Study Says," *Los Angeles Times,* March 1, 1999; Marla Cone, "State's Air Is Among Nation's Most Toxic," *Los Angeles Times,* March 22, 2006.

7 *Children bear the brunt of it:* National Environmental Trust, "Toxic Beginnings: Cancer Risks to Children from California's Air Pollution," September 2002.

7 *California has long been:* See "The History of the California Environmental Protection Agency," on the Air Resources Board Web site, http://www.calepa. ca.gov/About/History01/arb.htm; see also "California's Air Quality History Key Events," http://www.arb.ca.gov/html/brochure/history.htm.

8 *The fact that:* Bernard Endres and George V. Chilingar, "Environmental Hazards Posed by the Los Angeles Urban Oilfields: An Historical Perspective of Lessons Learned," presented on May 22, 2003, to the combined meeting of the Pacific Section of the American Association of Petroleum Geologists and the Western Region Society of Petroleum Engineers.

8 *Crude oil and pressurized gases:* Interview Floyd Leeson, April 2003.

8 *Twenty years earlier:* James Slosson, "Oil Is Where You Find It: The History of Oil Along the Newport-Inglewood Fault Trend," a field trip, May 20, 2003, Joint Meeting of Society of Petroleum Engineers, Western Region, and American Association of Petroleum Geologists, Pacific Section.

8 *In 1999:* Howard Blume, "Quaking over Belmont," *L.A. Weekly,* December 13–19, 2002.

8 *Like earthquakes or fires:* Interview John Jepson, California Division of Oil, Gas, and Geothermal Resources, April 2003.

8 *While checking:* Katsumi Keeler e-mail to Ben Shaw, February 6, 2003, 5:21 p.m., "Venoco."

8 *Normally, Venoco, Inc.:* Interview Mike Edwards, vice president, Venoco, April 2003.

8 *Later that evening:* Interview Barry Wallerstein, April 2003.

8 *Having won awards:* Venoco Web site, "Welcome to Venoco, Inc./A New Kind of Oil Company," http://www.venocoinc.com.

9 *He rarely communicated with his chief:* Interview Katsumi Keeler, February 2004; Keeler e-mail, February 6, 2003.

9 *A 1971 graduate:* Interview Barry Wallerstein, April 2003.

9 *After receiving:* William Greenburg, "Smog for Export," from *Sierra Club Bulletin* (1977), 22, in John and Laree Caughey, *Los Angeles: Biography of a City* (Berkeley: University of California Press, 1976), 460.

10 *In a stinging rebuke:* Marla Cone, "Nine AQMD Advisors Quit in Protest of New Smog Plan," *Los Angeles Times,* August 9, 1996.

10 *Griffin asked Wallerstein:* Interview Barry Wallerstein, April 2003.

11 *And it was Wallerstein:* Ibid.

11 *Five days later:* Keeler e-mail to Ben Shaw and Steve Jones, February 12, 2003, 7:52 a.m.

12 *I can't stress enough:* Ibid.

12 *Wallerstein appeared on the* Today *show:* Transcripts Today, May 5, 2003.

12 *And, he told* People: Susan Horsburgh, "Beverly Hills Mystery: Is There a Cancer Cluster at a Famed L.A. High School? Erin Brockovich Thinks So," *People,* May 19, 2003.

12 *In San Francisco:* Interview Jack Broadbent, October 2003.

12 *I told him that:* SCAQMD Notice of Violation No. P 43257 served to Bill Giardino, Venoco Inc. production foreman, February 7, 2003. Violations: "Failure to comply with permit conditions and Construction and Operation of one amine scrubber without a permit to construct/permit to operate." SCAQMD Table 7, "Sample Collected on February 11, 2003, Venoco Leaking Tank, SCAQMD Result of Analysis."

13 *The day after:* Interview Lori Moss, March 2003.

14 *"You have to go":* Interview Randy Moss, March 2004.

14 *Lori and Randy stood in line:* Interviews Lori Moss, Randy Moss, Erin Brockovich-Ellis, March 2003.

14 *The real-life story:* John W. Morgan, Desert Sierra Cancer Surveillance Program, Region Five of the California Cancer Registry, "Community Cancer Assessment in Hinkley California, 1988–1993, Updated: September 25, 2000," http:www.dscso.com.publications/Healthy Cancer Assessment.pdf.

14 *A registered Republican:* Interview Erin Brockovich-Ellis, September 2003.

15 *At the front of the line:* Interviews Erin Brockovich-Ellis, March 2003, Lori Moss, March 2003.

16 *She began to keep:* Interview Lori Moss, March 2003.

16 *Through the friend of a friend:* Interview Stephanie Meyers, October 2003.

16 *"A couple hundred bucks":* Ibid.

16 *A 1997 National Cancer Institute study:* http:www.cancer.gov/newscenter/pressrelease/benzene.

16 *A more recent NCI benzene study:* Quin Lan et al., "Hematotoxicity in Workers Exposed to Low Levels of Benzene," *Science* 306 (December 3, 2004): 1774–76.

16 *In response:* Wendy Benjamin, "Petroleum Industry Funds Challenge to Benzene Study," Associated Press, April 29, 2005.

17 *What constitutes a "safe" level of benzene:* www.epa.gov/ttn/atw/hlthef/benzene.html; EPA—Air Toxics Web site—Benzene; A. Hricko, "Rings of Controversy Around Benzene," *Environmental Health Perspectives* 102, no. 3 (March 1994): 276–81; see also http://ehp.niehs.nih.gov/docs/1994/102-3/focus.html.

17 *Barry Wallerstein's air samples:* SCAQMD Monitoring and Analysis (page 1 of 1, revised) To: Rudy Eden; Source: Venoco Benzene, ppm 4.5 (SS Canister 54049) and 4.3 (SS Canister 54091).

17 *"It's unsettling":* Interview Stephanie Meyers, October 2003.

17 *"I'd start a sentence":* Interview Carrie Powers, May 2004.

17 *She learned that:* Interview Dr. Brian Durrie, May 2004.

18 *"We were little surf rats":* Interview Carl Wilson, September 2003.

18 *Still, not all of:* Interview Dr. Peter Boesberg, July 2003.

19 *Tom Fries:* Interview Debi Genson-Fries, May 2003.

19 *"We're road warriors":* Interview Erin Brockovich-Ellis, March 2003.

20 *But before the field:* From City of Beverly Hills, letter from J. E. Brooks, Division Land Manager, Standard Oil Company of California, to Oil Committee, Beverly Hills City Council, April 30, 1973.

20 *In April 1985:* Beverly Hills Environmental Review Board Hearing, March 21, 1984, "Brief of Century Park East Homeowners Association in Opposition Application and in Support of Requirement of Environmental Impact Report," David C. Wheeler, Esq., Cox, Castle & Nicholson.

20 *Brockovich began wading:* "Final Environmental Impact Report, Beverly Hills High School Urban Drill Site," May 1978, prepared for City of Beverly Hills by Atlantis Scientific, Beverly Hills, California.

21 *Her brother, Tommy:* Erin Brockovich, *Take It from Me: Life's a Struggle but You Can Win* (New York: McGraw-Hill, 2002).

21 *Drury had already:* Interview Jim Drury, July 2003.

21 *"This is goddamn Beverly Hills":* Interview Erin Brockovich-Ellis, May 2003.

21 *No one understood:* Interview Denny Larson, January 2005; see also Steve Lerner, *Diamond: A Struggle for Environmental Justice in Louisiana's Chemical Corridor* (MIT Press, 2005) and "Coming Clean," Handbook Case Study, Monitoring chemicals in the Environment, Communities for a Better Environment (CBE), http://www.chemicalbodyburden.org/hb_cs_cbe.htm.

23 *On average:* Interview Brian Pannish, June 2005.

23 *Not only did the Bush administration:* Natural Resources Defense Council, news release: "The Bush Record: EPA Scales Back Monitoring of Smokestack Pollution," January 22, 2004; "Top EPA Official Resigns in Protest of Bush's Pro-Polluter Policies," February 27, 2002; "The Bush Record: EPA Goes Soft on Pollution Control for Oil Refineries," June 25, 2004. See also Miguel Bustillo, "Air Polluter Fines Called Too Small," Los Angeles Times, July 29, 2004; "Paying Less to Pollute: The Decline of Environmental Enforcement at EPA Under the Bush Administration," Environmental Integrity Project, January 2003.

23 *At the same time:* "Above the Law: How California's Big Air Polluters Get Away with It," Environmental Working Group, News Release, July 29, 2004.

23 *A 2004 review of toxic air emissions:* "Who's Counting? The Systematic Underreporting of Toxic Air Emissions," June 2004, a joint study of the Environmental Integrity Project and the Galveston-Houston Association for Smog Prevention.

24 *In 2005, a scathing report:* Marla Cone, "EPA Is Faulted As Failing to Shield Public from Toxins: A Federal Report Says the Environmental Agency Has Insufficient Data on Chemical Dangers," *Los Angeles Times,* July 13, 2005. The vast majority of chemicals used in commercial products have never had any federal review to evaluate potential toxicity to infants, children, developing fetuses, or adults. Biomonitoring tests have shown that a fetus, infant, or child in the U.S. today often has many synthetic chemicals in her blood or tissue. In the summer of 2005, the Kids Safe Chemicals Act was introduced in Congress by Senator Frank R. Lautenberg (D-NJ) to give more authority to the EPA.

24 *"When Erin first told me":* Interview Edward Masry, September 2003.

24 *The law firm's air sampling:* Columbia Analytical Services Inc., Masry & Vititoe, Beverly Hills High School, January 5, 2003: 56 micrograms per cubic meter is a cancer risk of 1,600 in a million; the federal government advises 1 in a million as the appropriate risk."Komax H2o Science Findings" in Masry & Vititoe Beverly Hills High School Press Kit.

24 *Instead, she sent:* Interview Gwen Gross, June 2003.

25 *Those air tests revealed:* "Data Evaluation of Indoor Air Quality Monitoring Reports for Beverly Vista, El Rodeo, Hawthorne and Horace Mann Elementary Schools, and Beverly Hills High School, Beverly Hills, CA," prepared by the Phylmar Group Inc., August 19, 1999; see figure 11, page 15.

25 *"I was worried about people with cancer":* Interview Erin Brockovich-Ellis, May 2003.

25 *"The superintendent stood us up":* Interview Jim Drury, July 2003.

26 *"This is kind of a family deal":* Interview Ed Masry, September 2003.

26 *Even so, troubles: Kissandra Cohen v. Masry & Vititoe,* no. BC228935 (Los Angeles County, California, Superior Court); see also Paul Lieberman, "Small Fry in a Big Net," *Los Angeles Times,* February 18, 2006, http://www.latimes.com/entertainment/news/la-et-pellicano18feb18,1,1015584.story?page=3&coll=la-utilities-entnews.

27 *"I was always a party freak":* "The Accidental Lawyer" in Mike Marriner, Nathan Gebhash Joanne Gordon, *Roadtrip Nation: A Guide to Discovering Your Path in Life* (New York: Ballantine Books, 2006); Also at http//www.usatoday.com/educate/college/careers/rtn/masry.htm.

28 *MTBE, a fuel additive:* "Senators Want More Data on Gas Additive," Associated Press, July 22, 2005.

28 *"We filed that on behalf":* Interview Ed Masry, September 2003.

30 *No righteous rants:* Hearing of the California Senate Health and Human Services Committee, "Possible Interference in the Scientific Review of Chromium VI Toxicity," February 28, 2003, www.sen.ca.gove/ftp/Sen/Committee/Standing/Health_home/chromium_VI_transcript_28Feb03.doc.

30 *Her New Year's resolution:* Interview Erin Brockovich-Ellis, March 2003.

30 *Weeks before:* Army Archerd. "Brockovich, Masry Head to Beverly Hills," *Daily Variety,* February 19, 2003.

31 *'"In Los Angeles, the oil industry'":* "Oil Wells in Los Angeles," USEPA Oil Spill Program Update, April 2001.

32 *Dahlgren, who received:* Interview James Dahlgren, March 2003.

33 *She had begged:* Interview Jody Kleinman, March 2003.

34 *"They're a bunch of slime":* Interview Norma Zager, March 2003.

34 *What shocked Barbara Wilson:* Interview Barbara Wilson, November 2003.

35 *Geneva Day later recalled:* Deposition of Geneva Day, law offices of Latham & Watkins, Los Angeles, Monday, August 2, 2004, volume 1, page 83, *Moss v. Venoco,* Los Angeles Superior Court, BC297083.

CHAPTER TWO: THE TOWER OF HOPE: A MITZVAH MAKEOVER

Page

39 *Named for the so-called:* Margaret Leslie Davis, *Dark Side of Fortune: Triumph and Scandal in the Life of Oil Tycoon Edward L. Doheny* (Berkeley: University of California Press, 1998).

39 *In recent years:* Interview Mina Solomon, August 2003.

39 *At Doheny's southern tip:* Southern California Petroleum Engineers Conference, May 2003, Oil Tour of Los Angeles.

39 *Arguably the most opulent:* "The Story of Greystone," Pamphlet for City of Beverly Hills Recreation and Parks Department at Greystone Mansion.

40 *Built of limestone:* Davis, *Dark Side of Fortune.*

40 *It was the first murder:* Dan La Botz, *Edward L. Doheny: Petroleum, Power, and Politics in the United States and Mexico* (New York: Praeger, 1991), 173.

40 *Though Doheny:* Ibid.

40 *"It's kinda a hidden secret":* Interview Steve Clark, May 20, 2004.

42 *His partner, Burton Green:* "History of Beverly Hills," City of Beverly Hills Web site, http://www.beverlyhills.org/presence/connect/CoBH/Homepage/For+Visitors/Facts+and+Figures/History+ of+Beverly+Hills/.

42 *About 23 million years ago:* Interview Don Clarke, August 2003; Susan F. Hodgson, "Oil and Gas Seeps in California," California Division of Oil and Gas Publication, TR 26, 1987.

42 *By geological standards:* Interview Don Hallinger, November 2003.

43 *In the past century:* Interview John Jepson, April 2003.

43 *Once Doheny:* Interviews Don Clarke, August 2003, John Jepson, April 2003.

43 *Los Angeles had an oil surfeit:* Interview John Jepson, April 2003.

43 *Standard Oil, a prime employer:* www.elsegundo.org/business/history/.

43 *After World War II:* Interview Don Clarke, August, 2003.

43 *Even the official:* Nancy Wride, "Oilmen Upset About New County Seal," *Los Angeles Times,* September 13, 2004.

43 *Oil company executives:* Interviews Mike Edwards, April 2003, Don Clarke, May 2003.

44 *Since 1900:* Interview Floyd Leeson, April 2003.

44 *Some experts:* Interview Brent Miyazaki, June 2003; B. L. Evans et al., "Well Abandonment in the Los Angeles Basin: A Primer," paper prepared for presentation at the SPE Western Regional/AAPG Pacific Section joint in Long Beach, California, May 19–24, 2003.

44 *What's left:* Interview Floyd Leeson, April 2003.

44 *The wells on the site:* Ibid.

44 *In the 1950s: Moss v. Venoco,* Joint Status Conference report.

44 *The ground beneath:* Ellen Summerfield, "Oil Well Watches Normandyland Change," *Highlights,* October 15, 1965.

45 *"If we had all the money":* Associated Press, September 5, 1982.

45 *To accommodate:* Beverly Hills Municipal Code, 10-5-302: Drilling Restriction Order 79-0-1720, effective February 15, 1979.

45 *Even when new:* Freedom of Information Act Request response from City of Beverly Hills: Interoffice Communication, City of Beverly Hills, "Chevron Letter of January 15, 1988," from Robert C. Bammes, Public Works Administrator, to City Manager Edward S. Kreins, April 14, 1988; letter from Chevron USA Land Department to BH Residents, January 15, 1988, and form letter from Kit Armstrong, Chevron USA's legislative affairs coordinator, in regard to notice regarding the use of hazardous substances: "[I]t is highly unlikely that we have caused or will cause any 'hazardous substance' to become permanently located in the subsurface oil and gas property you lease to us. However, if a molecule of a chemical that could be legally defined as 'hazardous' might be found in that property deep below the surface of the earth as a result of our oil and gas activities, the law may require us to notify you. So we did."

45 *Over the years:* "Environmental Assessment of Beverly Hills Oil and Gas Production Facility, Venoco, Inc.," Avanti Environmental Inc., January 3, 1997, from City of Beverly Hills; "Phase I Environmental Assessment Wainoco Oil and Gas Co. Facility," Intera West, February 1995 (prepared for Venoco, Inc.).

45 *And the city manager:* "Application by Venoco, Inc., for Permits to Drill Well Numbers BH-15, BH-16, BH-17 and BH-18," City of Beverly Hills City Council Agenda Statement, July 15, 1997, p. 5.

45 *Since 1995:* Interview Mike Edwards, April 2003; "Welcome to Venoco, Inc./A New Kind of Oil Company," http://www.venocoinc.com/.

46 *Begun in 1992:* Tahl Raz, "Oil Slicks," *Inc. Magazine,* October 2003, 78–86.

46 *Oil wells don't normally:* Interview Floyd Leeson, April 2003.

46 *It was, after all:* Miles Corwin, "The Oil Spill Heard 'Round the Country!" *Los Angeles Times,* January 28, 1989.

46 *But Marquez and Eson:* http://www.venocoinc.com.

46 *Not only did the company:* Jim Hendon, "Winning Minds by Winning Hearts: California Producers Make a Difference," America Association of Petroleum Geologists, *Explorer* magazine, June 2003, http://www.aapg.org/explorer/2003/06june/venoco/cfm.

46 *By 2000:* "Venoco, Inc., Was Named Business of the Year by the Hispanic Business Council," Press Release, January 15, 2000, http://www.venocoinc.com/news/archives/00_01_05.html.

46 *On April Fools' Day:* Raz, "Oil Slicks".

46 *Not long after:* "Inc. Magazine Ranks Venoco Among the Fastest Growing," Press Release, November 26, 2001, http://www.venocoinc.com/news/archives/inc500.htm.

47 *Bill Richardson:* "Former Secretary Bill Richardson Joins Venoco, Inc., Board," Venoco press release, May 2, 2001, http://www.venocoinc.com/news/archives/010502_richardson.html.

47 *It was, by all accounts:* http://www.project9865.org/TheTower.htm.

47 *Less prominent:* Proposition 65 is California's Safe Drinking and Toxic Enforcement Act of 1986. It requires the state to provide a list of chemicals known to cause cancer or birth defects or reproductive harm. It also requires businesses to notify the public about significant amounts of chemicals that are released into the environment.

47 *After Erin Brockovich:* "Tower of Hope You Don't Get Cancer," cartoon, *Highlights,* March 2003.

48 *"This Tower symbolizes":* Board of Education Gerald Lunn, CUB no. 10, http://www.geraldlunn.com/cub10.htm; Barry Brucker, Community Update Bulletin, April–June 2000.

48 *The mood was jubilant:* Interviews Leonard Stern, Eddie and Bernie Massey, October 2003.

48 *The governor:* http://www.project9865.org/tower.html.

48 *Donors of $150:* Interviews Leonard Stern and Ann Korman, October 2003.

48 *Even ardent environmentalists:* http://www.project9865.org/supporters.html.

48 *In the weeks after:* Tabby Davoodi, "Derrick Gets a Makeover," *Highlights,* May 26, 2000.

48 *"In retrospect":* Interview Lynn Koff, March 2003.

49 *"The response we got":* Interview William Guo, April 2003.

49 *The state Department of Conservation's:* Interview Floyd Leeson, April 2003.

49 *In July 2000:* "Energy Department Gives Community Service Award to Venoco, Inc.," Venoco press release, July 25, 2000, http://www.venocoinc.com/news/archives/00_07_25.html.

49 *Even so:* South Coast Air Quality Management District, Engineering and Compliance Division, Violation Notice Report by Jeannette Holtzman, inspector, Roger Christopher, supervisor, Steve Jones, AQAC supervisor, July 10, 2003: "On 3/9/2000 Venoco submitted Application No. 366919 for an amine treating unit which was installed without a Permit to Construct."

49 *After all:* Interview John Jepson, April 2003.

49 *In Long Beach:* http://www.consrv.ca.gov/DOG/photo_gallery/drilling_rigs/ photo_01.htm. See also Deborah Schoch, "Toasting Industry as Art," *Los Angeles Times,* September 13, 2006.

49 *At the 20th Century Fox studio lot:* William Rintoul, *Drilling Through Time: 75 Years with California's Division of Oil and Gas* (Sacramento: California Department of Conservation, 1990).

49 *Comedian Jack Benny:* Ibid.

50 *By the time:* Ibid.

50 *A former staffer with:* Robert Eshman, "Flower Tower," *Jewish Journal of Greater L.A.,* September 12, 1997.

51 *A press release from the City of Hope:* "City of Hope Pediatric Cancer Patients to Help Create the Largest Art Monument in the Western United States," press release, June 1999.

51 *For Hathaway Dinwiddie:* http://www.hathawaydinwiddie.com/projects. asp?chvPage Name=landmark&iPageNum=9.

51 *Originally, Eddie Massey:* Interview Eddie Massey, September 2003.

51 *Though the lease agreement:* "Agreement and Amendment to Oil and Gas Lease," Beverly Hills Unified School District, November 8, 1978, p. 17; Interviews Bernie and Eddie Massey, October 2003.

51 *"Kids would ask":* Interview Eddie Massey, October 2003.

51 *their flower-powered crusade:* http://www.portraitsofhope.org.

51 *To convince the Beverly Hills City Council:* Kathryn Kranhold, "Where Others Saw a Derrick, One Man Saw Only a Canvas," *Wall Street Journal,* February 26, 1997.

52 *"I have sat up here":* http://www.project9865.org/supporters.html.

52 *"They're selling this":* "Flower Children," *Los Angeles Magazine,* February 1998.

52 *"You don't dare":* Interview Peggy Kaus, December 2003.

52 *"No one thought we could do it":* Interviews Bernie and Eddie Massey, October 2003.

52 *One of her patients:* Interview Leonard Stern, September 2003.

52 *And with the support:* Patti Tannenbaum and Eileen Traub, "Community Service/REAL Service Learning Final Report," Beverly Hills Unified School District/PTA Advisory Board, June 2000, p. 3.

53 *"It was a wonderful":* Ibid.

53 *"My whole life":* Ibid.

53 *"Why not decorate":* Ibid.

53 *He had learned that despite:* W. James Gauderman et al., "The Effect of Air Pollution on Lung Development from 10 to 18 Years of Age," *New England Journal of Medicine,* 351, no. 11 (September 9, 2004), pp. 1057–67; Jonathan Shaw, "Clearing the Air: How Epidemiology, Engineering, and Experiment Finger Fine Particles as Airborne Killers," *Harvard Magazine,* May–June 2005.

53 *At the Harvard School of Public Health:* T. J. Woodruff et al, "The Relationship Between Selected Causes of Postneonatal Infant Mortality and Particulate Air Pollution in the U.S.," *Environmental Health Perspectives* 105, no. 6 (1997): 608–12.

53 *The green dots on the map:* Communities for a Better Environment, "People of Color and Toxic Release Facilities in L.A. County," Sources 1996 Toxic Release Inventory (U.S. EPA), 1990 U.S. Census.

54 *"I basically got yelled at":* Interview William Guo, April 2003.

55 *"I thought it was cute":* Interview Jeffry Prang, April 2003.

55 *"I am not convinced":* Letter from City of West Hollywood mayor Jeffry Prang to mayor of Beverly Hills Vicki Reynolds, May 1, 2000.

55 *In the meantime: Beverly Hills Unified School District vs. Venoco, Inc.,* case no. SC066503, May 2, 2001, Los Angeles Superior Court, Exhibit F: City of Beverly Hills Department of Building and Safety Stop Work Order, March 30, 2000; Exhibit G: City of Beverly Hills Correction Notice, April 27, 2001.

56 *One evening in August 2001: Timothy Marquez v. Jesse E. "Jempy" Neyman et al.,* case no. 01094619, July 15, 2002, Santa Barbara Superior Court.

56 *"If Venoco wants to":* Ibid.

56 *In the months that followed: Venoco, Inc. v. Eson, et al.,* Delaware Court of Chancery, June 6, 2002; Maria Zate, "Company Founder Now Suing Venoco for $10 Million," *Santa Barbara News-Press,* August 1, 2002.

56 *Meanwhile, a Delaware judge:* Ibid.

56 *"I used to think":* Raz, "Oil Slicks," p. 86.

57 *"What does it":* Interview Mike Edwards, April 2003.

57 *I felt as if I had:* California Air Resources Board, Facility Search Results, 2002 South Coast AQMD, Venoco Inc., 10609: 9.2 tons/yr total organic gases; 5.1 tons/yr reactive organic gases.

58 *A 2002 report:* Claudia Zagrean Nagy, "Oil Exploration and Production Wastes Initiative," California Environmental Protection Agency, Department of Toxic Substance Control, Hazardous Waste Management Program, Statewide Compliance Division, May 2002.

58 *Not long after:* Jim Hendon, "California Producer Makes Difference: Winning Minds by Winning Hearts," American Association of Petroleum Geologists, *Explorer,* June 2003. http://www.aapg.org/explorer/2003/06jun/venoco.cfm.

CHAPTER THREE: BLAME IT ON JULIA ROBERTS

Page

62 *When people in Beverly Hills:* BC297083, *Moss v. Venoco;* BC308673 *Bussel et al. v. Venoco Inc. et al.;* BC315885 *Steiner et al. v. Venoco Inc. et al.;* BC331173 *Kalcic et al. v. Venoco Inc. et al.;* BC317676 *Ashley et al. v. City of Beverly Hills et al.;* BC300164 *Yeshoua et al. v. Venoco Inc. et al.; Ibraham et al. v. City of Beverly Hills et al.,* Los Angeles Superior Court.

62 *Others meant not the allegations: Today,* May 5, 2003; *Good Morning America,* June 18, 2003, *Real Sports with Bryant Gumbel,* July 22, 2003; *NewsNight with Aaron Brown,* May 8, 2003.

63 *It began with:* http://www.bhusd.org/environmental/environment.02.11.03.htm; Norma Zager, "Venoco Up at Beverly Hills High School As Cancer Specialists Reassure District," *Beverly Hills Courier,* February 28, 2003; BHUSD-Courier Article February 28, 2003, http://www.beverlyhills.k12.ca.us/environmental/courier.2.28.03.htm, Supplemental Results; BHUSD-Courier Article May 23, 2003.

63 *The environmental fact sheet did not:* Memo to Ben Bushman, from Business Education Building Faculty, Re: Air Quality of Business Education Building, February 23, 2003.

63 *Nor did it refer:* Brittany Darwell, "This School Stinks . . . in More Ways Than One," *Highlights,* Opinion/Editorial, November 22, 2002.

63 *This, after all:* Interview Don Oblander, finance director, City of Beverly Hills, March 2003.

63 *How could the legendary town:* Interview Ellen Stern Harris, March 2003.

64 *Beverly Hills mayor MeraLee Goldman:* Interview MeraLee Goldman, March 2003.

64 *The town boasted:* Interview Tom Levyn, May 2003.

64 *"I feel it's absolutely safe":* Ibid.

64 *"I hate to be Chicken Little":* Interview Amy Heckerling, December 2003.

65 *As it happened:* EPA Office of the Inspector General: "Evaluation Report: EPA's Response to the World Trade Center Collapse, Report 2003-P-00012," August 21, 2003; see also Elizabeth Shogren, "EPA's 9/11 Air Ratings Distorted, Report Says," *Los Angeles Times,* August 23, 2003.

65 *"I didn't like":* Interview Amy Heckerling, December 2003.

65 *Olive finished:* Ibid.; Bill Oakley and Josh Weinstein, "Who Shot Mr. Burns? Part One," *The Simpsons,* May 21, 1995, http://www.snpp.com/episodes/2F16.html.

65 *"I just hate to see":* Interview Joel Pressman, November 2003. For a published case of an outbreak of "mass psychogenic illness" caused by a teacher noticing a "gasoline-like" smell in her classroom, see Timothy F. Jones, "Mass Psychogenic Illness Attributed to Toxic Exposure at a High School," *New England Journal of Medicine,* January 13, 2000, pp. 96–100.

66 *Parents, desperate for information:* Interview Jody Kleinman, March 2003; Gwen Gross, Beverly Hills High School Board Meeting, March 2003.

66 *What was not discussed:* Interview Mark Katchen, June 2003; Interview Dean Vlahos, March 2003.

67 *But now he insisted:* Interview Tom Levyn, May 2003.

68 *So when Beverly parent:* Interview Jody Kleinman, March 2003.

68 *"They're worried about their lawsuit":* Ibid.

69 *Like many others in his field:* Richard Doll and Richard Peto, "The Causes of Cancer: Quantitative Estimates of Avoidable Risks of Cancer in the United States Today," *Journal of the National Cancer Institute* 66 (1981): 1191–308.

69 *Over the years:* Richard W. Clapp et al, "Environmental and Occupational Causes of Cancer Re-visited," *Journal of Public Health Policy* 27 (2006): 61–76.

69 *Though his statistical analysis:* Thomas M. Mack, *Cancers in the Urban Environment: Patterns of Malignant Disease in Los Angeles County and Its Neighborhoods* (San Diego: Elsevier Academic Press, 2004), p. 645.

69 *What Kleinman didn't yet know:* Martha Groves, "Brockovich, Masry Take on Beverly Hills over Oil Fumes," *Los Angeles Times,* April 29, 2003; *Los Angeles Times,* For the Record: "Beverly Hills Oil Well," May 3, 2003.

69 *"How credible is the suggestion":* Interview Thomas Mack, March 2003.

69 *After signing:* Barry Brucker, Beverly Hills School Board Meeting, March 25, 2003; Norma Zager, "City Hires Tort Firm for Oil Facility," *Beverly Hills Courier,* March 28, 2003.

69 *By the end of March:* http://www.sugermangroup.com/scg_clients.html; http://www.sugermangroup.com/scg_experience.html; http://www.sourcewatch.org/index.php?title=Sugerman_Communication_Group.

70 *To oversee the legal:* Interview Larry Wiener, July 2003.

70 *Zager was captivated:* Norma Zager, "Weiner [sic] Has Starring Role in Oil Wells Saga," *Beverly Hills Courier,* May 21, 2004.

70 *Tall and portly:* http://www.lbbslaw.com/index.asp; http://www.lbbslaw.com/attorneybio.asp?AttyID=21.

70 *But if Bisgaard:* Interview Tom Levyn, May 2003; "L.A.'s Hired Gun," California Lawyer Magazine, March 1996.

70 *In May 2000:* In the Matter of Louis R. Miller no. 54141, case no. 96-0-05734-CEV, State Bar of California, April 10, 2000.

70 *When he was first:* Editorial: "Louis 'Skip' Miller Is the Wrong Lawyer for Beverly Hills at the Wrong Time," *Beverly Hills Weekly,* May 15, 2003.

70 *In any case:* $1 million for Miller's firm + $1 million for Weiner + $1 million for Bisgaard; $3 million + $25,000 for cost of Rowe Mawe + cost of CDM - $250,000 (interview Gwen Gross, June 2003) + cost of Sugerman; "Resolution of the Council of the City of Beverly Hills Approving an Agreement Between the City of Beverly Hills and Richards, Watson, Gershon for 3 Years";

"A Change Order in the amount of $200,000 to the blanket purchase order to Christensen, Miller, Fink, Jacobs for Claims Liability Legal Services for a Not-to-Exceed Total of $650,000 for ongoing legal services in connection with the City Council's Legislative Subpoenas"; Beverly Hills City Council minutes, November 5, 2003, #7 Item A, "A blanket purchase order in the amount of $450,000 to Christensen, Miller, Fink, Jacobs, Glaser & Shapiro for special litigation counsel service"; Beverly Hills City Council minutes, July 19, 2005; Approval for Special Services for *Moss v. Venoco* for Greines, Martin, Stein & Richland not to exceed $200,000.

70 *Together, they embarked on a stealth campaign:* Ron Matus, "The Erin Brockovich Effect: Influence, Inference," *St. Petersburg Times,* April 11, 2004, posted on Venoco's Web site: http://www.venocoinc.com/bh/ebeffect.pdf; Leon Jaroff, "Erin Brockovich's Junk Science," *Time,* July 17, 2003, posted on Venoco's Web site: http://www.venocoinc.com/bh/030711_time.pdf; Michael Fumento, "The Siege of Beverly Hills High," Scripps Howard News Service, March 13, 2003; Michael Fumento, "Brockovich's Beverly Hills Blues," Scripps Howard News Service, April 22, 2004; Michael Fumento, "Erin Brockovich Is Back," *American Spectator,* December 14, 2004. Michael Fumento is a senior fellow of the Hudson Institute, a right-wing think tank funded, in part, by ExxonMobil.

71 *"That bitch is going down":* Interview Norma Zager, December 5, 2003.

71 *Since the city was under attack:* Sam Atwood, "Atmospheric Venting Reported by Venoco," e-mail, September 5, 2003, 12:28 p.m.; Travis Brooks, SCAQMD Engineering and Compliance Division Violation Notice Report, May 8, 2003: "NOP38793 multiple days 4/6, 4/10, 4/19/03 Failing to properly maintain and operate clarifier in good operating condition, allowing VOCs to escape to the atmosphere from seals of 5 hatches," "detected leaks of 20,000–30,000 ppm at the hatch of the test tank"; "During Inspector Holtzman's re-inspection of the hatch on the test tank, she discovered it was still leaking at about 3,000 ppm"; a leak re-inspection on April 19, 2003, of the wastewater system found readings of 100,000 ppm at "4 significant leaks" from openings in the roof; interview Jack Broadbent, October 2003; SCAQMD Title V Permit application, July 25, 1997.

71 *Venoco too had been identified:* H. Stoddard, Engineering and Compliance Division, South Coast Air Quality Management District, Venoco: "Permit to Construct Application Processing and Calculations," Title V, May 14, 2003 (revised June 13, 2003), p. 21.

71 *The city's savvy legal strategy:* Interview (declined) Barry Brucker, March 2003.

71 *Her proclamations:* Interview Gwen Gross, June 2003.

71 *Masry disputed this:* Interview Edward Masry, September 2003.

71 *But he also:* Edward Masry, "Community Meeting," April 14, 2003.

71 *I asked her why:* Interview *Hamid Saebfar,* March 2003.

72 *"I'm not going":* Interview Gwen Gross, June 2003.

72 *"I can't answer":* Ibid.

72 *The following month:* http://www.thebeverlyhillscourier.com/08012003/MN1. htm.

72 *Known for his willingness:* School Board Meeting Farewells, June 20, 2003.

72 *He was especially proud:* http://bhhs.beverlyhills.k12.ca.us/bluerib/summary. htm.

72 *When the oil well story broke:* "Cool School," *In Style,* June 2003.

72 *When Venoco was shut down:* Interview Floyd Leeson, April 2003.

72 *As Bushman walked:* Ibid.

73 *Leeson was intimately familiar:* Ibid.

73 *"I was a mud man":* Ibid.

73 *"This site":* Ibid.

73 *"I didn't see pyres":* Ibid.

73 *Ben Bushman stormed:* The scene is based on interviews with Jennifer Moulton in September 2003 and Parinaz Farzinfarid in October 2003.

74 *An editorial published in* Highlights: Opinion, "A Little More Conversation," *Highlights,* February 28, 2003.

74 *The following school year:* Interview Jennifer Moulton, March 2004; see also http://www.splc.org/newsflash_archives.asp?id=7818year=2004_18k.

74 *"I'm neither":* Interview Menashi Cohen, February 2005.

74 *The principal agreed:* Menashi Cohen memorandum from AQMD files, fax transmission from Mark Katchen, the Phylmar Group Inc. to Mohsen Nazemi, March 4, 2003.

75 *In a March 4:* Mohsen Nazemi, "Beverly Hills High School," e-mail to Barry Wallerstein, March 4, 2003, 6:47 p.m.

75 *"I thought I'd get":* Interview Menashi Cohen, February 2005.

75 *Knowing that the school:* Interview Abraham Assil, April 2003.

75 *Weeks later:* Beverly Hills Parents for Safe Schools flyer, March 2003.

75 *One couple:* Interview Dean and Peggy Vlahos, March 25, 2003.

75 *"He's an athlete":* Interview Peggy Vlahos, ibid.

76 *"Everybody was terrified":* Interview Abraham Assil, April 2003.

76 *"He was insulting me":* Ibid.

76 *While parents asked:* Interview Joe Cannon, April 2003.

76 *Neither was forthcoming:* Letter from Patricia Coe-Withington, senior account executive, Travelers Property Insurance, to Mark Jubelt, Orbach & Huff, LLP, October 3, 2003. Acknowledging receipt of $26,347.18 from Mark Katchen of the Phylmar Group Inc. retained by Weston, Benshouf.

76 *Frustration also arose:* Interviews Abraham Assil, April 2003; Hamid Saebfar, March 2003.

77 *"It's just so sad":* Interview (declined) Ben Bushman, March 2004.

77 *She was stunned to learn:* Interview Jody Kleinman, April 2003.

77 *Several parents:* Interview Laraine Mestman, March 2003.

77 *There was also:* Interview Lee Bova, April 2003.

77 *"In the second game":* Interview Brittany Darwell, April 2003.

78 *She injected words like "standard of care":* Jody Kleinman testimony before Beverly Hills School Board, April 29, 2003.

78 *Through her research:* Air Resource Board Web site, Facility Search Form for Sempra Energy, Century City (11034) and for Venoco, Inc., Beverly Hills (106009).

78 *Anna Harari:* Interview Anna Harari, May 2004.

80 *On Wednesday morning:* Interview Pang Mueller, May 2003.

80 *One test showed:* SCAQMD Source Test Report, Venoco, April 11, 2003, "Toxic Air Pollution Investigation," April 18, 2003; interview Jack Spengler, January 2004.

80 *The AQMD has set:* Interview Barry Wallerstein, April 2003.

80 *"The problem":* Interview Pang Mueller, May 2003.

81 *Each time:* Barry Wallerstein memorandum, "Air Sample Analysis—Beverly Hills," February 11, February 19, February 28, March 6, April 10, April 15, April 22, 2003.

81 *What Wallerstein:* AQMD Photograph number 2, April 6, 2003, "top of clarifier was uneven and rusted"; Photograph number 3, "example of weathered and cracking seal and uneven surface, allowing multiple openings and VOC emissions"; Photograph number 7, April 19, 2003, "west-side skimmer drive rod location of VOC emissions"; Photograph number 8, April 19, 2003, "vapor leak at overlap of three bolted plates on roof of water injection tank"; Photograph number 9, "The bull plug . . . was resting on top of an open threaded connection, allowing VOC emissions from Flange #1412 at top of water injection tank," April 19, 2003; AQMD privileged and confidential attorney-client communication: Engineering and Compliance Violation Cover Letter from Jeanette Holtzman, Notice #P40557, issued to Venoco Inc, "Violation could have been prevented," March 20, 2003; "liquid carbon filters and associated piping; carbon drums and associated piping," Pang Mueller, senior enforcement manager, July 10, 2003; #P43257 on May 8, 2003 from Travis Brooks, "merge with existing NOV's: Violation involved poor maintenance; violation could have been prevented." See also SCAQMD Notice of Violation No. P38793 May 8, 2003, for "multiple days" for "failing to operate equipment in good condition: failing to properly maintain and operate the clarifier; operating the clarifier with multiple openings in the seals of 5 hatches; failing to properly maintain and operate hatch on test tank; operating wastewater tank with openings in the roof; failing to properly maintain and operate water level boot." For detailed description, see "inspector's findings" attachment to NOV P38793, re: "multiple leaks from the hatches on top of the

Wemco clarifier ranging from 1,000 to 100,000 ppm . . . probable violation of 500 ppm VOC emission limit."

81 *One was found:* "Venoco Monitoring April 10, 2003" AQMD e-mail correspondence from Air Quality Inspector Jeannette Holtzman to Carol Coy et al, April 11, 2003: "I detected a reading of 500,000 ppm at the rusted spot (on top of the water clarifier hatch)."

81 *Historically, according to internal AQMD reports:* AQMD Engineering Division, memorandum from R. Thrash, July 29, 1981, engineering evaluation report for Beverly Hills Oil Associates.

81 *The permit:* Interview Mohsen Nazemi, October 2003.

81 *"I don't want":* Interview Barry Wallerstein, April 2003.

81 *"There's so many of us":* Interview Lori Moss, May 2003.

CHAPTER FOUR: THE CURSE OF THE ENGLISH DEPARTMENT

Page

82 *The so-called new building:* Interview Gerald Carpenter, December 2003.

82 *The most striking shift:* http://www.centuryplazatowers.com/century_plaza/building_data/; Lark Ellen Gould, "Century City," Travel Agent, February 17, 1997; http://www.seeing-stars.com/Studios/FoxStudios.shtml.

82 *Encroaching budget cuts:* http://bhhs.beverlyhills.k12.ca.us/bluerib/summary.htm.

83 *But when the price:* John L. Mitchell, "To Raise Funds for School District Beverly Hills High Lends Name as a Designer Label," *Los Angeles Times,* September 16, 1988.

83 *While the annual:* Beverly Hills Unified School District, "Budget Facts at a Glance," General Fund Expenditure per Student, 2002–3 Projected, http://bhusd.org/accountability/pdf/sarc.bhhs.03-04.pdf.

83 Interview Lou Versace, August 2003.

84 Interview Gerald Carpenter, December 2003.

84 Interview "Mickey" Freedman, March 2004.

84 Interview Herbert Dodge, September 2003; "In the Summer: As Private As Public Can Be," *Time,* July 19, 1963.

86 Interview Jane Wortman, February 2003.

86 Interview Leonard Stern, September 2003.

86 Interview Dick Schreiber, February 2004.

86 Interview F. Willard Robinson, March 2004.

87 *I wish to report:* Letter from Kenneth Peters, superintendent of schools, to Clifford Enger, Beverly Hills Oil Company, October 31, 1963.

87 Interview Joyce Banzhaf, February 2004.

87 Interview "Coach" Chuck Kloes, May 2003.

88 *It's disgusting:* Mari-Ann Strandwall quoted in Michael Ross and Sue Frankel, "The Oil Well Is Not Well; Causes Problems in PE," *Highlights,* April 13, 1973.

88 Interview Jason Newman, April 2003.

88 Interview Linda Tromblestein, May 2003.

89 Interview Jane Gifford, December 2003.

90 Interview Susan Messenger, September 2003.

91 Interview Joel Goodman, May 2004.

91 *"But schoolteachers in California":* Leslie Bernstein et al., "High Breast Cancer Incidence Rates Among California Teachers: Results from the California Teachers Study (United States)," *Cancer Causes and Control* 13 (2002): 625–35.

93 Interview Mary Ann Baum, August 2003.

94 Interview Gary Thorpe, March 2003.

96 Interview Ken Peters, May 2004.

96 Interview Arthur Malin, March 2004.

96 Interview Bernie Grenell, March 2004.

CHAPTER FIVE: THE "STEAM" NEXT DOOR

Page

98 *When Zack Anderson:* Interview Zack Anderson, November 2003.

98 *"Jokingly":* Ibid.

99 *"The school is kind of going along":* Ibid.

99 *On his Web site:* http://www.beverlyunderground.com/editorials.htm.

99 *Beneath a photograph:* http://www.beverlyunderground.com/features.

99 *The son of a school board member:* Interview Zack Anderson, November 2003.

99 *Over time:* Ibid.

100 *Saebfar was a veteran:* Interview Hamid Saebfar, November 2003.

100 *In practice:* Claudia Zagrean Nagy, "Oil Exploration and Production Wastes Initiative," Department of Toxic Substances Control, Hazardous Waste Management Program, Statewide Compliance Division, May 2002, p. 37.

100 *But "economic concerns":* Interview Claudia Zagrean Nagy, April 2003.

100 *"The biggest problem":* Interview Hamid Saebfar, November 2003.

101 *"At first":* Interview Jennifer Jones, November 2003.

101 *They worried:* Interviews Hamid Saebfar and Jennifer Jones, November 2003.

102 *Public records:* From TACS AQMD 2001–2 AER, "Toxic Air Contaminants and Ozone Depleter Emissions / Fee Summary: Acrolein Annual Net Emissions 4 lbs., 011034 Central Plants Inc."

102 *According to the federal:* http://www.atsdr.cdc.gov/MHMI/mmg124.html.

102 *Acrolein, which the EPA:* "EPA NE Air Toxics" Web site, http://www.epa.gov/region1/eco/airtox/acrolein.html.

102 *"That's when the project died":* Interview Hamid Saebfar, November 2003.

102 *Wallerstein was convinced:* Interview Barry Wallerstein, May 2003; interview Mohsen Nazemi, May 2003.

103 *Unless the contract "is signed promptly":* Letter from Hamid Saebfar, Division Chief, School Property Evaluation and Cleanup Division, to Dr. Gwen Gross, superintendent, June 2, 2003.

103 *According to schools superintendent:* Interview Gwen Gross, June 2003.

103 *As the weeks passed:* Johndmillan@yahoo.com e-mail, June 12, 2003, 10:12 a.m., to Ed Lowry, director, Department of Toxic Substances Control.

103 *"When there's money involved":* Interview Hamid Saebfar, November 2003.

103 *Larry Wiener:* Interview Larry Wiener, July 2003.

104 *"That's a lie":* Interview Hamid Saebfar, November 2003.

104 *Not only did:* "Environmental Assessment of Soil and Soil Gas, Beverly Hills High School," prepared by CDM: David Jensen and James M. LaVelle, p. 1, 4.

104 *In the third issue:* http://www.beverlyunderground.com/issue3/topstories.htm.

104 *In it, he cast:* http://www.sempra.com/companies.htm.

104 *"It is important":* http://www.beverlyunderground.com/issue3/topstories. htm.

105 *Sempra, in compliance:* "A Proposition 65 Public Notice," *Beverly Hills Courier,* April 18, 2003, p. 2.

105 *The only other: Moss v. Venoco.*

105 *Despite demurrers: Moss v. Venoco,* Amended Notice of Demurrer and Demurrer of Sempra Energy, etc., September 16, 2003; See also 2-15-05 Notice of Ruling, on Plant Defendants' Motion to Quash Subpoena Issued to Custodian of Records for Southern California Gas Co.

105 *Opened in 1965: Moss v. Venoco,* Plaintiff's Second Amended Complaint.

105 *In essence:* http://www.sempra.com/companies.htm.

105 *According to the U.S. EPA:* Title V permit application, Larry Engel, vice president, 7-25-97.

105 *In 2000, Sempra:* http://www.arb.ca.gov/ap . . . /facdet.php?co_=19&ab_=SC&facid_= 11034&dis_=SC&dbyr=200.

106 *AQMD documents:* Toxic Air Contaminants and Ozone Depleters Emissions / Fee Summary, AQMD 2001–2 AER, 11034 Central Plants Inc.

106 *The amount of pollution:* Form S—Fees Due Summary, AQMD 97–98 Annual Emissions Report: $4,332; 96–97: $10,683.64 and $1,116 for toxic air contaminants; 95–96: $13,260.11.

106 *The company also:* South Coast Air Quality Management District NOV P16446, 1-21-2003, "emissions in excess of NOX annual allocation"; NOV P14378, 3-4-1998, "not properly reporting NOX emissions data from two boilers"; NOV P14386, 7-1-1996, "no CEMs on boiler #3; exceeded NOX allocation."

106 *That same year:* "In the matter of Central Plants, Inc., order granting a regular variance, Section 42350 of the California Health & Safety Code," case no. 3447-35: Findings and Decision of the Hearing Board, April 3, 1997, Marti L. Klein, p. 4.

106 *Basically, the program:* NOV P16446, 7-1-2001, Christian Hynes; see also Trade Registrations 6398 Natsource LLC, seller, Sempra Energy, buyer, 5,500 pounds, 7-29-2003; 6538 Sempra Energy, seller, Cantor Fitzgerald Brokerage, NOX 200,000 pounds, 10-1-2003.

106 *Until 1990:* AQMD Enforcement Division, 10-5-1991, Point Source Inspection: "For cooling tower fans, plant no longer uses hexachromium for O Tower."

106 *While "chromium 6":* SCAQMD 1989 Agenda #34—Adopt Proposed Rule 1404; http://es.epa.gov/techinfo/facts/ca.htmfact3.html.

107 *Of the two hundred:* Interview John Froines, April 2003.

107 *When in the fall:* Interview Sam Atwood, December 2004.

107 *"Whether the toxins":* http://www.beverlyunderground.com/issue3/topstories. htm.

107 *Already, Dunstan:* Interview Roger Dunstan, November 2003.

CHAPTER SIX: PR WARS

Page

109 *"Nobody's looked":* Interview Robert Lifson, May 2003.

110 *He had heard:* Interview Joel Pressman, November 2003.

110 *In the weeks prior:* Interview Robert Lifson, May 2003.

110 *But the alumni:* Interview Robert Fox, May 2003.

110 *Ten days earlier:* Martha Groves, "Cancer Study Finds No Elevated Risk in Beverly Hills," *Los Angeles Times,* May 7, 2003.

110 *The report:* Wendy Cozen, "Community Cancer Assessment Regarding Beverly Hills, California," USC Keck School of Medicine/Cancer Surveillance Program, April 2003.

111 *But her report did quote from:* Nancy Mueller, "Hodgkin's Disease," *Cancer Epidemiology and Prevention,* David Schottenfeld and Joseph F. Fraumeni Jr., editors (New York and Oxford: Oxford University Press, 1996), pp. 899–900.

111 *Cozen's negative findings:* Groves, "Cancer Study."

111 *In turn, county:* Interview Marilyn Underwood, March 2004.

112 *In a seminal study:* David Ozonoff and Leslie I. Boden, "Truth and Consequences: Health Agency Responses to Environmental Health Problems," *Science, Technology and Human Values* 70 (1987).

112 *Moreover, Underwood said:* Interview Marilyn Underwood, March 2004.

112 *For Lifson:* Interview Robert Lifson, August 2003.

113 *Lifson had developed:* http://www.beverlyhillsoilwellhealthstudy.com, http:// www.envirotoxicology.com/o2expert10.htm.

113 *Lifson had a theory:* Interview Robert Lifson, August 2003.

113 *He and Dahlgren:* http://www.lundydavis.com/html/attorneys/hunter_w_ lundy.html.

113 *In previous weeks:* Hunter Lundy meeting at Beverly Hilton Hotel, May 14, 2003. "Beverly Hills Oil & Gas Production Summary," Attorney Retainer Agreement "Authorization to Furnish Medical Information."

113 *As if there weren't enough:* Masry & Vititoe Law Offices Letter, "Re: Beverly Hills High School Litigation/Notice of Improper Attorney Contact; Media Contact" from Edward L. Masry, Erin Brockovich, Allen M. Stewart, Baron & Budd, May 16, 2003; Interview Erin Brockovich, April 2003.

114 *Not everyone:* Yahoo! groups BHHS1971, message 1852 of 1879, From: Phillip Berman, Date: Wednesday, July 30, 2003, 4:06 p.m.

114 *Less than a year:* Phillip Berman, personal e-mail correspondence.

115 *Since 1972:* Interviews Thomas Mack and Wendy Cozen, April 2003; Thomas Mack, *Cancers in the Urban Environment* (San Diego: Elsevier Academic Press 2004).

116 *Only a handful:* Michael J. Thun and Thomas Sinks, "Understanding Cancer Clusters," *CA: A Cancer Journal for Physicians* 54 (2004): 273–80.

116 *According to one recent study:* Ellen T. Chang et al, "Childhood Social Environment and Hodgkin's Lymphoma: New Findings from a Population-Based Case-Control Study," *Cancer Epidemiology Biomarkers & Prevention*, 13 (August 2004): 1361–70.

117 *"Cancer clusters are just a big mess":* Interview Wendy Cozen, April 2003.

117 *Unlike infectious diseases:* "America's Environmental Health Gap: Why the Country Needs a Nationwide Health Tracking Network," Pew Environmental Health Commission, September 2000.

117 *In 1996:* Richard Jackson, Director, National Center on Environmental Health, Testimony on cancer clusters before the Senate Environment and Public Works Committee, Field Hearing at Adelphia University, June 11, 2001. Accessed at http://hhs/gov/asl/testify/to10611.html.

118 *In all of medical history:* E-mail Raymond Neutra, March 6, 2003. See also: Raymond Richard Neutra, "Counterpoint from a Cluster Buster," *American Journal of Epidemiology,* July 1990; see also Atul Gawande, "The Cancer-Cluster Myth," *New Yorker,* February 8, 1999.

118 *in Fallon, Nevada:* Craig Steinmaus et al., "Probability Estimates for the Unique Childhood Leukemia Cluster in Fallon, Nevada, and Risks Near Other U.S. Military Aviation Facilities," *Environmental Health Perspectives* 112, no. 6 (May 2004).

118 *Since scientific methods for showing:* Ulysses Torassa, "Breast Cancer Amid Affluence; High Rate in Marin County Appears Tied to Wealth, Education," *San Francisco Chronicle,* Sunday, January 26, 2003. See also M. Wrensch et al, "Risk Factors for Breast Cancer in a Population with High Incidence Rates," Breast

Cancer Research, 5 (2003): 232–3. http://www.ncbi.nlm.nih.gov/entrez/query.feg
i?db=pubmed&cmd=Retrieve&dopt=AbstractPius&list_uids=12817999&query_
h1=27& itool=pubmed_DocSum.

118 *On the other hand:* Interview Julia Brody, September 2003; see also Julia
Green Brody and Ruthann A. Rudel, "Environmental Pollutants and Breast
Cancer," *Environmental Health Perspectives* 111, no. 8 (June 2003).

118 *Frustrated by years:* Interview Peggy Reynolds, April 2003. See also Peggy
Reynolds et al., "Childhood Cancer Incidence Rates and Hazardous Air
Pollutants in California: An Exploratory Analysis," *Environmental Health
Perspectives* 111, no. 4 (April 2003).

118 *At UCLA:* Interview John Froines, April 2003; see also Gary Polakovic,
"Air Particles Linked to Cell Damage," *Los Angeles Times,* April 7, 2003;
Ning Li et al., "Ultrafine Particulate Pollutants Induce Oxidative Stress
and Mitochondrial Damage," *Environmental Health Perspectives* 111, no. 4
(April 2003).

118 *Contacted by the city:* Interview Wendy Cozen, April 2003.

119 *"This increase":* Thomas Mack e-mail to author, May 2003.

119 *To the contrary:* Steve Sugerman, "City of Beverly Hills to Issue Subpoenas for
Masry Data; City Acts Aggressively to Demand Full Account of Testing Data,"
City of Beverly Hills Press Release, June 4, 2003. See also Steve Sugerman,
"Masry & Vititoe Law Firm Fails to Provide Data Demanded by Subpoena," City
of Beverly Hills Press Release, July 2, 2003; "Scientific Evidence and Public
Policy," *American Journal of Public Health* 95, supplement 1 (2005).

119 *While Cozen professed "neutrality":* Groves, "Brockovich, Masry Take On
Beverly Hills over Oil Fumes," *Los Angeles Times,* April 29, 2003.

120 *He had already signed:* Interview Thomas Mack, May 2003.

120 *In an article:* Eric Umansky, "Erin Brockovich's Weird Science," *New Republic,*
November 2003.

120 *Umansky used:* Eric Umansky, "Muckraker 90210," *Columbia Journalism
Review,* March–April 2004.

120 *"Oh, God":* Interview Thomas Mack, May 2003.

120 *Despite his contrition:* Interview Marrina Waks, December 2003. See also:
Nancy Rivera Brooks, "Digging for Oil on Campus," *Los Angeles Times,*
December 14, 2003.

121 *Just a week before:* Martha Groves, "Brockovich, Masry Take on Beverly Hills
over Oil Fumes," *Los Angeles Times,* April 29, 2003.

121 *"There is no basis":* Thomas D. Blackman, "Preliminary Summary of Findings
Ambient Air Investigation Beverly Hills High School," CDM, May 7, 2003.

121 *Dean Vlahos:* Interview Dean Vlahos, June 2003.

122 *He had last taken:* Phylmar Group Inc., "Data Evaluation of Indoor Air Quality
Monitoring Reports for Beverly Vista, El Rodeo, Hawthorne, and Horace
Mann Elementary Schools, and Beverly Hills High School, Beverly Hills,

California," prepared for Beverly Hills Unified School District, Draft, August 19, 1999; Phylmar Group, "Indoor Air Quality Monitoring Report for Beverly Vista Elementary School and Beverly Hills High School," January 3, 2000.

122 *When parents asked:* Interview Larraine Mestman, April 2003; interview Joe Cannon, April 2003.

122 *According to documents:* William Ireland, Haight Brown & Bonesteel LLP, "Re: Yeshoua et al. v. Beverly Hills Unified School District," to Patricia A. Coe-Withington, Senior Account Executive, Travelers Property Casualty, December 24, 2003.

123 *Justin Greenberg had graduated:* Interview Justin Greenberg, May 2003.

123 *Recent studies:* Interview John Peters, January 2004. See also Rob McConnell et al., "Asthma in Exercising Children Exposed to Ozone," *Lancet* 359, no. 9304 (February 2, 2002); W. James Gauderman et al., "The Effect of Air Pollution in Lung Development from 10 to 18 Years of Age," *New England Journal of Medicine,* September 9, 2004.

123 *Another athlete:* Interview Ralph Punaro, May 2003.

123 *His widow:* Interview Debi Genson-Fries, May 2003.

125 *"I'm just a farm boy":* Interview Al Stewart, August 2003.

126 *It was during: NewsNight with Aaron Brown,* transcript, May 8, 2003.

126 *Without a studio monitor:* Interview Tom Levyn, May 2003.

127 *"We're not going to":* Ibid.

127 *Despite her weakened state:* Sheila Weller, "Why Does This Woman Have Cancer?" *Glamour,* June 2003, 246–70.

128 *"I just felt like":* Diane Sawyer, "Cancer 90210?" *Good Morning America,* June 18, 2003.

128 *She had been:* Interview Michael DeWitt, June 2003.

128 *"This case": Moss v. Venoco.*

129 *There was one:* Interview Lori Moss, August 2003.

CHAPTER SEVEN: RAZZLE-DAZZLE

Page

133 *I find school board minutes:* BHUSD public records act response: Beverly Hills Unified School District, board of education minutes from November 14, 1978, Re: Beverly Hills Oil Company; see also Orbach & Huff letter from David M. Orbach to Joy Horowitz, March 4, 2004, Re: Request to Inspect and Copy Public Records and Haight Brown & Bonesteel letter from Jeffrey A. Vinnick to Joy Horowitz, Re: *Moss v. Venoco,* March 15, 2004.

134 *Initially, the promise:* Letter from Standard Oil of California, J. E. Brooks, division land manager, to Oil Committee of the Beverly Hills City Council, April 30, 1973, p. 2, from Beverly Hills public records act request and Beverly Hills High School "press kit," Masry & Vititoe Law Offices.

134 *In a June 20, 2003, letter:* Mayer Brown Rose & Maw letter from Peter K. Rosen, Re: City of Beverly Hills, June 20, 2003.

134 *In the file:* Orbach & Huff letters from David M. Orbach to Claims Department, St. Paul Surplus Lines Insurance Company Inc., Re: Venoco Oil Company and Beverly Hills Unified School District, May 1, 2003; Claims Department, Lexington Insurance Company Inc., Re: Beverly Hills Unified School District claims by former students, Venoco Oil Company and Wainoco Oil & Gas Company, July 22, 2003; Robert Plotz, environmental claim specialist, St. Paul Surplus Lines Insurance Company Inc., Re: Venoco Oil Company, Beverly Hills Unified School District, October 3, 2003; Natalie McMeans, Highlands Insurance Group, Environmental and Mass Tort Claim, Re: Wainoco Oil & Gas Company, Beverly Hills Unified School District, July 22, 2003.

135 *On August 7, 2003:* Letter from Natalie McMeans, Highlands Insurance Group, to David M. Orbach.

135 *Other insurance carriers:* Letter to David M. Orbach from David C. Lawther, claims specialist, Royal& Sun Alliance, Re: Wainoco Oil & Gas Company, October 2, 2003.

136 *On a bright, breezy Tuesday:* "Rigs to Roofs, Pumps to Parks: The Oilfields of the Newport Inglewood Fault," a field trip of the American Association of Petroleum Geologists and Society of Petroleum Engineers, Western Region, conference in Long Beach, California, May 21–23, 2003.

137 *In 2002, the Harvard:* Paul R. Epstein, and Jesse Selber, "Oil: A Life Cycle Analysis of Its Health and Environmental Impacts," report by the Center for Health and the Global Environment of the Harvard Medical School, March 2002. www.med.harvard.edu/chge/oil.html.

138 *In 2006, for example:* Cornelia Dean, "Truth? Fiction? Journalism? Award Goes to . . ." *New York Times,* February 9, 2006.

138 *Never mind that:* Aaron S. Katzenstein, Lambert A. Doezema, Isobel J. Simpson, Donald R. Blake, and F. Sherwood Rowland, "Extensive Regional Atmospheric Hydrocarbon Pollution in the Southwestern United States," Proceedings of the National Academy of Sciences, October 14, 2003. http://www.pnas.org/cgi/content/abstract/100/21/11975.

138 *At the same time:* Andrew Revkin, "Editor of Climate Reports Resigns," *New York Times,* June 10, 2005.

138 *At Beverly High:* AQMD Engineering and Compliance Division Violation Notice Report of Venoco Inc. by Yasmine Stutz, inspector, and Mark Van Der Au, February 20, 2003; South Coast Air Quality Management District, Source Test Report Conducted at Venoco Inc., April 11, 2003, by Mei Wang, air quality engineer, and reviewed by Michael Garibay, senior air quality engineer.

139 *According to studies:* K. H. Kilburn, "Evaluating Health Effects from Exposure to Hydrogen Sulfide: Central System Dysfunction," *Environmental Epidemiology*

and Toxicology 1: (1992): 207–16. See also Bernard Endres and George V. Chilingar, "Environmental Hazards Posed by the Los Angeles Basin Urban Oilfields: An Historical Perspective of Lessons Learned," presented at technical sessions on May 22, 2003, combined meeting Pacific Section American Association of Petroleum Geologists and Western Region Society of Petroleum Engineers.

139 *"Nobody knows":* Interview Mel Wright, May 2003.

139 *At Beverly Hills High School:* South Coast Air Quality Management District Notice of Violation, No. P 43257, Venoco, Inc., Office of Stationary Source Compliance, February 6, 2003, and February 11, 2003.

139 *By April:* South Coast Air Quality Management District Source Test Report 03-203, Venoco, Inc. "Volatile Organic Compound, Aromatic Hydrocarbon, and Sulfur Compound Emissions from a Gas Production Amine Treating Unit," April 18, 2003, p. 11.

140 *The highest allowable airborne exposure:* NIOSH Publication No. 2005-151: NIOSH Pocket Guide to Chemical Hazards, September 2005, http://www.cdc. gov/niosh/npg/npgd0049.html. See also http://www.osha.gov/pls/oshaweb/ owadisp.show_document?p_table=STANDARDS&p_id=10042.

140 *The amount of benzene:* SCAQMD Source Test 03-203.

141 *Weeks earlier:* SCAQMD, notice of violation March 19, 2003, P39438, "failure to keep equipment free from oil and sludge."

141 *Six months later:* SCAQMD NOV P28606, November 19, 2003; Exhibit D-2 City of Beverly Hills Staff Report, Re: Breit Burn, February 21, 2006, David D. Gustavson, director of public works and transportation to Mayor and City Council, "Subject: Lending Application for Permits to Drill Oil Wells Underneath the City of Beverly Hills from Drill Sites Located within the City of Los Angeles."

141 *What she learned:* National Center for Environmental Health, Centers for Disease Control and Prevention, http://www.cdc.gov/nceh/; Dr. Philip Landrigan, speech, September 7, 2004, Physicians for Social Responsibility, Los Angeles.

141 *In California:* Peggy Reynolds et al., "Childhood Cancer Incidence Rates and Hazardous Air Pollutants in California: An Exploratory Analysis," *Environmental Health Perspectives* 111, no. 3 (March 2003): 663; Michelle Wilhelm and Beate Ritz, "Residential Proximity to Traffic and Adverse Birth Outcomes in Los Angeles County, California, 1994–1996," *Environmental Health Perspectives* 111, no. 2 (February 2003): 207–16. Also interviews with Peggy Reynolds, April 2003, Beate Ritz, April 2003, and John Froines, April 2003.

142 *The federal government:* United States Environmental Protection Agency, "Chemical Hazard Data Availability Study: What Do We Really Know About the Safety of High Production Volume Chemicals?" Office of Pollution Prevention and Toxic Substances, April 1998, http://www.epa.gov/oppt/

chemtest/hazchem.htm; United States Environmental Protection Agency, Voluntary Children's Chemical Evaluation Program, December 26, 2000, Federal Register 65 (248): 81699–718.

142 *One of the few known:* Andrea Hricko, "Rings of Controversy Around Benzene," *Environmental Health Perspectives* 102, no. 3 (March 1994): 276–81, http://www.ehponline.org/docs/1994/102-3/focus.html; interview Myron Mehlman, November 2004.

142 *Questions about chronic:* Qing Lan, "Hematotoxicity in Workers Exposed to Low Levels of Benzene," *Science,* December 3, 2004, 1774–76. See also Agency for Toxic Substances and Disease Registry, "ToxFaq's on Benzene," 2005, www.atsdr. cdc.gov/tfacts3.html; American Cancer Society, Cancer Facts and Figures 2006, http://www.cancer.org/docroot/PED/content/PED_1_3X_Benzene.asp?sitearea= PED&viewmode=print&; Environmental Protection Agency, "Carcinogenic Effects of Benzene," 1998, www.epa.gov/NCEA/pdfs/benzenef.pdf; International Agency for Research on Cancer (IARC). IARC Monographs on the Evaluation of the Carcinogenic Risk of Chemicals to Humans. Some Industrial Chemicals and Dyestuffs, vol. 29 (Lyon, France: IARC, 1982 benzene supplement 7, 1987. National Toxicology Program, Eleventh Report on Carcinogens, Benzene, http:// ntp-server.niehs.nih.gov/ntp/roc/eleventh/profiles/s019benz.pdf.

142 *When she called:* Interview Jody Kleinman, April 2003. Sempra Energy Facility Information, 2004, California Air Resources Board: 6.2 tons total organic gases; 1.6 tons reactive organic gases; 19.5 tons carbon monoxide; 15.7 tons nitrous oxides; .1 tons sulfuric oxides; 1.8 tons particulate matter. See also Toxic Air Contaminants Emissions Summary for 011034 Central Plants Inc, AQMD 2001–2002.

142 *The differences in the biology of children:* Interview Dr. Melanie Marty, California Office of Environmental Health Hazard Assessment, February 2006.

142 *At Clark University:* Interview Dale Hattis, January 2004. See also D. Hattis, R. Goble, A. Russ, M. Chu, and J. Ericson, "Age-Related Differences in Susceptibility to Carcinogenesis. II. Approaches for Application and Uncertainty Analyses for Individual Genetically Acting Carcinogens," Environmental Health Perspectives 113, no. 4 (April 2005): 509–16. www.ehponlines.org/ members/2005/7564/7564.pdf.

143 *Like Hattis:* Frederic Perera, et al, "Molecular Evidence of an Interaction Between Prenatal Environmental Exposures and Birth Outcomes in a Multiethnic Population," *Environmental Health Perspectives* 112, no. 5 (April 2004): 626–30, http://www.ehponline.org/docs/2004/6617/abstract.html?section=children.

143 *In 2000, air pollution:* http://www.aqmd.gov/matesiidf/matestoc.htm.

144 *He had done consulting:* Interview Bill Piazza, May 2003; Steven Korenstein and Bill Piazza, "An Exposure Assessment of [PM. Sub. 10] from a Major Highway Interchange: Are Children in Nearby Schools at Risk?" *Journal of Environmental Health* 65 (2002): 9–17.

144 *In 1977:* William J. Blot et al., "Cancer Mortality in U.S. Counties with Petroleum Industries," *Science,* October 7, 1977, 51–53.

144 *At the time:* Brian E. Henderson, et al, "Lung Cancer and Air Pollution in South Central Los Angeles County," *American Journal of Epidemiology,* 101 (1975): 477.

144 *Studies from Russia:* World Health Organization International Agency for Research on Cancer, IARC Monographs on the Evaluation of Carcinogenic Risks to Humans, vol. 45, Occupational Exposures in Petroleum Refining, Crude Oil and Major Petroleum Fuels, p. 79, referencing study by Shamsadinskaya et al., 1976.

144 *Moreover, U.S. government scientists:* Blot, "Cancer Mortality."

145 *In 1980, for instance:* Philip Shabecoff, "E.P.A. Sees No Need for New Rules on Oil Wastes," *New York Times,* December 30, 1987; Michael Weisskopf, "EPA Urges Continuation of Exemptions for Oil Wastes; on Hill, Agency Cites Enforcement Problems, Costs," *Washington Post,* December 30, 1987.

145 *In 1991:* National Research Council, Committee on Environmental Epidemiology, *Environmental Epidemiology, vol. 1, Public Health and Hazardous Wastes* (Washington: National Academy Press, 1991), 256.

145 *Calling for action:* Ibid., 270.

145 *The EPA's Science Advisory Board:* EPA, An SAB Report: Review of Disproportionate Impact Methodologies, a Review by the Integrated Human Exposure Committee (IHEC) of the Science Advisory Board (SAB), EPA SAB-IHEC-99-007 (Washington: 1998).

145 *Even so:* http://www.epa.gov/oar/caa/caa112.txt.

145 *In a 1999 congressional investigation:* U.S. Congress, House, Minority Staff, Special Investigations Division, Committee on Government Reform, "Oil Refineries Fail to Report Millions of Pounds of Harmful Emissions" (prepared for Representative Henry A. Waxman, November 10, 1999).

145 *In 2001:* United States General Accounting Office, "Air Pollution: EPA Should Improve Oversight of Emissions Reporting by Large Facilities" (GAO-01-46, April 2001).

145 *Not surprisingly:* United States Environmental Protection Agency, Office of Inspector General, "EPA's Method for Calculating Air Toxics Emissions for Reporting Results Needs Improvement" (Report No. 2004-P-00012, March 31, 2004). See also Environmental Integrity Project and the Galveston-Houston Association for Smog Prevention, "Who's Counting? The Systematic Underreporting of Toxic Air Emissions," July 2004.

146 *The National Emissions Standards for Hazardous Air Pollutants:* Interview John Brock, EPA Region 9, February 2004.

146 *As director of health and safety:* Interview Bill Piazza, June 4 and July 1, 2003.

147 *"I couldn't stop crying":* Interview Jody Kleinman, April 2003.

148 *The first published medical reports:* Peter F. Infante, "Benzene: An Historical Perspective on the American and European Occupational Setting," in European Environment Agency, ed., *Late Lessons from Early Warnings: The Precautionary Principle 1896–2000* (Luxembourg: Office for Official Publications of the European Communities, 2001), 38–51.

149 *In 1922:* Alice Hamilton, "The Growing Menace of Benzene Poisoning in American Industry," *Journal of the American Medical Association* 78, no. 9 (March 4, 1922): 627.

149 *Today, benzene:* Andrea Hriko, "Rings of Controversy." See also National Library of Medicine, "Toxic Chemicals and Environmental Health Risks Where You Live and Work, Chemical: Benzene," http://toxtown.nlm.nih.gov/text_version/chemical.php?name=benzene and Agency for Toxic Substances and Disease Registry ToxFAQs for benzene, http://www.atsdr.cdc.gov/tfacts3.html.

149 *In 1948:* American Petroleum Institute, Department of Safety, API Toxicological Review on Benzene, September 1948 (prepared at the Harvard School of Public Health under the direction of Professor Philip Drinker; review prepared by Marshall Clinton, M.D.).

150 *Though benzene is known:* William J. Nicholson and Philip J. Landrigan, "Quantitative Assessement of Lives Lost Due to Delay in the Regulation of Occupational Exposure to Benzene," *Environmental Health Perspectives* 82 (1989): 185–88.

150 *That standard was challenged:* Ilise L. Feitshans, "Law and Regulation of Benzene," *Environmental Health Perspectives* 82 (1989): 299–307. See also *Industrial Union Department, AFL-CIO v. American Petroleum Institute et al,* no. 78-911, 448 U.S. 607, 608 (1980); slip opinion at p. 1.

150 *The day after:* Joanne Omang, "Scope of Benzene Ruling Viewed as Limited," *Washington Post,* July 3, 1980.

151 *According to Dr. Philip Landrigan:* Nicholson and Landrigan, "Quantitative Assessment."

151 *Dr. Peter Infante:* Interview Peter Infante, December 2003.

151 *As director:* Interview Myron Mehlman, November 2004. See also *Mehlman v. Mobil Oil Corp.,* 707 A2d 1000, 1002–3 (N.J. 1998).

152 *Still, he called:* Tony Cantu, "Whistleblower Says Win over Mobil Is Global Warning," *Princeton Packet,* March 31, 1998.

152 *In his den:* http://www.collegiumramazzini.org/.

152 *The American Public Health:* "American Public Health Association Adopts 19 New Policies," January 19, 2006, from News Release for APHA Web site, www.apha.org/news/press/2006/19 policies.htm.

152 *"Just listen very carefully:"* Interview Myron Mehlman, November 2004.

153 *One stunning example:* Elizabeth Delzell, Nalini Sathiakumar, Philip Cole, and Ilene Brill, "A Case-Control Study of Leukemia, Non-Hodgkin's Lymphoma,

and Multiple Myeloma Among Employees of Union Oil Company of California Submitted to Union Oil Company of California," September 8, 1992, cited at www.epa.gov/opptintr/tsca8e/pubs/8esub/2005/8e1003_101405.htm.

153 *Delzell's positive findings:* D. Pyatt, "Benzene and Hematopoietic Malignancies," *Clinical Occupational Environmental Medicine* 4, no. 3: 529–55; S. H. Lamm, et al., "Non-Hodgkin Lymphoma and Benzene Exposure: A Systematic Literature Review," *Chemico-Biological Interactions* 153–154 (2005): 231–37; D. E. Bergsagel et al., "Benzene and Multiple Myeloma: Appraisal of the Scientific Evidence," *Blood* 94, no. 4 (1999): 1174–82; S. Bezabeh et al., "Does Benzene Cause Multiple Myeloma? An Analysis of the Published Case-Control Literature," *Environmental Health Perspectives* 104, supp. 6 (1996): 1393–98. See also letter from Raphael Metzger, "Re: Failure of American Petroleum Industry to Submit to EPA"; "Delzell et al., "Case-Control Study," http://www.epa.gov/opptintr/tsca8e/pubs/8enq/2005/october05/behq-0905-16223a.pdf.

153 *In testimony:* Allen P. Soape, Sr. v. Atlantic Richfield Company et al., no. D-157, in the District Court, Jefferson County, Texas, 136th Judicial District, videotaped deposition of Elizabeth Delzell, November 19, 1998, 420 North 20th Street, Suite 1600, Birmingham, Alabama.

153 *"This is a case":* Interview Raphael Metzger, February 2006.

153 *I spoke to a Toxic Substances:* Interview Terry O'Bryan, February 2006.

153 *"The amazing thing":* Interview Raphael Metzger, October 2006.

153 *Days after:* Interview Jody Kleinman, June 2003.

154 *Instead, the city council had voted:* Interview Tom Levyn, June 2003.

154 *Data from the Masry law firm:* Masry & Vititoe's Air Sample, "Komex H2O Science Findings," Beverly Hills High School press kit.

156 *In the weeks that followed: City of Beverly Hills vs. Masry & Vititoe, et al.,* case no. 55011900, Los Angeles Superior Court, Department L, July 17, 2003.

156 *The local newspaper:* Norma Zager, "Masry's Attorney Admits in Court NO Study Done by Them to Establish Cancer Rates at Beverly Hills High School," *Beverly Hills Courier,* July 17, 2003.

156 *Among his findings:* Interview Dr. Richard Clapp, January 2004.

157 *If anyone in town:* Interview Judy Okun, October 2003. See also George W. Pring and Penelope Canan, *SLAPPS: Getting Sued for Speaking Out* (Philadelphia: Temple University Press, 1996), discussion under "Maple Properties: Not Seeing the Forest for the Trees," p. 37. See also Thomas A. Waldman, "SLAPP Suits, Weaknesses in First Amendment Law and in the Court's Responses to Frivolous Litigation," *UCLA Law Review,* 39, 1016–18 (1992): "Okun is a SLAPP defendant's worst-case scenario because the suit took . . . years to resolve. . . . The extended time frame and cost of the litigation penalized the defendants for petitioning the government." In a SLAPP suit, the person who is accused of illegal activities turns the table on the accuser. The lawsuits are usually filed to retaliate or silence critics.

159 *Piazza also issued:* Air Quality Dynamics report, "Re: Ambient Air Report—
     Beverly Hills High School," June 28, 2003.

159 *Perhaps most telling:* CDM, "Methane Assessment Report, ABC Entertain-
     ment Center, 202 Avenue of the Stars," October 3, 2001. lacity.org/pln/eir/zk_
     Ave_of_Stars/appendices/index.htm.

159 *As it happened:* Interview Jody Kleinman, July 2003.

161 *A growing body of scientific evidence:* http://www.aqmd.gov/ej/docs/SchoolAd-
     visory.doc; http://www.oehha.ca.gov/public_info/facts/pdf/Factsheetparent.pdf
     and http://www.oehha.ca.gov/public_info/facts/pdf/Factsheetschools.pdf.

161 *She learned that were she:* Toxic Air Pollution Higher Inside Vehicles: Fact
     Sheet, http://www.aqmd.gov/news1/1999/in_car_facts.htm.

162 *But here, at this small theater:* Interviews Jody Kleinman and Susan Messen-
     ger, September 2003.

162 *She was aware:* L. Bernstein, et al., "High Breast Cancer Incidence Rates
     Among California Teachers: Results from the California Teachers Study
     (United States)," *Cancer Causes Control* 13, no. 7 (September 2002): 625–35,
     http://www.calteachersstudy.org/publications.html.

CHAPTER EIGHT: *VELL MOALTALLI*

Page

163 *Beverly Hills, birthplace:* Interview Leah Sawyer, February 2006. Todd S. Pur-
     dum, "Beverly Hills Journal; Once Again, Tinseltown Brings Down the House,"
     New York Times, July 31, 1998.

163 *In the weeks:* BHUSD letter from Gwen E. Gross and Jeffrey C. Hubbard to par-
     ents, August 2003, "Environmental Investigation Questions and Answers."

163 *His report was not:* http://www.cato.org/pubs/regulation/about.html; Center
     for Media and Democracy, Source Watch, "Cato Institute," http://www.source-
     watch.org/index.php?title=Cato_Institute, March 20, 2006. See also People
     for the American Way Web site, "Right Wing Watch," http://www.pfaw.org/
     pfaw/general/default.aspx?oid=9261.

164 *Mahshid Soleimani:* Interview Mahshid Soleimani, July 2003.

164 *"For God's sake":* Ibid.; interview Nelli Emrani, July 2003.

167 *California may once have:* "How California Ranks: The State's Expenditures
     for K-12 Education," *EdSource,* August 2003, http://www.edsource.org/pdf/
     RankingsFinal03.pdf, retrieved March 17, 2006. See also Rand News Release,
     "Rand Report Shows California Schools Lag Behind Other States on Almost
     Every Objective Measurement," January 3, 2005.

168 *"We have nothing":* Interview Mahshid Soleimani, July 2003.

168 *"They think I'm the provocateur":* Interviews Jody Kleinman, Mahshid Solei-
     mani, Nelli Emrani, Janet Morris, July 2003.

169 *When she called:* Interview Mahshid Soleimani, July 2003.

170 *They researched state law:* California Code of Regulations, Section 14010 (h), http://www.cde.ca.gov/ls/fa/sf/schoolsiteguide.asp.

170 *They studied the city's municipal code:* Beverly Hills Municipal Code, 10-5-306, "Drilling Within the City Limits" (Ord. 79-O-720, eff. 2-15-1979).

170 *"People in Beverly Hills":* Interview Nelli Emrani, July 2003.

171 *After several weeks:* Interview Jody Kleinman, August 2003.

171 *Much as he wanted:* Interview Dan Wright, August 2003.

171 *He told her:* California Health and Safety Code, Section 42400.7.

172 *What Dan Wright didn't yet know: Moss v. Venoco.*

172 *That summer, hundreds:* Interview Sam Atwood, August 2003. Petition to South Coast Air Quality Management District, Re: Application No. 415342. Letters to Pang Mueller and Barry Wallerstein from Debbie Rashti, August 18, 2003, Jody Kleinman August 22, 2003, Mahshid Soleimani, August 19, 2003; Venoco Public Notice Telephone Record from John Yee, 8-13-03–8-15-03.

172 *Indeed, after intensive lobbying:* Notice of Exemption from Barry Wallerstein, South Coast Air Quality Management District to County of Los Angeles, "Proposed Venoco Amine Gas Treating Unit Project," October 21, 2003, http://www.aqmd.gov/permit/Formspdf/Basic/AQMDForm400-CEQA.pdf; Letter to Jody Kleinman from Mohsen Nazemi, AQMD Engineering and Compliance Division, October 17, 2003.

173 *"This facility has generated":* SCAQMD, Engineering and Compliance Application Processing and Calculations, Appl. No. 415342, 5/15/03 (revised 6/13/03), H. Stoddard, CEQA.

173 *Even though his inspectors:* AQMD Notice of Violation issued to Venoco, Inc. No. P40557, Office of Stationary Source Compliance, Jeannette Holtzman, June 24, 2003.

173 *When Venoco's lawyer:* Letter from Gisele Goetz, General Counsel, Venoco, to Peter Mieras, SCAQMD legal enforcement office, September 16, 2003.

173 *The AQMD denied:* AQMD Response to Comment Letter No. 1, Letter to Jody Kleinman from Mohsen Nazemi, Engineering and Compliance, October 17, 2003.

174 *He later admitted:* Martha Groves, "Panelist's $500,000 'Finder's Fee' Raises Questions in Beverly Hills," *Los Angeles Times,* November 27, 2004.

176 *Beverly Hills, in fact:* Julie Gruenbaum Fax, "Hancock Park Shul War Back in Court," *Jewish Journal of Greater Los Angeles,* August 22, 2003, http://www.jewishjournal.com/home/preview.php?id=10929, retrieved March 20, 2006.

180 *In a move:* Josh Gross, editorial: "Cronyism Is Alive and Well in Beverly Hills," *Beverly Hills Weekly,* October 21–27, 2004.

181 *Just when it seemed:* Sam Atwood, SCAQMD New Release, "Venoco to Monitor Air Quality at Beverly Hills High School," October 17, 2003.

181 *In an October 17, 2003,* letter: Letter to John McCarthy, Venoco, from Mohsen Nazemi, assistant deputy executive officer, engineering and compliance, re:

"Venoco Inc. Beverly Hills Facility, ID No. 106009 Amine Gas Treating Unit, Application No. 415342."

181 *According to Venoco's own documents:* Venoco, Inc. Beverly Hills Facility, SCAQMD Permit A/N 415342, "Vent Gas Monitoring Plan," October 17, 2003, p. 3.

181 *According to inspection reports:* South Coast Air Quality Management District Permit to Operate, M22109, Southern California Gas Company, "The Gases displaced during all phase of transfer of odorant or depressuring of this facility must be vented through an activated charcoal filter," May 6, 1982, on file with city of Beverly Hills.

181 *With expansion of drilling:* Response to Freedom of Information Act Request of City of Beverly Hills: "Contaminated Water Report" to City Engineer Gene Littig (and later George DeChellis) from Wainoco Oil & Gas Company: 843 barrels in September 1987; 363 barrels in August 1987; 732 barrels in July 1987; 2,946 barrels in May 1987; 936 barrels in April 1987; 280 barrels in March 1987; 849 barrels in February 1987; 1329 barrels in January 1987; 1206 barrels in December 1986 (and delivery of a new gas-handling system for hydrogen sulfide removal from sales gas); 360 barrels in November 1986; 483 barrels in October 1986; 243 barrels in September 1986; 978 barrels in August 1986; 723 barrels hauled off-site for disposal in July 1986; "Problems continued to plague the gas-handling system during June 1986"; 840 barrels April 1986; 1680 barrels in March 1986 after an "acid stimulation job" was performed on a well; 5043 barrels in February 1986. Also, construction of two roof extensions "to improve the aesthetics of the drillsite with regard to the overhead view from Century Park East Condominiums. This is one of the conditions imposed by the Beverly Hills City Council for the granting of a negative declaration of environmental impact with a resumption of drilling at the site." For January 1986, 3363 barrels of water hauled for off-site disposal; 2643 barrels in December 1985, when plans to replace a gas scrubber were made due to "frequent breakdowns over the past year due to contamination of the compressor oil." In November 1985, 4560 barrels of water hauled for off-site disposal.

181 *In a confidential memo:* Division of Oil and Gas "Notice of Intention to Drill New Well," ("Request well be classified as 'confidential'), Beverly Hills Oil Associates, 1-15-82, Re: "O.S." 8.

181 *On August 5, 1986:* from City of Beverly Hills, Public Records Act request: Division of Oil and Gas letter from Kenneth M. Carlson to Wainoco Oil Company, August 5, 1986.

181 *On September 19, 1986:* (from City of Beverly Hills, Public Records Act request): Division of Oil and Gas letter from Kenneth M. Carlson, lead environmental engineer, to Benjamin Gillette, Wainoco Oil & Gas Company, September 29, 1986.

182 *On October 17, 1986:* Kenneth M. Carlson, lead environmental engineer, Department of Conservation Division of Oil and Gas, October 28, 1986 letter to Benjamin Gillette, Wainoco Oil and Gas Co., "Re: Safety inspection made on October 17, 1986."

182 *Four months later:* Kenneth M. Carlson, lead environmental engineer, Department of Conservation Division of Oil and Gas, letter to Benjamin Gillette, Wainoco Oil and Gas Co., "Re: Safety System and Environmental Inspections," February 9, 1987.

182 *Carlson reported again:* Kenneth Carlson, lead environmental engineer, Department of Conservation Division of Oil and Gas, letter to Benjamin Gillette, Wainoco, November 9, 1987.

182 *Despite efforts to complete:* Ibid.

182 *Two months later:* Kenneth Carlson letter to Wainoco, January 22, 1988, follow-up by John Jepson.

182 *In July 1991:* California Department of Conservation Division of Oil and Gas Letter to Benjamin Gillette, Wainoco Oil and Gas Co. from John D. Jepson, environmental engineer, and Michael J. Kratovil, environmental supervisor, "Re: Safety System and Environmental Inspection," July 19, 1991.

182 *"It means it didn't work":* Interview Melvin Wells, April 2003.

183 *She looked up acetone:* ATSDR Fact Sheet DHHS/Agency for Toxic Substances and Disease Registry, Division of Toxicology, Centers for Disease Control and Prevention, September 1, 1995: http://wonder.cdc.gov/wonder/prevguid/p0000467/p0000467.asp.

183 *Soleimani also found:* I. Johansson and M. Ingelman-Sundberg, "Benzene Metabolism by Ethanol-, Acetone-, and Benzene-Inducible Chyocrome P-450 (IIE1) in Rat and Rabbit Liver Microsomes," *Cancer Research* 48, no. 19 (October 1, 1988): 5387–90.

183 *In its tests:* SCAQMD Draft report, Beverly Hills High School, PM—well "at vent pipe," February 11, 2003.

183 *But in its final report:* SCAQMD Analyses Results, Table 5, "Samples Collected on February 6, 2003, Well Vent—Undiluted Natural Gas," Can #54089, 54157.

183 *Even though the agency's:* SCAQMD Lab Report, #03098-01, Laboratory Analysis, 3.2 ppm acetone; 3.5 ppm benzene; April 25, 2003, Rudy Eden, senior manager. Summary of AQMD activities at Venoco in 2003, #19 Research re: MEK, acetone in air samples; collected MSDS sheets, May 28, 2003.

183 *In fact, when he met:* Interview Mahshid Soleimani, December 2003.

184 *At issue was the agency's:* http://www.aqmd.gov/hb/2004/0401min.html.

184 *A month earlier:* SCAQMD public comment hearing re: Rule 1148.1, December 4, 2003, letter from Ivan Tether, California Independent Petroleum Association, environmental chair, to Kennard Ellis, SCAQMD air quality engineer, "Re: Proposed Rule 1148.1—Oil and Gas Production Wells," October 8, 2003.

185 *An AQMD engineer:* Larry Bowen, planning and rules manager, at http://www. aqmd.gov/hb/2004/0401min.html.

185 *how could the AQMD:* SCAQMD Engineering and Compliance Division, Violation Notice Report, Venoco Inc., wastewater treatment system, attachment to P38793, May 8, 2003.

186 *Records Kleinman had received:* "Southern California Gas Company Measurement Collection System Gas Volume Detail Report from 2-1-2003 to 2-28-2003," Venoco Inc. CONFIDENTIAL—TRADE SECRET, produced pursuant to Government Code 6254.7(d).

187 *Even though Venoco's settlement agreement:* SCAQMD News Release, "Venoco to Monitor Air Quality at Beverly Hills High School," October 17, 2003, p. 2.

187 *In a January 21, 2004, e-mail:* Jeannette Holtzman e-mail to Roger Chistopher, Wednesday January 21, 2004, 10:12 a.m., "re: well workovers."

187 *In fact, during the administration:* Michael Janofsky, "Judges Overturn Bush Bid to Ease Pollution Rules," *New York Times,* March 18, 2006.

187 *In March 2006: State of New York et al. v. EPA,* No. 03-1380. U.S. District Court of Appeals for the District of Columbia, March 17, 2006. www.cadc. uscourts.gov/docs/common/opinions/200603/03-1380a.pdf.

188 *In a remarkable:* AQMD Jeannette Holtzman handwritten notes, January 21, 2004, from California Public Records Act request.

CHAPTER NINE: CHERNOBYL, 90212

Page

189 *A short, affable:* Interview Lee Bova, April 2003.

190 *Of course, she was curious:* "PCB, Furan Exposure Increases Risk of Non-Hodgkin's Lymphoma," Reuters Health Information, December 14, 2005, www.medscape.com/viewarticle/519773. See also: N. Rothman, K. P. Cantor, A. Blair, D. Bush, J. W. Brock, K. Helzlsouer, S. H. Zahm, L. L. Needham, G. R. Pearson, R. N. Hoover, G. W. Comstock, and P. T. Strickland, "A Nested Case-Control Study of Non-Hodgkin Lymphoma and Serum Organochlorine Residues," *Lancet* 350 (July 26, 1997): 240–44.

191 *"You could see the smokestacks":* Interview Tiffany Smith, May 2003.

191 *In 1997, nine teenage:* Interview Lisa Lewis, January 2004; interview David Aftergood, July 2003.

191 *One oncologist:* Interview Barry Rosenblum, December 2003.

192 *Waks believed:* Interview Abraham Waks, April 2004.

193 *But the main danger:* U.S. Department of Labor Occupational Safety and Health Administration, OSHA Hazard Information Bulletins, January 26, 1989, Memorandum for Regional Administrators from Edward Baier, directorate of technical support, "Potential Health Hazards Associated with

Handling Pipe Used in Oil and Gas Production," http://osha.gov/dts/hib/hib_
data/hib19890126.html.

193 *In New Orleans:* "Supreme Court Rejects ExxonMobil in Norm Case," Associated
Press, May 15, 2006.

194 *At some oil-field sites:* "Naturally Occurring Radioactive Materials (NORM) in
Produced Water and Oil-Field Equipment—An Issue for the Energy Indus-
try," U.S. Department of the Interior U.S. Geological Survey Fact Sheet
FS-142-99, September 1999.

195 *Medical studies about Chernobyl:* V. K. Ivanov et al., "Dynamics of Thyroid
Cancer Incidence in Russia Following the Chernobyl Accident," *Journal of
Radiological Protection* (1999): 305–18; Furio Pacini et al., "Post-Chernobyl
Thyroid Carcinoma in Belarus Children and Adolescents: Comparison with
Naturally Occurring Thyroid Carcinoma in Italy and France," *Journal of Clini-
cal Endocrinology & Metabolism* 82, no. 11, (1997): 3563–69. T. Parfitt, "Cher-
nobyl's Legacy," *Lancet* 363, no. 9420 (May 8, 2004): 1534 Y. Shibata et al.,
"Fifteen Years After Chernobyl: New Evidence of Thyroid Cancer," *Lancet*
358 (2001): 1965–66.

195 *Referencing a 1999 study:* P. Jacob et al., "Childhood Exposure Due to the
Chernobyl Accident and Thyroid Cancer Risk in Contaminated Areas of
Belarus and Russia," *British Journal of Cancer* 80 (1999): 1461–69; M. Santoro,
et al., "Gene Rearrangement and Chernobyl Related Thyroid Cancers," *British
Journal of Cancer* 82 (2000): 315–22.

196 *One evening, she reminded:* City of Beverly Hills Water Quality Report, 2002.

196 *On another evening:* Paul R. Epstein and Jesse Selber, "Oil: A Life Cycle Analysis of Its Health and Environmental Impacts," Center for Health and the
Global Environment, Harvard Medical School, Boston, March 2002.

196 *According to documents:* Fax correspondence from Christopher P. Bisgaard,
Lewis Brisbois Bisgaard & Smith LLP, to Stephen J. O'Neil, Sheppard, Mullin,
Richter & Hampton LLP, October 21, 2003, "Re: Confirmation of Venoco,
Inc.'s Use of I-131 at BHHS," obtained through a California Freedom of Infor-
mation Act Request, Beverly Hills Unifed School District, April 2004.

196 *Not long after:* Christine Pelisek, "Radioactive High: Beverly Hills High Family
Alleges Radiation Risk from Oil Wells," *L.A. Weekly,* July 4–10, 2003, http://
www.laweekly.com/ink/printme.php?eid=45313, retrieved February 11, 2005.

197 *The investigation concluded:* Los Angeles County Department of Health Services Environmental Health memo, October 28, 2003, "Beverly Hills High
School," and "Beverly Hills High School—Supplemental Report on Radiological Surveys," prepared by California Department of Health Services, Radiologic Health Branch, December 2003.

197 *The mapping survey:* California Department of Health Services, Radiologic
Health Branch, "Report of Radiological Survey of Beverly Hills High School
and Venoco Oil Well Site," October 2003, p. 1.

197 *Mysteriously, five of twelve:* "Beverly Hills High School—Supplemental Report on Radiological Surveys," December 2003, California Department of Health Services, Radiologic Health Branch, p. 7.

197 *While state oil and gas officials:* Interview Michael Edwards, April 2003. See also Division of Oil, Gas, and Geothermal Resources, "Class II Injection Wells," Frequently Asked Questions, Web site at http://www.consrv.ca.gov/DOG/general_information/class_injection_wells.htm.

197 *Initially, the state Health Department report:* "Report of Radiological Survey of Beverly Hills High School and Venoco Oil Well Site," prepared by California Department of Health Services, Radiologic Health Branch, October 2003, p. 2.

197 *But the words:* "Report of Radiologial Survey of Beverly Hills High School and Venoco Oil Well Site," prepared by California Department of Health Services, Radiologic Health Branch, November 2003, retrieved from BHUSD Web site in December 2003, http://www.beverlyhills.k12.ca.us/environment/?rn=8111.

197 *Even so, health officials insisted:* Interview Kathleen Kaufman, July 2003.

198 *The U.S. Committee on the Biological Effects of Ionizing Radiation:* National Academy of Sciences press release, "Low Levels of Ionizing Radiation May Cause Harm," June 29, 2005, http://www4.nationalacademies.org/news.nsf/isbn/030909156X?OpenDocument. Full report available from Committee to Assess Health Risks from Exposure to Low Levels of Ionizing Radiation, National Research Council, *Health Risks from Exposure to Low Levels of Ionizing Radiation: BEIR VII Phase 2* (Washington, D.C.: National Academies Press, 2006).

198 *"We follow Nuclear Regulatory Commission guidelines":* Interview Robert Miller, July 2003.

198 *Not only had she never inspected:* Interview Kathleen Kaufman, July 2003.

199 *As for parents' outrage:* 10 Code of Federal Regulations 20.1905, "Exemptions to Labeling Requirements," posted at http://www.nrc.gov.edgesuite.net/reading-rm/doc-collections/cfr/part020/part020-1905.html. See also http://www.epa.gov/radiation/understand/health_effects.htm, http://www.epa.gov/radiation/understand/protection_basics.htm.

199 *Both times, the stated reason:* Letter from Ken August, deputy director, Office of Public Affairs, California Department of Health Services, to Joy Horowitz, "Re: Public Records Act Request," June 19, 2003; letter from Ken August, deputy director, Office of Public Affairs, California Department of Health Services, to Joy Horowitz, "Re: Public Records Act Request," August 6, 2003.

199 *More specifically:* Letter from Michael B. Lumbard, senior counsel, California Department of Health Services, to Howard Gest, Burhenn & Gest LLP, "Re: Public Records Act Request: Joy Horowitz—Documents Referring or Relating to Beverly Hills High School Oil Wells," December 30, 2003.

199 *Or that the records had been destroyed:* Interview Mitch Findlay, August 2003; FIRST Energy Services Inc. Radiation Safety Manual, revised July 2000.

See also http://www.dhs.ca.gov/rhb/PDF/Licensing%20Checklist%20for%20
Portable%20Nuclear_%20Moisture%20Density%20Gauge.pdf.

199 *"We were way ahead":* Interview Floyd Leeson, March 2005.

200 *In an e-mail:* Department of Health Services for Los Angeles County, Kathleen
Kaufman e-mail, Friday April 2, 2004 11:57 a.m. to csalgado, doesterl, RGreger,
SFoerfle,V Anderso, Cyrus Rangan, Richard Wagener, "Subject: BHHS."

201 *"the crazies have the company":* Interview Floyd Leeson, March 2005.

202 *They spotted a blue van:* Interviews Jody Kleinman and Marrina Waks,
April 2004.

202 *Kleinman asked why the trucks:* Ibid.

203 *"There was not supposed to be":* Interview Abraham Waks, April 2004.

203 *"We were expecting":* Interview Kathleen Kaufman, April 2004.

203 *"The explanation by Kaufman":* Interview Daniel Hirsch, Committee to Bridge
the Gap, July 2004.

204 *"No radiation above background":* "April 5, 2004 Visit to BHHS Venoco Site,"
p. 2.

204 *"Based on information today":* Interview Kathleen Kaufman, April 2004.

204 *One, on the southwest:* Kathleen Kaufman and Steve Doerfler, "Venoco Air
Sampling: April 5, 2004 Visit to the BHHS and the Venoco Site, Los Angeles
County Radiation Management," p. 2.

205 *At 11:47:* E-mail from Robert Greger to Kathleen Kaufman, "Subject: FW:
Venoco Air sampler results."

205 *On Monday, May 10:* E-mail from Kathleen Kaufman to Robert Greger,
Monday, May 10, 2004, 4:04 p.m., "Re: Venoco Air sampler results."

CHAPTER TEN: BUTT-ASS WRONG

Page

207 *On most winter mornings:* Interview Phil Berman, June 2005.

208 *The incidence for the disease:* National Cancer Institute fact sheet, http://
www.cancer.gov/cancertopics/factsheet/Sites-Types/testicular.

208 *Scientists have postulated:* "Declining Semen Quality and Increasing
Incidence of Testicular Cancer: Is There a Common Cause?" et al., E. Carlsen,
Environmental Health Perspectives 7, suppl. (Oct. 1995): 137–39.

209 *Thousands of e-mails:* Interview Erin Brockovich-Ellis, February 2004.

209 *There was, for example:* Howard Kurtz, "Monsanto's Man," *Washington Post,* January 16, 2006, http://www.washingtonpost.com/wp-dyn/content/article/2006/01/
15/AR20006011501113_pf.html.

209 *Fumento:* http://www.frontpagemag.com/Articles/ReadArticle/asp?ID=19663
http://sixtyminutes.ninemasn.com.au/sixtyminutes/stories/2005_04_10/
story_1347.asp; Michael Fumento, "Brockovich's Beverly Hills Blues," Scripps
Howard News Service, April 22, 2004, http://www.fumento.com/pollution/

brockoamspec.html; Michael Fumento, "Erin Crockovich Is Back," December 14, 2004.

209 *And soon there would be:* Civil Justice Association of California, press release, John H. Sullivan, "California Reporter, Not Erin Brockovich, Should Receive Harvard Health Award," October 17, 2005.

210 *Her one-woman crusade:* Eric Umansky, "Muckraker 90210: A Most Unlikely Reporter Nails Erin Brockovich," *Columbia Journalism Review,* March–April 2004; Eric Umansky, "Erin Brockovich's Weird Science," *New Republic,* November 24, 2003.

211 *It exposed:* Transcript of "Possible Interference in the Scientific Review of Chromium VI Toxicity," informational hearing of the California Senate Health and Human Services Committee, 2003. Chaired by Senator Deborah Ortiz, April 2, 2003, state capitol, Sacramento, California; interview Gary Praglin, September 2003; Andrew Bridges, "Allegations of Corporate Meddling Dog Calif. Report on Chromium 6," Associated Press, February 28, 2003. See also "Chrome-Plated Fraud: How PG&E's Scientists-for-Hire Reversed Findings of Cancer Study," Environmental Working Group report, at http://ewg.org/reports/chromium/printerfrinedly.php. Peter Waldman, "Study Tied Pollutant to Cancer; Then Consultants Got Hold of It," *Wall Street Journal,* December 23, 2005.

211 *But her bill:* Harrison Shephard, "State May Launch Biomonitoring," *Los Angeles Daily News,* March 30, 2006, www.dailynews.com/news/ci_3652606.

212 *Not only was it impossible:* www.dtsc.ca.gov/schools/index.cfm; California Health and Safety Code Section 424007.

213 *"The AQMD is a shill":* Moss v. Venoco, Declaration of Linda Mills, public records coordinator for South Coast Air Quality Management District Pursuant to Evidence Code Section 1561(a), Exhibit A: Privilege Log; "Southern California Gas Company Measurement Collections Systems Gas Volume Detail Report from 3-1-2003 to 3-31-2003," Confidential Trade Secret; "Attachments to letter from Gisele Goetz at Venoco Inc to Pang Mueller re: Daily Oil and Gas production information per your request," Confidential Trade Secret; "Southern California Gas Company Measurement Collections System Gas Volume Detail Report—2002 Production," Confidential Trade Secret; "Southern California Gas Company Measurement Collections System Gas Volume Detail Report—(redacted)," Confidential Trade Secret.

213 *What especially galled her:* Privilege Log ibid, page 7: AQMD 2001–2002 Air Emissions Report, Confidential Trade Secret, 9/5/2002; AQMD 2001–2002 Air Emissions Report, Confidential Trade Secret, 8/19/02; AQMD 2001–2002 Air Emissions Report, Confidential Trade Secret 8/20/02; AQMD 2000–2001 Air Emissions Report, Confidential Trade Secret 8/15/01; AQMD 2000–2001 Air Emissions Report, Confidential Trade Secret 1/23/01; AQMD 2000–2001 Air Emissions Report, Confidential Trade Secret, 11/21/01; 1999–2000 Annual

Emissions Report, Confidential Trade Secret, 8/28/00; AQMD 2000–2001 Air Emissions Report, Confidential Trade Secret, 9/8/00.

216 *In the preceding days:* Interview Roger Dunstan, March 2003.

216 *The city had doled out:* "Lobbyists for the City of Beverly Hills—GCG Rose & Kindel," City of Beverly Hills Web site; http://www.beverlyhills.org/presence/connect/CoBH/Homepage/Local+Government/City+Officials/City+Manager/LG-CI_Lobbyists; "Rose & Kindel Issue Management and Support Generation," Rose & Kindel Web site; http://www.rosekindel.com/issuues.shtml.

217 *Ortiz gaveled:* http://www.senate.ca.gov/ftp/sen/committee/standing/health/_home/health_risks_schools_transcript.doc.

217 *California passed the Children's:* Transcript of the Joint Informational Hearing of the Senate Committees on Health and Human Services, Senator Deborah Ortiz, chair, and Environmental Quality, Senator Byron Sher, chair, "State and Local Governments' Role in Preventing and Mitigating Environmental Health Risks in California Schools," March 12, 2004, http://www.senate.ca.gov/ftp/SEN/COMMITTEE/STANDING/HEALTH/_home/HEALTH_RISKS_SCHOOLS_TRANSCRIPT.DOC.

224 *Normal levels for toluene:* http://www.arb.ca.gov/adam/toxics/sitepages/tolubbnk.html.

224 *CDM, the city's testing firm:* http://bhusd.com/environmental/enviro_reports/4th_round_AA_Summary_Report.pdf; http://www.dhs.ca.gov/ohb/HESIS/toluene.htm.

225 *Under amendments to the law:* Interview Jack Broadbent, October 2003. See also www.epa.gov/oar.oaqps/permits/requirem.html.

225 *In the months following:* E-mail from AQMD media liaison Tiny Cherry to Joy Horowitz; "Notice of Proposed Title V Permits," Distribution Date: July 15, 2004.

225 *That is undoubtedly because:* Sempra emissions data at http://www.arb.ca.gov/app/emsinv/facinfo/faccrit.php?dd=&grp=1&sort=FacilityNameA&dbyr=2004&ab_=&dis_=SC&co_=19&fname_=Sempra+&city_=&fzip_=&fsic_=&facid_=011034&_all_fac=C&displayit=Pollutant&showpol=50000&showpol2.

227 *Brockovich's testimony dominated:* "Committees Discuss Oil Well on Beverly Hills High School Campus," City News Service, March 15, 2004; http://abclocal.go.com/kabc/news/print_031304_nw_school_oil_well.html.

228 *Several months earlier:* Letter from Edward Masry, Erin Brockovich, Allen M. Stewart, "Re: Beverly Hills High School Litigation; Notice of Improper Attorney Contact; Media Contact," May 16, 2003.

228 *Lori Moss:* Interview Lori Moss, March 2004.

CHAPTER ELEVEN: CASE MANAGEMENT ORDER

Page

233 *It is the only:* Interview Arthur Blech, September 2004.

233 *He'd lain awake:* Interview Al Stewart, January 2004.

234 *"I wouldn't want":* Ibid.

234 *In recent months: Moss v. Venoco,* Amended Notice of Demurrer and Demur-
     rer of Sempra Energy, August 25, 2003; Chevron Texaco's Notice of Demur-
     rer, Demurrer and Joinder to City of Beverly Hills' Demurrer, August 22,
     2003; Notice of Demurrer to First Amended Complaint (Wainoco Oil and Gas
     Company and Frontier Oil Corporation), August 13, 2003; Beverly Hills Uni-
     fied School District's Notice of Demurrer and Demurrer to Plaintiff's First
     Amended Complaint, August 8, 2003; Notice of Demurrer and Demurrer of
     Defendant Venoco, Inc. to First Amended Complaint, August 7, 2003.

234 *Toxic torts are no different:* Interview Raphael Metzger, May 2004. See also V.
     Thomas Meador III et al., "Anti-Toxins: Defense Counsel in Toxic Tort Cases
     Can Frequently Prevail by Challenging Plaintiffs' Proof of Both General and
     Specific Causation," *Los Angeles Lawyer,* July–August 2003, http://www.lacba.
     org/Files/LAL/Vol26No5/1422.pdf.

235 *Contrary to press reports: Moss v. Venoco;* see also related cases: *Yeshoua et al. v.
     Venoco et al.,* no. BC 300164; Ibraham et al. v. City of Beverly Hills et al., no.
     SC078058; *Jacobs et al. v. Wainoco Oil & Gas Co. et al.,* no. SC080117; *Bussel et al.
     v. Venoco Inc,* et al., no. BC 308673; *Steiner et al. v. Venoco et al.,* no. BC 315885;
     Ashley et al. v. City of Beverly Hills et al., no. BC 317676; *Kalcic et al. v. Venoco Inc.
     et al.,* no. BC 331173.

236 *In recent days:* Tom Hamburger and Alan C. Miller, "Mercury Emissions Rule
     Geared to Benefit Industry, Staffers Say; Buffeted by Complaints, EPA Ad-
     ministrator Michael Leavitt Calls for Additional Analysis, *Los Angeles Times,*
     March 16, 2004. See also Juliet Eilperin, "EPA Wording Found to Mirror
     Industry's; Influence on Mercury Proposal Probed," *Washington Post,*
     September 22, 2004.

237 *Mortimer, who had been named:* Chuck Welch, "Profile: Judge Wendell Mor-
     timer, Los Angeles Superior Court," *Los Angeles Daily Journal,* August 9, 1996.

237 *In the 2004 presidential election:* Nathan Vardi, "Demonizing for Dollars," Forbes.
     com, November 15, 2004, at http://forbes-global.com/forbes/2004/1115/17.

237 *The 2003 settlement agreement:* Jose Casuso, "Lawyers Turn to Council to
     Collect Record Fees," *Surf Santa Monica,* April 12, 2005, http://www.surfsanta-
     monica.com/ssm_site/the_lookout/news/News-2005/April-2005/04_12_05_Law-
     yers_Turn_to_Council.htm.

237 *a charge that . . . Fred Baron called "silly":* Ibid.

237 *At issue on this morning: Bockrath v. Aldrich Chemical Co.,* 21 Cal 4th 71 (1999).

238 *Stewart's complaint had listed: Moss v. Venoco.*

238 *"I'm an expert":* Interview Al Stewart, August 2003.

238 *Bravado aside:* "40 Under 40—Most Successful Young Litigators in America,"
     National Law Journal, July 29, 2002; "45 Under 45—Rising Stars of the Private
     Bar," *American Lawyer,* January 20, 2003.

238 *No doubt:* Interview Al Stewart, August 2003.

239 *"You can live":* Ibid.

240 *Despite how obvious:* Interview Eddie Greenwald, January 2004; interview Bruce Greenwald, January 2005.

241 *In the weeks prior:* BC297083 Joint Initial Status Conference Report, October 7, 2003.

242 *But even more important: Moss v. Venoco,* Draft Report of Richard W. Clapp, February 25, 2006; Deposition of Richard W. Clapp, pp. 90–93.

242 *They wanted:* BC297083, January 23, 2004 status conference hearing.

242 *He handed out:* "Preliminary Data on BHHS Litigation Plaintiffs (From all Complaints as of January 21, 2004)," prepared by Latham & Watkins.

242 *Getto had been litigating:* Interview Ernest Getto, January 2004.

243 *Getto had authored:* Ernest J. Getto and Cynthia H. Cwik, "Keep 'Junk" Science Off the Stand," *National Law Journal,* April 19, 1993, p. 15. See also Ernest J. Getto and Cynthia H. Cwik, "Court Sets Principles on Scientific Evidence," *California Law Business,* July 26, 1993; *Daubert v. Merrell Dow Pharmaceuticals,* 509 U.S. 579 (1993).

243 *In 1997, Getto had represented: Stadish v. Southern California Gas Company,* June 16, 1997, Los Angeles Superior Court B100536, nonpublished opinion.

243 *The trial judge: Stadish v. Southern California Gas Company,* California Court of Appeals, Second Appellate District, B147579, June 2, 2002. In an unpublished opinion, the case was affirmed on appeal. The appellate panel noted: "[T]here is no evidence that the amount of benzene in the pipes resulted in an abnormally high amount of benzene in the ambient air sufficient to cause appellant illness."

243 *Getto felt certain:* Interview Ernest Getto, January 2004.

243 *Getto had also negotiated:* Deborah Schoch, "Some Refinery Foes Upset with Settlement; Lawsuit: Plaintiffs Claimed Mobil's Torrance Plant Created Health Hazards. Several Call Their Award Too Small and Say Terms of Pact Should Not Be Secret," *Los Angeles Times,* December 27, 1994.

243 *To prove his point:* "Preliminary Data on BHHS Litigation Plaintiffs," Latham & Watkins fax, January 26, 2004.

245 *"No one ever returned":* Interview Madeline Cantillon Fries, August 2006.

245 *They had worked together:* Interview Ernest Getto, January 2004.

245 *The company reportedly paid:* Jean Guccione, "Lockheed to Settle Final Claims over Toxins," *Los Angeles Times,* April 17, 2002.

245 *Even before:* See also City of Beverly Hills Minutes of August 23, 2003, Item F-22: Adopted RES #03-R-11459 issuing a legislative subpoena to Chevron USA.

246 *In Santa Monica: City of Beverly Hills v. Law Offices of Masry & Vititoe,* Los Angeles Superior Court, Department L, No. SS011900. Reporter's transcript, November 19, 2003.

247   *On February 10, 2004:* Moss v. Venoco, Defendant City of Beverly Hills Motion
for Revocation of Pro Hac Vice Status of Baron & Budd Attorneys.

247   *After Judge Mortimer:* Interview Al Stewart, February 2004.

247   *"What defendants say":* Interview Al Stewart, September 2006.

247   *After collecting $1.1 million:* Beverly Hills City Council Minutes of June 15,
2004, Item G ($650,000 allotted); Minutes of October 7, 2003, Item F-11F;
Minutes of November 5, 2003 ($450,000 "blanket purchase order"); Item F7A
and Minutes of October 19, 2004.

247   *In order to avoid:* Tina Spee, "Former Beverly Hills Mayor Joins Christensen
Miller," *Los Angeles Daily Journal Extra,* Industry Watch, November 8, 2004.

247   *In the spring of 2006:* Andrew Blankstein and Greg Krikorian, "Lawyer In-
dicted in PI Inquiry," *Los Angeles Times,* February 16, 2006; Kim Christensen,
"Top Lawyer to Leave Firm Over Pellicano Case, Sources Say," *Los Angeles
Times,* May 2, 2006.

248   *They dumped nearly everything:* Response by City of Beverly Hills to public
records act request of Joy Horowitz.

248   *"I hope they have fun":* Interview Edward Masry, January 2004.

248   *Those documents:* Response to Freedom of Information Act request by city of
Beverly Hills, November 2004.

248   *It was the frequency:* Letter to Clifford Enger, Beverly Hills Oil Company,
from Beverly Hills Fire Marshall, "Re: Well Installation, Entrance Off Olympic Blvd," November 26, 1963. See also Correction to 1978 EIR by Peter Gardett, oil consultant for city of Beverly Hills, to Environmental Review Board:
"a transformer fire that occurred on the existing drill site in the early 1960s
probably should be reported." Letter to Clifford Enger from K. L. Peters, superintendent of schools, October 31, 1963. California Regional Water Quality
Control Board, Letter from Raymond M. Hertel, executive officer, to Beverly
Hills Oil Company, August 25, 1976. "The prohibition on discharge of oil field
brines to Ballona Creek is effective September 1, 1976. Any discharge after
that date would be in violation of both State and Federal law and would subject you to civil and criminal penalties." See also Interoffice Communication,
city of Beverly Hills, George E. Morgan, city manager, to Robert Bammes, civil
engineer, "Re: Beverly Hills Oil Company Waste Discharge Permit Status."
See also Wainoco Oil and Gas Company, "Contaminated Water Report" to
Beverly Hills City Engineer, November 1985 (162 barrels a day) to November
1988 (13 barrels a day), Beverly Hills Public Works Department 00413; Argo
Petroleum Operating Corporation, "Contaminated Water Report" to Beverly
Hills City Engineer and Peter Gardett, oil consultant; November 1984 (490
barrels a day) to October 1985 (136 barrels a day). Beverly Hills Oil Company,
"Contaminated Water Report," to Beverly Hills City Engineer and Peter Gardett, oil consultant; December 1982 (7,600 barrels, or 245 barrels a day) to October 1985 (533 barrels a day). See John L. Mitchell, "Firm That Pumps Beverly

Hills Oil Seeks Bankruptcy," *Los Angeles Times*, April 19, 1984; and John L. Mitchell, "Takeover of Troubled Oil Firm Sought; 3 Major Banks Want to Keep Beverly Hills Wells in Operation," *Los Angeles Times*, October 18, 1984. See also Los Angeles Fire Department Abstract of Fire Station 92 Journal, 5-9-96, Incident Number 0983, Address 2052 Century Park East. "An explosion involving one of the boilers occurred. Handled LAPD on scene."

248 *In the fall of 1963:* Letter to Clifford Enger, Beverly Hills Oil Company, from Beverly Hills Fire Marshal, "Re: Well Installation, Entrance Off Olympic Blvd.," November 26, 1963. See also Correction to 1978 EIR by Peter Gardett, oil consultant for city of Beverly Hills, to Environmental Review Board: "a transformer fire that occurred on the existing drill site in the early 1960s probably should be reported." Letter to Cliffor Enger from K. L. Peters, Superintendent of Schools, October 31, 1963.

249 *Next door:* Application by Central Plants, November 10, 1964, to Air Pollution Control District: "boilers supply saturated steam of 265 psi to equipment which serves three buildings in the CC development." See also Engineering Field Report by Re Keelogg, Sr, Air Pollution Control District, 1-4-73, "Central Plants, Inc."

249 *With the expansion:* South Coast Air Quality Management District, Equipment Breakdown with Excess Emissions, Central Plants Inc., #4 Boiler, "loss of power to plant due to failure of main breaker," 3-29-94.

249 *But in May 1996:* Title V application for permit, South Coast Air Quality Management District, Central Plants Inc. ID # 011034, 2052 Century Park East, Stanley Zison, director environmental compliance, July 25, 1997.

249 *Firefighters from Station 92:* Los Angeles Fire Department Abstract of Fire Station 92 Journal, 5-9-96, Incident Number 0983, Address 2052 Century Park East. "An explosion involving one of the boilers occurred. Handled LAPD on scene."

249 *Two months later:* South Coast Air Quality Management District, Enforcement Division Report Form, Central Plants Inc., ID #011034, Complaint #95570, Jim Molde, 5-15-96. South Coast Air Quality Management District, NOV P14386, Central Plants Inc., "No CEMS on boiler #3; Exceed NOX allocation," July 1, 1996, Jimedel C. Molde.

249 *In 1997:* South Coast Air Quality Management District, Air Quality Complaint Report, #104234, Inspector John D. Eckert, 5-2-97.

249 *Just two weeks later:* Title V application for permit, Central Plants, 1997.

249 *This time, though:* Petition for a Variance before the Hearing Board of the South Coast Air Quality Management District, Case No. 3447-36, Central Plants Inc., July 31, 1997.

249 *If strict compliance:* Findings and Decision of the Hearing Board, "In the Matter of Central Plants, Inc.," Order Granting a Regular Variance, Case No. 3447-35, in Title V permit application. South Coast Air Quality Management

District, "Toxic Air Contaminants and Ozone Depleters Emission/Fee Summary," #011034 Central Plants Inc.

249 *As for Venoco:* AQMD 1998–1999 Annual Emissions Report, ID 106009, Venoco Inc., Pat Corcoran, 8-27-99. "Non-Permitted Annual Emissions from the Use of Organics": 4.46 tons. Material Description: Emulsion Breaker. Taraway Degreaser.

249 *Defense lawyers could only guess: Moss v. Venoco,* log entry from Venoco foremen, July 2002, Bates #VCO81960.

250 *When he began to formulate:* In re "Agent Orange" Products Liability Litigation," (MDL no. 381), 597F. Sup 740 (1984).

250 *In 1956:* Letter from Universal Consolidated Oil Company to Beverly Hills Board of Education, November 9, 1956. See also 1957 "Gardett report" from consultant Peter Gardett on oil development possibilities: "It is considered most probable that deeper production could be obtained beneath the high school property . . . and that some of the unused wells are currently draining oil from adjacent property in BH. Deep zone exploration and development of substantial development of the Fox Studio properties located adjacent to the city of BH and to the high school grounds has forced consideration by the BH Schools and citizens of means of protecting their property from drainage. No reliable estimate can be made at this time regarding potential income to the city of oil royalties; however under the terms of Richfield-Signal's bid, it is considered highly probable that the city of Beverly Hills could realize several millions of dollars from this source."

250 *After Standard Oil:* City of Beverly Hills Interoffice Communication from George DeChellis, city engineer, to Edward S. Kreins, city manager, "Oil Report," December 5, 1979.

251 *Drilling within Beverly Hills:* City Of Beverly Hills Inter-Office Communication to mayor and members of council from Oil Committee, "Re: "Standard Oil Request for Drill Site in Beverly Hills," May 8, 1974. See also letter from J. E. Brooks, division land manager, Standard Oil Company, to Beverly Hills Oil Committee, April 30, 1973.

251 *The problem, though:* "The History of Chevron—Exploration and Discovery," Chevron Web site. www.chevron.com/products/learning-center/history/topic/explore.

251 *At the behest of King Faisal:* Robert A. Rosenblatt, "Standard Oil of California Asks Stockholder Support for Arabs," *Los Angeles Times,* August 2, 1973.

251 *His letter set off:* "Oil Firm's Letter on Arabs Draws Rebuke from Jews," *Washington Post,* August 4, 1973.

251 *The mayor, Phyllis Seaton:* Letter to Otto M. Miller, chairman of the board, Standard Oil Co. of California, from Phyllis Seaton, mayor of Beverly Hills, August 10, 1973.

251 *Nine months later:* City of Beverly Hills, Inter-Office Communication to mayor and members of council from Oil Committee, "Re: Standard Oil Request for Drill Site in Beverly Hills," May 8, 1974.

251 *However, in an unzoned:* Letter from J. E. Brooks, land manager, Standard Oil Company of California, to Honorable George Slaff and Honorable J Stuchen, Oil Committee, March 18, 1974: minimum case was $26 million. Maximum case (with crude at $9 per barrel) $50.5 million for city and residents. City of Beverly Hills Interoffice communication, from George DeChellis, city engineer, to George E. Morgan, city manager et al, April 21, 1976. "GE Morgan stated that at the previous meeting between Enger and Mayor Ellman and George Slaff, the Oil Company stated that the City would have certain royalty rights." Memo to George Morgan, city manager, from George DeChellis, city engineer, "Re: Beverly Hills Oil Company, Slant Drilling, Beverly Hills High School," May 18, 1976. "The legality of the royalty payment to the City must be established." Atlantis Scientific, addendum to final environmental impact report, Beverly Hills High School Urban Drill Site, May 1978: "The City of Beverly Hills agrees to permit the BHOC to drill under and through and to produce oil and gas from beneath all roadways, alleys, curbs, parks, playgrounds and any and all properties which may be owned by the City of Beverly Hills within the area described in Exhibit 'A.'"

252 *According to public hearings:* City of Beverly Hills "Agreement of February 18, 1975, Between Beverly Hills Oil Company and Standard Oil Company of California."

252 *Based on its lease:* John L. Mitchell, "Firm That Pumps Beverly Hills Oil Seeks Bankruptcy," *Los Angeles Times*, April 19, 1984. John L. Mitchell, "Takeover of Troubled Oil Firm Sought; 3 Major Banks Want to Keep Beverly Hills Wells in Operation," *Los Angeles Times*, October 18, 1984.

252 *The school district:* Memorandum, Planning and Community Development Department, City of Santa Monica Planning Division, "Public Hearing to Consider a Landmark Designation Application," July 12, 2004.

253 *Under the heading:* California Division of the State Architect: Change Order No. 70 from Rowland Crawford, architect, to Montgomery Ross Fisher, Inc., "Re: Beverly Hills High School Additions and Alterations," March 3, 1970.

253 *"In my twenty-five years here":* Interview Jack Bruce, October 2004.

253 *But at the top:* California Division of the State Architect, Beverly Hills High School, 1971.

254 *When I contacted:* Interview (declined) Jeffrey Hubbard, October 2004.

254 *Kenneth Peters:* Interview Kenneth Peters, May 2004.

254 *Strategy was everything:* Interview Al Stewart, August 2003.

254 *In toxic tort cases:* Interview Jody Freeman, July 2003.

255 *He had also filed: Moss v. Venoco;* Privilege log from SCAQMD: Southern California Gas Company Measurement Collections Systems Gas Volume Detail

Report: Confidential—Trade Secret; Daily Oil and Gas production information at Venoco: Confidential—Trade Secret; AQMD Air Emissions
Report, 1999–2002: Confidential—Trade Secret.

255 *They already knew:* South Coast Air Quality Management District, "Sampling
Results by Location (Calculated Risk per million)," Table 14, Benzene at
Venoco: 117.1 per million risk (per parts per billion of benzene) compared
to MATES II Annual Average 102.4 risk; AQMD 2001–2001 AER, Form
TACS, 011034 Central Plants Inc., "Toxic Air Contaminants and Ozone
Depleters Emissions/Fee Summary:" 1.5 pounds benzene annual gross
emissions: Fee $4.86; 1.4 pounds 1,3-Butadiene annual gross emissions:
Fee $3.62; 36 pounds Formaldehyde: $9.00 fee. Central Plants Inc. SCAQMD
inspection by M. Morris, 4-2-90: "Cooling tower on premises does not use any
chrome."

255 *By the time Judge Mortimer: Moss v. Venoco,* Case Management Order, March
2004.

256 *"There will be a sit-down":* Interview Al Stewart, March 2004.

CHAPTER TWELVE: DISCOVERY

Page

258 The account of the plaintiffs' gathering of evidence at Beverly Hills High
School as part of discovery is based on notes I took of the process on
September 17, 2004. Unless otherwise noted, references to depositions are
from court filings and transcripts of depositions in *Moss v. Venoco.*

259 *The issue of migration:* California Environmental Protection Agency Department of Toxic Substance Control, "Guidance for the Evaluation and Mitigation
of Subsurface Vapor Intrusion to Indoor Air," February 7, 2005. http://
www.dtsc.ca.gov/AssessingRisk/upload/HERD_POL_Eval_Subsurface_Vapor_
Intrusion_interim_final.pdf.

259 *According to the school district's testing:* Ravi Subramanian et al., "CDM Summary Report—Comparison of Plaintiff and CDM Shadow Sampling VOC Results," Beverly Hills High School, April 11, 2005, Project No. 22293-44479-RT.
OVERSIGHT.RPT.

260 *These were the bungalow classrooms:* Phylmar Group Inc., "Data Evaluation of
Indoor Air Quality Monitoring Reports for Beverly Vista, El Rodeo, Haw-
thorne, and Horace Mann Elementary Schools, and Beverly Hills High
School," prepared for Beverly Hills Unified School District, draft report,
August 19, 1999. See also Phylmar Group Inc., "Indoor Air Quality Monitor-
ing Report for Beverly Vista Elementary School and Beverly Hills High
School," prepared for Beverly Hills Unified School District, January 3, 2000.

260 *But by the time:* Deposition Randy Darrell Horsak, *Moss v. Venoco,* June 22,
2005.

261 *"I expect people":* Telephone interview William Ireland, September 20, 2004.

261 *"I've got my own":* Telephone interview Edward Masry, September 20, 2004.

261 *No independent testing:* Interview Hamid Saebfar, November 2003.

261 *They also asked:* Baron & Budd, "Re: Beverly Hills High School Litigation; Case Update," April 28, 2005.

262 *And then: Moss v. Venoco,* Amended Case Management Order, March 2004.

262 *Each step of the way: Moss v. Venoco,* Plaintiffs Opposition to Defendants' ex parte Motion to Enforce Demand for Physical Examination of Plaintiffs Pursuant to Protocol of Donald F. Nortman, M.D., October 29, 2004; Declaration of William E. Ireland in Support of Motion to Compel Plaintiffs to Attend Independent Medical Examinations on November 10, 11, and 12, 2004, in Accordance with Dr. Donald Nortman's Proposed Protocol, October 29, 2004; The Beverly Hills Unified School District's Ex Parte Application For an Order Compelling Plaintiffs to Attend and Submit to Independent Medical Exams . . . October 29, 2004.

262 *The building: The 9/11 Commission Report,* http://www.9-11commission.gov/report/911Report.pdf.

262 *Just past the security guard:* Telephone interview Geneva Day, January 2005.

263 *"I thought it was necessary":* Telephone interview Geneva Day, January 2005.

264 *She had begun taking:* Interview Lori Moss, September 2004.

267 *Active in Republican:* Lewis Brisbois, Bisgaard & Smith Web site, http://www.lbbslaw.com/attorneybio.asp?AttyID=21.

267 *Penny Newman:* Interview Penny Newman, October 2003.

272 *For two hours:* Interview John Link, January 2005.

272 *The number one payout:* Ibid.

274 *After bypass surgery:* Interview Erin Brockovich-Ellis, March 2005.

275 *But even after:* David M. Halbfinger and Allison Hope Weiner, "A Detective to the Stars Is Accused of Wiretaps," *New York Times,* February 7, 2006.

275 *Many of his clients:* Greg Kirkorian et al., "Sources Date Pellicano Probe to 2001," *Los Angeles Times,* November 13, 2003.

275 *Cohen's lawsuit against Masry:* Amanda Bronstad, "Law Firms Settle in Calif. Wiretapping Suit," *National Law Journal,* April 4, 2006.

275 *In a case of spy:* David M. Halbfinger and Allison Hope Weiner, "Pellicano Case Casts Harsh Light on Hollywood Entertainment Lawyers," *New York Times,* May 23, 2006.

CHAPTER THIRTEEN: TRADE SECRETS AND OTHER PRIVILEGES

Unless otherwise specified, all depictions in this chapter of courtroom scenes and testimony from depositions are derived entirely from court filings, reporters' transcripts, or my own notes from proceedings in Department 307 on the *Moss v. Venoco* litigation.

Page

276   *On Friday, August 26:* "Fisherman Wins $14 Million From Dupont," Associated Press, August 27, 2005.

276   *"They were taking":* Interview Al Stewart, September 2005.

276   *"I know y'all":* Ibid.

277   *A published opinion: Transwestern Pipeline Co. v. Monsanto Co.,* 46 Cal. App. 4th 502, 514; 53 Cal. Rptr. 2d 887, 893 (1996). See also "Monsanto Hit Big for PCB Liability," *National Law Journal,* March 7, 1994, p. 17. *Transwestern Pipeline Co. v Monsanto Co.* C643857. Los Angeles Superior Court. http://rsowin.netwiz.net/index%20/PCB%20Award%20.html.

277   *Potentially dangerous levels:* "Polychlorinated Biphenyls (PCBs) Health Effects," U.S. Environmental Protection Agency, Office of Prevention, Pesticides and Toxic Substances Web site, http://www.epa.gov/opptintr/pcb/effects/html. See also "Dioxin Research at the National Institute of Environmental Health Sciences (NIEHS) Factsheets and Pamphlets," http://www.niehs.nib.gov/oc/facthseets/dioxin/htm and "Dioxins: Technical Information for California Health Officials," California Department of Health Services, Environmental Health Investigations Branch, May 2003.

278   *According to the appellate court:* Transwestern Pipeline, p. 510.

279   *On November 29, 2004: Moss v. Venoco,* Joint Status Conference Report, January 31, 2005 (hearing February 4, 2005) p. 4.

279   *All the papers:* Interview Jody Kleinman, March 2004. See also Southern California Gas Company, "Measurement Collections System Gas Volume Detail Report," Customer: Whittier Pipeline Corp., Beverly Hills, California, 2003.

280   *The gas company's lawyer: Moss v. Venoco,* Joint Status Conference Report, January 31, 2005. See also Sempra Energy letter from Leiton S. Hashimoto, custodian of records for Southern California Gas Company, December 10, 2004, to James D. Piel.

280   *On this case:* V. Thomas Meador III and Dianne Miller, "Managing Mass Toxic Tort Litigation Risks: Effective Pretrial Tactics," American Corporate Counsel Associates ACCA Docket, April 2002.

281   *There, customers could read:* Southern California Gas Company Web site, Proposition 65; Polychlorinated Biphenyls (PCB's), http://www.socalgas.com/business/resource_center/aq_prop65.shtml.

281   *"These documents": Moss v. Venoco,* "Stipulation for Protective Order as to Production of Documents by Southern California Gas Company," April 21, 2005.

281   *Despite his willingness: Moss v. Venoco,* Notice of Entry of Order, February 15, 2005, Wendell Mortimer Jr.

282 *But the defense lawyers: Moss v. Venoco,* Defendant City of Beverly Hills Reply Memorandum in support of motion to compel; Declaration of Steven R. Tannenbaum, PhD; March 18, 2005.

282 *Scott Frieling:* Baron & Budd letter, February 2, 2005, from Scott Frieling to John Shimada, Lewis Brisbois Bisgaard & Smith; attached as Exhibit B of Motion to compel further response to city of Beverly Hills special interrogatory no. 4 and to compel compliance with the court's November 23, 2004 order, February 10, 2005.

282 *"Just because": Moss v. Venoco,* March 25, 2005 hearing.

284 *It was their opinion:* Deposition of David E. Neff, June 16–17, 2005; depostion of James N. Tarr, May 24–25, 2005; Jack V. Matson, Final Expert Report: "Hexavalent Chromium Emissions from Cooling Towers at the Central Plants Inc. Facility, Century City, California," April 4, 2005; "An Evaluation of the Impact of Toxic Chemical Air Emissions from Industrial Facilities at Beverly Hills High School," Stone Lions Environmental Corporation, February 28, 2005; Robert N. Meroney, "Prediction of the Impact of Cooling Tower Drift Near BHHS," March 2005; Steven Hanna, "Deposition of Chromate Released to the Atmosphere in Drift Water from Cooling Towers Adjacent to BHHS," April 12, 2005; Barry Dellinger, "Calculation of PCDF Emissions from Natural Gas Fired Boilers Contaminated with PCBs," April 28, 2005.

286 *In early March:* "Urban Dispersion Program," New York City, U.S. Department of Homeland Security and U.S. Defense Threat Reduction Agency, http://urbandispersion.pnl.gov/docs/nyc-factsheet.pdf. See also Ian Urbin, "Antiterror Test to Follow Winds and Determine Airborne Paths," *New York Times,* February 11, 2005.

286 *Hanna, a professor:* http://hsph.harvard.edu/faculty/StevenHanna.html.

286 *"I really don't think":* Interview Steven Hanna, June 2005.

286 *Each year:* National Cancer Institute, "Fact Sheet," http://cancernet.nci.nih. gov/cancertopics/factsheet/Sites-Types/testicular/.

286 *At the same time:* Few studies not funded by industry have been conducted in petroleum exploration and producing workers. In one of two case-control studies, an excess risk for testicular cancer was observed among petroleum and natural gas extraction workers. See P. K. Mills, G. R. Newell, D. E. Johnson, "Testicular Cancer Associated with Employment in Agriculture and Oil and Natural Gas Extraction," *Lancet* 1, no. 8370 (Jan. 28, 1984): 201–10; No such excess was found in the other study: C. M. Sewell, S. P. Castle, H. F. Hull et al. "Testicular Cancer and Employment in Agriculture and Oil and Natural Gas Extraction," *Lancet* 1, no. 8470 (March 8, 1986): 553. Epidemiological studies of communities exposed to oil pollutants near oil fields are scarce. See Anna-Karin Hurtig and Miguel San Sabastian, "Geographical Incidence in Cancer Incidence in the Amazon Basin of Ecuador in Relation to Residence Near Oil

Fields," *International Journal of Epidemiology* 31 (2002): 1021–27. In that study, the authors found "cancers of the stomach, rectum, skin melanoma, soft tissue and kidney in men and for cancers of the cervix and lymph nodes in women. An increase in haematopoietic cancers was also observed in the population under 10 years in the exposed counties in both males and females." The authors concluded that "study results are compatible with a relationship between cancer incidence and living in proximity to oil fields."

286 *But even more crucial: Moss v. Venoco,* "Plaintiffs' Opposition to Defendants Motion In Limine to Exclude Evidence Of, or Reference to, Non-Initial Trial Plaintiffs, etc." May 5, 2006.

287 *In his report: Moss v. Venoco,* Draft Report of Richard W. Clapp, February 25, 2006.

287 *When Clapp had requested: Moss v. Venoco,* "Declaration of William E. Ireland in Support of Opposition to Plaintiffs' Motion to Compel Further Answers to Plaintiff John Laurie's Demand for Production of Documents, Set Two," January 26, 2005.

287 *Yet in December 1994, when it had not:* Memo from Sol Levine, superintendent of schools, to Dr. Arthur Fields, principal Horace Mann School, "Re: Response from Dr. Paul Papanek," January 4, 1995. Letter to Dr. Sol Levine, superintendent of Beverly Hills Unified School District from Toxics Epidemiology Program, County of Los Angeles Department of Health Services, Paul J. Papanek, Jr., chief, December 7, 1994.

288 *In a January: Moss v. Venoco,* Notice of Motion and Motion for Protective Order, January 26, 2005.

289 *"The pretense that the law":* Interview Al Stewart, September 2005.

289 *Dellinger was a member:* Maureen D. Avakian, Barry Dellinger, et al., "Workshop Summary: The Origin, Fate, and Health Effects of Combustion By-Products: A Research Framework," *Environmental Health Perspectives* 110, no. 11 (November 2002); U.S. EPA, Air Pollution Prevention and Control, "Real-Time Monitoring of Dioxins and Other Ambient Air Trace Organics," http://www.epa.gov/appcdwww/empact/; "LSU Team Receives $1.3 Million Grant from National Science Foundation; Researchers to Investigate Microscopic Particles That Cause Health Problems," *LSU News,* Louisiana State University, Office of University Relations, May 19, 2004.

290 *Since 1985:* Environmental Research Foundation, *Rachel's Hazardous Waste News* no. 173, March 21, 1990, http://www.ejnet.org/rachel/rhwn173.htm.

290 *In 1997:* International Agency for Research on Cancer, *Chlorinated Dibenzo-para-Dioxins and Polychlorinated Dibenzofurans,* IARC Monographs, vol. 69, http://monographs.iarc.fr/ENG/Monographs/vol69/volume69.pdf.

290 *In January 2001:* U.S. National Toxicology Program, 10th Report on Carcinogens, http://ntp.niehs.nih.gov/indexcfm?objectid=72016262-BDB7-CEBA-FA60E922B18C2540.

290 *In 2003:* D. Mackie, J. Liu, Y-S Loh, et al., "No Evidence of Dioxin Cancer Threshold," *Environmental Health Perspectives* 111 (2003): 1145–47.

290 *On April 28, 2005:* Telephone interview Barry Dellinger, June 2005.

290 *According to California's Office:* "Cancer Potencies Approved by the Scientific Review Panel from 1984 to 1996 (in Order of Cancer Potency)," Table 2, http://www.oehha.ca.go/air/toxic_contminants/leadrpt.html.

290 *They are also:* John Froines, "Findings Related to Disproportionate Impacts on Children of Toxic Air Contaminants," Scientific Review Panel, February 1, 2002, http://www.arb.ca.gov/srp/sb25.doc. See also "Hormone Disruptors: Emerging Evidence of a Future Threat," from *NRDC: Our Children at Risk: The Five Worst Environmental Threats to Their Health,* http://www.nrdc.org/health/kids/ocar/chap5e.asp.

291 *Scientific understanding:* Peter Montague, "How We Got Here—Part I: The History of Chlorinated Biphenyls (PCBs)," *Rachel's Hazardous Waste News* no. 327, Environmental Research Foundation, March 4, 1993. See also Eric Coppolino, "Pandora's Poison," *Sierra Magazine,* September 1994.

291 *When he analyzed:* Telephone interview Barry Dellinger, June 2005.

291 *Recent testing in California:* California Air Resources Board, Engineering and Laboratory Branch, "Evaluation Test Report: Determination of Emissions from the No. 3 Reformer at Tosco Refining Company San Francisco Area Refinery at Avon," California Environmental Protection Agency, 1999.

291 *According to a 2003 report:* "Dioxins: Technical Information for California Health Officials." California Department of Health Services, Environmental Health Investigation Branch, May 2003.

291 *Dellinger testified that:* EPA, National Center for Environmental Assessment, "The Inventory of Sources of Dioxin in the United States (External Review Draft 2005)," http://cfpub.epa.gov/ncea/cfm/recordisplay.cfm?deid=132080.

291 *The U.S. EPA's most recent:* "Draft Dioxin Reassessment," 2003, http://www.epa.gov/ncea/dioxinqa.htm. See also http://www.epa.gov/ncea/pdfs/dioxin/nas-review/pdfs/part1_vol1/dioxin_pt1_vol1_ch11_dec2003.pdf.

292 *"Now," Dellinger testified:* Interview Barry Dellinger, June 2005.

292 *"I was surprised":* Ibid.

292 *Even though PCBs:* Interview Sara McGurk, July 2005. See also "Caulking Found to Be Unrecognized Source of PCB Contamination in Schools and Other Buildings; Researchers Call for Survey to Identify Buildings for EPA-Mandated Remediation," Harvard School of Public Health press release, July 20, 2004, research by Robert Herrick, http://ehp.niehs.nih.gov/docs/2004/6912/abstract/html.

292 *Ever since 1983:* EPA Memorandum, "Approval of Enron/Transwestern Revised Natural Gas Pipeline PCB Compliance Monitoring Program (CMP) Plan" from Michael Calhoun, environmental scientist, Multimedia Enforcement Branch, through David Hindin, chief, Multimedia Enforcement Branch,

to Melissa Marshall, director, Multimedia Enforcement Division, December 24, 1996, http://www.epa.gov/pcb/pubs/cmp96.pdf.

292 *In February 2002:* U.S. Department of Justice, press release, "United States Settles Case with Natural Gas Pipeline Company," February 1, 2002.

292 *"It's sort of a Catch-22":* Interview Sara McGurk, July 2005.

293 *With headquarters:* "Energy Solutions from Sempra," Sempra Energy Web site, http://www.sempra.com/.

293 *Lawyers representing: Moss v. Venoco,* Defendants' Motion for Summary Judgment of Defendants Sempra Energy, Sempra Energy Global Enterprises and Pacific Enterprises, Inc: Memo of Points and Authorities, April 5, 2005.

294 *"He doesn't":* Interview Al Stewart, September 2005.

295 *With nine months:* Court of Appeal of the State of California, Second Appellate District, Division Four, petition for writ of mandate is denied by P. I. Epstein, J. Curry and J. Willhite, February 15, 2006.

295 *In a "white paper":* John P. Woodyard, "PCB White Paper; Behavior of PCBs in Natural Gas," March 20, 2005, http://www.northernnaturalgas.com/html/include/PCB%20White%20Paper%20080805.pdf.

296 *"I've never": Moss v. Venoco,* Woodyard deposition, p. 191.

300 *"They're two different": Moss v. Venoco,* Horsak deposition, March 21, 2005.

302 *This time: Moss v. Venoco,* Defendants' Motion in Limine Re: Barry Dellinger, September 29, 2006.

305 *She had devoted:* "Editorial: In Loving Memory," *Highlights,* March 22, 2002, http://64.233.167.104/search?q=cache:g7S9xSSuUAYJ:bhhs.beverlyhills.k12.ca.us/highlights/mar22_02/march22_pg2.pdf+Beverly+Hills+High+School+Susan+ Srere&hl=en&gl=us&ct=clnk&cd=3.

CHAPTER FOURTEEN: ACCEPTABLE RISKS

Page

306 *"During my last":* Harvard and Radcliffe Class of 1975: Twenty-fifth Anniversary Report (Cambridge, Mass., 2000).

307 *Now, since his lung cancer:* http://berman.redtoenail.org/.

307 *"I will tell you":* Interview Phil Berman, June 2005.

308 *Five-year survival:* American Cancer Society, "What Are the Key Statistics for Lung Cancer?" http://www.cancer.org/docroot/CRI/content/CRI_2_4_1x_What_Are_the_Key_Statistics_About_ Lung_Cancer_15.asp?sitearea=.

310 *A few years ago:* Ning Li et al., "Ultrafine Particulate Pollutants Induce Oxidative Stress and Mitochondrial Damage," *Environmental Health Perspectives* 111, no. 4 (April 2003), http://www.ehponline.org/docs/2003/6000/abstract.html.

311 *In California alone:* Bart Ostro et al., "Fine Particulate Air Pollution and Mortality in Nine California Counties: Results from CALFINE," *Environmental Health Perspectives* 114, no. 1 (January 2006).

311   *In September 2006:* Janet Wilson, "EPA Criticized for Not Toughening Soot
Law," *Los Angeles Times,* October 7, 2006. See also editorial, "Science Ignored,
Again," *New York Times,* October 14, 2006.

312   *"Why take chances?":* Interview John Peters, January 2004.

312   *So far, the federal Environmental Protection Agency:* Janet Wilson, "EPA's
Own Scientific Panel Chides Administrator: Proposed Clean Air Standards
Ignore Recommendations, Could Lead to Public Health Problems, Scientists
Say," *Los Angeles Times,* February 4, 2006.

313   *In 1994, the Government Accountability Office:* GAO Report, "Toxic Substances Control Act: Legislative Changes Could Make the Act More Effective,"
1994; GAO Report, "Toxic Chemicals: Long-Term Coordinated Strategy
Needed to Measure Exposures in Humans," May 2000; GAO Report, "Chemical Regulation: Options Exist to Improve EPA's Ability to Assess Health Risks
and Manage Its Chemical Review Program," GAO-05-458, July 2005. See also
Marla Cone, "EPA Is Faulted as Failing to Shield Public from Toxins: A
Federal Report Says the Environmental Agency Has Insufficient Data on
Chemical Dangers," *Los Angeles Times,* July 13, 2005.

313   *As a result:* T. E. Wirth, "Environment and Health: A Connection to the Current Debate on Education in America," presented at the Roundtable on Environmental Health Science, Research, and Medicine, the National Academy of
Sciences, Washington, D.C., June 2000.

313   *"We're sort of like":* Interview Melanie Marty, February 2006.

314   *California women have:* Myrto Petreas, "PDBE's in Tissues of Women with
and Without Breast Cancer," California Department of Health Services, California Breast Cancer Research Program, 2004, http:www.cabreastcancer.org/
research/PageGrant.asp?grant_id=3808.

314   *There is presently:* Voluntary Children's Chemical Evaluation Program, http://
www.epa.gov/chemrtk/vccep/index.htm.

314   *For example, human sperm counts:* Our Stolen Future, http://www.ourstolen-
future.org/newscience/reproduction/sperm/humansperm.htm; Shanna H.
Swann, "The Question of Declining Sperm Density Revisited: 101 Studies
Published 1934–1996," *Environmental Health Perspectives* 108, no. 10
(October 2000), http://www.ehponline.org/docs/2000/108p961-966swan/
abstract.html; Ben Harder, "Count Down: Chemicals Linked to Inferior
Sperm," *Science News Online* 163, no. 22 (May 31, 2003): 339.

314   *An explosion of new studies:* Frederick S. vom Saal, "An Extensive New Literature Concerning Low-Dose Effects of Bisphenol A Shows the Need for a New
Risk Assessment," *Environmental Health Perspectives* 113, no. 8 (August
2005), http://www.ehp.niehs.nih.gov/docs/2005/7713/abstract.html.

315   *In a study of fetuses:* "Ubiquitous Chemical Associated with Abnormal
Reproductive Development," Scientific American.com, May 27, 2005,
http://scientificamerican.com/print_version.cfm?articleID=000240B8-30B1-

1296-B0B183414B7F0000. See also Shanna H. Swan, "Decrease in Anogenital Distance Among Male Infants with Prenatal Phthalate Exposure," *Environmental Health Perspectives* 113, no. 8 (August 2005), http://www.ehponline.org/members/2005/8100/8100.html.

315 *Another study found:* Monica Muñoz-de-Toro, "Perinatal Exposure to Bisphenol A Alters Peripubertal Mammary Gland Development in Mice." *Endocrinology* 146 (2005): 4138–47.

315 *A Japanese study found:* Mayumi Sugiura-Ogasawara, et al., "Exposure to Bisphenol A Is Associated with Recurrent Miscarriage," *Human Reproduction,* June 9, 2005, http://humrep.oxfordjournals.org/cgi/content/abstract/deh888v1.

315 *Animal studies have offered:* Interview Melanie Marty, February 2006; interview Julia Brody, September 2003. See also Julia Green Brody, "Environmental Pollutants and Breast Cancer," *Environmental Health Perspectives* 111, no. 8 (June 2003); http://www.silentspring.org/newweb/research/ssa.html; http://www.cancer.gov/cancertopics/pdq/treatment/childhodgkins/HealthProfessional/page7.

315 *When a class of chemicals:* Matthew R. Bonner, "Breast Cancer Risk and Exposure in Early Life to Polycyclic Aromatic Hydrocarbons Using Total Suspended Particulates as a Proxy Measure," *Cancer Epidemiology Biomarkers & Prevention* 14 (January 2005): 53–60.

315 *In her role:* Letter from Melanie A. Marty, chair, Children's Health Protection Advisory Committee, to Michael Leavitt, administrator, United States Environmental Protection Agency, "Re: Regulation of Mercury from Coal-Fired Power Plants," June 8, 2004; http://democrats.senate.gov/dpc/hearings/hearing16/CHPAC%202004_0608_regulationofmercury.pdf; letter from Melanie A. Marty, chair, Children's Health Protection Advisory Committee, to Stephen Johnson, acting administrator, United States Environmental Protection Agency, "Re: Particulate Matter National Ambient Air Quality Standards," August 8, 2005; letter from Melanie A. Marty, chair, Children's Health Protection Advisory Committee, to Stephen Johnson, acting administrator, United States Environmental Protection Agency, "Re: Perchlorate PRG and Water Contamination," March 8, 2006; http://www.ewg.org/issues_content/perchlorate/20060315/chpac-epa_ltr.pdf.

315 *She's also lobbied:* Letter from Melanie A. Marty, chair, Children's Health Protection Advisory Committee, to Stephen Johnson, acting administrator, United States Environmental Protection Agency, "Re: Release of Supplemental Guidance for Assessing Cancer Susceptibility from Early-Life Exposures to Carcinogens," March 3, 2005.

315 *Under the leadership of John D. Graham:* Source Watch, Center for Media and Democracy, "Harvard Center for Risk Analysis and Big Tobacco," http:www.sourcewatch.org/index.php?title=Harvard_Center_for_Risk_Analysis_and_Big_Tobacco. Also Public Citizen, "John Graham Nomination Confirmed," http:www.citizen.org/congress/regulations/graham.html.

317 *"I used to like":* Interview Gina Solomon, February 2006.

317 *Solomon was referring:* Elisa K. Ong and Stanton A. Glanz, "Constructing 'Sound Science' and 'Good Epidemiology': Tobacco, Lawyers, and Public Relations Firms," *American Journal of Public Health* 91, no. 11 (November 2001): 1749–57. See also Joaquin Barnoya and Stanton A. Glantz, "The Tobacco Industry's Worldwide ETS Consultants Project: European and Asian Components," *European Journal of Public Health* 16 (2006): 69–77.

317 *As Donald Kennedy:* Iris Kuo, "What Constitutes Sound Science? No One Can Really Say. For Bush, Term Is All About Politics," *Detroit Free Press,* May 5, 2006.

318 *In fact, the head of TASSC:* Paul Thacker, "Pundit for Hire: Smoked Out," *New Republic,* January 27, 2006, https://ssl.tnr.com/p/docsub.mhtml?i=20060206&s=thacker020606. See also Source Watch, Center for Media and Democracy, "Steven J. Milloy," http://www.sourcewatch.org/index.php?title=Steve_Milloy and junkscience.com. See also Chris Mooney, "Some Like it Hot," *Mother Jones,* May–June 2005, http://www.motherjones.com/news/featurex/2005/05/exxon_chart.html.

318 *By "manufacturing uncertainty":* David Michaels, "The Art of 'Manufacturing Uncertainty," *Los Angeles Times,* June 24, 2005. See also David Michaels, "Doubt Is Their Product," *Scientific American* 292, issue 6 (June 2005): 96–101.

318 *According to journalist Paul Thacker:* Paul Thacker, "The Weinberg Proposal," *Environmental Science and Technology Online,* February 22, 2006, http://pubs/acs.org/subscribe/journals/esthag-w/2006/feb/business/pt_weinberg.html.

318 *That same year:* Jordan Rau, "Legislature Targets Toxic Risks in Products," *Los Angeles Times,* May 30, 2005.

318 *in January 2006:* Joseph A. Poltich, *Environmental Health Perspectives,* "Bisphenol-A and risk assessment (Perspectives Correspondence)," January 1, 2006.

319 *According to documents filed:* Interview Gary Praglin, September 2003; Hearing of the California Senate Health and Human Services Committee, 2003. "Possible Interference in the Scientific Review of Chromium VI Toxicity." February 23, 2003. Los Angeles, CA. Transcript available at: http://www.sen.ca.gov/health/CHROMIUM_VI_TRANSCRIPT_28FEB03.DOC. Peter Waldman, "Study Tied Pollutant to Cancer: Then Consultants Got Hold of It," *Wall Street Journal,* December 23, 2005; Environmental Working Group, "Chrome-Plated Fraud: How PG&E's Scientists-for-Hire Reversed Findings of a Cancer Study," March 2006, http://www.ewg.org/reports/chromium/ltr_cdc_20060313.php.

319 *When the issue was raised:* David Egilman, "Commentary: Corporate Corruption of Science—The Case of Chromium (VI)," *International Journal of Occupational and Environmental Health* 12 (2006): 169–76. Paustenbach is quoted in an e-mail to the journal editor as saying, "Ultimately, I should not have succumbed to the possible pressures brought to bear by special interests."

319 *As one state senator said:* State Senator Jack Scott is quoted in Miguel Bustillo, "PG&E Assailed in Hearing Over Chromium 6," *Los Angeles Times,* March 1, 2003.

319 *The most controversial aspect:* Peter Waldman, ibid.

320 *That finding:* Zhang Jiangdong and S. Li, "Cancer Mortality in a Chinese Population Exposed to Hexavalent Chromium in Water." *Journal of Occupational and Environmental Medicine* 39 (1997): 315–19.

320 *After Dr. Paustenbach resigned:* OMB Watch, "Administration Stacks Scientific Advisory Panels," March 19, 2003, http://www.ombwatch.org/article/articleview/1384/1/39.

320 *Not long after:* "Editorial Retraction," *Journal of Occupational and Environmental Medicine* 48, no. 7 (July 2006): 749.

320 *By February 2006:* Elliot Blair Smith, "PG&E Critic Erin Brockovich Doubtful about Legal Settlement," *USA Today,* February 6, 2006.

321 *In the summer of 2005:* 109th Congress, 1st Sess., Rep. 1391, introduced by Senators Lautenberg, Jeffords, Boxer, Kerry, Corzine, Clinton, and Kennedy, July 13, 2005: see http://www.theorator.com/bills109/s1391.html.

321 *As of this writing:* Chris VandenHeuvel, "Chemical Makers' Statement on Child, Worker and Consumer Safe Chemicals Act of 2005," American Chemistry Council press release, July 13, 2005.

321 *More recently, EPA officials:* John Heilprin, "EPA Seeks to Ease Reporting of Toxics; Agency Says It Wants to Reduce Business Burden," Associated Press, September 22, 2005.

321 *Dr. Costa: Moss v. Venoco,* Declaration of Max Costa, August 16, 2006.

321 *In response: Moss v. Venoco,* Defendants' Joint Consolidated Reply Memorandum of Points and Authorities in Support of Motions for Summary Judgment as to Plaintiffs Lee, Davidson, Laurie, Tackaberry, Day, and Busch, September 22, 2006, p. 30.

322 *Dr. Steven Patierno: Moss v. Venoco,* Declaration of Steven R. Patierno, PhD, June 22, 2006, p. 37. Dr. Patierno also testified that his research has shown that loss of DNA repair from chromium exposure leads to decreased mutagenesis.

323 *According to defense expert Mary Jane Wilson: Moss v. Venoco,* Defendants' Motion in Limine to Exclude Maximum Benzene Emissions Estimates Prepared by Plaintiffs' Expert James Tarr, June 16, 2006; Declaration of Mary Jane Wilson, June 14, 2006.

323 *During the evidentiary hearing: Moss v. Venoco,* Declaration of Jim Tarr, Exhibit 26, p. 28, August 11, 2006. Hearing of October 13, 2006.

324 *On November 7, 2006: Moss v. Venoco,* Minute Order, Judge Wendell Mortimer Jr., November 7, 2006.

325 *At the Suva Elementary School:* Interview Jack Broadbent, October 2003; http://www.calepa.ca.gov/EnvJustice/ActionPlan/PhaseI/March2005/EJrptSept2004.

pdf. See p. 4 of California EPA Environmental Justice Update, 2004 (on Suva Elementary).

326 *In the San Fernando Valley's:* Janie Shelton and Wendy Cozen, "Community Cancer Assessment Regarding Retinoblastoma in the West Valley," University of Southern California Cancer Surveillance Program, Los Angeles County, July 29, 2005. See also Kathy Braidhill, "Fallout: The Legacy of the Nation's Forgotten Nuclear Meltdown," *California Lawyer Magazine,* April 2006, http://californialawyermagazine.com/index.cfm?sid=&tkn=&eid=821931&evid=1.

326 *In Eldorado Hills:* http://www.epa.gov/region09/toxic/noa/eldorado/intro1.html.

326 *According to figures:* "Building Safe Schools: Invisible Threats, Visible Actions: A Report of Childproofing Our Communities Campaign and the Center for Health, Environment and Justice," December 2005, http://www.childproofing.org/buildingsafeschools.pdf.

326 *Even more children:* Robert W. Amler, Agency for Toxic Substances and Disease Registry (ATSDR), U.S. Department of Health and Human Services, http://www.cehn.org/cehn/ edconfabstracts.html, http://www. atsdr.cdc.gov/child/chw498-i.html.

326 *Recent research has suggested:* National Research Council, *Scientific Frontiers in Developmental Toxicity and Risk Assessment* (Washington, D.C.: National Academy Press, 2000). See also "Children's Environmental Health: Environmental Contaminants and Their Relation to Learning, Behavioral and Developmental Disorders," Fact Sheet of the National Institute of Environmental Health Sciences, http://www.niehs.nih.gov/oc/factsheets/ceh/contamin.htm.

AFTERWORD

Page

331 *On Wednesday afternoon: Moss v. Venoco* (consolidated with BC300164, BC308673, SC0058, SC080117, BC315885, BC317676), Ruling of Wendell Mortimer, Jr, November 22, 2006.

331 *Sitting in O'Hare:* Interview Ernest Getto, December 2006.

332 *As it turned out: Moss v. Venoco,* "Draft Report of Richard W. Clapp," Plaintiffs' Exhibit A; Declaration of William R. Sawyer, pp. 68–69.

332 *Since the plaintiffs':* Unless otherwise noted, the references to the litigation are from notes I took or from court transcripts from the hearings on motions for summary judgment before Judge Wendell Mortimer Jr. on November 20 and 21. The hearings were based on thousands of pages of testimony from expert depositions, motions filed by both plaintiffs and defendants, along with exhibits of peer-reviewed studies, and sworn declarations. See: Defendants Joint Evidentiary Objections and Motions to Strike the Declaration of William R. Sawyer, Max Costa, Richard Clapp and Nachman Brautbar and

Exhibits Thereto filed on September 22, 2006, and Plaintiffs' opposition filed October 10, 2006, and Plaintiffs' Consolidated Memorandum of Points and Authorities in Opposition to Defendants' Various Causation Motions for Summary Judgment Relating to the Claims of Karen Lee, Geneva Day, Stace Tackaberry, John Laurie, Gary Davidson, and Christine Busch.

333 *From the moment he launched:* Michael Liedtke, "Chevron's 4Q Profit Soars to Record High," Associated Press, January 27, 2006.

334 *It was an awkward omission:* For the discussion about IBM's suppression of Dr. Clapp's study, I relied on several secondary sources. Among them: Donald Kennedy, "Editorial: Science, Law and the IBM Case," *Science* 305, no. 5682 (July 16, 2004): pp. 340–42; Joseph LaDou, "A Challenge to Academic Freedom," *San Francisco Medicine,* February 2005, http://www.sfms.org/AM/Template.cfm?Section=Home&CONTENTID=1257&TEMPLATE=/CM/HTMLDisplay.cfm&SECTION=Article_Archives; William M. Bulkeley, "Study of Cancers at IBM Is Released," *Wall Street Journal,* October 19, 2006.

336 *Should such a study:* U.S. National Research Council Committee on Environmental Epidemiology, *Environmental Epidemiology: Public Health and Hazardous Wastes* (Washington, D.C.: National Academies Press, 1991): pp. 30–31.

337 *A National Cancer Institute study:* Qin Lan et al. "Hematotoxicity in Workers Exposed to Low Levels of Benzene," *Science* 306 (December 3, 2004): pp. 1174–76.

338 *In his nine-page opinion: Moss v. Venoco,* Ruling of Wendell Mortimer Jr. on motions for summary judgment, December 12, 2006, p. 7.

339 *In that regard:* Agency for Toxic Substances and Disease Registry (ATSDR), "Toxicological Profile for Polychlorinated Biphenyls (PCBs)" (Atlanta, GA: U.S. Department of Health and Human Services, Public Health Service, 2000). http://www.atsdr.cdc.gov/toxprofiles/tp17.html. "Scorecard: The Pollution Information Site," Chemical Profile for Polychlorinated Biphenyls, http://www.scorecard.org/chemical-profiles/summary.tcl?edf_substance_id=1336-36-3.

341 *The cold hard facts are these:* I've noted references on these points in earlier chapters.

343 *Back in Dallas:* Interview Al Stewart, December 2006.

344 *In that case:* Lockheed Litigation Cases (JCCP No. 2967), Sup.Ct.App.No. 5132167 ("Lockheed II").

345 *He asked a colleague:* Interview Al Stewart, December 2006.

345 *But even within his own camp:* Interview Jim Tarr, December 2006.

346 *In San Diego:* Phil Berman e-mail correspondence, November 24, 2006.

346 *"What strikes me as entirely tragic:"* Lou Versace e-mail, December 6, 2006.

346 *She and her husband:* Interview Lori Moss, November 2006.

346 *By happenstance that fall:* Interview Carol Malony, September 2006.

347 *"I don't know what I was expecting":* Carol Malony e-mail, January 2, 2007.

347 *"They always were hiding":* Interview Mahshid Soleimani, November 2006.

347 *He rarely gave much thought:* Zack Anderson e-mail, November 15, 2006.

347 *Jody Kleinman thought it was sad:* Interview Jody Kleinman, December 2006.

348 *With Judge Mortimer's ruling:* Interview Tom Meador, November 2006.

349 *One might have expected:* Interview Ernie Getto and Cindy Cwik, December 2006.

349 *Erin Brockovich was no longer:* Interview Erin Brockovich-Ellis, December 2006.

350 *The new mayor:* Kelly Hartog, "Judge Dismisses Beverly Hills Oil Well Cases," Beverly Hills Courier, November 24, 2006.

350 *For his part:* Beverly Hills City Council meeting, November 2004, in discussion prior to meeting with Jody Kleinman.

350 *And the lawyer:* Interview Chris Williamson, January 2007.

350 *"This is a victory:"* Quoted in Kelly Hartog, "Judge Dismisses Beverly Hills Oil Well Cases," *Beverly Hills Courier*, November 24, 2006.

351 *Now Wiener counted on the services:* Mark Hand, "API Highlights Oil Industry Challenges Despite Record Profits," *PR Week*, November 11, 2005. See also: Edelman, Source Watch: A Project of the Center for Media & Democracy Web site http://www.sourcewatch.org/index.php?title=Edelman Tom Goff bio in "CIRM Edelman Team Bios," Agenda Item #9C-iii, http://test-www.cirm.ca.gov/meetings/pdf/2005/08/05/080505_item_9g.pdf.

Agency for Toxic Substances and Disease Registry (ATSDR): The lead federal public health agency, part of the U.S. Department of Health and Human Services, responsible for determining human health effects of toxic exposures, assessing health hazards at Superfund sites, and mitigating risks from hazardous substances.

Air Quality Management District (AQMD): The air pollution control agency for Los Angeles and Orange County that is primarily responsible for controlling emissions from stationary sources of air pollution, including 28,000 businesses.

American Cancer Society: A nationwide, community-based voluntary health organization.

California Air Resources Board (CARB): Part of the California Environmental Protection Agency, it implements and enforces air pollution rules and regulations concerning mobile sources, such as cars and trucks, while considering the effects on the state's economy.

Center for Health, Environment and Justice, The: Nonprofit environmental group founded by the activist Lois Gibbs after the Love Canal disaster.

Centers for Disease Control and Prevention (CDC): Founded in 1946 to control malaria, the CDC is part of the U.S. Department of Health and Human Services. It conducts investigations to prevent and control infectious diseases, injuries, workplace hazards, disabilities, and environmental health threats.

Children's Health Environmental Coalition: A national nonprofit organization dedicated to educating the public about environmental toxins that affect children's health.

Children's Health Protection Advisory Committee: A committee of scientists and academics that advises the EPA on regulations, research, and communications issues relevant to children.

Coalition for Clean Air: Nonprofit organization dedicated to restoring clean air to California by advocating a responsible public health policy.

Communities for a Better Environment (CBE): A nonprofit environmental justice group based in southeast Los Angeles and Oakland, dedicated to improving environmental health in minority neighborhoods.

Department Of Health Services (DHS): The state agency that is part of the California Health and Human Services Agency, which oversees public health, environmental health, and medical care of Californians.

Department of Toxic Substance Control (DTSC): The California agency that assesses and oversees cleanup of hazardous materials at public schools.

Division of Oil, Gas and Geothermal Resources (DOGGR): One of the oldest agencies in California, it is part of the Department of Conservation and is responsible for ensuring the safety of subsurface operations of oil and gas operators.

Division of the State Architect: The California agency responsible for reviewing construction plans for the state's public schools and certifying projects for safety upon their completion.

Government Accountability Office (GAO): The investigative arm of Congress that is charged with keeping the federal government accountable and efficient.

International Agency for Research On Cancer (IARC): A part of the World Health Organization that conducts research on the causes of cancer.

National Cancer Institute (NCI): The federal government's principal agency for cancer research and training; it is part of the National Institutes of Health.

National Environmental Trust (NET): A nonprofit organization based in Washington, D.C., that seeks to inform the public about environmental problems and their health effects.

National Institute for Occupational Safety and Health (NIOSH): The research arm of OSHA, NIOSH is a federal agency that is a part of the Centers for Disease Control; it conducts research into occupational safety and health matters.

National Institute of Environmental Health Sciences (NIEHS): Part of the National Institutes of Health, NIEHS conducts research on environmental health and publishes the journal *Environmental Health Perspectives*.

National Toxicology Program: A part of the Department of Health and Human Services that conducts tests on the human health effects of chemical agents in the environment; it produces an annual report that lists known and suspected human carcinogens, first ordered by Congress in 1978. The eleventh annual report listed 58 "known" and 188 "reasonably anticipated" carcinogens.

Nuclear Regulatory Commission (NRC): The federal agency that regulates nuclear materials and facilities.

Occupational Safety and Health Administration (OSHA): A federal agency that enforces safety and health legislation in the workplace.

Office of Environmental Health Hazard Assessment (OEHHA): A well-respected California agency that provides toxicological and medical information for decisions involving public health to state and local agencies.

Office of Information and Regulatory Affairs: Part of the Office of Management and Budget, it oversees the implementation of government-wide policies.

Office of Prevention, Pesticides and Toxic Substances: An agency of the EPA that regulates the use of pesticides and chemicals.

Surveillance Epidemiology and End Results (SEER): A program of the National Cancer Institute that provides information on cancer incidence in the United States.

U.S. Environmental Protection Agency (EPA): The federal agency that is principally responsible for ensuring compliance with environmental laws enacted by Congress, such as the Clean Air Act, the Clean Water Act, and the Toxic Substances Control Act.

World Health Organization (WHO): The health agency of the United Nations, it monitors disease outbreaks.

CAST OF CHARACTERS

PLAINTIFFS AND FAMILIES

Berman, Phillip: 1971 Beverly graduate; testicular cancer and metastasized lung cancer.

Bova, Lee: Beverly Hills resident, lives across the street from school; non-Hodgkin's lymphoma.

Busch, Christine: Nurse at Century City Hospital; basal cell carcinoma.

Bussel, Ari: 1984 graduate with a brother with a rare cancer and a sister with an undiagnosed wasting disease.

Davidson, Gary: Attended Beverly 1981 to 1982; Hodgkin's lymphoma.

Day, Geneva: Mother of Janet Day.

Day, Janet: 1984 Beverly graduate; played basketball and was on the track team; Hodgkin's lymphoma; died 2002.

Frankel, Jeffrey: 1989 Beverly graduate; testicular cancer; stroke.

Freedman, Marilyn (Mickey): Beverly English and history teacher, 1967–2001; endometriosis.

Fries, Madeline: 1971 Beverly graduate; Graves' disease (dropped out of the case).

Fries, Tom: 1971 Beverly graduate; Hodgkin's disease; died in 2000 from complications arising from chemotherapy and radiation treatments for cancer.

Genson-Fries, Debi: Wife of Tom Fries.

Goodman, Dana: Beverly graduate who met Lori Moss in the oncologist's office; Hodgkin's disease.

Goodman, Joel: 1962 Beverly graduate and history teacher, 1967–1970; prostate cancer.

Greenberg, Justin: 1998 Beverly graduate; brain tumor.

Gross, Melissa: 1988 Beverly graduate; breast cancer.

Laurie, John: Played sports at the YMCA and at Beverly; one of the initial twelve plaintiffs whose case was selected to go to trial; thyroid cancer.

Lewinson, Judy: Mother of Lori Moss.

Messenger, Susan: Beverly AP Spanish teacher, 1977 to present; breast cancer three times.

Meyers, Stephanie: Beverly Hills resident (lived on South Roxbury Drive); non-Hodgkin's lymphoma.

Moss, Lori: 1992 Beverly graduate who started the litigation after meeting Erin Brockovich; Hodgkin's disease and thyroid cancer.

Moss, Randy: Husband of Lori Moss.

Powers, Carrie: 1974 Beverly graduate; brain tumor; multiple myeloma.

Punaro, Ralph: 1967 Beverly graduate and star athlete; non-Hodgkin's lymphoma and leukemia.

Revel, Monica: 1993 graduate; metastasized melanoma.

Smith, Tiffany: Beverly Hills resident who lived across the street from the high school; thyroid disease.

Srere, Susan: Beverly High English teacher; metastasized melanoma.

Wilson, Barbara: Psychotherapist and mother of Carl Wilson.

Wilson, Carl: 1990 Beverly graduate; Hodgkin's disease.

BEVERLY HILLS RESIDENTS

Assil, Abraham: Beverly parent of four children; he offered to make a donation for independent environmental tests of the school.

Brucker, Barry: 1977 Beverly graduate; school board president who would be elected to the city council.

Cohen, Menashi: UCLA visiting professor of engineering who sent his son to Harvard-Westlake when he wasn't convinced that data from the Air Quality Management District was reliable.

Delshad, Jimmy: First Iranian elected to the Beverly Hills City Council (spring 2003).

Egerman, Mark: Former school board member and Beverly Hills mayor.

Emrani, Nelli: Parent who joined the campaign to dump Venoco.

Goldman, Meralee: Former Beverly Hills mayor.

Gottfried, Abraham: Resident of Century Park East Condominiums, located across the street from the oil wells at Beverly High.

Greenwald, Ann: 1974 Beverly graduate; brain cancer.

Greenwald, Bruce: 1971 Beverly graduate and physician who thought the lawsuit was "bullshit."

Greenwald, Ed: 1964 Beverly graduate; prostate cancer.

Greenwald, John: 1966 Beverly graduate and physician; non-Hodgkin's lymphoma; died 2002; his college roommate, who also went to Beverly, died of testicular cancer.

Grenell, Bernie: Beverly Hills school board member, 1976–1980; died of leukemia, 2004.

Harris, Dawn: Dental hygienist and wife of Eddie Massey.

Harris, Ellen Stern: Longtime Beverly Hills resident and "mother" of the environmental movement in California; urged Jody Kleinman to keep fighting; died of breast cancer, 2006.

Heckerling, Amy: Beverly parent and film director who removed her daughter from the school after the principal told her she could skip PE.

Kleinman, Jody: Beverly parent who led the campaign to shut down the oil wells and kept her daughter in school there.

Levyn, Thomas: Beverly Hills mayor with daughter at the high school.

Lurie, Myra: PTA council president voted to school board.

Malin, Arthur: Psychiatrist and school board member, 1969–1977.

Massey, Bernie: 1980 Beverly graduate who launched the Tower of Hope campaign after seeing that the old covering for the derrick had grown dilapidated.

Massey, Eddie: Beverly graduate and artist who designed the flower motif for the Tower of Hope.

Meshkaty, Nooshin: PTA president of El Rodeo Elementary School, later elected to the school board.

Millan, John: School board member who was antagonistic to independent reviews by the state Department of Toxic Substances Control.

Morris, Janet: 1979 Beverly graduate and parent who joined the campaign to close down the oil wells on campus.

Okun, Judy: Photographer for the *Beverly Hills Weekly* whose husband was sued by developers in 1976 for writing a letter to the local paper critical of a land swap deal.

Rashti, Debbi: Parent who moved her daughter to Santa Monica High School because of concerns over toxic emissions from the oil wells on campus at Beverly.

Soleimani, Mahshid: Mother of three sons who led the unsuccessful petition drive to shut down the oil wells on campus.

Vlahos, Dean: Beverly parent who pulled his son off the baseball team over concerns about benzene leaks from the oil wells.

Waks, Abraham: Physician and parent who compared the incidence of thyroid cancer among students to the effects of Chernobyl and recommended the use of radiation monitoring badges for students.

Waks, Marrina: Parent who had her family's hair tested for heavy metals and found high levels of uranium in her daughters' hair samples; questioned the safety of using radioactive Iodine-131 at the oil wells.

Williams, Stephen: A toxicologist and oil company head hunter who moved his son from a private school to attend Beverly High.

BEVERLY HILLS HIGH SCHOOL FACULTY, STUDENTS, AND ADMINISTRATORS

Anderson, Zack: Beverly sophomore who started an underground student paper online after he claimed that school administrators censored coverage of the oil well controversy in *Highlights,* the school newspaper; the first to question what was in the "steam" from the power plant.

Banzhaf, Joyce: Beverly health education teacher, 1973–2001; she questioned the safety of the oil wells and power plant when her students' desks shook.

Baum, Mary Ann: Beverly AP English teacher who thought that concerns over the oil wells were a product of people in Beverly Hills' being out of touch with reality.

Bloch Oshansky, Lisa: 1975 Beverly graduate; lung cancer (never smoked); died 2006; sister Amy died of leukemia.

Bushman, Ben: Beverly High principal and former football coach, 1965–2004.

Carpenter, Gerald ("Carp"): Beverly history teacher and athletic coach whose three children attended the high school, 1964–1988.

Dodge, Herbert: Beverly history teacher (1962–1988) who created the school's AP program.

Farzinfarid, Parinaz: Beverly student who unsuccessfully tried to set up a debate between the superintendent and Ed Masry for the Norman News Service, the student TV journalism class.

Freedman, Marilyn "Mickey": Beverly English and history teacher, 1967–2001; plaintiff who joined the lawsuit for more information.

Gifford, Jane: Beverly substitute teacher, 1971–1983; special education teacher, 1984–1996.

Gross, Gwen: Beverly Hills superintendent of schools, 2001–2004.

Guo, Will: Beverly student, 1996–2000; he first questioned the safety of the oil wells in 2000.

Harari, Anna: Beverly student, 2001–2004; she operated the sound system for the student-run TV network, KBEV, that broadcasts school board meetings.

Kloes, Chuck: Beverly history teacher and track and football coach, 1965–2003.

Lewis, Lisa: 1999 Beverly graduate who thought the lawsuit was unfounded; thyroid cancer.

Moulton, Jennifer: Beverly journalism teacher whose contract wasn't renewed after she invoked her students' First Amendment rights about covering the oil well controversy.

Newman, Jason: 1969 Beverly graduate and PE coach for two decades; colon cancer and kidney tumor.

O'Brian, Barbara: Beverly English teacher, breast cancer.

Peters, Kenneth L.: Principal and superintendent of schools, 1950–1980.

Pressman, Joel: 1967 Beverly graduate; choral music teacher, 1976 to present.

Reilly, Chuck: Beverly basketball coach; brain tumor.

Robinson, Willard F: Beverly principal, 1959–1975.

Schenkel, Barbara: Beverly English teacher; breast cancer.

Schreiber, Dick: Beverly football and swimming coach, 1959–1997.

Shaffron, Gail: English teacher; lung cancer.

Stern, Leonard: Beverly English and history teacher, 1966–2001; he enlisted student volunteers, through "community service," to help paint the Tower of Hope.

Strandwall, Mari-Ann: Beverly track and tennis coach, 1967–1992; breast cancer.

Sussman, Barbara: Beverly teacher; breast cancer.

Thorpe, Gary: Beverly chemistry and biology teacher whose daughters attended the high school; plaintiff for "medical monitoring" in the future.

Tromblestein, Linda*: Beverly graduate and Beverly Hills Unified School District teacher.

Versace, Lou: Beverly English teacher, 1966–1986; he thought there was a "curse of the English department"; prostate cancer; also a plaintiff.

Wortman, Jane: 1971 Beverly graduate and math teacher, 1977 to present; thought the lawsuit was frivolous but worried about all of the cancers of her colleagues.

Willinger, Marilyn: Beverly home economics teacher; breast cancer.

GOVERNMENT OFFICIALS

Aanestad, Sam: Republican state senator from northern California; member of the Health and Human Services Committee who believed that Erin Brockovich was stirring up trouble in Beverly Hills.

Baker, Richard: Deputy supervisor for Division of Gas, Oil and Geothermal Resources in Los Angeles.

Broadbent, Jack: Director of U.S. Environmental Protection Agency's Air Division for California (Region 9); resigned in 2003 over frustration with the policies of the Bush adminstration, which he believed weakened enforcement of Clean Air Act.

Brock, John: Environmental engineer for EPA's Air Toxics Enforcement Division in California; believed there was no "regulatory hook" at Beverly High.

Bruce, Jack: Structural engineer and regional manager of the California Division of the State Architect, which oversees construction safety of public schools.

Burke, William: AQMD chairman.

Carlson, Kenneth: State engineer, California Division of Oil and Gas; he failed Wainoco Oil Company on two safety inspections, 1986 and 1987.

Dunstan, Roger: Consultant for the Health and Human Services Committee of the California State Senate.

Escutia, Martha: Democratic state senator and author of the Children's Environmental Health Act; member of the Health and Human Services Committee that held hearings about Beverly High.

Graham, John D.: Administrator of the Office of Information and Regulatory Affairs at the White House Office of Management and Budget; founder of the industry-sponsored Harvard Center for Risk Analysis.

---

*name changed.

Greger, Robert: Chief of inspection and enforcement, California Department of Health Services Radiologic health branch; he believes in "hormesis," the theory that radiation is good for you.

Holtzman, Jeanette: AQMD inspector who issued notices of violation to Venoco for illegal venting of gas and leaking equipment.

Jepson, John: Engineer, California Division of Oil, Gas and Geothermal Resources; he helped to organize a tour of oil fields in Los Angeles for petroleum engineers.

Jones, Jennifer: Program manager and scientist at the state Department of Toxic Substances Control; she claimed that the head of the AQMD refused to share his data with her agency.

Kaufman, Kathleen: Director, Radiation Management, Los Angeles County Health Department; she had no idea that oil wells used radioactive materials until parents at Beverly High told her.

Keeler, Katsumi: AQMD inspector worried about student safety at Beverly High.

Kuehl, Sheila: Democratic state senator and member of the Health and Human Services Committee whose district includes Beverly Hills; former child actor on the television series *The Many Loves of Dobie Gillis* and graduate of Harvard Law School; first openly gay member of the California legislature.

Leeson, Floyd: Operations engineer with the California Division of Oil, Gas and Geothermal Resources and former "mud man" at the oil well site at Beverly High.

McGurk, Sara: Chemist at the EPA's Office of Prevention, Pesticides and Toxic Substances; oversees regulation of PCBs.

Meroney, Robert N.: Professor of Environmental Engineering at Colorado State University; plaintiffs' wind expert.

Mieras, Peter: AQMD lawyer and enforcement prosecutor.

Mueller, Pang: AQMD chemical engineer who discovered high levels of benzene coming from a piece of equipment at Venoco, causing operations there to be shut down a second time in 2003.

Nazemi, Mohsen: AQMD assistant deputy executive officer assigned to speak to parents in Beverly Hills about the Venoco site.

Ortiz, Deborah: Democratic state senator from Sacramento and chair of the Health and Human Services Committee, which conducted hearings into possible contamination of Beverly High.

Saebfar, Hamid: DTSC chief of school property evaluation and cleanup who wanted to conduct an investigation of Beverly High; school officials refused to sign a contract with him.

Stoddard, Hamilton: AQMD engineer.

Underwood, Marilyn: Toxicologist, California Department of Health Services, Environmental Health Investigation Branch.

Wallerstein, Barry: AQMD executive officer and 1971 Beverly graduate.

Wells, Melvin: Inspector for state Division of Oil, Gas and Geothermal Resources who didn't get "out to Beverly Hills" as often as he was supposed to.

Williams, Stanley: L.A. Deputy District Attorney in charge of environmental unit, composed of three lawyers.

Wright, Dan: Prosecutor with L.A. district attorney's environmental unit; double jeopardy laws prevented him from filing criminal charges against Venoco for hazardous waste pollution.

ENVIRONMENTAL ADVOCATES

Brockovich, Erin: Masry & Vititoe's director of research; she first questioned whether Lori Moss's two cancers might be linked to environmental factors at Beverly Hills High School.

Carmichael, Tim: Director of the Coalition for Clean Air; he put William Guo in touch with West Hollywood officials when Beverly Hills ignored him.

Kuhn, Scott: Legal counsel for Communities for a Better Environment (CBE), an activist group working for low-income families living next to industrial pollution; CBE's map of toxic release inventories in Los Angeles spurred Will Guo to take action in Beverly Hills.

Guo, William: Sierra Club student coordinator whose concern in 2000 about the oil wells' safety was greeted by silence and derision among school and city officials in Beverly Hills.

Hirsch, Dan: Director of the Adlai Stevenson Program on Nuclear Policy at the University of California, Santa Cruz, and president of the Committee to Bridge the Gap, a nuclear watchdog group, who advised Jody Kleinman on regulatory issues.

Larson, Denny: Director of the Refinery Reform Campaign in Crockett, California, where Ed Masry first launched the "bucket brigade," so local residents could gather air samples when they suspected toxic fumes were being released from neighboring chemical plants into their homes or schools.

Schaeffer, Eric: Head of EPA's Office of Regulatory Enforcement until 2002, when he formed the Environmental Integrity Project to advocate for more effective enforcement of environmental laws; one of his reports found the EPA is underestimating toxic chemical releases by as much as 300 million pounds a year.

Solomon, Gina: Senior scientist at the Natural Resources Defense Council and assistant clinical professor of medicine at the University of California, San Francisco.

THE MEDIA

Bill-de la Pena, Claudia: KCBS-TV producer who sat on the Thousand Oaks City Council with Ed Masry.

Darwell, Brittany: Editor of *Highlights,* the student newspaper, who complained that the administration was leaning on her to be "objective" in her reporting.

Edwards, Mike: PR spokesman for Venoco, the Santa Barbara–based oil company operating at Beverly High.

Fumento, Michael: Senior fellow at the conservative Hudson Institute, financed by ExxonMobil, who portrays Erin Brockovich (or "Crockovich," as he called her) and Ed Masry as "sharks" whose allegations lacked scientific credibility; Fumento's column was cancelled by Scripps Howard in 2006 after it was disclosed that a book he wrote about agribusiness was financed by Monsanto.

Griffin, Drew: Investigative reporter at KCBS-TV who broke the story about Beverly High's being "toxic."

Gross, Josh: Beverly graduate and *Beverly Hills Weekly* publisher; he criticized Mayor Tom Levyn's move to Christensen Miller, the law firm to which the city paid $1 million for its representation in the lawsuit, as a "quid pro quo."

Groves, Martha: *Los Angeles Times* reporter who first reported that the head of the LA County Cancer registry, Dr. Thomas Mack, was working as a consultant to a lawyer from Irell and Manella, representing Wainoco, one of the oil companies in the litigation.

Milloy, Steven: Lawyer paid by ExxonMobil and tobacco companies who created The Advancement of Sound Science Coalition (TASSC) for Philip Morris to debunk science showing that secondhand smoke is a carcinogen; commentator for Fox News and operator of the junkscience.com Web site.

Sugerman, Steve: President of the Sugerman Communications Group, the PR firm specializing in "crisis" management, hired by the city of Beverly Hills to write press releases saying that there was no evidence of health problems at the high school.

Umansky, Eric: Freelance writer for *The New Republic* and *Columbia Journalism Review* whose articles concluded that Erin Brockovich's public allegations didn't match her evidence; he never bothered to look up public information about toxic releases from Sempra's Central Plants.

Zager, Norma: *Beverly Hills Courier* editor and former stand-up comic in Vegas who said she was out to destroy Erin Brockovich.

PLAINTIFFS' COUNSEL

Drury, Jim: Masry & Vititoe "environmental specialist" who took air and water samples at Beverly Hills High School to show the chemical "fingerprints" there.

Eichler, Nancy Seidler: Attorney at Masry & Vititoe.

Frieling, Scott R.: Baron & Budd associate.

Jensen, Steve Baughman: Baron & Budd attorney.

Masry, Edward: Senior partner at Masry & Vititoe made famous by Christopher Plummer's portrayal of him in the film *Erin Brockovich.*

Piel, James D.: Baron & Budd partner.

Stewart, Allen M.: Lead counsel and senior partner at Baron & Budd.

DEFENSE COUNSEL

Bisgaard, Christopher P.: Senior partner at Lewis Brisbois Bisgaard & Smith (city of Beverly Hills).

Bloomfield, Thomas A.: Gallagher & Gallagher (Frontier and Wainoco Oil Co.).

Cwik, Cindy H.: Latham & Watkins (San Diego, Chevron).

Ezell, Peter: Partner at Haight, Brown & Bonesteel (Beverly Hills Unified School District).

Getto, Ernest J.: Senior partner at Latham & Watkins (San Francisco, Chevron, Inc.).

Goetz, Giselle: General counsel for Venoco, Inc.

Howes, Marlin E.: Sempra Energy in-house counsel.

Ireland, William E.: Haight, Brown & Bonesteel (Beverly Hills Unified School District).

Johnson, David D.: Latham & Watkins (Los Angeles, Chevron).

Meador, V. Thomas III: Morgan, Lewis & Bockius (Sempra Energy, Inc.).

Miller, Deanne L.: Morgan Lewis & Bockius (Sempra Energy, Inc.).

Miller, Louis "Skip": Partner at Christensen, Miller, Fink, Jacobs, Glaser, Weil & Shapiro (city of Beverly Hills).

O'Neill, Stephen J.: Sheppard, Mullin, Richter & Hampton (Venoco, Inc.).

Orbach, David: Partner at Orbach & Huff (Beverly Hills Unified School District).

Philobosian, Robert: Former L.A. district attorney and partner at Sheppard, Mullin, Richter & Hampton (Venoco, Inc.).

Refkin, Martin N.: Gallagher & Gallagher (Frontier and Wainoco Oil Co.).

Riff, Lawrence P.: Partner at Steptoe & Johnson (Wainoco Oil Company).

Rosen, Peter: Mayer Brown Rose and Maw (city of Beverly Hills).

Vinnick, Jeffrey A.: Beverly High graduate and partner at Haight, Brown & Bonesteel (Beverly Hills Unified School District).

Wiener, Laurence S.: Beverly High graduate and partner at Richards Watson Gershon; Beverly Hills city attorney.

Wilkinson, Kirk A.: Latham & Watkins (Los Angeles, Chevron).

EXPERTS AND RESEARCHERS

Ashford, Nick: Professor of technology and policy at Massachusetts Institute of Technology who advanced the theory of toxic induced loss of tolerance—a two-pronged medical response to low-level chemical sensitivity.

Boesberg, Peter: Oncologist of Carl Wilson and Tom Fries.

Brautbar, Nachman: Physician and toxicologist at the University of Southern California; worked with Erin Brockovich on the Hinkley case and was hired by the plaintiffs as a medical causation expert.

Clapp, Richard: Professor of environmental health at Boston University's School of Public Health; hired by the plaintiffs to conduct an epidemiological report and found an excess incidence of three types of cancer among graduates from Beverly Hills High from 1975 to 2000.

Cole, Philip: Epidemiologist hired by the city of Beverly Hills.

Costa, Max: Chromium researcher and chair of the Department of Environmental Medicine at NYU's School of Medicine; plaintiffs' causation expert.

Cozen, Wendy: Epidemiologist at the University of Southern California Cancer Surveillance Program who prepared a report about Beverly Hills residents, not graduates of the high school, and found cancer rates "at the high end" of normal.

Dahlgren, James: Toxicologist hired by Masry & Vititoe.

Dellinger, Barry: Chemistry professor at LSU and expert on combustion of hazardous wastes; hired by plaintiffs as expert witness on dioxins.

Durrie, Brian: Multiple myeloma specialist at Cedars-Sinai Medical Center who believes exposure to toxic chemicals, especially dioxins, is a big risk factor for the disease.

Endres, Bernard: Geologist and lawyer hired by Masry & Vititoe to take samples at Beverly Hills High School.

Froines, John: Professor at UCLA's School of Public Health who directs the Center for Occupational and Environmental Health; he is on the scientific advisory panel of the California EPA.

Hagemann, Matt: Former senior science policy adviser for the EPA hired by the plaintiffs to conduct chemical exposure assessments.

Hanna, Steven: Professor of environmental health at Harvard School of Public Health; plaintiffs' expert on air dispersion.

Hattis, Dale: Environmental science and policy professor at Clark University who has quantified cancer risks for children and adolescents for the EPA.

Horsak, Randy: Plaintiffs' expert witness who runs an environmental engineering company in Texas.

Infante, Peter: Toxicologist formerly with the Occupational Safety and Health Administration who conducted a key study of benzene exposure among Goodyear tire workers in Ohio.

Katchen, Mark: Beverly Hills school district's environmental consultant; found high levels of formaldehyde and benzene inside portable classrooms in 1999; later hired as expert witness for the defense.

Lifson, Robert: 1971 Beverly graduate and emergency room physician; hired by plaintiffs' lawyer Hunter Lundy to sign up prospective clients for a medical "study."

Link, John: Breast cancer specialist who was Melissa Gross's doctor.

Mack, Thomas: Professor of preventive medicine at the USC Keck School of Medicine and epidemiologist retained as a consultant by the law firm Irell and Manella, representing Wainoco Oil Company; wrote a book about cancer in Los Angeles and concluded that there is no evidence of a malignancy caused by an environmental carcinogen.

Marty, Melanie: Toxicologist who heads the California EPA's Office of Environmental Health Hazard Assessment's branch on air toxicology and epidemiology, chair of the EPA's advisory committee on children's health.

Matson, Jack: Professor of environmental engineering at Pennsylvania State University; hired by plaintiffs.

Mehlman, Myron: Former director of toxicology at Mobil Oil Corporation who was fired after he advised a Mobil subsidiary in Japan to stop selling gasoline with hazardous levels of the carcinogen benzene.

Michaels, David: Professor at George Washington University's School of Public Health who has written about how industry has "manufactured uncertainty" to prevent regulatory action; runs the Project on Scientific Knowledge and Public Policy, funded by plaintiffs' lawyers from silicon breast implant cases.

Neff, David: Ph.D. student who created an animated depiction of toxic chemical dispersion at Beverly High.

Ozonoff, David: Environmental health professor and chair of the Department of Environmental Health at Boston University School of Public Health; believes public health agencies err on the side of finding "false negative" studies on cancer clusters.

Patierno, Steven: Professor of Environmental and Occupational Health and director of the George Washington Cancer Institute; hired by defense counsel.

Paustenbach, Dennis: Toxicologist and industrial hygienist hired by PG&E and forced to resign from California Blue Ribbon panel on hexavalent chromium over a conflict of interest.

Peters, John: Director of the Children's Health Study at the University of Southern California's Keck School of Medicine.

Piazza, Bill: Air modeling expert and director of Health and Safety for Los Angeles Unified School District; helped Jody Kleinman to interpret data from the AQMD.

Rosenbloom, Barry: Jeffrey Frankel's oncologist.

Sawyer, William P: Toxicologist hired by plaintiffs as causation expert.

Tarr, Jim: Environmental engineer from Los Angeles; plaintiffs' air-modeling expert.

VanSkoy-Mosher, Michael: Karen Lee's oncologist.

Vom Saal, Frederick: Biology professor at the University of Missouri whose work has been attacked by scientists hired by the plastics industry.

Wilson, Mary Jane: Petroleum engineer who received $1 million from defense counsel to refute the testimony of plaintiffs' expert Jim Tarr.

Woodyard, John: Natural gas industry consultant; Sempra's defense expert.

THE JUDGES

Baker, Valerie: Los Angeles Superior Court judge in Santa Monica; agreed with the city of Beverly Hills that its legislative subpoena was necessary for public health reasons.

Mortimer, Wendell, Jr. ("Mort"): Los Angeles Superior Court judge in Central Civil West courthouse assigned to the Beverly Hills mass toxic tort case.

Yaffee, David P: Los Angeles Superior Court judge downtown; refused to hold Ed Masry and Erin Brockovich in contempt of court.

ACKNOWLEDGMENTS

This book would not have been possible without the help and support of many remarkable people. I am indebted, especially, to those cancer survivors and their families who opened their hearts and homes to me: Lori Moss, Phil Berman, Debi Genson-Fries, Carl Wilson, Barbara Wilson, Carrie Powers, Lou Versace, Stephanie Meyers, Justin Greenberg, Susan Messenger, Lee Bova, Jason Newman, Ari Bussel, Adrienne Lowe, and Carol Malony.

For their patience and generosity in helping me to understand technical matters related to epidemiology, toxicology, oncology, and the health effects of chemical exposures, I owe special thanks to John Froines, Karl Kelsey, Nick Ashcroft, John Peters, Richard Clapp, Julia Brody, Dale Hattis, John Spengler, David Ozonoff, Melanie Marty, Bill Piazza, Jim Tarr, Marilyn Underwood, Beatte Ritz, Peter Infante, Myron Mehlman, Peter Boesberg, Matt and Melissa Dinolfo, John Link, Barry Rosenbloom, Scott Fruin, Peggy Reynolds, Raymond Neutra, Thomas Mack, Wendy Cozen, and Sandy Geschwind. I take full responsibility, however, for any glaring errors in the manuscript.

In Beverly Hills, it was the "wacko" soccer moms I most admired and who spent hours and hours with me, helping me to navigate the terrain of their hometown: Jody Kleinman, Mahshid Soleimani, Janet Morris, Marrina Waks, and Nelli Emrani. And the courageous students: Zack Anderson, Brittany Darwell, Anna Harrari, and William Guo. And my former teachers and classmates: Chuck Kloes, Gerald Carpenter, Herb Dodge, Mickey Freedman, Leonard Stern, and Jane Wortman. Ellen Stern Harris, grande dame of the environmental movement in California, died from breast cancer before this book was completed. But it was she who insisted I write it.

From the start, Erin Brockovich-Ellis shared public documents I wasn't savvy enough to obtain on my own. Ed Masry, Patty Weiss, and Nancy Eichler were also generous with their time. In Dallas, Al Stewart helped me to understand the limits of our justice system. This book wouldn't have been possible without their cooperation.

For reporters, the name of the game is getting your phone calls returned, especially by those who don't want to talk to you. For that, I'd like to thank Sam Atwood, Ernie Getto, Cindy Cwik, Jeff Vinnick, Bill Ireland, Larry Wiener, Nina Webster, MaraLee Goldman, Thomas Levyn, Thomas Meador, Mike Edwards, Ben Bushman, and Gwen Gross. There were also many people who spoke to me on condition of anonymity. You know who you are, and I trust you know how valuable your insights proved to be, time and again.

For dogged research assistance and courthouse runs, Mary Brisson was an integral part of this project. Cherie Rodgers was also generous with her time. Howard Gest provided pro bono legal support for public records searches. For helping me to navigate the paper trail of Los Angeles Superior Court, thank you to Robin Sanchez in Department 307, and Linda Biche, Earl Anderson, and Todd Tramel. Ellen Baskin, Katy Young, and Tiffany Smith also provided invaluable research help and Sue Clamage and Freddie Odlum offered skilled secretarial support.

This book began as an assignment from *Los Angeles* magazine. Though that article never saw the light of day, I owe special thanks to Kit Rachlis, Karen Wada, and Eric Mercado for getting me started. I was incredibly lucky that my friend April Smith called me up one day and introduced me to the irrepressible Molly Friedrich, who became my agent. Her unflappable support and good sense connected me to my wonderful editor, Molly Stern, who helped to shape an unwieldy manuscript. Her wisdom and sharp focus made every page better. She never gave up on me. Thanks, also, to Alessandra Lusardi, Laura Tisdel, Adam Goldberger, and Noirin Lucas at Viking for their great care and marvelous attention to detail. Andrew Celli asked essential questions that helped to strengthen the manuscript in countless ways.

I was ready to quit this project more times than I care to admit. But it was the love of friends and family that kept me going: Amy Spies, Liberty Godshall, Carol Patchett, Delia Ephron, and my sister Shari Epstein read early drafts of the manuscript and helped make it better. I am also deeply thankful to Mark Bransdorfer and Jacqueline Liebman. Jill Cherneff was always was there for me, as were Ed Zwick, Jerry Kass, Barry Siegel, Wendy Brandchaft, Charlie Plotkin, Laura Plotkin, Jan Cherubin, Roger Director, Carrie Frazier, Sarah Steinberg, Doug Brayfield, Karen Bell, Carla Tulchin, Milton Jay, Laurie Steig, and Ron McDevitt. My sister Peggy Horowitz and my brother, Steve Horowitz, never failed to offer kind words and encouragement.

Finally, I owe a great debt to my children and husband, who stuck by me when I had no business expecting them to do so as this project dragged on year after year. Trevor read early drafts and offered insightful edits; Gus reminded me of the importance of being a muckraker; Lucy's encouragement kept me sane. And, as always, my husband, Brock Walsh, offered guidance and counsel and phenomenal lasagnas when I needed them most. His love and double duty made it all possible.

INDEX